Horses and Tack

Books by M. E. Ensminger

The Stockman's Handbook
Animal Science
Beef Cattle Science
Dairy Cattle Science
Sheep and Wool Science
Swine Science
Poultry Science
Horses and Horsemanship
Horses! Horses! Horses!
Tack! Tack! Tack!
Complete Encyclopedia of Horses
The Complete Book of Dogs
China — The Impossible Dream
Food and Animals — A Global Perspective
Horses and Tack

Horses
and Tack

M. E. Ensminger

Illustrated with Drawings and Photographs

HOUGHTON MIFFLIN COMPANY

BOSTON

Library of Congress Cataloging in Publication Data

Ensminger, M   Eugene.

   Horses and tack.

   Bibliography: p.
   1. Horses.   I. Title.
SF285.E55   636.1   76-30463
ISBN 0-395-24766-7

Printed in the United States of America

A 13 12 11 10 9 8 7 6 5 4

Design by Roy Howard Brown

"Horse Power," made for the author
by his brother, Harry Edward Ensminger.

To
brother Harry
who lives again
in the hearts of people and in the classic craftsmanship
he left behind.

ABOUT PEGASUS

The word *Pegasus* is of Greek origin, meaning strong.
Legend has it that the winged horse, Pegasus, was
fashioned from the body of Medusa, daughter of a sea-god
who, in her youth, was as mortal as she was beautiful. At
his birth, the frisky colt flew to Mount Helicon, where he
created a fountain (Horsewell) with one swift blow of his
hoof. Using a golden bridle, Bellerophon coaxed the
curious animal from his favorite meadow, made him
captive, and rode him off. Later, Pegasus unceremoniously
dumped his venerable and conceited master and flew into
outer space where he became the constellation that bears
his name.

Preface

The unique thing about the horse business, not found in any other industry, is the human values behind it. It's a people's business, and a way of life for many.

Also, the horse industry is a big and important business, and it will get bigger. The following facts and figures attest to the magnitude and importance of the industry:

- There are approximately 8 million horses in the United States.
- Horses represent an estimated $13 billion investment.
- Annual expenditures for horse feed, drugs, tack, and equipment average about $1000 per horse.
- U.S. horses make for a gross business — from vitamins to saddlery — of $8 billion per year.
- Annual wages paid in the horse industry exceed $1 billion.
- There are more 4-H Club horse projects than beef cattle projects. In 1966, for the first time in history, 4-H Club horse and pony projects took the lead over 4-H beef cattle projects. Subsequently, this lead has been widened further and further. These figures are presented in Table 1.

Table 1 4-H Club Beef Cattle and Horse Projects[1]

	1965	1966	1970	1974
Beef cattle........	160,914	157,949	150,056	160,846
Horses...........	146,541	165,510	231,206	320,767

[1]U.S. Department of Agriculture.

- Horse shows are increasing in size and numbers. They have more than doubled during the past 20 years. In 1974, 1258 horse shows were sanctioned by the American Horse Shows Association, with prize money totaling $4,987,649. The horse show story is shown in Table 2.

Table 2 Horse Shows

Year	AHSA Sanctioned Shows (no.)	Major Shows (over 50% of Divisions with "A" Rating) (no.)	Prize Money ($)
1959	425	142	1,453,322
1968	825	275	2,879,280
1971	958	325	3,615,550
1973	1178	375	4,458,659
1974	1258	405	4,987,649

■ Horse racing continues to be America's leading spectator sport. In 1974, 78,799,936 people went to horse races (Thoroughbred and harness racing); 31,299,936 more than witnessed automobile racing — the second ranking spectator sport. That same year, the rankings in attendance of the other leading sports were: football, third; baseball, fourth; basketball, fifth; hockey, sixth; and Greyhound racing, seventh. The rankings and figures of the seven leading spectator sports are given in Table 3.

Table 3 U.S. Sports Attendance 1974[1]

Leading Sports	Fan Attendance
1. Horse Racing (Thoroughbred and harness)	78,799,936
2. Auto Racing	47,500,000
3. Football	42,910,071
4. Baseball	41,662,407
5. Basketball	33,785,097
6. Hockey	21,386,207
7. Greyhound Racing	16,274,471

[1] *1974 Survey of Sports Attendance,* Triangle Publications, Inc., Hightstown, N.J.

■ Saddle clubs are springing up everywhere, and more people are riding horses for pleasure than ever before.
■ On the western range, cow ponies are still used in the traditional manner; mechanical replacement for them has not yet been devised.
■ Horses are benefactors of mankind in numerous other ways. Limited numbers of them are used by the Forest Service; others are used as pack animals into remote areas not otherwise accessible by surface travel. They

are still the show in many motion pictures and in parades. Those responsible for law enforcement have found that mounted patrols are one of the most effective ways in which to handle crowds and riots.

In the laboratory, horses serve as a factory for the manufacture of antitoxins that are used for rendering animals and people immune to certain diseases, such as tetanus. Also, medical doctors use equine-produced estrogens (female sex hormones), obtained from the urine of pregnant mares, to relieve the menopause (change of life) of women.

Despite the magnitude of the U.S. horse industry, horse owners suffer appalling losses. They are —

- Spending millions of dollars on needless concoctions and using unbalanced and deficient rations.

- Producing only a 50 percent foal crop, which means that they are keeping 2 mares a whole year to produce 1 foal.

- Keeping a stallion for each 7.3 foals produced.

- Maintaining horse-breeding establishments that return little or nothing on investment.

- Retiring an appalling number of horses from tracks, shows, and other uses due to unsoundnesses.

- Losing through inefficiency and deaths millions of dollars due to diseases and parasites.

Such wanton losses prompt the question: If the horse industry is so good, why not better?

This book is designed to impart sound, scientific information relative to breeding, feeding, housing, care and management, and health of horses; to give instruction in the arts of selecting and judging, and trimming the feet and shoeing; to present the basic principles of training and horsemanship; to give impetus to the rapidly expanding horse industry; and to make for greater knowledge and enjoyment in the grandest sport of all.

The author gratefully acknowledges the contributions of all those who worked so diligently on the manuscript of this book. Special appreciation is expressed to my wife, Audrey, for her inspiration, encouragement, and assistance; to Pat Logoluso Long, for editing and format; to Virginia Watkins, for typing; to artists Ruth Geary and Professor Richard Johnson, for the many line drawings; and to Joan Wright, who "whipped" the manuscript into final form. Also, I wish to thank most sincerely, but inadequately, all those who responded so liberally to my call for pictures and information, due acknowledgment of which is given at appropriate places in the book.

M. E. Ensminger

January 1977
Clovis, California

CONTENTS

Horses and Tack

1. History and Development of Horses

The story of the horse covers a period of approximately 58 million years; but man hunted him as recently as 25,000 years ago, domesticated him a mere 5000 years ago, and returned him to the New World less than 500 years ago.

Figure 1.1 Prehistoric wild horses were hunted for food as recently as 25,000 years ago. (After painting by Ernest Griset; courtesy, Smithsonian Institution)

EVOLUTION

Fossil remains prove that members of the horse family roamed the plains of America (especially what is now the Great Plains area of the United States) during most of Tertiary time, beginning about 58 million years ago. Yet, no horses were present on this continent when Columbus discovered America in 1492. Why they perished, only a few thousand years before, is still one of the unexplained mysteries of evolution.

Through fossils, it is possible to reconstruct the evolution of the horse, beginning with the ancient 4-toed ancestor, the *Eohippus* (meaning "dawn horse"). This was a small animal, scarcely more than a foot high, with 4 toes on the front feet and 3 toes on the hind feet, and with slender legs, a short neck, and even teeth. It was well adapted to traveling in and feeding on the herbage of swamplands. Gradually, the descendants of *Eohippus* grew in size and changed in form, evolving into a 3-toed animal known as *Mesohippus,* which was about 24 inches in height or about the size of a Collie. Further changes continued, transforming the animal from a denizen of the swamp to a creature of the prairie. In conformation, the animal grew taller, the teeth grew longer, the cannon bones lengthened, and the middle toe (third toe) grew longer and stronger — forming a hoof. The horse is an excellent example, therefore, of the slow adaptation of animal life to changing conditions in environment, climate, food, and soil.

Figure 1.2 Evolution of the horse, spanning 58 million years, as portrayed by the hind feet. Beginning with *Eohippus* (left), the descendants grew taller, the cannon bone lengthened, and the middle toe (third toe) grew longer and stronger — forming a hoof (right). (Courtesy, The American Museum of Natural History, New York, New York)

Figure 1.3 *Przewalsky's* horse. This is the only surviving species of original wild horses (horses not feral or escaped from domestication) known to exist at the present time. Note that the animals are small, with an erect mane and no forelock. (After painting by Charles Knight; courtesy, The American Museum of Natural History, New York, New York)

ZOOLOGICAL CLASSIFICATION

In the zoological scheme, the horse is classed as *Equus caballus.* He is distinguished from asses and zebras — the other members of the genus *Equus* — by the longer hair of the mane and tail, the presence of the "chestnut" on the inside of the hind leg, and by other less constant characteristics such as larger size, larger hoofs, more arched neck, smaller head, and shorter ears.

DOMESTICATION

The horse was probably the last of the present-day farm animals to be domesticated by man. According to early records, after subduing the ox, the sheep, and the goat, man domesticated the ass and then the camel; and, finally, the horse became his servant. Horses appear to have been domesticated first in Central Asia or Persia more than 5000 years ago.

Of course, it seems incredible that all the various breeds, colors, and types of draft, light, and pony horses should have descended from a common, wild ancestor. Rather, there were probably many different wild stocks giving descent to domestic horses.

MAN'S USE OF THE HORSE

The name "horse" is derived from the Anglo-Saxon, *hors,* meaning swiftness; and the word horseman comes from the Hebrew root "to prick or spur." Within themselves, these early characterizations tell somewhat of a story.

The horse was first used as a source of food. Records dating back some 25,000 years ago reveal that, prior to their domestication, these animals were hunted by Paleolithic (Old Stone Age) man. Following domestication, mares were milked for human food — a practice still followed in certain parts of the world. Next, man learned to use the horse to wage war. About 1500 B.C., Pharaoh pursued the Israelites to the Red Sea, using chariots and horses; and the Great Horse of medieval times was the knight's steed. As early as 1450 B.C., the sports-loving Greeks used the horse in the Olympic games, in both chariot and horse races. The use of horses in pulling loads and tilling the soil was a comparatively recent development. The improved roads that the Romans constructed during Caesar's campaigns, beginning about 55 B.C., were largely instrumental in encouraging the breeding of horses for use in transportation — for drawing heavy loads. However, there is no evidence to indicate that the horse was used in Europe to draw the plow prior to the 10th Century, and few of them replaced oxen as the main source of agricultural power until the end of the 18th Century.

Figure 1.4 Man's use of the horse.

INTRODUCTION INTO THE UNITED STATES

Horses were first brought directly into what is now the United States by de Soto in the year 1539. Upon his several vessels, he had 237 horses. Beginning in the year 1600, the Spaniards established a chain of Christian missions among the Indians in the New World, extending from the eastern coast of Mexico up the Rio Grande, thence across the mountains to the Pacific Coast. Each mission brought horses from the mother country.

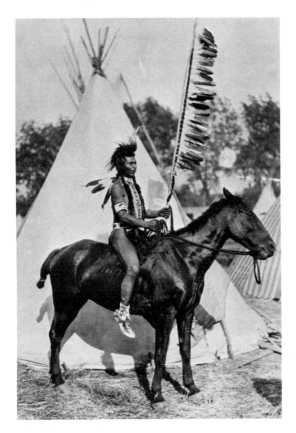

Figure 1.5 American Indian mounted on horse of Spanish extraction. The coming of horses among the Indians led to greater infringement on the hunting grounds of the tribes, which was ever a cause for war. (Courtesy, Jeff Edwards, Brislawn-Edwards, Porterville, California)

HISTORICAL

The golden age of the horse extended to the advent of the automobile, truck, and tractor. During this period, everybody loved the horse. The town livery stable, watering trough, and hitching post were trademarks of every town and village. People wept when the horse fell on an icy street, and they jailed men who beat or mistreated him. The oat bag, carriage, wagon, buggy whip, axle grease, horseshoe, and horseshoe nail industries were thriving and essential parts of the national economy. Every schoolboy knew and respected the village blacksmith.

During this era, much romance and adventure surrounded the horse. Again and again, he proved his worth through such dramatic performances as the Pony Express. Also, the horse served as a status symbol, the ultimate expression of which was a fantastic dinner staged on horseback in the plushest restaurant of the day by the New York Riding Club.

Figure 1.6 The statue of the Pony Express which stands in the St. Joseph, Missouri, Civic Center. It was erected in 1941, when the Postal Department honored the riders of the Pony Express with a commemorative postage stamp. (Courtesy, St. Joseph Museum, St. Joseph, Missouri)

PONY EXPRESS

This mail service operated as a private venture under contract, and carried U.S. mail on horseback from St. Joseph, Missouri, to Placerville, California, before railways or telegraph. It was started in 1861, and it had a brief existence of but 18 months before it was supplanted by a telegraph line. The riders' steeds were fleet horses, not ponies. The horses were stationed at points 10 to 15 miles apart, and each rider rode 3 to 7 animals successively, covering about 75 miles before passing the pouch to his successor. There were 80 riders, some 420 horses, and 190 relay stations. Riders were paid $25 per week.

The fastest trip ever made was in 7 days and 17 hours, when Lincoln's first inaugural address was carried to the West Coast. But the normal schedule was 8 days, which was about 24 days faster than the schedule of Butterfield's Overland Stage Line on the southern route. The maintenance of the schedule through the wilderness, often in blinding snows and howling storms and in the face of Indian dangers, won for the service a fame that has not been diminished with the passing of time.

The Pony Express lost money. The average charge for sending a letter during the period was $3, but it cost about $16 per letter to operate the service; thus, the private venture lost $13 per letter, and it is estimated that the Pony Express cost its backers $390,000.

Despite its short life, the Pony Express was credited with many important contributions, not the least of which was its help in keeping East and West joined together during the early crucial days of the Civil War.

HIPPIES ON HORSEBACK

A horseback dinner was staged in Louis Sherry's restaurant, corner of Fifth Avenue and 44th Street, New York City, on March 28, 1903, with Cornelius K. G. Billings — Chicago utilities heir, racing enthusiast, and self-styled "American Horse King" — as host. To publicize his newly opened $200,000 stable at 196th Street and Fort Washington Road (now Fort Tryon Park), Mr. Billings converted the grand ballroom of Sherry's into a woodland paradise by means of $10,000 worth of full-scale scenic props, artificial foliage, potted palms, and a tanbark floor covering, borrowed, at Mr. Sherry's insistence, from the Barnum and Bailey circus. Thirty-six mystified horses were conveyed up to the ballroom by freight elevators, and the uncomfortable guests — members of the New York Riding Club — attired in white ties and tails, gingerly astride their favorite mounts, drank and ate to the merriment of music, while their steeds munched oats out of troughs decorated with gold foil, and costumed lackeys cleaned up behind them.

Miniature tables were attached to the saddle pommels (drive-in style), and apprehensive waiters dressed in riding attire served drink after drink, and course after course, topped off by Jack Horner pies — huge, ornamental concoctions which, when cut open, revealed a covey of nymphs in their birthday suits. Only one guest fell off his horse.

GROWTH AND DECLINE OF U.S. HORSES

Ironic as it may seem, the development of manufacturing and commerce was responsible for both the rise and fall of the horse and mule industry in the United States. The early growth of American industry created a large need for horses to transport the raw and manufactured goods and to produce needed agricultural products for those people who lived in the cities and villages. However, the relentless wheels of progress steadily lifted from the horse his role in both agriculture and war.

A century ago, muscles provided 94% of the world's energy needs; coal, oil, and waterpower provided the other 6%. Today, the situation is reversed in the developed nations. They now obtain 94% of their energy needs from coal, oil, natural gas, and waterpower, and only 6% from the muscle power of men and animals.

At their height, in 1915, there were 21,431,000 horses in the United States, most of which were draft animals. Mules reached a peak in 1925,

Figure 1.7 Power.

at 5,918,000 head. With the advent of the machine age — the automobile, truck, and tractor — the draft horse and mule declined.

Today, the horse is rising to a more happy position in contributing to the fields of recreation and sport; and further expansion in light horses appears inevitable.

Based on the 1971 VEE vaccination program conducted by the U.S. Department of Agriculture, the 10 leading states in horse numbers, by rank, were: Texas, California, Tennessee, Oklahoma, Ohio, Mississippi, Michigan, Missouri, Kentucky, and Kansas.

WORLD HORSE NUMBERS

Table 1.1 shows the size and density of the horse population in ten countries in 1970–71. As shown, the numbers totaled 66.3 million head. This was far below the 1934–38 prewar figure of 96.4 million head. This decline in numbers since 1938 can be attributed chiefly to mechanization of agriculture in certain areas.

The leading countries in horse numbers, by rank, were: Brazil, United States, U.S.S.R., China, Mexico, Argentina, Poland, Mongolia, Ethiopia, and Yugoslavia.

CLASSIFICATION OF HORSES

Horses may be classified as light horses, draft horses, or ponies, according to size, build, and use.

■ *Light horses* stand over 14-2 hands high[1], weigh 900 to 1400 pounds, and are used primarily for riding, driving, racing, or utility purposes on

[1] A hand is 4 inches; thus, 14–2 hands is 58 inches.

Table 1.1 Size and Density of Horse Population of Ten Leading Horse-Producing Countries of the World in 1970–71, by Rank

Country	Horse[1] Population	Human Population[2]	Size of Country[2]		Horses per Capita	Horses per Sq. Mile	Horses per Sq. Km
			(sq. mi)	(sq. km)			
Brazil.................	9,050,000	98,081,000	3,286,473	8,511,965	.09	2.75	1.06
United States.........	7,800,000	204,765,770	3,536,855	9,160,454	.03	2.2	.85
U.S.S.R.	7,400,000	245,070,000	8,647,172	22,396,175	.03	.86	.33
China................	7,200,000	697,260,000	3,746,453	9,703,313	.01	1.92	.74
Mexico	5,026,000	50,830,000	758,259	1,963,890	.10	6.63	2.56
Argentina............	3,600,000	23,550,000	1,079,520	2,795,957	.02	3.3	1.29
Poland...............	2,570,000	32,750,000	120,664	312,520	.08	21.3	8.22
Mongolia	2,320,000	1,280,000	604,000	1,564,360	1.81	3.84	1.48
Ethiopia	1,415,000	25,900,000	457,256	1,184,293	.55	3.09	1.19
Yugoslavia...........	1,230,000	20,550,000	98,766	255,804	.60	1.25	.48
WORLD TOTAL ..	66,312,000	3,631,797,000	135,781,867	351,675,036	.02	.49	.19

[1] *Statistical Yearbook 1972*, United Nations, New York, N.Y., 1972, pp. 118–126, 1970–71 data.
[2] *The 1973 World Almanac*, Newspaper Enterprise Association, Inc., New York, N.Y., 1972.

the farm. Light horses generally are more rangy and are capable of more action and greater speed than draft horses.

- *Draft horses* stand 14-2 to 17-2 hands high, weigh 1400 pounds or more, and are used primarily for drawing loads and other heavy work.
- *Ponies* stand 14-2 hands high and under and weigh up to 900 pounds. The breeding, feeding, care, and management are essentially the same for ponies as for larger light horses; the only differences result from their diminutive size.

Figure 1.8 The way it used to be done.

2. Types, Uses, and Breeds of Horses

The improvement of horses dates back to the time when man first domesticated them and sought to improve them more nearly to fulfill his needs. Through selection, different types and breeds evolved, better adapted to different uses and better meeting different human desires.

TYPES AND USES OF HORSES

In no class of animals have so many diverse and distinct types been developed as in the horse. The descendants of the Oriental light-legged horse have, for generations, been bred and used for riding and driving purposes — first as the chariot and riding horses of Egypt, Greece, and Arabia; later, as the running horse of England; and, finally, for purposes

Figure 2.1 Bronze horse with one foot on a swallow to indicate its swiftness. Note that this horse is literally floating through the air, with head up, tail high, and three feet off the ground. Note, too, that this horse is doing the rack — a fast, flashy, four-beat gait in which each foot meets the ground separately at equal intervals. (Contrary to many reports, he is not galloping.)

This was among the artifacts found in a tomb of the late Eastern Han Dynasty (25 A.D. to 220 A.D.) in China. (Photo by A. H. Ensminger)

of recreation and sport in the United States and throughout the world. In due time, further refinements in breeding light horses were made, and these animals were adapted for more specific purposes. In this manner, light horses specifically adapted to the purposes enumerated in Table 2.1 have evolved.

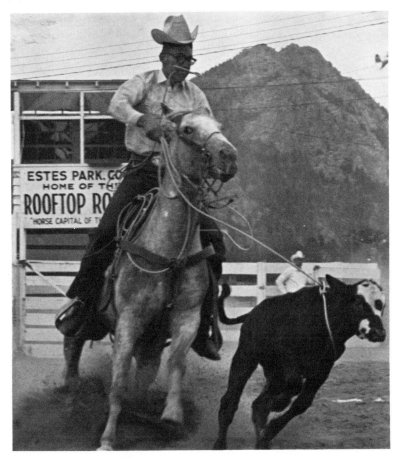

Figure 2.2 Stock horse in action — calf roping. For this purpose, the horse is trained to come to a sliding stop the moment his rider lays an arm on his neck in preparation for leaving his saddle and running to the roped calf to hog-tie its legs. The horse keeps the rope on the calf taut until its legs are hog-tied. (Courtesy, McLaughlin Photography, Morrison, Colorado)

In attempting to produce animals to meet these specific purposes, new breeds of light horses have been developed. In certain cases, however, the particular use or performance is so exacting that only one breed appears to be sufficiently specialized; for example, in running races the Thoroughbred is used almost exclusively, and harness races are now synonymous with the Standardbred breed.

Table 2.1 Light Horse Summary

Type	Primary Use	Breeds
Riding Horses	Three-gaited saddle horses	American Bashkir Curly American Paint Horse American Saddle Horse American White; American Creme Andalusian Appaloosa Arabian Cleveland Bay Galiceno Hanoverian Hungarian Horse Lipizzan Morab Morgan Morocco Spotted Horse Palomino Pinto Quarter Horse Rangerbred Spanish-Barb Thoroughbred Trakehner Ysabella
	Gaited horses	American Saddle Horse Missouri Fox Trotting Horse Paso Fino Peruvian Paso Tennessee Walking Horse
	Stock horses	Grades, crossbreds, or following purebreds: American Buckskin American Mustang American Paint Horse Appaloosa Arabian Chickasaw Hungarian Horse Morgan Pinto Horse Quarter Horse Spanish-Barb Spanish Mustang Thoroughbred
	Polo mounts	Grades, crossbreds, and purebreds of all breeds, but predominantly of Thoroughbred breeding.

(Cont.)

Table 2.1 Light Horse Summary (*Cont.*)

Type	Primary Use	Breeds
Riding Horses .... (*Cont.*)	Hunters and Jumpers.............	Grades, crossbreds, and purebreds of all breeds, but predominantly of Thoroughbred breeding.
	Ponies for riding	American Gotland Horse American Walking Pony Connemara Pony National Appaloosa Pony Pony of the Americas Shetland Pony Welsh Pony
Racehorses[1]	Running racehorses	Thoroughbred
	Harness racehorses (trotters and pacers)............	Standardbred
	Quarter racehorses	Quarter Horse
Driving Horses	Heavy harness horses.............	Hackney
	Fine harness horses	American Saddle Horses (predominantly, although other breeds are so used)
	Roadsters..........................	Standardbred
	Ponies for driving: 1. Harness show ponies 2. Heavy harness ponies	Hackney Shetland Pony Welsh Pony

[1]In a few states, Appaloosa and Arabian horses are also being raced under saddle.

BREEDS OF HORSES

A breed of horses may be defined as a group of horses having a common origin and possessing certain well-fixed, distinctive, uniformly transmitted characteristics that are not common to other horses. There are about 300 breeds of horses in the world, of which 34 breeds of light horses, 7 breeds of ponies, and 6 breeds of draft horses are found in the United States.

There is scarcely a breed of horses that does not possess one or more distinctive breed characteristics in which it excels all others. Moreover, any one of several breeds is often well adapted to the same use. Certainly, if any strong preference exists, it should be an important factor in determining the choice of a breed, although it is recognized that some breeds are better adapted to specific purposes than others.

A discussion of the common U.S. breeds of light horses and ponies and their characteristics follows.[1] It is noteworthy that most U.S. breeds of

[1]No person or department has authority to approve a breed. The only legal basis for recognizing a breed is contained in the Tariff Act of 1930, which provides for the duty-free admission of purebred breeding

light horses are American creations. There are two primary reasons for this: (1) the diverse needs and uses for which light horses have been produced; and (2) the fact that many men of wealth have bred light horses. For detailed information about any of the breeds, write to the appropriate breed registry, the names and addresses of which are given in this chapter in the section entitled, "Breed Registry Associations."

Figure 2.3 American Bashkir Curly stallion, Curly Q, first Permanent Stud in the American Bashkir Curly Registry. Owned by Sarge and Sunny Martin, Ely, Nevada. (Courtesy, American Bashkir Curly Registry, Ely, Nevada)

AMERICAN BASHKIR CURLY

Horses with curly hair are known to have been raised centuries earlier by the people of Bashkiria on the eastern slopes of the Ural Mountains; hence, the name Bashkir. In this rugged climate, the Bashkiri people depended upon their curly horses for transportation, clothing, meat, and milk. In their native land, mares give three to six gallons of milk per day, which is highly prized. In addition to being consumed as fresh milk, cream, and butter, it makes a delicious cheese. Also, the milk is fermented to make a drink called "Kumiss," which the natives drink both as an

horses provided they are registered in the country of origin. But this applies to imported animals only. In this book, therefore, no official recognition of any breed is intended or implied. Rather, every effort has been made to present the factual story of the breeds. In particular, information about the new or less widely distributed breeds is needed and often difficult to obtain.

intoxicating liquor and for medicinal purposes. History also records that the nomadic Mongols rode curly horses.

The modern history of curly horses in America began in 1898, when Peter Damele of Ely, Nevada, cut three curly animals from a herd of wild horses in the Peter Hanson Mountain Range. Most of today's curly horses trace to Damele ranch breeding. The American Bashkir Curly Registry was formed August 14, 1971.

The curly coat, with corkscrew mane and wavy tail, is the outstanding characteristic of the breed. The mane hair, and often the tail hair, falls out completely each summer and grows back during the winter. In build, Curlies are medium size and chunky, somewhat resembling the early-day Morgan in conformation. The breed is noted for small nostrils, a gentle disposition, and heavy milking. Many of the animals have a natural fox-trot gait. All colors are accepted. Horses weighing in excess of 1350 pounds or having faulty conformation are disqualified for registry.

The American Bashkir Curly is used as a pleasure horse and for utility purposes — including light draft work. Because of their ruggedness, endurance, and gentle dispositions, they make ideal family trail horses and children's mounts.

Figure 2.4 American Creme stallion, "Polar Bar," owned by Edward Bales, Prineville, Oregon. (Photo by Paul Zinn; courtesy, American Albino Association, Inc., Crabtree, Oregon)

AMERICAN CREME HORSE
Pale cream horses have been around for a very long time, primarily in Oregon and Washington. However, they were not given breed status until

1970, at which time the American Albino Association, Inc., established a separate American Creme Horse Division for their registration.

The following color classifications of American Creme Horses are registered:

A — Body ivory white, mane white (lighter than body), eyes blue, skin pink.

B — Body cream, mane darker than body, cinnamon buff to ridgeway, eyes dark.

C — Body and mane of the same color, pale cream; eyes blue, skin pink.

D — Body and mane of same color, sooty cream; eyes blue, skin pink.

Combinations of the above classifications are also acceptable.

American Creme horses are used as pleasure and stock horses, for exhibition purposes, and as parade and flag bearer horses.

Both the American Creme Horse and the American White Horse are registered by the American Albino Association, Inc., Crabtree, Oregon, with separate divisions provided for each.

Figure 2.5 American Gotland stallion, Gulldson 40, sire of show, pleasure, jumping, and trot racing ponies. (Courtesy, USDA)

AMERICAN GOTLAND HORSE

American Gotland Horses originated on the Baltic island of Gotland, a part of Sweden. Coat colors are bay, brown, black, dun, chestnut, roan, or palomino, and some leopard and blanket markings. They average about 51 inches high, with a range of 11 to 14 hands.

American Gotland Horses are used for harness racing (trotting), as pleasure horses and jumpers, and as riding horses for children and medium-sized adults.

Pintos and animals with large markings are disqualified for registration.

Figure 2.6 American Mustang stallion, El Mano De Oro, National Grand Champion Stallion of 1976, owned by Sally Crouse, Banning, California. (Courtesy, American Mustang Association, Yucaipa, California)

AMERICAN MUSTANG

American Mustang horses originated along the Barbary Coast of North Africa, from which they were taken to Spain by the conquering Moors, propagated in Andalusia, and brought to America by the Conquistadores. The American Mustang Association was formed in 1962.

They may be any color, but they must be between 13–2 and 15 hands high.

American Mustangs are used for pleasure riding, show, trail riding, endurance trails, stock horses, and jumping.

AMERICAN PAINT HORSE

American Paint Horses[2] originated in the United States. Coat colors are white plus any other color, but the coloring must be a recognizable paint. No discrimination is made against glass, blue, or light-colored eyes.

---

[2] Two different associations have evolved for the registration of these varicolored horses. In the Pinto Horse Association of America, Inc., which is the older of the two registries, the breed is known as Pinto Horse, whereas in the American Paint Horse Association, the breed is known as the American Paint Horse. Both groups of horses are similar in color.

Figure 2.7 American Paint Horse mare, Skip Again, a sorrel tobiano, winner of 26 Grand Champion-ships. Owned by Larry Wiescamp, Alamosa, Colorado. (Courtesy, American Paint Horse Association, Ft. Worth, Texas)

American Paint Horses are used as stock horses, pleasure horses, and for showing and racing.

Animals are disqualified for registration unless they have natural white markings above the knees or hocks, except on the face; if they have Appaloosa coloring or breeding; if they are adult horses under 14 hands high; or if they are five-gaited horses.

AMERICAN SADDLE HORSE

American Saddle Horses originated in the United States, in Fayette County, Kentucky. Coat colors are bay, brown, gray, roan, chestnut, black, or golden. Gaudy white markings are undesirable. Animals have a long, graceful neck and proud action. They furnish an easy ride with great style and animation.

American Saddle Horses are used as three- and five-gaited saddle horses, and as harness, pleasure, and stock horses.

AMERICAN WALKING PONY

American Walking Ponies originated near Macon, Georgia, in 1968. There is no coat color stipulation. Since it is a cross between Welsh Pony

Figure 2.8 American Saddle stallion, Beau Fortune. (Courtesy, American Saddle Horse Breeders Association, Louisville, Kentucky)

Figure 2.9 American Walking Pony mare, BT Sunday Summer, the highest selling animal of the breed to date, owned by Floyd F. Scott, Willingboro, New Jersey. Summer is pictured with her foal. (Courtesy, American Walking Pony Association, Macon, Georgia)

and Tennessee Walking Horse, the colors of both parent breeds occur. They range in height from 13 to 14-2 hands.

American Walking Ponies must perform the running walk gait. They are used for pleasure riding, and as mounts for children or small adults.

Figure 2.10 American White Horse gelding, "Soapsuds Smith." Owned by Neva Hahn, Muscatine, Iowa. (Courtesy, American Albino Association, Inc., Crabtree, Oregon)

AMERICAN WHITE HORSE

The American White Horse originated on White Horse Ranch, Naper, Nebraska. They have hair as white as clean snow, with pink skin. The eyes are light blue, dark blue (near black), brown, or hazel, but never pink.

American White Horses are used as pleasure horses. Their snow-white color makes them attractive as trained horses for exhibition purposes and as parade and flag bearer horses.

Both the American White Horse and the American Creme Horse are registered by the American Albino Association, Crabtree, Oregon, with separate divisions provided for each.

ANDALUSIAN

Andalusian horses originated in Spain. Whites, grays, and bays are most common, but there are a few blacks, roans, and chestnuts.

Andalusian horses are used for bullfighting, parade, dressage, jumping, and pleasure riding.

Animals not tracing to the Spanish Registry, which is supervised by the army in Spain, are not eligible for registry.

APPALOOSA

Appaloosa horses originated in the United States — by the Nez Percé tribe of American Indians in Oregon, Washington, and Idaho — from

Figure 2.11 Andalusian stallion, Pregonero, Central American Grand Champion of the Andalusian breed, owned by Sr. don Mario Rey Rosa, Guatemala City, Guatemala. Shown in action at age 20, Pregonero was foaled in Spain. (Courtesy, Sr. Rafael Aycinena, Asociación Guatemalteca de Criadores de Caballos de Pura Raza Española, Guatemala City, Guatemala)

Figure 2.12 Appaloosa stallion, Little Navajo Joe, a champion stallion. (Courtesy, USDA)

animals that first came from Fergana, Central Asia. They have variable coat coloring but usually there is white over the loin and hips, with round or egg-shaped dark spots on the white areas.

The eyes show more white encirclement than most breeds, the skin is mottled, and the hoofs are striped vertically black and white. Appaloosas are used as stock, parade, race, and pleasure horses.

Animals are disqualified for registration unless they have Appaloosa characteristics; if they have draft horse, pony, albino, or pinto breeding; if they are gray or non-Appaloosa roan, or the progeny of a gray or non-Appaloosa roan; if they are cryptorchids; or if they are under 14 hands high at maturity, at 5 years of age or more.

Figure 2.13 Arabian mare, Fire Music, by Bask. In 1973, she was both Canadian and U.S. National Champion Mare; and in 1974, she was U.S. National Champion Arabian English Pleasure Horse. Fire Music is owned by Lasma Arabians, Scottsdale, Arizona. (Courtesy, International Arabian Horse Association, Burbank, California)

ARABIAN

Arabian horses originated on the Arabian Peninsula. Coat colors usually are bay, gray, or chestnut, and occasionally white or black. White marks on the head and legs are common. The skin is always dark.

These animals have a beautiful head, short coupling, docility, great endurance, and a gay way of going. They are used as saddle, stock, show, race, and pleasure horses.

Figure 2.14 Buckskin stallion, Leo Reno; a golden buckskin, with dorsal stripe and dark ear tips and ear outline. Owned by Holiday Farm, Dyer, Indiana. (Courtesy, International Buckskin Horse Assn., St. John, Indiana)

BUCKSKIN

Buckskin horses originated in the United States. Coat colors are buckskin, red dun, or grulla (mouse-dun).

Buckskins are used as stock horses, pleasure horses, and show horses. Disqualifications for registration are:

1. American Buckskin Registry Association: Palominos, chestnuts, sorrels, or bays with dorsal stripe; draft type; blue or glass eyes; white spots on body (indicating Pinto or Appaloosa blood) or white markings above knees or hocks.

2. International Buckskin Horse Association: Excessive white; showing Paint, Pinto, or Appaloosa characteristics.

CHICKASAW

Chickasaw horses were developed by the Chickasaw Indians of Tennessee, North Carolina, and Oklahoma, from horses of Spanish extraction. Coat colors are bay, black, chestnut, gray, roan, sorrel, and palomino.

The breed is characterized by a short head and ears; a short back; a short neck; square, stocky hips; a low-set tail; a wide chest; and great width between the eyes. The preferred height: 53 to 59 inches.

Chickasaw horses are used as cow ponies.

Figure 2.15 Cleveland Bay stallion, "Cleveland Farnley." (Courtesy, USDA)

CLEVELAND BAY

Cleveland Bay horses originated in England, in the Cleveland district of Yorkshire. The coat color is always solid bay on the body and black on the legs. These horses are larger than most light horse breeds; they weigh from 1150 to 1400 pounds.

Cleveland Bays are used for riding, driving, and all kinds of farm work. They also are used in crossbreeding to produce heavyweight hunters.

Animals are disqualified for registration if they are any color but bay, although a few white hairs on the forehead are permissible.

Figure 2.16 Connemara stallion, Oak Hills Trocadi, owned by Mavis Connemara Farm, Rochester, Illinois. (Courtesy, Mr. Mavis)

CONNEMARA PONY

Connemara Ponies originated on the west coast of Ireland. Coat colors usually are gray, black, bay, dun, brown, or cream, and occasionally roan or chestnut.

These ponies are heavy boned, hardy, and docile. They range rather widely in height; hence, the American Connemara Society registers in two sections: *Section 1,* "pony," 13 to 14-2 hands; *Section 2,* "small horse," over 14-2 hands. Connemara Ponies are used as jumpers, as show ponies under saddle or in harness, and as riding ponies for medium-sized adults and children.

Animals are disqualified for registration if they are piebald, skewbald, or cream with blue eyes.

Figure 2.17 Galiceno mare, Vestido Azul, owned by Glenn H. Bracken, Tyler, Texas. (Courtesy, Galiceno Horse Breeders Assn., Tyler, Texas)

GALICENO

Galiceno horses originated in Galicia, a province in northwestern Spain. Horses of this lineage were first brought to America by the Conquistadores, but these horses were not introduced to the United States as a breed until 1958. The most common coat colors are bay, black, chestnut (sorrel), dun (buckskin), gray, brown, or palomino. Solid colors prevail.

At maturity, Galicenos are 12 to 13 hands high and weigh 625 to 700 pounds. They are used as riding horses.

Animals are disqualified for registration if they have albino, pinto, or paint coloring, or if they are cryptorchids or monorchids.

HACKNEY

Hackney horses originated on the east coast of England, in Norfolk and adjoining counties. The most common colors are chestnut, bay, or brown, and occasionally roan or black. White marks are common and desirable.

In the show-ring, custom decrees that Hackney horses and ponies be docked and have their manes pulled. They have a high natural action.

Figure 2.18 Hackney stallion, "May Day Creation," Champion Stallion and Sire of Champion Ponies. (Courtesy, USDA)

Hackneys are used as heavy harness or carriage horses and ponies, and for crossbreeding purposes to produce hunters and jumpers.

HANOVERIAN

The Hanoverian breed originated in the Hanover section of Germany, beginning in 1732. An Englishman went to Hanover and became its prince. Later, he returned to England and became King George II. During his stay in Germany he assembled outstanding individuals of certain breeds for the purpose of developing a superior horse for military use, with emphasis on size, intelligence, and temperament. Out of this effort evolved the Hanoverian breed of horses.

In Germany, the breeding, selection, and registration of Hanoverian horses are under government supervision. The State Stud, at Celle, was founded in 1735. Today, 160 stallions are maintained at Celle. Each spring, these stallions are sent out to 60 stallion stations, where they breed more than 12,000 registered Hanoverian mares. Without doubt, the breeding and selection program followed with Hanoverian horses in

Germany is the finest equine production testing program in the world. It involves a rigid inspection of all stallions at $2\frac{1}{2}$ years of age, with only 60 selected, and the 15 top ones of these sent to the State Stud at Celle. Next, the stallions are put in intensive training and performance tested for one year in pulling, jumping, and dressage. During this time, temperament is also noted. If an animal does not measure up in any category, he is gelded.

Today, 70 percent of the horses of Germany are Hanoverians, and it is the most numerous light horse breed in Europe. In Europe, they are used for riding, driving (carriage horses), hunting, jumping, dressage, and utility purposes. In the United States, the breed is used for all light-horse purposes, especially for hunting, jumping, and dressage.

Hanoverian horses are big and powerful. Many of them stand $16\frac{1}{2}$ hands or better and weigh 1200 pounds or more. They combine nobility, size, and strength in a unique way.

In 1973, the American Hanoverian Society was formed, with headquarters in Carmel, Indiana.

Figure 2.19 Hungarian mare, "Hungarian Barna." (Courtesy, USDA)

HUNGARIAN HORSE

This very old breed originated in Hungary. The coat may be any color, either broken or solid.

These horses possess a unique combination of style and beauty, with ruggedness. They are used as stock, cutting, and pleasure horses, as hunters and jumpers, and for trail riding.

Animals are disqualified for registration if they are cryptorchids or have glass eyes.

Figure 2.20 Lipizzan stallion, Maestoso Brezova II, purchased directly from the Spanish Riding School, Vienna, Austria. Owned by Evelyn L. Dreitzler, Snohomish, Washington. (Courtesy, Mrs. Dreitzler)

LIPIZZAN

Lipizzan horses originated in Lipizza, Yugoslavia, the town from which the breed takes its name. Most mature animals of the breed are white. But Lipizzan foals are born dark (brown or gray), then turn white at 4 to 6 years of age. About 1 in 600 remains black or brown throughout life. When the latter happens, it is considered good luck.

Lipizzan horses have an elastic walk, with considerable knee action. They are used for dressage (for which purpose they are without a peer), harness horses, pleasure horses, hunters, jumpers, and parade horses.

Animals having glass eyes, extreme Roman nose, or deformed or crooked limbs are disqualified for registration.

Figure 2.21 Missouri Fox Trotting stallion, winner in the Show and Celebration. (Courtesy, Missouri Fox Trotting Horse Breed Association, Ava, Missouri)

MISSOURI FOX TROTTING HORSE

Missouri Fox Trotting Horses originated in the United States, in the Ozark Hills of Missouri and Arkansas. They usually are sorrel, but any color is accepted.

These horses are distinguished by the fox trot gait. They are used as pleasure and stock horses and for trail riding.

Animals are disqualified for registration if they cannot fox trot.

MORAB

The Morab Horse Registry of America was formed in Fresno County, California, on July 19, 1973, based on the foundation stock of Martha Doyle Fuller. On her ranch at Clovis, California, she bred Morgan mares to Arabian stallions, to produce stock horses. In 1955, she began selecting and perpetuating animals based on this cross. However, crosses of this kind occurred in the 1800s; and many people crossed Morgans and Arabians following World War I. William Randolph Hearst, Sr., bred Morabs for his ranch operations in the 1930s and 1940s.

The Morab is predominantly Morgan and Arabian, although it may be part Thoroughbred. The breed possesses the muscular strength and

Figure 2.22 Morab mare, Tezya, bred by Martha Doyle Fuller, founder of the breed. Tezya was the first registered Morab. (Courtesy, Morab Horse Registry of America, Clovis, California)

ruggedness of the Morgan and the refinement and beauty of the Arabian. Mature animals average about 15 hands in height.

Morabs are used for show, pleasure riding, endurance rides, and ranch work.

Animals are disqualified if they have breed characteristics other than Morgan, Arabian, and Thoroughbred; if they have albino, appaloosa, paint, or pinto color; or if they are under 14 hands at maturity.

MORGAN

Morgan horses originated in the United States, in the New England states. Coat colors are bay, brown, black, or chestnut; extensive white markings are uncommon.

Morgan horses are noted for their easy keeping qualities, endurance, and docility. They are used as saddle and stock horses.

Animals are disqualified for registration if they are walleyed or have white markings above the knee or hock, except that white markings on the face are acceptable.

Figure 2.23 Morgan mare, Hanover Super Lady, Grand Champion Mare at the 1973 Grand National Morgan Horse Show. (Courtesy, American Morgan Horse Association, Inc., Hamilton, New York)

Figure 2.24 Morocco Spotted Horse, a chestnut and white stallion. (Courtesy, USDA)

MOROCCO SPOTTED HORSE

Morocco Spotted Horses originated in the United States. As the name suggests, they are spotted. The secondary color, white, must comprise not less than 10 percent, not including white on the legs or face.

Morocco Spotted Horses are used for parade horses, saddle horses, stock horses, pleasure horses, and harness horses.

Animals that are under 14–2 hands, or that are of draft or pony breeding, or that show such characteristics, are not eligible for registration.

NATIONAL APPALOOSA PONY

National Appaloosa Ponies originated in the United States, near Rochester, Indiana. They are varicolored, but leopard, blanket-type, snowflake, or roan are most popular. The skin, nose, and area around the eyes are mottled. White sclera encircles the eyes.

National Appaloosa Ponies are used as working ponies, show ponies, and for trail riding, jumping, and racing.

Albino, pinto, or paint-colored animals are not eligible for registration.

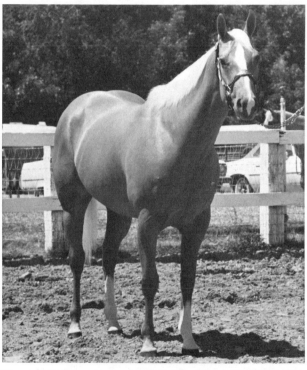

Figure 2.25 Palomino mare, Better Be Sweet, 1974 High Point Palomino of the nation, with a total of 443 points. Also, she was Grand Champion Mare 20 times in 1974. (Courtesy, Palomino Horse Breeders of America, Mineral Wells, Texas. Photograph by Don Shugart)

PALOMINO

Palomino horses originated in the United States, from animals of Spanish extraction. These horses are golden colored. They have a light-colored mane and tail of white, silver, or ivory; the mane and tail may not have more than 15 percent dark or chestnut hair. White markings on the face or below the knees are acceptable.

Palominos are used as stock, parade, pleasure, saddle, and fine harness horses.

The Palomino Horse Breeders of America lists the following disqualifications: Patches of stained or blackened discoloration; dorsal stripe along the spine; zebra stripes or lighter or darker color running around the legs or across the shoulders or withers; or patches of white hair except as caused by an injury or saddle.

The Palomino Horse Association, Inc., lists the following disqualifications: Excessive dark hair in mane or tail; white stockings above knees or hocks.

Figure 2.26 Paso Fino stallion. (Courtesy, Cantlebrook Farms, Durango, Colorado)

PASO FINO

Paso Fino horses[3] originated in the Caribbean area, where they have existed for over 400 years. They have been registered in stud books in Peru, Puerto Rico, Cuba, and Colombia.

---

[3] In the United States, four different breed associations have evolved for the registration and promotion of horses which come under the general heading of "Paso" horses. Each of the registries has slightly different standards. The American Paso Fino Horse Association, Inc., and the Paso Fino Owners and Breeders Association, Inc., call their breed "Paso Fino"; the American Association of Owners and Breeders of Peruvian Paso Horses and the Peruvian Paso Horse Registry of North America call their breed "Peruvian Paso."

The coat may be any color, although solid colors are preferred. Bay, chestnut, or black with white markings are most common. Occasionally, palominos and pintos appear.

Paso Finos are used as pleasure, cutting, and parade horses and for endurance riding and drill team work.

Paso fino is Spanish, meaning fine step. The Paso Fino gait may be described as a broken pace. The legs on the same side move together, but the hind foot strikes the ground a fraction of a second before the front foot, producing a four-beat gait.

Animals that do not possess the Paso Fino gait or do not trace directly to the purebred Paso Fino ancestry are not eligible for registration.

Figure 2.27 Peruvian Paso stallion, Broche del Oro. (Courtesy, USDA)

PERUVIAN PASO

The Peruvian Paso[4] is original only to Peru. In this respect it should not be confused with the Paso Fino breeds whose ancestors were scattered throughout the Caribbean area.

The trademark of the breed is the piso, or gait, a natural (inborn), smooth, four-beat, lateral gait — in essence, a broken pace. Breed enthusiasts insist that the Peruvian Paso does only two acceptable gaits, the *paso llano* and the *sobreandando;* they do not admit to a canter.

Peruvian horses come in all basic solid colors, as well as grays, roans, and palominos, with some rather striking variations of these colors.

[4]See footnote 3.

Peruvian Paso Horse Registry of North America disqualifies for registry animals with light forequarters, coarseness, or extreme height.

American Association of Owners and Breeders of Peruvian Paso Horses disqualifies those with paint, pinto, or albino coloration.

Figure 2.28 Pinto stallion, King Storm Cloud, Pinto Champion. A black-and-white tobiano. Owned by Mr. and Mrs. Leonard Brown, Brooklyn, Michigan. (Courtesy, Pinto Horse Association of America, San Diego, California)

PINTO

Pinto horses[5] originated in the United States, from horses brought in by the Spanish Conquistadores. The coat should be half color (or colors) and half white, with many spots well-placed.

The two distinct pattern markings are overo and tobiano. Overo is a colored horse with white areas extending upward from the belly and lower regions, and there may be other white markings; in tobiano the white areas on the back extend downward, and there may be other white markings as well. Glass eyes are acceptable. The registry association has a separate registry for ponies and horses under 14 hands high.

Pintos are used for any light-horse purpose, but especially as show, parade, novice, pleasure, and stock horses.

[5]Refer to footnote 2 under American Paint Horse.

Figure 2.29 Pony of the Americas stallion, Siri Chief, owned by Golden Rod Farms, Chariton, Iowa. (Courtesy, Pony of America Club, Inc., Mason City, Iowa)

PONY OF THE AMERICAS

Pony of the Americas originated in the United States, in Mason City, Iowa. Their coloring is like the Appaloosa. They have white over the loin and hips and round or egg-shaped dark spots on the white areas.

These ponies have the characteristics of Arabian and Quarter Horses in miniature. They range in height from 46 to 54 inches and are used as western-type riding ponies for children.

Animals are disqualified for registration if they are not within the height range; if they do not have Appaloosa coloring, including mottled skin and large whites of the eyes; if they have pinto markings; or if they are loud-colored roans.

QUARTER HORSE

Quarter Horses originated in the United States. The most common colors are chestnut, sorrel, bay, or dun, and sometimes black, palomino, roan, brown, or copper color.

These horses are well muscled and powerfully built; they have small, alert ears and sometimes heavily muscled cheeks and jaw. They are used as stock, race, and pleasure horses.

Animals are disqualified for registration if they have pinto, Appaloosa, or albino coloring or white markings on the underline.

Figure 2.30 Quarter Horse stallion, an excellent type western cow pony. (Courtesy, Quarter Horse Journal)

Figure 2.31 Racing type Quarter Horse, Truly Truckle, winner of Santa Anita, 3 furlongs (³⁄₈ mile) — straight course. To 1975, sire of 141 Quarter Horse starters, with official earnings of his get totaling $794,053. Stud fee $3000. Owned by Sid Huntley, Huntley Ranch, Madera, California. (Courtesy, Mr. Huntley)

Figure 2.32 Rangerbred stallion, Sonny's Diplomat, Grand Champion Halter Stallion. (Courtesy, Colorado Ranger Horse Assn., Inc., Woodbine, Maryland)

RANGERBRED (COLORADO RANGERS)

The Rangerbred (or Colorado Rangers) originated in the United States, in Colorado, in 1937. However, the two prized foundation stallions of the breed — Leopard, an Arabian, and Linden Tree, a pure Barb — were imported from Turkey by Ulysses S. Grant, retired general and ex-president of the United States, in 1878. They were a gift and token of deep friendship from Sultan Abdul Hamid II, of Turkey.

The breed registry known as the Colorado Ranger Horse Association, was formed in 1937. The name Colorado Rangers was selected for the breed to signify that they were Colorado-bred and that they were bred under range conditions. The breed traces to the two Turkish-bred stallions primarily through their influence on Mustang mares in the Colby Ranch, near Beatrice, Nebraska, and Mike Ruby's Lazy J Bar Ranch, of Thurman, Colorado.

Color is neither an objective of the breed nor a prerequisite for eligibility to registry. Nevertheless, it is noteworthy that many Rangerbreds are spotted. The breed registry eloquently states its position on color as follows: "Color is a fickle jade. It is merely pigment in the skin. It cannot be ridden. Fads fade. Bloodlines endure."

In type, Rangerbreds are similar to Appaloosas. They are used primarily as stock horses.

Animals of draft or pony breeding are not eligible for registration.

Figure 2.33 Shetland Pony stallion, C-Jo's Topper, a many times Grand Champion. (Courtesy, USDA)

SHETLAND PONY

Shetland Ponies originated in the Shetland Islands. The coat may be any color, either broken or solid.

These ponies are small. Two class sizes are recognized by the breed registry: (1) 43 inches and under, and (2) 43 inches to 46 inches. They are used as mounts for children, harness and racing ponies, and roadsters.

Animals are disqualified for registration if they are over 46 inches high.

SPANISH-BARB

The Barb horse was taken from Africa to Spain with the conquest of Spain by the Moors in 711 A.D. From Spain, they were taken to Cuba in 1511, to Mexico in 1519, to southwestern United States in 1540, and to Florida in 1565. The Spanish-Barb Breeders Association was organized in 1972.

Spanish-Barbs are small horses (the standard height is 13–3 to 14–1 hands), with short coupling (usually 5 lumbar vertebrae; at times 17 thoracic vertebrae), deep bodies, good action, and without extreme muscling. All colors are represented in the breed, but dun, grulla, sorrel, and roan are most common. Most animals are solid colored. A dorsal stripe and zebra markings occur in all duns and grullas and in some sorrels. Spanish-Barbs are used for cow ponies, western riding, English riding, and packhorses.

Figure 2.34 Spanish-Barb mare, Coche-Tres, a sorrel. Bred and owned by Susan Banner, Colorado Springs, Colorado. (Courtesy, Spanish-Barb Breeders Association, Colorado Springs, Colorado)

Figure 2.35 Spanish Mustang stallion, Syndicate. (Courtesy, USDA)

SPANISH MUSTANG

The Spanish Mustang originated in the United States. They trace to the feral and the semi-feral (Indian-owned) horses of Barb and Andalusian ancestry that were brought to America by the Spanish Conquistadores in the early 1500s and 1600s. Beginning about 1925, Robert

Figure 2.36 Robert E. Brislawn ("Mr. Mustang"), Cayuse Ranch, Oshoto, Wyoming, originator of the Spanish Mustang Breed. (Courtesy, Jeff Edwards, Brislawn-Edwards, Porterville, California)

E. Brislawn, Sr., and his brother, Ferdinand L. Brislawn, began gathering pure Spanish Mustangs. To retain the purity of the strain, The Spanish Mustang Registry, Inc., was founded in 1957, at Sundance, Wyoming. Spanish Mustangs run the whole gamut of equine colors, including all the solid colors and all the broken colors. They stand 13 to $14\frac{1}{2}$ hands, and some have 5 to $5\frac{1}{2}$ lumbar vertebrae. Spanish Mustangs are used for cow ponies, western riding, English riding, and packhorses.

The breed is characterized by having only five lumbar vertebrae (most breeds have six), short ears, a low-set tail, and round leg bones.

Spanish Mustangs are used primarily for cow ponies and trail riding.

STANDARDBRED

Standardbred horses originated in the United States. The most common colors are bay, brown, chestnut, or black, and occasionally gray, roan, or dun.

Standardbreds are smaller, less leggy, and more rugged than Thoroughbreds. They are used for harness racing, either trotting or pacing, and as harness horses in horse shows.

- DAN PATCH — Famous Standardbred

This great Standardbred horse made history soon after the turn of the century, from 1902 to 1910. In 1906, he paced the world's fastest mile, 1:55, at the Minnesota State Fair. That record stood until 1938, but it was not recognized, because a windshield was pulled in front of the sulky to break the wind. However, to the 93,000 rabid fans who witnessed the feat, and to his worshippers everywhere, the record stood.

The great horse's owner, Will Savage, was a fabulous and colorful

Figure 2.37 Standardbred stallion, "Adios," leading sire of money winners of the breed. (Courtesy, USDA)

character. Will and Dan Patch belonged to each other, when winning — yes, even in death. Mr. Savage made headlines of a sort when he paid $60,000 for the six-year-old Standardbred pacer in 1902. Even his friends referred to the deal as "Savage's folly." But subsequent events proved how wrong they were.

Dan Patch brought fame and fortune to his master and to himself. A railroad line — The Dan Patch Line — was named after him. There were also Dan Patch sleds, coaster wagons, cigars, washing machines (a two-minute performer like Dan), and shoes for kiddies. And Mr. Savage built

Figure 2.38 Dan Patch. (Courtesy, United States Trotting Association, Columbus, Ohio)

the great horse an empire, surroundings befitting his station in life. The stable was equipped with modern living quarters for 60 caretakers. Two racetracks were constructed; the best mile strip ever built, and a covered half-miler with 8400 panes of glass. Even during a Minnesota blizzard, Dan and his stable mates could train in comfort — and style.

Dan Patch was the idol of his day — the Babe Ruth, the Bing Crosby, and the Beatles. People came to see him, as they do any other notable. Lili Langtry, the famous actress, arranged to have her train stopped near Dan's so that she could go to his private car for a visit. Men vied for his shoes, women fought to pluck hair from his mane and tail, small boys played Dan Patch in the backyard, and people wept when he became ill.

The town of Hamilton changed its name to Savage, in honor of the man who had put it on the map.

But there was more than a platonic relationship between horse and owner — there was something almost supernatural between Dan and Will. On July 4, 1916, Dan Patch and Will Savage both took ill on the same day. Those keeping vigil over the horse saw him snuff out his last race — the race with life itself — on July 11. He died at age 20. Thirty-two hours later, Dan's master, Will Savage, was dead at age 57. Both were buried at the same hour; Mr. Savage in Lakewood cemetery, and Mr. Patch under the shade of an oak tree on the bank of the Minnesota river.

Figure 2.39 Tennessee Walking Horse stallion, Sun's Delight, a world Grand Champion. (Courtesy, USDA)

TENNESSEE WALKING HORSE

Tennessee Walking Horses originated in the United States, in the Central Basin of Tennessee. Coat colors are sorrel, chestnut, black, roan, white, bay, brown, gray, or golden. White markings on the face and legs are common.

These horses are characterized by their running walk. They are used as plantation walking horses and as pleasure and show horses.

Figure 2.40 The Darley Arabian, imported in 1706 by King Charles II of England, immortal foundation Thoroughbred stallion from which the Eclipse line sprang. (Courtesy, The Mercaldo Archive, Ozone Park, New York)

Figure 2.41 Thoroughbred stallion, Tentam, holder of the world record for a mile and an eighth on the grass. (Courtesy, Windfields Farm, Chesapeake City, Maryland)

THOROUGHBRED

Thoroughbred horses originated in England. The most common coat colors are bay, brown, black, or chestnut, and, less frequently, roan or gray. White markings on the face and legs are common.

These horses are noted for their fineness of conformation and their long, straight, well-muscled legs. They are used as race, saddle, stock, and polo horses, and as hunters.

■ MAN O'WAR — Famous Thoroughbred

Ask the person on the street — one who may never have gone to a race — to name the greatest horse of all time and chances are that he'll say Man O' War. If there is any absolute against which greatness in a horse may be measured, it is the legendary Man O' War. "Big Red," as he was known, seemed to have limitless speed. Only once in his 21 starts did his machine-like power fail to propel him first across the finish line; that was when he was beaten by the aptly named, "Upset," at Saratoga on August 13, 1919, after an unfortunate start. As if to redress that wrong, Man O' War trounced Upset with authority the next 3 times they met. In 8 times of his 11 starts as a 3-year-old, he broke either a track or world's record.

Man O' War was born in 1917. Samuel D. Riddle bought him as a yearling at the Saratoga sale, on August 17, 1918, for $5000.

During his career, talented writers and eloquent speakers extolled him with such superlatives as "look of eagles" and "living flame." But it fell to his groom, Will Harbut, who had quite a way with words as well as with horses, to devise the most fitting description of all. "Man O' War," as Will never tired of telling the thousands who came to see him, "was de mostest hoss dat ever was." During his lifetime, more visitors went to see Man O' War than Mammoth Cave.

Physically, Man O' War was a glowing chestnut, almost red, standing 16 hands $1\frac{5}{8}$ inches. He measured $71\frac{3}{4}$ inches at the girth and weighed 1100 pounds in training. As a stallion, his weight reached 1370 pounds. He was unusually long bodied and powerfully muscled in the gaskins. Estimates of his stride varied anywhere from 25 to 28 feet, although, oddly enough, it was never officially measured.

When training, Big Red's morning came early. He was given his first meal at 3:30 A.M. At 7:30 A.M., he was brushed and massaged; the bandages that he wore at all times except when in action were removed, and his legs were washed; his face, eyes, and nostrils were sponged; and he was given a rubdown with a soft cloth. After work on warm days, he was washed; then he was rubbed thoroughly, his feet were cleaned and dressed, and he was left to rest in his stall. He was fond of his caretaker; he liked to snatch his hat and carry it around as he showed off for visitors.

Most Thoroughbred horses share a universal birthday — January 1.

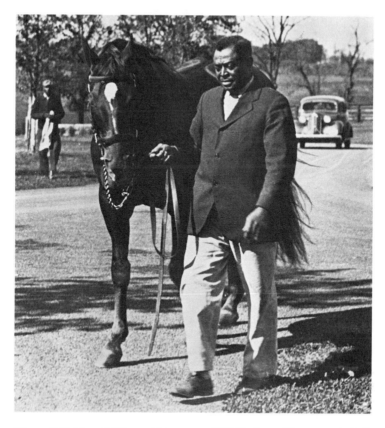

Figure 2.42 Man O'War and his groom, Will Harbut. (Courtesy, J. C. Skeets Meadors and Keeneland Library, Lexington, Kentucky)

But Big Red was different! At Faraway Farm, near Lexington, where he spent most of his life, his actual foaling date, March 29, was duly observed as a special occasion. He received telegrams, carrots, and other tokens of recognition from all over the country.

The great horse, who was the first to command a $5000 service fee, was maintained largely for private use. He sired over 300 offspring who won over 1200 races and earned more than $3½ million.

Big Red died in 1947, at the age of 30. Ira Drymon, as the Thoroughbred Club's representative, delivered the eulogy before the 2000 people assembled and over a nationwide radio hookup. As taps was sounded and the mammoth coffin of polished oak containing the body of Man O' War was lowered to his final resting place, men, women, and children wept unashamedly. Today, above the grave stands a lifesize-and-a-half statue of the great champion.

The Man O' War legend continues on, for he lived and died and won a lasting name and fame — a rare achievement by any beast, or man.

TRAKEHNER

The breed originated in Trakehnen, East Prussia, in 1732. It evolved from the blending of the indigenous Prussian horses, Thoroughbreds, and Arabians. Although the breeding goals have changed through the years to meet the needs of the times, generally speaking the emphasis has been on the development of a horse with the size of the Thoroughbred, but more rugged, and possessing the elegance of the Arabian.

The American Trakehner Association, Inc., was formed in September, 1974.

Figure 2.43 Welsh Pony stallion, "1740 Liseter Shooting Star." (Courtesy, USDA)

WELSH PONY

Welsh Ponies originated in Wales. The coat may be any color except piebald or skewbald, but gaudy white markings are not popular. These ponies are an intermediate size between Shetland Ponies and other light horse breeds. The American Welsh Stud Book stipulates two height divisions: Division A cannot exceed 12–2 hands, and Division B must be over 12–2 and not more than 14 hands.

Welsh Ponies are used for racing, trail riding, parading, stock cutting, and hunting, and as roadsters and mounts for children and small adults.

Piebald or skewbald animals are not eligible for registration.

YSABELLA

Ysabella horses originated in the United States, on McKinzie Rancho, Williamsport, Indiana. The foundation animals were American Saddlers. Coat colors are gold, white, or chestnut, with flaxen, silver, or white mane and tail. There may be white markings on the face and legs.

Ysabellas are used for pleasure riding and as exhibition horses.

Animals having bay color, spots, or black mane and tail are not eligible for registration.

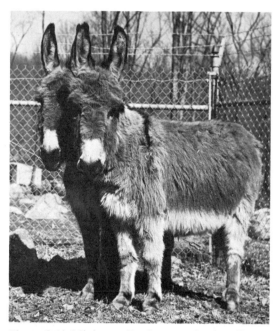

Figure 2.44 Miniature Donkeys used primarily as children's pets. These small animals, standing under 38 inches high at the withers, originated in Sardinia and Sicily. They vary from mouse color to almost black, and a dorsal stripe forms a cross with a stripe over the withers and down the shoulders. (Courtesy, Daniel Langfeld, Jr., Danby Farm, Millard, Nebraska)

DONKEYS

Small members of the ass family, *Equus asinas,* are known as donkeys. The males are known as jacks, and the females as jennets. Compared with the horse, the ass is smaller; has shorter hairs on the mane and tail; does not possess the "chestnuts" on the inside of the hind legs; has much longer ears; has smaller, deeper hoofs; possesses a louder and more harsh voice, called a bray; is less subject to founder or injury; is more hardy; and has a longer gestation period — jennets carry their young about 12 months.

Donkeys should be fed and cared for in the same manner as horses, lessening their feed and space requirements in keeping with their smaller size.

BREED NUMBERS

Table 2.2 shows (1) the 1974, and (2) the total registrations to date of the breeds of light horses, ponies, and donkeys. The recent annual figures reflect the current popularity of the different breeds, although it is recognized that only one year's data fails to show trends. It is noteworthy that about 200,000 horses are being registered annually in the United States at the present time.

Table 2.2 1974 and Total Registrations of Horses, Ponies, and Donkeys in United States Breed Associations

Class	Breed	1974 Registrations	Total Registrations (since Breed Registry Started)
	Quarter Horse..............	77,202[1]	1,044,281
	Thoroughbred..............	27,143	639,902
	Appaloosa	20,361	214,000
	Arabian		
	Purebred	13,500	110,000
	Half-Arabian	13,920	141,384
	Anglo-Arabian	306	3473
	Standardbred................	14,652[2]	392,020
	Tennessee Walking Horse ...	5000	150,754
	American Paint Horse	4752	31,750
	American Saddle Horse	4536	153,593
	Morgan	3700	56,000
	Pinto	2321	23,111
	Palomino	1762[3]	41,340
	Buckskin.....................	1260[4]	4696
Light Horses	Pony of the Americas........	1200	18,000
and Ponies:........	Missouri Fox Trotting		
	Horse......................	1171	9791
	Paso Fino....................	740[5]	3256
	Shetland Pony	645	130,592
	American Part-Blooded......	523	10,039
	Hackney......................	461	19,908
	Welsh Pony..................	443	24,942
	Peruvian Paso...............	341[6]	1472
	Connemara Pony............	151	1689
	U.S. Pony Trotting	120	1300
	Rangerbred..................	111	1518
	Spanish Mustang	70	550
	American White[7]	66	638
	Galiceno.....................	51	1998
	Trakehner...................	45	—
	Morab........................	38	68
	Spanish-Barb................	25	47

(Cont.)

[1] American Quarter Horse Association: 1974 registrations, 76,559; total registrations, 1,038,340. Standard Quarter Horse Association: 1974 registrations, 643; total registrations, 5941.

[2] United States Trotting Association: 1974 registrations, 12,578; total registrations, 392,020. National Trotting & Racing Association: 1974 registrations, 2074.

[3] Palomino Horse Breeders of America: 1974 registrations, 1603; total registrations, 32,699. The Palomino Horse Association, Inc.: 1974 registrations, 159; total registrations, 8641.

[4] American Buckskin Registry Association: 1974 registrations, 360; total registrations, 2796. International Buckskin Horse Association, Inc.: 1974 registrations, 900; total registrations, 1900.

[5] Paso Fino Owners and Breeders Association: 1974 registrations, 540; total registrations, 1056. American Paso Fino Horse Association, Inc.: 1974 registrations, 200; total registrations, 2200.

[6] Peruvian Paso Horse Registry of North America: 1974 registrations, 197; total registrations, 401. American Association of Owners & Breeders of Peruvian Paso Horses: 1974 registrations, 144; total registrations, 1071.

Table 2.2 1974 and Total Registrations of Horses, Ponies, and Donkeys in United States Breed Associations (*Cont.*)

Class	Breed	1974 Registrations	Total Registrations (Since Breed Registry Started)
Light Horses and Ponies:........ (*Cont.*)	American Walking Pony.....	20	114
	American Gotland............	20	278
	Andalusian	19	187
	American Mustang...........	16	712
	American Creme[7]	15	164
	American Bashkir Curly.....	10	35
	Chickasaw.....................	8	631
	American Fox Trotting Horse.......................	—	1873
	American Lipizzan	—	7
Donkeys and Mules:........	Donkeys and Mules..........	179	675
	Miniature Mediterranean Donkey.....................	129	3937

[7]The American Creme and the American White are registered as separate divisions by the American Albino Association, Inc. The American Albino Association and its predecessor, American Albino Horse Club, have registered the following numbers in all divisions: In 1974, 81; total in period 1936–1974, 3237.

RACING

According to some historians, the Greeks introduced horse racing in the Olympic games in 1450 B.C. Also, it is reported that a planned horse race of consequence was run in 1377 between animals owned by Richard II and the Earl of Arundel. The sporting instinct of man being what it is, it is reasonable to surmise, however, that a bit of a contest was staged the first time that two proud mounted horsemen chanced to meet.

The development of horse racing in Britain dates from the 17th Century, although it is known to have taken place much earlier. Records exist of racing during the Roman occupation, and during the reign of Henry II races took place at Smithfield, which was the great London horse market at the time. But it was in the reign of James I that racing first began to be an organized sport. He took a great liking to Newmarket, where he had a royal palace and a racecourse built. Also, he established public races in various parts of the country.

The famous Rowley Mile Course at Newmarket, the home of English flat racing, is named after Charles II. "Old Riley" was his nickname, after his favorite hack by that name. Charles II loved racing; he rode in matches, founded races called the Royal Plates, and sometimes adjudicated in the disputes.

The Jockey Club came into existence at Newmarket in 1752, with many rich and influential men among its members. It gradually became the governing body of English racing.

Figure 2.45 Mandan Indian horse race. (From an oil painting by George Catlin; courtesy, Smithsonian Institution)

Figure 2.46 Running race-horse, a Thoroughbred, in action — at the extended gallop. (Courtesy, Alfred Gwynne Vanderbilt, Sagamore Farm, Glyndon, Maryland)

RACEHORSE(s)

The term "racehorse" refers to a horse that is bred and trained for racing. Today, two types of horse races are run: (1) running races (including steeplechase races) and (2) harness races.

RUNNING RACEHORSES

Racehorses used for running (an extended gallop) under the saddle are now confined almost exclusively to two breeds: Thoroughbreds and Quarter Horses. Also, the Thoroughbred breed (including both purebreds and crossbreds) has been used widely for other purposes — especially as polo mounts, hunters, and cavalry horses. Quarter Horses are the cow pony of the West.

Although trials of speed had taken place between horses from the earliest recorded history, the true and unmistakable foundation of the Thoroughbred breed, as such, traces back only to the reign of Charles II, known as the "father of the British turf."

Although the length of race, weight carried, and type of track have undergone considerable variation in recent years, the running horse always has been selected for speed and more speed at the run. The distinguishing characteristics of the running horse, as represented by the Thoroughbred, are the extreme refinement, oblique shoulders, well-made withers, heavily muscled rear quarters, straight hind legs, and close travel to the ground.

Quarter Horse running races are increasing in importance. Also, Appaloosa and Arabian running races have been approved in a few states.

HARNESS RACEHORSES
(TROTTERS AND PACERS)

Prior to the advent of improved roads and the automobile, but following the invention of the buggy, there was need for a fast, light-harness type of horse. This horse was used to draw vehicles varying in type from the light roadster of the young gallant to the dignified family carriage. In the process of meeting this need, two truly American breeds of horses evolved — the Morgan and the Standardbred. The first breed traces to the foundation sire, Justin Morgan, and the latter to Hambletonian 10, an animal which was linebred to imported Messenger.

As horse and buggy travel passed into permanent oblivion except for recreation and sport, Standardbred breeders wisely placed greater emphasis upon the sport of racing, whereas Morgan enthusiasts directed their breeding programs toward transforming their animals into a saddle breed.

The early descendants of Messenger were sent over the track, trotting (not galloping) under the saddle, but eventually the jockey races in this

Figure 2.47 Harness racehorse, a trotter, in action. (Courtesy, U.S. Trotting Association, Columbus, Ohio)

country came to be restricted to a running type of race in which the Thoroughbred was used. With this shift, beginning in 1879, qualifying standards — a mile in 2:30 at the trot and 2:25 at the pace when hitched to the sulky — were set up for light harness races, and those animals so qualifying were registered. On January 1, 1933, registration on performance alone was no longer granted, and registration of both sire and dam was required.

The pneumatic-tire racing vehicles, known as sulkies, were first introduced in 1892. With their use that year, the time was reduced nearly four seconds below the record of the previous year. Thus were developed harness racing and the Standardbred breed of horses, which today is the exclusive breed used for this purpose.

Trotters and pacers are of similar breeding and type, the particular gaits being largely a matter of training. In fact, many individuals show speed at both the trot and the pace. It is generally recognized, however, that pacers are handicapped in the mud, in the sand, or over a rough surface.

In the beginning, horses of this type found their principal use in harness races at county and state fairs. However, in recent years pari-mutuel harness racing has been established at a number of tracks. Today, harness racehorses are almost exclusively of the Standardbred breed.

RACING COLORS

The Jockey Club assigns colors to racing stables. They may be assigned for one year, or they may be assigned for a lifetime. Sometimes colors are reassigned when no longer in use, but this is not the case with the colors of very famous stables. Jockeys must wear the colors assigned to the stable.

RACING ATTENDANCE

In 1974, 78.8 million fans went to Thoroughbred and harness racing. Auto racing ranked second, with 47.5 million fans; football (pro and college) ranked third, with 42.9 million fans; baseball (major and minor leagues) was in a close fourth place, with an attendance of 41.7 million; and basketball (pro and college) stood fifth, with an attendance of 33.8 million.[6]

RACING RECORDS

In running races (Thoroughbreds), Dr. Fager holds the world's record for a mile at $1:32\frac{1}{5}$ (equal to a speed of 45.4 miles per hour), set at Arlington Park, Chicago, in 1968; and Man O' War set the world's record for $1\frac{3}{8}$ mile at $2:14\frac{1}{5}$, in 1920.

In quarter races (Quarter Horses), Joe Sherry set the U.S. record for a quarter mile (440 yards) at 21.5, in 1965.

In harness racing (Standardbreds), Nevele Pride holds the world's trotting record for a mile at $1:54\frac{4}{5}$ minutes, which was established in 1969; and Steady Star set the world's pacing record for a mile at 1:52 minutes in 1971.

BREED REGISTRY ASSOCIATIONS

A breed registry association consists of a group of breeders banded together for the purposes of (1) recording the lineage of their animals, (2) protecting the purity of the breed, (3) encouraging further improvement of the breed, and (4) promoting interest in the breed. A list of the horse breed registry associations is given in Table 2.3.

---

[6]Statistics courtesy of *Triangle Publications, Inc.*

Table 2.3 Breed Registry Associations

Class of Animal	Breed	Association	Address
Light Horses:..	American Bashkir Curly............	American Bashkir Curly Registry	Box 453, Ely, NV 89301
	American Creme Horse.............	American Albino Association	Box 79, Crabtree, OR 97335
	American Mustang..................	American Mustang Assn., Inc.	P.O. Box 338, Yucaipa, CA 92399
	American Paint Horse	American Paint Horse Assn.	P.O. Box 13486, Ft. Worth, TX 76118
	American Part-Blooded.............	American Part-Blooded Horse Registry	4120 S.E. River Drive, Portland, OR 97222
	(Morgans, American Saddle Horses, Standardbreds, Hackneys, Tennessee Walking Horses, Quarter Horses)		
	American Saddle Horse.............	American Saddle Horse Breeders Assn.	929 S. Fourth St., Louisville, KY 40203
	American White Horse.............	American Albino Assn.	Box 79, Crabtree, OR 97335
	Andalusian	American Andalusian Assn.	P.O. Box 1290, Silver City, NM 88061
	Appaloosa	Appaloosa Horse Club, Inc.	P.O. Box 8403, Moscow, ID 83843
	Arabian-Purebred..................	Arabian Horse Registry of America, Inc.	3435 South Yosemite St., Denver, CO 80231
	Buckskin..........................	American Buckskin Registry Assn.	P.O. Box 1125, Anderson, CA 96007
		International Buckskin Horse Assn., Inc.	P.O. Box 357, St. John, IN 46373
	Chickasaw.........................	Chickasaw Horse Assn., Inc., The	P.O. Box 8, Love Valley, NC 28677
		National Chickasaw Horse Assn.	Route 2, Clarinda, IA 51232
	Cleveland Bay.....................	Cleveland Bay Assn. of America	Middleburg, VA 22117
	Galiceno	Galiceno Horse Breeders Assn., Inc.	111 E. Elm St., Tyler, TX 75701
	Hackney	American Hackney Horse Society	P.O. Box 630, Peekskill, NY 10566
	Hanoverian	American Hanoverian Society	809 W. 106th St., Carmel, IN 46032
	Hungarian	Hungarian Horse Assn.	Bitterroot Stock Farm, Hamilton, MT 59840
	Lipizzan..........................	American Lipizzan Horse Registry	P.O. Box 415, Platteville, WI 53818
	Missouri Fox Trotting Horse.......	Missouri Fox Trotting Horse Breed Assn. Inc.	P.O. Box 637, Ava, MO 65608
	Morab.............................	Morab Horse Registry of America	P.O. Box 143, Clovis, CA 93612

(Cont.)

Table 2.3 Breed Registry Associations (Cont.)

Class of Animal	Breed	Association	Address
	Morgan	American Morgan Horse Assn., Inc.	Box 29, Hamilton, NY 13346
	Morocco Spotted Horse	Morocco Spotted Horse Co-operative Assn. of America	Route 1, Ridott, IL 61067
	Palomino	Palomino Horse Assn., Inc, The	P.O. Box 324, Jefferson City, MO 65101
		Palomino Horse Breeders of America	Bpx 249, Mineral Wells, TX 76067
	Paso Fino	American Paso Fino Horse Assn., Inc.	Mellan Bank Bldg., Room 3018, 525 William Penn Pl., Pittsburgh, PA 15219
		Paso Fino Owners & Breeders Assn., Inc.	c/o Blue Shadows, Rt. 1, Box 45, Tryon, NC 28782
	Peruvian Paso	American Assn. of Owners & Breeders of Peruvian Paso Horses	P.O. Box 2035, California City, CA 93505
		Peruvian Paso Horse Registry of N.A.	P.O. Box 816, Guerneville, CA 95446
	Pinto	Pinto Horse Assn. of America, Inc.	P.O. Box 3984, San Diego, CA 92103
Light Horses... (Cont.)	Quarter Horse	American Quarter Horse Assn.	Box 200, Amarillo, TX 79105
		Standard Quarter Horse Assn.	4390 Fenton, Denver, CO 80212
	Rangerbred	Colorado Ranger Horse Assn., Inc.	7023 Eden Mill Rd., Woodbine, MD 21797
	Spanish-Barb	Spanish-Barb Breeders Assn.	P.O. Box 7479, Colorado Springs, CO 80907
	Spanish Mustang	Spanish Mustang Registry, Inc., The	Route 2, Box 74, Marshall, TX 75670
	Standardbreds	United States Trotting Assn.	750 Michigan Ave., Columbus, OH 43215
		National Trotting & Pacing Assn., Inc.	575 Broadway, Hanover, PA 17331
	Tennessee Walking Horse	Tennessee Walking Horse Breeders Assn. of America	P.O. Box 286, Lewisburg, TN 37091
	Thoroughbred	Jockey Club, The	300 Park Avenue, New York, NY 10022
	Trakehner	American Trakehner Assn., Inc.	P.O. Box 268, Norman, OK 73069
	Welsh Cob	Welsh Cob Society of America, Inc.	225 Head of the Bay Road, Buzzards Bay, Mass. 02532
		Trakehner Breed Assn. and Registry of America, Inc.	Rt. 1, Box 177, Petersburg, VA 23803
	Ysabella	Ysabella Saddle Horse Assn., Inc.	c/o Prairie Edge Farm, Rt. 3, Williamsport, IN 47993

(Cont.)

Table 2.3 Breed Registry Associations (*Cont.*)

Class of Animal	Breed	Association	Address
	Half-bred Thoroughbreds: .... Foals by registered Thoroughbred stallions and out of mares not registered in the American (Jockey Club) Stud Book, or in the Arabian Stud Book.	American Remount Assn.	P.O. Box 1006, Perris, CA 92370
Half Breds:.....	Half-bred Arabian: .... 1. In the Half-Arabian Stud Book: Foals by registered Arabian stallions and out of mares that are not registered in either the American (Jockey Club) Stud Book or the Arabian Stud Book. 2. In the Anglo-Arab Stud Book: (a) Foals by registered Thoroughbred stallions and out of registered Arabian mares. (b) Foals by registered Arabian stallions and out of registered Thoroughbred mares. (c) Foals by registered Thoroughbred or Arabian stallions and out of registered Anglo-Arab mares. (d) Foals by registered Anglo-Arab stallions out of registered Thoroughbred, Arabian, or Anglo-Arab mares.	International Arabian Horse Assn.	224 E. Olive Ave., Burbank, CA 91503

(*Cont.*)

Table 2.3 Breed Registry Associations (*Cont.*)

Class of Animal	Breed	Association	Address
Ponies:..........	Connemara Pony	American Connemara Pony Soc.	R.D. 1, Hoshiekon Farm, Goshen, CT 06756
	Gotland Horse	American Gotland Horse Assn.	R.R. 2, Box 181, Elkland, MO 65644
	National Appaloosa Pony	National Appaloosa Pony, Inc.	122 E. Eighth St., Rochester, IN 46975
	Pony of the Americas	Pony of the Americas Club	P.O. Box 1447, Mason City, IA 50401
	Shetland Pony..........	American Shetland Pony Club	P.O. Box 435, Fowler, IN 47944
	Walking Pony..........	American Walking Pony Assn.	Rt. 5, Box 88, Upper River Rd., Macon, GA 31201
	Welsh Pony..........	Welsh Pony Society of America	P.O. Drawer A, White Post, VA 22663
Draft Horses:...	American Creme Draft Horse	American Creme Draft Horse Assn.	Hubbard, IA 50122
	Belgian..........	Belgian Draft Horse Corp. of America	P.O. Box 335, Wabash, IN 46992
	Clydesdale	Clydesdale Breeders Assn. of the United States	Rt. 3, Waverly, IA 50677
	Percheron..........	Percheron Horse Assn. of America	R.R. 1, Belmont, OH 43718
	Shire	American Shire Horse Assn.	6960 Northwest Dr., Ferndale, WA 98248
	Suffolk	American Suffolk Horse Assn., Inc.	672 Polk Blvd., Des Moines, IA 50312
Jacks, Jennets, and Donkeys:...	Donkeys, Mules, & Hinnys	American Donkey & Mule Society, Inc.	2410 Executive Dr., Indianapolis, IN 46241
	Miniature Donkeys..........	Miniature Donkey Registry of the United States, Inc.	1108 Jackson St., Omaha, NB 68102
	Jacks and Jennets..........	Standard Jack and Jennet Registry of America	Rt. 7, Todds Road, Lexington, KY 40502

3. Selecting and Judging Horses

Relatively few horses are inspected and evaluated by experienced judges. Most of them are bought by persons who lack experience in judging but who have a practical need for the animal and take pride in selecting and owning a good horse. Before buying a horse, an amateur should enlist the help of a competent horseman.

HOW TO SELECT A HORSE

When selecting a horse, the buyer must first decide what kind of horse he needs. This means that he must consider the following points:

1. The mount should be purchased within a price range that the buyer can afford.

2. The amateur or child should have a quiet, gentle, well-broken horse that is neither headstrong nor unmanageable. The horse should never be too spirited for the rider's skill.

3. The size of the horse should be in keeping with the size and weight of the rider. A small child should have a small horse or pony, but a heavy man should have a horse of the weight-carrying type. Also, a tall man or woman looks out of place if not mounted on a horse of considerable height.

4. Usually the novice will do best to start with a three-gaited horse and first master the three natural gaits before attempting to ride a horse executing the more complicated gaits.

5. Other conditions being equal, the breed and color of horse may be decided on the basis of preference.

6. The mount should be suited to the type of work to be performed.

After deciding on the kind of horse needed and getting an ideal in mind, the buyer is ready to select the individual horse. Selection on the basis of body conformation and performance is the best single method of obtaining a good horse. Of course, when animals are selected for breeding purposes, two additional criteria should be considered. These are (1) the record of the horse's progeny if the animal is old enough and has reproduced, and (2) the animal's pedigree. Also, show-ring winnings may be helpful.

Proficiency in judging horses necessitates a knowledge of: (1) the parts of a horse; (2) correct conformation and stance; (3) the proper value assigned to each part (a scorecard may be used for this purpose); (4) how to determine age; (5) how to measure a horse; (6) blemishes and unsoundnesses; (7) vices; (8) the gaits; (9) defects in action; and (10) colors and markings.

PARTS OF A HORSE

In selecting and judging horses, horsemen usually refer to parts rather than the individual as a whole. Nothing so quickly sets a real horseman apart from a novice as a thorough knowledge of the parts and the language commonly used in describing them. Figure 3.1 shows the parts of a horse.

It is noteworthy that the knee joint in the horse is the counterpart of the wrist joint in man; the stifle joint in the horse is the counterpart of the knee joint in man; and the hock joint in the horse is the counterpart of the ankle joint in man.

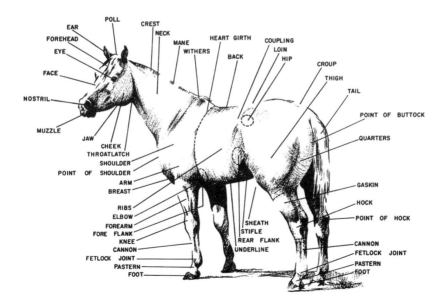

Figure 3.1 Parts of a horse.

CONFORMATION

A good horse must conform to a specific type which fits him for the function that he is expected to perform. Secondly, he should be true to the characteristics of the breed that he represents.

Anyone selecting a horse should have clearly in mind the ideal for which he is looking, recognizing full well that few animals meet this high standard and that he may have to settle for less. Table 3.1 (Figures 3.2 to 3.13) is a handy judging guide.

Table 3.1 Handy Judging Guide for Light Horses (Figures 3.2 to 3.13)

Procedure for Examining, and What to Look for	Ideal Type	Common Faults
FRONT VIEW:		
1. Head.	1. Head well proportioned to rest of body, refined, cleancut, with chiseled appearance; broad, full forehead with great width between the eyes; jaw broad and strongly muscled; ears medium sized, well carried, and attractive.	1. Plain headed.
2. Sex character.	2. Refinement and feminity in the broodmare; boldness and masculinity in the stallion.	2. Mares lacking feminity; stallions lacking masculinity.
3. Chest capacity.	3. A deep, wide chest.	3. A narrow chest.
4. Set to the front legs.	4. Straight, true, and squarely set.	4. Crooked front legs.
REAR VIEW:		
1. Width of croup and through rear quarters.	1. Wide and muscular over the croup and through the rear quarters.	1. Lacking width over the croup and muscling through the rear quarters.
2. Set to the hind legs.	2. Straight, true, and squarely set.	2. Crooked hind legs.

(Cont.)

Table 3.1 Handy Judging Guide for Light Horses (*Cont.*)

Procedure for Examining, and What to Look for	Ideal Type	Common Faults
SIDE VIEW:		
1. Style and beauty.	1. High carriage of head, active ears, alert disposition, and beauty of conformation.	1. Lacking style and beauty.
2. Balance and symmetry.	2. All parts well developed and nicely blended together.	2. Lacking in balance and symmetry.
3. Neck.	3. Fairly long neck, carried high; clean-cut about the throat latch; with head well set on.	3. A short, thick neck; ewe-necked.
4. Shoulders.	4. Sloping shoulders (about a 45 degree angle).	4. Straight in the shoulders.
5. Topline.	5. A short, strong back and loin, with a long, nicely turned, and heavily muscled croup, and a high, well-set tail; withers clearly defined and of the same height as the high point of the croup.	5. Sway-backed; steep croup.
6. Coupling.	6. A short coupling as denoted by the last rib being close to the hip.	6. Long in the coupling.
7. Middle.	7. Ample middle due to long, well sprung ribs.	7. Lacking middle.
8. Rear flank.	8. Well let down in the rear flank.	8. High cut rear flank or "wasp-waisted."
9. Arm, forearm, and gaskin.	9. Well-muscled arm, forearm, and gaskin.	9. Light-muscled arm, forearm and gaskin.
10. Legs, feet and pasterns.	10. Straight, true, and squarely set legs; pasterns sloping about 45 degrees; hoofs large, dense, and wide at the heels.	10. Crooked legs; straight pasterns, hoofs small, contracted at the heels, and shelly.
11. Quality.	11. Plenty of quality, as denoted by clean, flat bone, well-defined joints and tendons, refined head and ears, and fine skin and hair.	11. Lacking quality.
12. Breed type (size, color, shape of body and head, and action true to the breed represented).	12. Showing plenty of breed type.	12. Lacking breed type.

(*Cont.*)

Table 3.1 Handy Judging Guide for Light Horses (*Cont.*)

Procedure for Examining, and What to Look for	Ideal Type	Common Faults
SOUNDNESS:		
1. Soundness, and freedom from defects in conformation that may predispose unsoundness.	1. Sound, and free from blemishes.	1. Unsound; blemished (wire cuts, capped hocks, etc).
ACTION:[1]		
1. At the walk.	1. Easy, prompt, balanced; a long step, with each foot carried forward in a straight line; feet lifted clear of the ground.	1. A short step, with feet not lifted clear of the ground.
2. At the trot.	2. Rapid, straight, elastic trot, with the joints well flexed.	2. Winging, forging, and interfering.
3. At the canter.	3. Slow, collected canter, which is readily executed on either lead.	3. Fast and extended canter.

[1]The three most common gaits are given here. Five-gaited horses must perform two additional gaits. In selecting for gait, (1) observe horse at each intended gait, and (2) examine trained horses while performing at use for which they are intended.

STANCE

Proper stance, or underpinning, is requisite to correct movement. The legs should be straight, true, and squarely set, and the bone should be clearly defined. The pasterns should be sloping; and the feet should be large and wide at the heels. The hock should be large, clean, wide from front to back, deep, clean-cut, and correctly set. The knee should be deep from front to rear, wide when viewed from the front, straight, and tapered gradually into the leg. Since the hock and knee joints of the horse are subject to great wear and are the seat of many unsoundnesses, they should receive special attention.

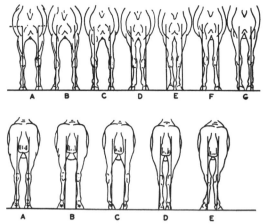

Figure 3.14 The proper and faulty conformation of (top) the forelegs when viewed from the front, and (bottom) the hind legs when viewed from the rear. The forelegs: A, represents correct conformation; B, splay-footed or base-narrow forefeet, toes cut out, heels in; C, bowed legs; D, knock-kneed, knees set close together with toes pointing outward; E, conformation predisposing to interfering; F, knees set close together; G, pigeon-toed or toe narrow — a conformation which will cause the animal to wing or throw out the feet as they are elevated. The hind legs: A, represents correct conformation; B, hind legs set too far apart; C, bandy-legged — wide at the hocks and hind feet toe in; D, hind legs set too close together; E, cow-hocked. The direction of the leg and the form of the foot are very important in the horse. (Courtesy, USDA)

Figure 3.15 The proper and faulty conformation of (top) the forelegs when viewed from the side, and (bottom) the hind legs when viewed from the side. The forelegs: A, correct conformation; B, forelegs too far under the body; C, forelegs too far advanced; D, knee-sprung or buck-kneed — over in the knees; E, calf-kneed — standing with knees too far back. The hind legs: A, correct conformation; B, sickle hocked — hind legs too far under the body; C, legs set too far back; D, hock joint is too straight. The direction of the legs and the form of the foot are very important in the horse. (Courtesy, USDA)

ALL-BREED HORSE SCORECARD

Characteristics	Points or percent	Name or number of horse:	Name or number of horse:	Name or number of horse:	Name or number of horse:
Breed type	15				
Form	35				
Feet and legs	15				
Head and neck	10				
Quality	10				
Action	15				
Total points or percent	100				

Breed type 15

Animals should possess the distinctive characteristics of breed represented, including
Color:
Height at maturity:
Weight at maturity:

Form 35

Style and beauty: Attractive, good carriage, alert, refined.
Balance and symmetry: All parts well developed and nicely blended together.
Body: Nicely turned; long well-sprung ribs; heavily muscled.
Back and loin: Short and strong, wide, well muscled, and short coupled.
Croup: Long, level, wide, muscular, with a high-set tail.
Rear quarters: Deep and muscular.
Gaskin: Heavily muscled.
Withers: Prominent, and of the same height as the high point of the croup.
Shoulders: Deep, well laid in, and sloping about a 45 degree angle.
Chest: Fairly wide, deep, and full.
Arm and forearm: Well muscled.

Feet and legs 15

Legs: Correct position and set when viewed from front, side, and rear.
Pasterns: Long, and sloping at about a 45 degree angle.
Feet: In proportion to size of horse, good shape, wide and deep at heels, dense texture of hoof.
Hocks: Deep, clean-cut, and well supported.
Knees: Broad, tapered gradually into cannon.
Cannons: Clean, flat, with tendons well defined.

Head and neck 10

Alertly carried, showing style and character.
Head: Well proportioned to rest of body, refined, clean-cut, with chiseled appearance; broad, full forehead with great width between the eyes; ears medium sized, well carried, and attractive; eyes large and prominent.
Neck: Long, nicely arched, clean-cut about the throatlatch, with head well set on, gracefully carried.

Quality 10

Clean, flat bone; well-defined and clean joints and tendons; and fine skin and hair.

Action 15

Walk: Easy, springy, prompt, balanced, a long step, with each foot carried forward in a straight line; feet lifted clear of the ground.
Trot: Prompt, straight, elastic, balanced, with hocks carried closely, and high flexion of knees and hocks.
Discrimination:
Any abnormality that affects the serviceability of the horse.
Disqualification:
In keeping with breed registry or show regulations.

Total points or percent 100

HORSE SCORECARD

A horse must conform to the specific type that is needed for the function he is to perform. Secondly, he should conform to the characteristics of the breed that he represents. The use of a scorecard is a good way to make sure that no part is overlooked and a proper value is assigned to each part.

A scorecard is a listing of the different parts of an animal, with a numerical value assigned to each part according to its relative importance. Also, breed characteristics may be considered in a scorecard. An all-breed horse scorecard is presented on page 66.

HOW TO DETERMINE AGE

The lifespan of horses averages about 20 years, a little more than one-third that of man. Horses generally are at their best between 3 and 12 years of age. This may vary because of individual differences in animals or because of differences in the kind of work they do. The age of horses is, therefore, important to breeder, seller, and buyer.

The approximate age of a horse can be determined by noting time of appearance, shape, and degree of wear of temporary and permanent teeth. Temporary, or milk, teeth are easily distinguishable from permanent ones because they are smaller and whiter.

The best way to learn to determine age in horses is by examining the teeth of individual horses of known ages.

A mature male horse has 40 teeth and a mature female has 36, as shown in Table 3.2.[1] A foal of either sex has 24. The mare does not have tushes as a rule.

Figure 3.16 How to look a horse in the mouth. With the tongue held in one hand and the lower jaw grasped with the other hand, you can look at the teeth for as long as you like.

---

[1]Quite commonly, a small, pointed tooth, known as a "wolf tooth," may appear in front of each molar in the upper jaw, thus increasing the total number of teeth to 42 in the male and 38 in the female. Less frequently, 2 more wolf teeth in the lower jaw increase the total number of teeth in the male and female to 44 and 40, respectively.

Table 3.2 Types and Number of Teeth in Horses

Types of Teeth	Number of Teeth		
	Mature Male	Mature Female	Young Animal, Either Sex
Molars or grinders.	24	24	12
Incisors or front teeth .... The 2 central incisors are known as centrals or nippers; the next 2, 1 on each side of the nippers, are called intermediates or middles; and the last, or outer pair, are the corners.	12	12	12
Tushes or pointed teeth .... These are located between the incisors and molars in males. Females do not have tushes as a rule.	4	0	0
Total teeth	40	36	24

Figure 3.17 Temporary incisors to 10 days of age: first or central upper and lower temporary incisors appear.

Figure 3.18 Temporary incisors at 4 to 6 weeks of age: second or intermediate upper and lower temporary incisors appear.

Figure 3.19 Temporary incisors at 6 to 10 months: third or corner upper and lower temporary incisors appear.

Figure 3.20 Temporary incisors at 1 year: crowns of central temporary incisors show wear.

Figure 3.21 Temporary incisors at 1½ years: intermediate temporary incisors show wear.

Figure 3.22 Temporary incisors at 2 years: all show wear.

Figure 3.23 Incisors at 4 years: permanent incisors replace temporary centrals and intermediates; temporary corner incisors remain.

Figure 3.24 Incisors at 5 years: all permanent; cups in all incisors.

Figure 3.25 Incisors at 6 years: cups worn out of lower central incisors.

Figure 3.26 Incisors at 7 years: cups worn out of lower intermediate incisors.

Figure 3.27 Incisors at 8 years: cups worn out of all lower incisors, and dental star (dark line in front of cup) appears on lower central and intermediate pairs.

Figure 3.28 Incisors at 9 years: cups worn out of upper central incisors; dental star on upper central and intermediate pairs.

Figure 3.29 Incisors at 10 years: cups worn out of upper intermediate incisors, and dental star is present in all incisors.

Figure 3.30 Incisors at 11 or 12 years: cups worn in all incisors (smooth mouthed), and dental star approaches center of cups.

Figure 3.31 Characteristic shape of lower incisors at 18 years.

Figure 3.32 Side view of 5-, 7-, and 20-year-old mouth. Note that as the horse advances in age, the teeth change from nearly perpendicular to slanting sharply toward the front.

Even experienced horsemen cannot determine the age of an animal accurately after it is 12 years old. After this age, the teeth change from oval to triangular and they project or slant forward more and more as the horse becomes older.

Side views of the mouths of 5-, 7-, and 20-year-old horses are shown in Figure 3.32.

An animal's environment can affect wear on the teeth. Teeth of horses raised in dry sandy areas, for example, will show more than normal wear; a 5-year-old western horse may have teeth that would be normal in a 6- to 8-year-old horse raised elsewhere. The teeth of cribbers also show more than normal wear. The age of such animals is hard to determine, and the age of horses with a parrot mouth also is difficult to estimate.

JANUARY 1 BIRTH DATE

Regardless of when a foal is born, its birth date is always considered as January 1. Thus, a foal born May 1, 1970, will be 15 years old on January 1, 1985. This is done from the standpoint of racing and showing. As a result, horsemen who race or show make every effort to have foals arrive as near January 1 as possible, thereby getting the advantage of more growth than animals born later in the year. This is especially important in the younger age groups; for example, when racing or showing a 2-year-old.

A shift of the date of birth (the January 1 birthday, for purposes of racing and showing) to somewhere between March 1 and May 1 would improve conception rate and foaling percentage, simply because mares would be bred under more natural and ideal spring conditions. Thus, it would have considerable virtue from the standpoint of the horse producer. On the other side of the ledger, however, it would create problems in racing and in registrations, both here and abroad. Also, such a deep-rooted tradition would be difficult to change; in fact, much consideration has been given to this matter from time to time. In the final analysis, therefore, stepping up breeding research is the primary avenue through which the deplorably low percentage foal crop may be improved.

OLDEST HORSE

Authentic records of very old horses are difficult to obtain. Old Bill, a horse owned throughout his lifetime by a Mr. Petrie of Edinburgh, Scotland, is reputed to have lived to age 62, according to B. S. Dystra, hippologist, of Holland.[2]

An ex-Italian army horse, Topolino, was foaled on February 24, 1909, and died in February, 1960, at the age of 51.

Old Nellie, a black mare of draft breeding, raised by a Missouri farmer, was 53 years and 8 months old when she died in 1969.

Since the average life span of a horse is a little more than one-third the life expectancy of a person in the United States, in terms of human life a 50-year-old horse would be equivalent to a man more than 150 years old.

HOW TO MEASURE A HORSE

The measurements considered important to a horse are his height, weight, girth, and bone.

Height at the withers

Figure 3.33 The height of a horse is measured from the highest point of the withers to the ground. The experienced horseman deftly estimates the height of a horse in relation to his own stature, and does not use any measuring device.

[2]*American Shetland Pony Journal,* November 1969, p. 25.

1. *Height* of a horse refers to the distance from the highest point of the withers to the ground. It is expressed in hands, each hand being 4 inches (derived from the average width of the human hand). The experienced horseman estimates the height of a horse in relation to his own stature, by standing opposite the front limbs and sighting across to the top of the withers. Height may also be determined by actual measurements.

2. *Weight* is best determined by using a scale.

3. *Girth* refers to the circumference of the chest, in inches, as measured with a tape from behind the withers and in front of the back.

4. *Bone* is the circumference, in inches as recorded on a tape measure, around the cannon bone halfway between the knee and fetlock joints.

BLEMISHES AND UNSOUNDNESSES

An integral part of selecting a horse lies in the ability to recognize common blemishes and unsoundnesses and the ability to rate the importance of each. A thorough knowledge of normal, sound structure makes it easy to recognize imperfections.

Any deviation from normal in the structure or function of a horse constitutes an unsoundness. From a practical standpoint, however, a differentiation is made between abnormalities that do, and those that do not, affect serviceability.

Blemishes include abnormalities that do not affect serviceability, such as wire cuts, rope burns, nail scratches, or capped hocks.

Unsoundnesses include more serious abnormalities that affect serviceability. Unsoundnesses may be caused by any one or various combinations of the following: (1) an inherent or predisposing weakness; (2) subjecting the horse to strain and stress far beyond the capability of even the best structure and tissue; (3) accident or injury; and (4) nutritional deficiencies, particularly minerals. Unsoundnesses that can be definitely traced to the latter three causes should not be considered as hereditary. Unless one is very positive, however, serious unsoundnesses should always be regarded with suspicion in the breeding animal. Probably no unsoundness is actually inherited, but the fact that individuals may inherit a predisposition to an unsoundness through faulty conformation cannot be questioned.

A buyer should consider the use to which he intends to put the animal before he buys a blemished or unsound horse.

The locations of common blemishes and unsoundnesses are shown in Figure 3.34.

Definitions and descriptions of some common blemishes and unsoundnesses follow.

1. *Undershot jaw* — Lower jaw is longer than the upper jaw, causing malocclusion of the teeth.

2. *Parrot mouth* (overshot jaw) — Lower jaw is shorter than upper jaw.

3. *Blindness* — Partial or complete loss of vision. Blindness can

Locations
OF UNSOUNDNESSES

1. *Undershot jaw*
2. *Parrot mouth*
3. *Blindness*
4. *Moon Blindness*
5. *Poll evil*
6. *Fistulous withers*
7. *Stifled*
8. *Thoroughpin*
9. *Capped hock*
10. *Stringhalt*
11. *Curb*
12. *Bone spavin or jack*
13. *Bog spavin*
14. *Blood spavin*
15. *Bowed tendons*
16. *Sidebones*
17. *Cocked ankles*
18. *Quittor*
19. *Ring bone*
20. *Windpuffs*
21. *Splints*
22. *Knee sprung*
23. *Calf kneed*
24. *Capped elbow*
25. *Sweeney*
26. *Contracted feet, corns, founder, thrush, quarter or sand crack, scratches or grease heel.*

General: heaves, hernia, roaring, thick wind.

Figure 3.34 Location of points of common unsoundnesses.

usually be detected by very erect ears, a hesitant gait, discoloration of the eye, or by moving the hand gently as it is held close to the eye.

4. *Moon blindness* — A cloudy or inflamed condition of the eye that recurs at periodic intervals (periodic opthalmia).

5. *Poll evil* — An inflamed or infected condition in the region of the poll, usually caused by bruising.

6. *Fistulous withers* — An inflamed or infected condition in the region of the withers caused by a bruise or ill-fitting harness.

7. *Stifled* — The patella (cap) of the stifle joint has been displaced.

8. *Thoroughpin* — a puffy condition in the web (tissue) of the hock.

9. *Capped hock* — An enlargement at the point of the hock.

10. *Stringhalt* — An excessive flexing upward of the hind legs when moving forward or backward.

11. *Curb* — Swelling at the rear of the leg and just below the point of the hock.

12. *Bone spavin or jack* — A bony enlargement on the inside of the hock at a point where the hock tapers into the cannon bone.

13. *Bog spavin* — A filling of the natural depression on the inside and front of the hock.

14. *Blood spavin* — A varicose vein that appears on the inside of the hock just above the location of a bog spavin.

15. *Bowed tendons* — Swollen tendons behind the cannon bones in both the front and hind legs. Descriptive terms of "high" or "low" bow are

Figure 3.35 Front legs of the horse, as viewed from the front: A, sound leg; B, splint; C, wind puffs; D, ringbone; and E, sidebone.

Figure 3.36 Front legs of the horse, as viewed from the side: A, sound leg; B, bowed tendon; and C, filled tendon.

Figure 3.37 Hind legs of the horse, a three-quarter view: A, sound leg; and B, bog spavin.

used by horsemen to denote the location of the injury; the high bow appears just under the knee and the low bow just above the fetlock.

16. *Sidebones* — Hardened lateral cartilage immediately above and toward the rear quarter of the coronet.

17. *Cocked ankles* — Fetlocks bent forward in a cocked position, usually the hind ones.

Figure 3.38 Hind legs of the horse, a front view: A, sound leg; and B, bone spavin.

Figure 3.39 Hind legs of the horse as viewed from the side: A, sound leg; B, thoroughpin; C, capped hock; D, curb; and E, cocked ankle.

Figure 3.40 A, sound hoof; B, contracted heel.

Figure 3.41 Most common causes, ranked in order, for retiring horses from the track: (1) bowed tendons; (2) knee injury; (3) osselets; (4) bucked shin; (5) splint; (6) fractured sesamoid; (7) fractured fibula; (8) sand crack; and (9) suspensory ligament damaged.

18. *Quittor* — A deep-seated running sore at the coronet.

19. *Ringbone* — A bony growth on the pastern bone, generally on the front foot.

20. *Windpuff* — An enlargement of the fluid sac, or bursa, just above the pastern on the fore and rear legs.

21. *Splints* — Bony growths on the cannon bone, usually on the inside of the front legs.

22. *Knee-sprung* — The knees are bent forward; also called buck-kneed.

23. *Calf-kneed* — Knees tend to bend backward; opposite of buck-kneed. This condition causes more trouble than knee-sprung or buck-kneed.

24. *Capped elbow or shoe boil* — Swelling at the point of the elbow.

25. *Sweeney* — A depression in the shoulder because of an atrophied muscle.

26. *Foot ailments:*

a. *Contracted heel* — A drawing in or contracting of the heel.

b. *Corns* — A bruise in the soft tissue underlying the horny sole of the foot.

c. *Founder* — A serious inflammation of the fleshy laminae under the horny wall of the hoof, characterized by ridges running around the hoof.

d. *Thrush* — A disease of the frog (bottom middle) of the hoof.

e. *Splayfoot* — Front toes turned out, heels turned in.

f. *Pigeon-toed* — Front toes turned in, heels turned out.

g. *Quarter or sand crack* — A vertical split in the horny wall of the hoof.

h. *Scratches or grease heel* — A scabby inflammation of the posterior surface of the fetlocks.

Some general ailments that affect horses are defined as follows:

1. *Heaves* — Difficulty in forcing air out of the lungs.

2. *Hernia* — The protrusion of any internal organ through the wall that contains it.

3. *Roaring* — Whistling or wheezing when breathing is speeded up.

4. *Thick wind* — Difficulty in breathing.

VICES

Stable vices are bad habits which are observed in confinement. Many of them originate with incompetent handling and lack of exercise; but once acquired they are difficult to cope with or to correct. The common ones are:

1. *Bolting* — Eating too fast; usually rectified by placing some baseball-sized stones in the feed box, or by adding chopped hay to the animal's grain ration.

2. *Cribbing* — Biting or setting the teething against the manger (or other object) and sucking in air; remedied by buckling a strap around the neck and compressing the larynx without discomfort.

3. *Halter pulling* — Pulling on the halter when tied. It is usually a man-made vice, caused by tying the horse too low, too short, or so long that he gets a foot over the tie rope. Also, it may result when a horse has been tied to a pole or tree at the proper height but so loosely that the rope slides down on the pole or tree. At other times, the horse may be tied with a halter or rope that is too light or flimsy, or tied too closely to something terrifying, with the result that he pulls back in fright and breaks the rope.

The number of times required to make a horse into a confirmed halter puller will vary according to the first traumatic experience and the temperament of the horse. One bad experience may make a confirmed halter puller that is hard to break.

There are many methods of breaking a halter puller. Either a rope under the tail, or a rope around the belly, so arranged that it will tighten up when the horse flies back and breaks his halter, appears to be very successful; and there is no danger of serious injury from the use of either method.

4. *Kicking* — Striking with the hind feet without provocation. Unusual excitement or injury may cause a gentle horse to kick.

5. *Tail rubbing* — Rubbing the tail against the side of the stall or other objects; rectified by installing a tail board. A tail board is a board projecting from the wall of the stall high enough to strike just below the point of the buttock, instead of the tail of the rubbing horse.

6. *Weaving* — Rhythmical swaying back and forth while standing in the stall.

Figure 3.42 The gaits of horses.

7. *Other vices* — Balking, rearing, shying, striking with the front feet, running away, and objection to harnessing, saddling, and grooming.

GAITS

A gait is a particular way of going, either natural or acquired, that is characterized by a distinctive rhythmic movement of the feet and legs (see Figure 3.42).

In proper show-ring procedure, horses are brought back to the walk each time before they are called upon to execute a different gait. An exception is made in five-gaited classes where the rack may be executed from the slow gait.

The walk is a natural, slow, flatfooted, four-beat gait. A four-beat gait is one in which each foot leaves and strikes the ground at separate intervals. The walk should be springy, regular, and true.

The trot is a natural, rapid, two-beat diagonal gait in which a front foot and the opposite hind foot take off and strike the ground simultaneously. There is a brief moment when all four feet are off the ground and the horse seems to float through the air.

This gait varies considerably with different breeds. The trot of the

Standardbred is characterized by length and rapidity of individual strides; the trot of the Hackney shows extreme flexion of the knees and hocks that produces a high-stepping show gait.

The canter is a slow, restrained, three-beat gait. Two diagonal legs are paired and produce a single beat that falls between the successive beats of the two unpaired legs. The canter imposes a special wear on the leading forefoot and its diagonal hindfoot. It is important, therefore, to change the lead frequently.

In the show-ring, the lead should be toward the inside of the ring; a right foot lead when going clockwise (see Figure 3.43), and a left foot lead when moving counterclockwise. The lead is changed by reversing direction of travel (when the ringmaster calls for "reverse and canter"). The canter should be executed in such a slow collected manner that the animal may perform in a relatively small circle.

The lope is the western adaption of a very slow canter. It is a smooth, slow gait in which the head is carried low.

The run or *gallop* is a fast, four-beat gait in which the feet strike the ground separately — first one hind foot, then the other hind foot, then the front foot on the same side as the first hind foot, and then the other front

Figure 3.43 The right lead at the lope, which should be toward the inside of the ring when going clockwise.

foot, which decides the lead. There is a brief interval when all four feet are off the ground. The gallop is the fast natural gait of both wild horses and Thoroughbred racehorses.

The pace is a fast two-beat gait in which the front and hind feet on the same side start and stop simultaneously. The feet rise just above the ground level. There is a split second when all four feet are off the ground and the horse seems to float through the air.

The pace is faster than the trot but slower than the run or gallop. It allows for a "quick getaway," but it produces an objectionable side or rolling type of motion. This gait is not suited to travel in mud or snow; a smooth, hard footing and easy draft are necessary for its best execution.

The pace was once popular in England, but it lost favor soon after the development of the Thoroughbred in the 18th Century.

The stepping pace (or slow pace) is the preferred slow gait for five-gaited show horses. It is a modified pace in which the objectionable side or rolling motion of the true pace is eliminated because the two feet on each side do not move exactly together. Instead, it is a four-beat gait with each of the four feet striking the ground separately. In the takeoff, the hind and front feet start almost together, but the hind foot touches the ground slightly ahead of the front foot on the same side, and each foot strikes the ground separately.

The fox trot is a slow, short, broken type of trot in which the head usually nods. In executing the fox trot, the horse brings each hind foot to the ground an instant before the diagonal forefoot. This gait is accepted as a slow gait, but it is not as popular as the stepping pace.

The running walk is a slow, four-beat gait, intermediate in speed between the walk and rack. The hind foot oversteps the front foot from a few to as many as 18 inches, giving the motion a smooth gliding effect. It is characterized by a bobbing or nodding of the head, a flopping of the ears, and a snapping of the teeth (none of which should be excessive) in rhythm with the movements of the legs. This is a necessary gait in Tennessee Walking Horses.

The running walk is easy on both horse and rider; it is the all-day working gait of the South, executed at a speed of 6 to 8 miles per hour.

The rack (formerly, but now incorrectly called single-foot) is a fast, flashy, unnatural, four-beat gait in which each foot meets the ground separately at equal intervals; hence it was originally known as the "single-foot," a designation now largely discarded. The rack is easy on the rider, but hard on the horse. It is the most popular and flashy gait in the American show-ring. On the tanbark, greater speed at the rack is requested with the command "rack on."

The traverse or *side step* is simply a lateral movement of the animal to the right or left as desired, without moving forward or backward. This trick will often assist in (1) lining up horses in the show-ring, (2) opening and closing gates, and (3) taking position in a mounted drill or a posse.

DEFECTS IN ACTION

The feet of an animal should move straight ahead and parallel to a center line drawn in the direction of travel. Any deviations from this way of going constitute defects. Some defects in action are:

1. *Cross-firing,* which is generally confined to pacers, consisting of a scuffing on the inside of the diagonal fore and hind feet.

2. *Dwelling,* most noticeable in trick-trained horses, consisting of a noticeable pause in the flight of the foot, as though the stride were completed before the foot reaches the ground.

3. *Forging,* the striking of the forefoot by the toe of the hind foot.

4. *Interfering,* the striking of the fetlock or cannon by the opposite foot that is in motion. This condition is predisposed in horses with base-narrow, toe-wide, or splayfooted standing positions.

5. *Lameness,* which can be detected when the affected foot is favored when standing. In action, the load on the ailing foot is eased, and there is characteristic bobbing of the head of the horse as the affected foot strikes the ground.

6. *Paddling,* the throwing of the front feet outward as they are picked up. This condition is predisposed in horses with toe-narrow or pigeon-toed standing positions.

7. *Pointing,* a perceptible extension of the stride with little flexion. This condition is likely to occur in the Thoroughbred and Standardbred breeds — animals bred and trained for great speed with a long stride.

8. *Pounding,* a condition in which there is heavy contact with the ground in contrast to the desired light, springy movement.

9. *Rolling,* excessive lateral shoulder motion, characteristic of horses with protruding shoulders.

10. *Scalping,* that condition in which the hairline at the top of the hind foot hits the toe of the forefoot as it breaks over.

11. *Speedy cutting,* a condition of a horse at speed in which a hind leg above the scalping mark hits against the shoe of a breaking-over forefoot. In trotters, legs on the same side are involved; in pacers, diagonal legs are involved.

12. *Stringhalt,* characterized by excessive flexing of the hind legs. It is most easily detected when backing a horse.

13. *Trappy,* a short, quick, choppy stride. This condition is predisposed in horses with short, straight pasterns and straight shoulders.

14. *Winding* or *rope-walking,* a twisting of the striding leg around in front of the supporting leg so as to make contact in the manner of a "rope-walking" artist. This condition most often occurs in horses with very wide fronts.

15. *Winging,* an exaggerated paddling, particularly noticeable in high-going horses.

COLORS AND MARKINGS

Within certain breeds, some colors are preferred or required, and others are undesirable or constitute disqualifications for registration. A good horseman needs a working knowledge of horse colors and patterns because they are the most conspicuous features by which a horse can be described or identified.

BODY COLORS

The five basic body colors of horses are:

1. *Bay* — Bay is a mixture of red and yellow. It includes many shades, from a light yellowish tan (light bay) to a dark, rich shade that is almost brown (dark bay). A bay horse usually has a black mane and tail and black points.

2. *Black* — A black horse is completely black, including the muzzle and flanks. If in doubt whether the horse is dark brown or black, note the color of the fine hairs on the muzzle and the hair on the flanks; tan or brown hairs at these points indicate the horse is not a true black, but a seal brown.

3. *Brown* — A brown horse is almost black but can be distinguished by the fine tan or brown hairs on the muzzle or flanks.

4. *Chestnut* (*sorrel*) — A chestnut horse is basically red. The shades vary from light washy yellow (light chestnut) to a dark liver color (dark chestnut). Between these come the brilliant red-gold and copper shades. Normally, the mane and tail of a chestnut horse are the same shade as the body, although they may be lighter. When they are lighter, the coloring is called flaxen mane and tail. Chestnut color is never accompanied by a black mane and tail.

5. *White* — A true white horse is born white and remains white throughout life. White horses have snow-white hair, pink skin, and brown eyes (rarely blue).

Besides the five basic colors, horses have five major variations to these coat colors. The variations are:

1. *Dun* (*buckskin*) — Dun is a yellowish color of variable shading from pale yellow to a dirty canvas color. A dun horse has a stripe down the back.

2. *Gray* — This is a mixture of white and black hairs. Sometimes a gray horse is difficult to distinguish from a black horse at birth, but gray horses get lighter with age.

3. *Palomino* — This is a golden color. Palomino horses have a light-colored mane and tail of white, silver, or ivory.

4. *Pinto* (*calico or paint*) — Pinto is a Spanish word that means painted. The pinto color is characterized by irregular colored and white areas in either piebald or skewbald patterns. Piebald horses are black and white, and skewbald horses are white and any other color except black.

5. *Roan* — Roan is a mixture of white hairs with one or more base

colors. White with bay is red roan; white with chestnut is strawberry roan; and white with black is blue roan.

HEAD MARKS

When identifying an individual horse, it is generally necessary to include more identification than just body color. For example, it may be necessary to identify the dark sorrel as the one with the blaze face. Some common head markings are shown in Figure 3.44.

(A) Star   (B) Stripe   (C) Snip   (D) Star and Stripe

(E) Star, Stripe, and Snip   (F) Blaze   (G) Bald

Figure 3.44 The head marks of horses: (A) Star is any white mark on the forehead located above a line running from eye to eye; (B) stripe is a narrow white marking that extends from about the line of the eyes to the nostrils; (C) snip is a white mark between the nostrils or on the lips; (D) star and stripe includes both a star and stripe; (E) star, stripe, and snip includes all three of these marks — star, stripe, and snip; (F) blaze is a broad, white marking covering almost all the forehead but not including the eyes or nostrils; (G) bald is a bald, or white, face including the eyes and nostrils, or a partially white face.

LEG MARKS

Leg marks are often used, along with head marks, to describe a horse. The most common leg marks are shown in Figure 3.45.

Figure 3.45 The leg marks of horses: (A) coronet, a white stripe covers the coronet band; (B) pastern, white extends from the coronet to and including the pastern; (C) ankle, white extends from the coronet to and including the fetlock; (D) half stocking, white extends from the coronet to the middle of the cannon; (E) stocking, white extends from the coronet to the knee, and when the white includes the knee the mark is called a full stocking; (F) white heels, both heels are white; (G) white outside heel, outside heel only is white; (H) white inside heel, inside heel only is white.

OTHER CONSIDERATIONS WHEN BUYING A HORSE

In addition to the desirable qualities in conformation and action already enumerated, there should be style and beauty, balance and symmetry, an abundance of quality, an energetic yet manageable disposition, freedom from vices, good wind, suitable age, freedom from disease, and proper condition. The buyer should also be on the alert for possible misrepresentations.

4. Training the Horse

There are as many successful ways to train horses as there are to train children. The author has observed several top professional trainers. Each used a different technique, yet all ended up with the same result — a champion. Most of them follow the basic principles given herein.

The good horseman who has followed a program of training and educating the foal from the time it was a few days old has already eliminated the word "breaking." To him, the saddling and/or harnessing of the young horse is merely another step in the training program, which is done with apparent ease and satisfaction.

Figure 4.1 Training a yearling on "how to be a racehorse." Learning to gallop beside a lead pony is one of the first lessons. (Courtesy, *From Dawn to Destiny*, by Frank Jennings and Allen F. Brewer, Jr., published by The Thoroughbred Press, Lexington, Kentucky)

Figure 4.2 Spanish Mustangs at play. (Photo by Mrs. Buddy Banner, Willow Springs Ranch, Oracle, Arizona)

BEHAVIOR OF HORSES

Each animal species has characteristic ways of performing certain functions and rarely departs therefrom. The horse is no exception. A good understanding of horse behavior enhances horse training. Some noteworthy horse behavior patterns follow.

■ *Communication* — The signals consist of patterns of sound, produced by motions of the respiratory and upper alimentary tract. A *snort* is a danger signal to the whole herd; a *neigh* is a distress call; a *nicker* is a sign of relief; and a *whinny* is a call of pleasure and expectancy.

Without doubt, this trait — being able to communicate — accounts for the foundation stock of the American Indians and the hardy bands of Mustangs — the feral horses of the Great Plains. In some mysterious manner, the abandoned and stray horses of the expeditions of de Soto and Coronado found and communicated with each other; otherwise, they could not have reproduced.

■ *Courtship* — The sight of a mare elicits characteristic courtship by the stallion, including smelling the external genitalia and groin of the mare, extending his neck with an upcurled upper lip, and pinching the mare with his teeth by grasping the folds of her skin in the loin-croup area.

Heat (estrus) in mares is marked by the mare allowing the stallion to smell and bite her, frequent urination in small quantities, mucus discharge from the vulva, spreading the hind legs, and lifting the tail sideways.

■ *Dominance* — Any group of horses develops a hierarchical structure, or "peck order," in which each animal assumes a position of relative dominance. This order is maintained by sounds and gestures; challenging is kept to a minimum.

■ *Fighting* — Under wild conditions, natural enemies are avoided by flight or fight, according to the situation. The teeth and hind feet are used for fighting.

■ *Hearing* — Horses hear over a great range in frequencies, and they can pick up sounds too slight for man to hear.

■ *Leadership* — In wild bands, there is always a stallion leader.

■ *Lookout* — During the day, it is rare to see all members of a herd lying down together. One horse is almost always on the lookout.

■ *Pawing* — The modern domestic horse paws the ground when excited in much the same way as did Przewalsky's Horse.

■ *Vision* — In its natural habitat, the adult horse keeps a sharp lookout for its natural enemies, even while grazing. Also, it is noteworthy that the eye of the horse is adapted in several ways for darkness, as in nocturnal animals. Also, its eyes are set on the sides of the head so that each eye receives a very wide and largely different scene. The lens of the horse's eye is nonelastic, but the retina is arranged on a slope, the bottom part being nearer the lens than the top part. Thus, in order to focus on objects at different distances, the horse has to raise or lower his head so that the image is brought onto that part of the retina at the correct distance to achieve a sharp image. This arrangement is advantageous to wild horses because while the head is down grazing, both near objects on the ground and distant ones on the horizon are in focus simultaneously.

Color vision in horses has not been established.

MEMORY OF HORSES

To a very considerable degree the horse's aptitude for training is due to his memory. Many examples substantiating the excellent memory of horses could be cited, but only one will be related. Legend has it that the Arabs selected their mounts for memory and discipline by shutting them in a corral without water until they were extremely thirsty. Then they would turn them out so that they could go drink from a nearby stream. But before they reached the water, they would call them by blowing a bugle. The ones who remembered — who responded to the bugle and returned to the corral, rather than quench their thirst — were retained; the ones who forgot — who ignored the call and went for water — were culled.

CONTROLLING THE HORSE

The horse has whims and ideas of his own. But the horseman should be the boss, with the animal promptly carrying out his wishes. With the experienced horseman, this relationship is clear-cut, for he is able to relay his feelings to the horse instantly and unmistakably. For complete control and a finished performance, the horse should have a proud and exalted opinion of himself; but, at the same time, he should subjugate those undesirable traits that make a beast of his size and strength so difficult to handle by a comparatively frail and small person.

Complete control, therefore, is based on mental faculties rather than muscular force. The faculties of the horse which must be understood and played upon to obtain skillful training and control at all times are:

1. *Memory* — The horse remembers or recognizes the indications given him, the manner in which he responded, and the rewards or punishments that followed his actions.

2. *Confidence and fear* — In a well-mannered horse, it is necessary that confidence in the horseman replace the fear which accompanied his existence in the wild state.

3. *Association of ideas* — Horses are creatures of habit, hence the schooling of a horse should be handled by the same competent horseman, who allows the animal an opportunity to associate the various commands with the desired response.

4. *Willingness* — A willing worker or performer is obtained through the judicious employment of rewards and punishments.

5. *Rewards* — The most common rewards are a praising voice, a gentle stroking of the hand, and treats such as sugar and carrots. Sometimes, stopping work at the right moment (when a horse just begins to master something) may be used effectively as a reward.

6. *Punishment* — The two most common types of equine punishment are the spur and the whip.

TRAINING THE FOAL

The foal should be given daily lessons of 15 to 30 minutes each, for 7 to 10 days. If trained early in life, it will be a better disciplined, more serviceable horse. Give it one lesson at a time, and in sequence; that is, be sure the pupil masters each learning experience before it is given the next one.

Put a well-fitted halter on the foal when it is 10 to 14 days old. When it has become accustomed to the halter, in a day of so, tie it securely in the stall beside the mare. Try to keep the foal from freeing itself from the rope or from becoming tangled up in it.

Leave the foal tied 15 to 30 minutes each day for 2 to 3 days. Groom the animal carefully while it is tied. Rub each leg and handle each foot so that the foal becomes accustomed to having its feet picked up. After it has been groomed, lead it around with the mare for a few days and then lead

Figure 4.3 Teaching the foal to lead. After the foal has been gentled to a halter, a non-skid loop slipped over the hindquarters will teach him to move forward promptly.

it by itself. Lead it at both the walk and the trot. Many breeders teach a foal to lead simply by leading it with the mare from the stall to the paddock and back again.

At this stage of the training, be sure the foal executes your commands to stop and go as soon as you give them. When halted, make it stand in show position — squarely on all four legs with its head up.

Use all your patience, gentleness, and firmness in training the foal. Never let your temper get the best of you.

TRAINING THE YEARLING

The yearling should be given daily lessons of 30 minutes each, repeated until each learning experience is mastered. The horse learns by repetition. Thus, teach only one thing at a time, and repeat it in the same manner daily until mastered; then proceed to the next learning experience. Teach the yearling the following, in order:

1. *The meaning of "Whoa" and his name* — The yearling should be taught "whoa" means stop. Always give the command, then call his name, as "Whoa, Duke."

Figure 4.4 Front feet of a yearling hobbled with a large, soft cotton rope. This training lesson is designed to teach the young horse to stand still (as if tied) and not get excited if he gets caught in a fence.

2. *To stand when hobbled* — Next, the young horse should be hobbled; first the two front feet, then "sideline" (tie a front foot and a hind foot on the same side together). Hobbling is for the purpose of teaching the horse to stand still (as if tied) and not get excited if he gets caught in a fence. Many a valuable horse has mutilated himself for lack of this kind of training.

3. *To become accustomed to the saddle blanket* (*put the saddle blanket on; repeat for two days* — Gently place the saddle blanket on the young horse's back, and move it from head to tail, until he is not afraid of having an object on his back.

4. *To get used to the saddle* (*saddle him, repeat for 5 or 6 days*) — Next, put the saddle on and off several times; then tighten the girth moderately and lead him around.

Thus, the gentling of the yearling is for the purposes of teaching him the meaning of the word "whoa"; to stand patiently when hobbled or caught in a wire fence; and to get used to the saddle blanket and the saddle. After a few days of gentling like this, the yearling may be turned to pasture for a time.

TRAINING AT 18 MONTHS OF AGE

At 18 months of age, the young horse should receive additional training. At this stage, each lesson should be for 30 minutes daily, with each step mastered before moving on to the next. The trainer should always be gentle, but firm, and should not make a pet out of the horse. Let him know who is boss. When he must be punished for wrongdoing, use the whip — one time only; and do so immediately after the horse commits the act. Never discipline a horse by gouging him with spurs. When he does well, reward him by stroking his neck or shoulder and calling his name: "That's a good boy, Duke." At 18 months of age, teach the following:

1. *To drive, turn, stop, and back up; by using plowlines* — Tie the stirrups together under the horse, then run plowlines through them. Stand behind the horse and use the plowlines to drive, turn, stop, and back up.

2. *To flex his neck and set his head* — This may be accomplished either by (a) tying the reins to the stirrups, or (b) using rubber reins made from strips of old inner tube. Then turn the young horse loose in the corral or training ring for 30 minutes (he can't hurt himself).

Figure 4.5 When the horse is approximately 18 months of age, use plowlines to teach him to drive, turn, stop, and back up.

Figure 4.6 At about 18 months of age, teach the young horse to flex his neck and set his head. This shows rubber reins, made from strips of an old inner tube, being used for this purpose.

Figure 4.7 Dumb jockey, a bitting contrivance for training a young horse to place his head in the desired position.

Also, a dumb jockey bitting rig — a contrivance fastened on a young horse — may be used to train him to place his head in the desired position. The rigging consists of surcingle, back strap, crupper, side reins, overcheck or sidecheck, standing martingale, and some sort of projection above the top of the surcingle to which reins may be attached.

It is noteworthy that fashions in head sets change, and that not all horses should have their heads set. For example, hunters, jumpers, and cutting horses must "use" their heads.

3. *To respond to the bosal or hackamore, ride him; introduce leg pressure* — During the first few months of riding, use a bosal or hackamore; it will alleviate the hazard of hurting his mouth with bits. Do some light riding; introduce leg pressure.

TRAINING THE TWO-YEAR-OLD

At this stage, each lesson should be of 30 minutes duration daily, repeated until mastered. The two-year-old is ready for the following advance training:

1. *To respond to the aids* — Mount the horse and put him in motion by use of the aids — the legs, hands, and reins, and voice. After riding him for 5 or 6 days at the walk and trot, move him into the lope or canter; always on the proper lead — a right foot lead when going clockwise, a left foot lead when moving counterclockwise.

2. *To back* — From the ground, teach the horse to back. Hold the reins near the bosal or bit; push back (push and release) and command "Back, Duke." If necessary, push on his shoulder and/or switch him on the forelegs. Next, mount the horse and, from his back, teach him to stop and back up. If he won't back when you're mounted, have a friend stand in

front of him and switch him back while you pull (pull and release) on the reins and command "Back, Duke." Backing teaches the horse to get his feet under him, which is essential for pivots and sharp turns.

3. *To pivot* (Western horse) — Each time the horse is stopped and backed up, pause for a few seconds, then collect him (with the reins, and apply a little leg pressure) and pivot. Always teach the young horse to turn on his hind feet; pull him back until his hind feet are under him, then pull diagonally on the reins.

4. *To make a sliding stop* (Western horse) — Teach the horse to make a proper sliding stop — to "stick his tail in the ground." When properly done, the rider's reining hand is low, the horse's head is low and his front feet are near the ground. Most judges prefer a stop with 3 or 4 feet on the ground, rather than the more spectacular 2 hind-leg stop. If the stop is on 3 feet, 1 forefoot is up slightly, ready to turn or roll back either way. Most expert western horsemen don't like a sliding stop with both front feet up in the air because the horse is not balanced and can fall over backward.

It takes months of training to get a horse to do the sliding stop right. First he should be stopped at the walk, then the trot, next the short lope, and finally when wide open.

In executing the sliding stop, the western rider uses his aids as follows: (a) squeezes with his legs; (b) says "Ho"; (c) sits back deep in the saddle; and (d) pulls up on the reins. The leg pressure is to alert the horse. Throwing the rider's weight back, when properly timed, drives the horse's hind feet up under him. The reins are pulled no harder than necessary, then the pressure is released so that the horse can use his head to maintain his balance.

Figure 4.8 A good sliding stop. Note that the reining hand is low, the horse's head is low, and three of the feet are on the ground.

Figure 4.9 Well-trained and well-ridden barrel racing horse. This is the only woman's event in rodeo. It is an excellent test of training and speed, for it is a race against time, coupled with ease of maneuverability. Each contestant must ride a cloverleaf pattern around three barrels. (Courtesy, McLaughlin Photography, Morrison, Colorado)

Proper timing is important. The rider squeezes when the lead foot is off the ground and the hind feet are getting ready to come off. As his hind feet come up, he shifts his weight back and starts making contact with the horse's mouth. He does not jerk, for jerking hurts the horse's mouth and makes his head fly up and his mouth gape open. Another important thing relative to timing is this: If the rider "applies the brakes" when the horse is stretched out and his front feet are in the air, he forces the horse to throw all his weight on his front feet and he'll bounce.

The really good sliding stop is performed with rhythm and balance, and is easy and smooth.

Some good horsemen train horses on the longe line — a light strap of webbing or leather 30 feet long. When the author visited the Spanish Riding School of Vienna, where the famed Lipizzaner stallions perform, he learned that all basic training — including gaits, leads, stops, rollbacks, etc. — is given on the longe. Starting at age four, they work these horses from the ground for one year before they are ever mounted.

Figure 4.10 Skillful training, bitting, and shoeing made for the high natural action exhibited by this Hackney stallion. (Photo by Carl Klein, New York, New York; courtesy, Mrs. J. Macy Willets, Cassilis Farm, New Marlboro, Massachusetts)

The only exception to use of the longe line in training is a roping horse, because, when on the end of a rope, a roping horse is taught to run straight back from the trainer, rather than around him.

BLOOD TESTING FOR FITNESS

Blood testing (hematology) is a means of evaluating physical fitness.

All body cells require oxygen. With strenuous exercise, as in racing, the oxygen requirement increases. Oxygen is transported by hemoglobin, the protein-iron coloring matter in blood. It follows that any reduction in the hemoglobin content, or in total blood volume, will lower the oxygen-carrying capacity of the blood. When this condition is marked, anoxia (or anemia) develops, fatigue sets in, and there is lowered stamina and endurance.

Anoxia may be caused by many conditions. Usually it is due either to (1) nutritional deficiency, or (2) blood worms — both of which may be aggravated by the stress and strain of racing, endurance trials, and showing.

Most trainers accept one or more of the following as indicative of the lack of "fitness": loss of appetite; loss of weight; excessive "blowing" following work; a dry, harsh cough; rough coat; dull eye; watery instead of beady sweating; and "blowing up" over the loins. In an effort to be more exacting, some veterinarians who attend racing stables, endurance trials, and show strings now use blood examinations as a means of evaluating physical fitness.

It appears that, although there are breed differences, most horses which show consistent, good racing form have hemoglobin levels between 14 and 16 grams per milliliter, red cell counts between 9 and 11 million per cubic millimeter, and packed cell volumes between 40 percent and 45 percent. Also, other blood determinations are sometimes made. The blood testing approach is interesting and appealing. However, much more information on the subject is needed. Proof of this assertion becomes evident when it is realized that all horses whose blood pictures fall within the above range are not necessarily good performers; neither are horses with blood pictures outside this range incapable of winning. Some horses do respond to treatment, but, generally, the results have been inconsistent and disappointing. One needs to know if horses which have lower blood values, but which do not respond to treatment, carry all of the red cells and hemoglobin that they are capable of developing — and whether they have less potential for racing. Even more perplexing is the fact that this blood count can be too high, producing polycythemia. A horse with polycythemia frequently loses appetite, fails to thrive in the stable, performs unsatisfactorily, and may show cyanosis (dark bluish or purple coloration of the skin and mucus membrane due to lack of oxygen). It is also noteworthy that absolute polycythemia occurs at high altitudes or when there is heart disease or fibrosis of the lungs.

Racehorses with anemia are sometimes treated by either (1) injecting iron and/or vitamin B_{12}, or (2) giving orally (in the feed or water) one of several iron preparations. Sometimes vitamin C (ascorbic acid), folic acid, and the other B-complex vitamins are added.

At this time, there is insufficient knowledge of equine anemia, or of ways of stimulating the making of blood (hematopoiesis), to make a winner. The true role of therapy, if any, remains unknown.

The most that can be said at this time is that prevailing treatments usually satisfy the owner or trainer who insists that his charges "get the works." Most scientists are agreed, however, that "quickie" miracle shots or concoctions will never replace sound nutrition and parasite control on a continuous basis.

5. Breeding Horses

Horse owners who plan to breed one or more mares should have a working knowledge of heredity and know how to care for breeding animals and foals. The number of mares bred that actually conceive varies from about 40 to 85 percent, with the average running about 50 percent. Some mares that do conceive fail to produce living foals. This means that, on the average, 2 mares are kept a whole year to produce 1 foal, and even then, some foals are disappointments from the standpoint of quality.

Figure 5.1 The most reliable and obvious indications of potency and doing things right are a large number of healthy, vigorous foals from a season's service. (Courtesy, Mr. and Mrs. J. Cecil Ferguson, Broadwall Farm, Greene, Rhode Island)

HEREDITY IN HORSES

Until very recent times, the general principle that "like begets like" was the only recognized concept of heredity. That the application of this principle over a long period of time has been effective in modifying animal types in the direction of selection is evident from a comparison of present-day types of animals within each class of livestock. Thus, the speed of representatives of the modern Thoroughbred — coupled with their general lithe, angular build and nervous temperament — is in sharp contrast to the slow, easy gaits and docility of the Tennessee Walking Horse. Yet there is good and substantial evidence to indicate that both breeds descended from a common ancestry. Because of the diversity of genes carried by the original parent stock, it has been possible, through selection, to develop two distinct breeds — one highly adapted to fast running at extended distances and the other to a slow, ambling gait. Also, through selection accompanied by planned matings, this same parent stock has been altered into horses especially adept as hunters, jumpers, stock horses, polo mounts, three- and five-gaited park hacks, harness racehorses, etc.

THE GENE AS THE UNIT OF HEREDITY

The gene is the unit that determines heredity. In the body cells of horses there are many chromosomes. In turn, the chromosomes carry pairs of minute particles, called genes, which are the basic hereditary material (Figure 5.2). The nucleus of each body cell of horses contains 32 pairs of chromosomes, or a total of 64, whereas there are thousands of pairs of genes.

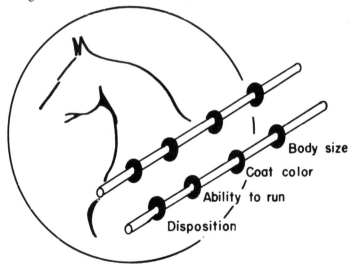

Figure 5.2 A pair of bundles, called chromosomes, carrying minute particles, called genes. The genes determine all the hereditary characteristics of horses, from length of leg to body size.

When a sex cell (a sperm or an egg) is formed, only one chromosome and one gene of each pair goes into it. Then, when mating and fertilization occur, the 32 single chromosomes from the germ cell of each parent unite to form new pairs, and the chromosomes with their genes are again present in duplicate in the body cells of the embryo. Thus, with all possible combinations of 32 pairs of chromosomes and the genes that they bear, it is not strange that full sisters (except identical twins from a single egg split after fertilization) are so different. Actually we can marvel that they bear as much resemblance to each other as they do.

Because of this situation, the mating of a mare with a fine track record to a stallion that transmits good performance characteristics will not always produce a foal of a merit equal to its parents. The foal could be markedly poorer than the parents, or, in some cases, it could be better than either parent.

SIMPLE AND MULTIPLE GENE INHERITANCE

Simple and multiple gene inheritance occurs in horses, as in all animals. In simple gene inheritance, only one pair of genes is involved; thus, a pair of genes may be responsible for some one specific trait in horses. However, most characteristics, such as speed, are due to many genes; hence, they are called multiple-gene characteristics.

For most characteristics, many pairs of genes are involved. For example, growth rate in foals is affected by (1) appetite and feed consumption, (2) the proportion of the feed eaten that is absorbed, and (3) the use to which the nutrients are put, whether they are used for growth or fattening — and each in turn is probably affected by different genes. Because multiple characteristics show all manner of gradation from high to low performance, they are sometimes referred to as quantitative traits. Thus, quantitative inheritance refers to the degree to which a characteristic is inherited. For example, all racehorses can run and all inherit some ability to run, but it is the degree to which they inherit the ability that is important.

DOMINANT AND RECESSIVE FACTORS

Dominant and recessive factors exist in horses. Some genes have the ability to prevent or mask the expression of others, with the result that the genetic makeup of such animals cannot be recognized with accuracy. This is called dominance. The gene that is masked is recessive. Because black is dominant to chestnut, all of the offspring will be black when a pure black stallion is crossed with a chestnut mare.

The resulting black offspring are not genotypically pure; they are Bb, where B stands for the dominant black and b for the recessive chestnut. These black, or F_1 (first cross, or first generation), animals will produce germ cells carrying black and chestnut genes in equal proportion (Figure 5.3). Then if an F_1 stallion is crossed with F_1 mares, the F_2 (second cross,

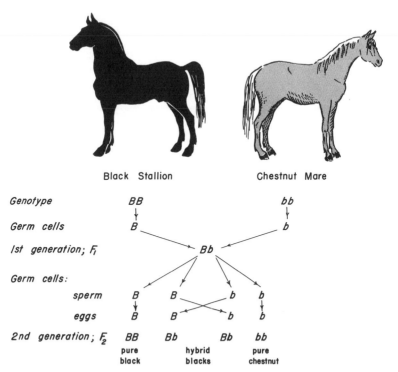

Black Stallion   Chestnut Mare

Figure 5.3 Gene inheritance in horses. Note: 1. That each horse has at least a pair of genes for color, conveniently represented by symbols.

2. That each reproductive cell (egg or sperm) contains but one of each pair.

3. That the Bb genotypes, in the first (F_1) generation, can vary in the degree of blackness, thus tending to resemble the one black parent.

4. That the second (F_2) generation has the ratio of three blacks to one chestnut (phenotypically). The Bb may be black or shading into brown.

5. That the pure blacks and certain hybrid blacks may not be distinguished on the basis of appearance, because the B gene obscures the b gene in varying degrees.

6. That the chestnut (bb) is quite likely the only pure color, in this example, that can be detected on sight.

or second generation) population will on the average consist of three blacks to one chestnut.

The chestnut in the F_2 population, being a recessive, will be pure for color. That is, the mating of any two chestnut horses will always produce chestnut offspring; this is the situation in the Suffolk breed of draft horses where all animals of the breed are chestnuts. Of the three blacks in the F_2, however, only one is pure for black with the genetic constitution BB. The other two will be Bb in genetic constitution and will produce germ cells carrying B and b in equal proportion.

Dominance often makes it difficult to identify and discard all animals carrying an undesirable recessive factor. In some cases, dominance is neither complete nor absent, but incomplete, or partial, and expressed in a variety of ways. The best known case of partial dominance in horses is the palomino coloring.

HEREDITY AND ENVIRONMENT
Heredity and environment in quantitative traits function in horses just as they do in all animals. Generally, horse trainers believe that heredity is most important, whereas horse owners believe that environment, particularly training, is most important — especially if they lose a race. Actually, maximum development of characteristics of economic importance such as growth, body form, or speed cannot be achieved unless horses receive proper training, nutrition, and management.

The problem of the horse breeder is to select the best animals available genetically to be parents of the next generation. Because only 15 to 30 percent of the observed variation among animals may be due to heredity, and because environmental differences can produce misleading variations, mistakes in the selection of breeding animals are inevitable.

SEX IS DETERMINED BY CHROMOSOMES
The sex of an animal is determined by chromosomes. The mare has a pair of similar chromosomes called X chromosomes, and the stallion has a pair of unlike sex chromosomes called X and Y chromosomes.

Figure 5.4 Diagrammatic illustration of the mechanism of sex determination in horses, showing how sex is determined by the chromosomal makeup of the individual.

The sex chromosomes in each pair separate from one another when the germ cells are formed. Thus, each of the ova or eggs produced by the mare contains the X chromosome; but the sperm of the stallion are of two types, one-half containing the X chromosome and the other half the Y chromosome (Figure 5.4). Since, on the average, the eggs and sperm unite at random, it can be understood that half of the progeny will contain the chromosomal makeup XX (female) and the other half XY (male).

OTHER FUNDAMENTALS OF HEREDITY

Other hereditary fundamentals of importance are the following:

■ Both the stallion and the mare are equally important to any one off-spring. But a stallion generally can have many more offspring than a mare and, from a hereditary standpoint, is more important to the herd or breed.

■ Prepotency is the ability of an animal to stamp its characteristics on its offspring so the offspring resemble that parent or each other more than usual.

■ Nicking results when the right combination of genes for good characteristics is contributed by each parent. Thus, animals nick well when their respective combinations of good genes complement each other.

■ Family names of horses have genetic significance only if (1) they are based on a linebreeding program that keeps the family closely related to the admired stallion or mare carrying the particular name, and (2) members of the family have been rigidly culled. Family names, therefore, lend themselves to speculation, and often have no more significance than human family names.

SYSTEMS OF BREEDING

Systems of breeding, whether planned or by chance, have made it possible to produce horses specially adapted to riding, racing, or driving. There is no one best system of breeding or secret of success for all conditions. Each breeding program is an individual case, requiring careful study. The choice of the system of breeding should be determined primarily by the size and quality of the herd, by the finances and skill of the operator, and by the ultimate goal ahead.

The systems of breeding from which the horseman may select are:

1. Purebreeding, in which the lineage, regardless of the number of generations removed, traces back to the foundation animals accepted by the breed or to animals that have been subsequently approved for infusion. Purebreeding may be conducted as either inbreeding or outcrossing, or part of each.

2. Inbreeding is the mating of animals more closely related than the average of the population from which they came. It may be done either by closebreeding or linebreeding.

a. Closebreeding is breeding closely related animals such as sire to daughter, son to dam, or brother to sister.

b. Linebreeding is breeding related animals so as to keep the offspring closely related to some highly admired ancestor such as half brother to half sister, female descendant to grandsire, or cousin to cousin.

3. Outcrossing is the mating of animals that are members of the same breed but that show no relationship in the pedigree for at least four to six generations.

4. Grading up is breeding a purebred sire of a given breed to a native, or grade, female.

5. Crossbreeding is mating animals of different breeds.

PERFORMANCE TESTING

The breeders of racehorses have always followed a program of mating animals of proved performance on the track. For example, it is interesting to note that the first breed register which appeared in 1791 — known as "An Introduction to The General Stud Book" — recorded the pedigrees of all the Thoroughbred horses winning important races. In a similar way, the Standardbred horse — which is an American creation — takes its name from the fact that, in its early history, animals were required to trot a mile in 2 minutes and 30 seconds, or to pace a mile in 2 minutes and 25 seconds, before they could be considered as eligible for registry. The chief aim, therefore, of early-day breeders of racehorses was to record the pedigree of outstanding performers rather than all members of the breed.

The simplest type of progeny testing in horses consists of the average record or merit of an individual stallion's or mare's offspring. Thus, the offspring of Thoroughbred or Standardbred animals bred for racing may be tested by timing on the track. Less satisfactory tests for saddle horses and fine harness horses have been devised. However, it is conceivable that actual exhibiting on the tanbark in the great horse shows of the country may be an acceptable criterion for saddle-bred animals.

THE STALLION

A stallion may become the parent of a great number of progeny. Therefore, he should be a purebred animal, a good representative of the breed selected, and a superior individual in type and soundness. If he is an older horse with progeny, the progeny should be of uniformly high quality and of approved type and soundness.

Each stallion should be studied as an individual, and his feeding, care, exercise, and handling should be varied accordingly.

We haven't improved on nature in percent foal crop. In the wild state, each band of 30 to 40 mares was headed by a stallion leader who sired all the foals in that band. With plenty of outdoor exercise on natural footing, superior nutrition derived from plants grown on unleached soils, regular production beginning at any early age, little possibility of disease or infection, and frequent services during the heat period, 90 percent or higher foaling rates were commonplace. The low fertility usually encountered under domestication must be caused to a large extent by the relatively artificial conditions that have been created.

REPRODUCTIVE ORGANS OF THE STALLION

The stallion's functions in reproduction are (1) to produce the male reproductive cells, the sperm or spermatozoa, and (2) to introduce sperm into the female reproductive tract at the proper time. Figure 5.5 is a schematic drawing of the reproductive organs of the stallion.

The two testicles are the primary sex organs of the stallion. They produce the sperm and a hormone called testosterone, which regulates and maintains the male reproductive tract in its functional state and is responsible for the masculine appearance and behavior of the stallion.

Sperm are produced in the inner walls or surface of the seminiferous tubules, which are a mass of minute, coiled tubules. These tubules merge into a series of larger ducts that carry the sperm to a coiled tube called epididymis. The epididymis is the place where the sperm are stored and where they mature, or ripen.

The testicles and epididymides are enclosed in the scrotum, the chief function of which is thermoregulatory. The scrotum maintains the testicles at temperatures several degrees cooler than the rest of the body.

From the epididymis, the sperm move through a tube, the vas deferens, into the urethra. The urethra has a dual role. It carries urine from the bladder through the penis and sperm from the junction with the vas deferens to the end of the penis.

Along the urethra are the accessory glands. These are the prostate, the seminal vesicles, the Cowper's gland. Their fluids nourish and preserve the sperm and provide a medium that transports the sperm. The fluids and sperm combined are called semen.

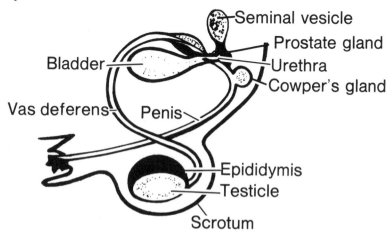

Figure 5.5 Reproductive organs of the stallion.

Figure 5.6 The Thoroughbred stallion, Talgo, and his inseparable mascot — a sheep; on Rancho San Pedro Coxtocan, Corretera, Mexico. Other common mascots include ponies, goats, dogs, cats, and chickens. (Photo by A. H. Ensminger)

CARE AND MANAGEMENT OF THE STALLION

The following points are pertinent to the care and management of the stallion.

1. *Quarters* — The most convenient arrangement is a roomy box stall that opens directly into a two- or three-acre pasture.

2. *Feeding* — The feed requirements are covered in chapter 6.

3. *Exercise* — Allow the stallion the run of a sizeable pasture but also provide additional, unhurried exercise either under saddle or hitched to a cart; by longeing; or by leading.

4. *Grooming* — Groom the stallion daily to make him more attractive and to assist in maintaining his good health and condition.

5. *Age and service* — Limit the mature stallion to not more than 2 services per day, one early in the morning and the other late in the afternoon; allow one day of rest each week.

The number of hand matings per year for stallions of different ages should be limited as follows: 2 years old, 10 to 15; 3 years old, 20 to 40; 4 years old, 30 to 60; mature horses, 80 to 100; and over 18 years old, 20 to 40. Limit the 2-year-olds to 2 to 3 services per week; the 3-year-olds to 1 service per day; and the 4-year-olds or over to 2 services per day. A stallion may remain a vigorous and reliable breeder up to 20 to 25 years of age.

There are breed differences. Thus, when first entering stud duty, the average 3-year-old Thoroughbred should be limited to 20 to 25 mares per season, but a Standardbred of the same age may breed 25 to 30 mares. A 4- to 5-year-old Thoroughbred should be limited to 30 to 40 mares per season, but a Standardbred of the same age may breed 40 to 50 mares.

STALLION BREEDING CONTRACT

Stallion breeding contracts should always be in writing; and the higher the stud fee, the more important it is that good business methods prevail. Neither "gentlemen's agreements" nor barn door records will suffice.

From a legal standpoint, a stallion breeding contract is binding to the parties whose signatures are affixed thereto. Thus, it is important that the contract be carefully read and fully understood before signing.

A sample stallion breeding contract is shown in Figure 5.7. The contract should be executed in duplicate for each mare, one copy to be retained by each party.

INCENTIVE BREEDING CONTRACT

In addition to the provisions made in the sample stallion breeding contract, the author suggests that consideration be given to incorporating an incentive basis. Here are some guidelines for the latter:

Generally, stallion owners guarantee a live foal, which means that the foal must stand and nurse; otherwise, the stud fee is either refunded or not collected, according to the stipulations. Of course, it is in the best interest of both parties that a strong, healthy foal be born. One well-known horse establishment reports that their records reveal that of all mares settled during a particular 3-year period, 19 percent of them subsequently either resorbed or aborted fetuses, or the foal or mare died. Further, their investigation of these situations showed that the vast majority of these losses could have been averted by better care and management. They found many things wrong — ranging from racing mares in foal to turning them to pastures where there was insufficient feed. To alleviate many, if not most, of these losses — losses that accrue after the mare has been examined and pronounced safe in foal, then taken away from the stallion owner's premises — the author suggests that an incentive basis be incorporated in the stallion breeding contract. For example, the stallion owner might agree to reduce the stud fee (1) by 10, 15, or 20 percent (state which) provided a live foal is born, or (2) by 25 to $33\frac{1}{3}$ percent provided the mare owner's veterinarian certifies that the mare is safe in foal 30 days after being removed from the place where bred, with payment made at that time and based on conception rather than the birth of a live foal.

Breeding Contract

This contract for the breeding season of _____ made and entered into by and between _____ ,
(year)   (owner of stallion)

_____ , herein after designated stallion owner, and _____ , _____ ,
(address)   (owner of mare)   (address)

hereinafter designated mare owner.

This contract covers—

The stallion, _____ , whose service fee is $ _____ ; $ _____ of which is paid
(name of stallion)

with this contract and the balance will be paid before the mare leaves _____ .
(name of farm or ranch)

and

The mare, _____ , reg. no. _____ , by _____ out of _____ ,
(name of mare)   (sire)   (dam)

age _____ , color_____ .

The mare owner agrees that—

Upon arrival, the mare will (a) be halter broken, (b) have the hind shoes removed, and (c) be accompanied by a health certificate signed by a veterinarian, certifying that she is healthy and in sound breeding condition.

Stallion owner will not be responsible for accident, disease, or death to the mare, or to her foal (if she has a foal).

Stallion owner may, at his discretion, have his veterinarian (a) check and treat the mare for breeding condition or diseases, and (b) treat her for parasites if needed, with the expenses of such services charged to the mare owner's account and paid when the mare leaves the farm or ranch.

He will pay the following board on his mare at the time the mare leaves the farm or ranch: Feed and facilities $ _____ per day.

Should the mare prove barren, or should the foal die at birth, he will send notice of same, signed by a licensed veterinarian, within 5 days of such barren determination or death.

Should he fail to deliver the above mare to the stallion owner's premises on or before _____ , stallion
(date)

owner shall be under no further obligation with respect to any matter herein set forth.

This contract shall not be assigned or transferred. In the event the mare is sold, any remaining unpaid fee shall immediately become due and payable and no refund shall be due anyone under any circumstances.

The stallion owner agrees that—

He will provide suitable facilities for the mare and feed and care for her in a good and husbandlike manner.

Mare owner will not be responsible for any disease, accident, or injury to stallion owner's horses.

A live foal is guaranteed—meaning a foal that can stand up alone and nurse.

The stallion owner and mare owner mutually agree that—

This contract is not valid unless completed in full.

Should the above named stallion die or become unfit for service, or should the above named mare die or become unfit to breed, this contract shall become null and void and money paid as part of this contract shall be refunded to mare owner.

Should the mare prove barren, or should the foal die at birth, with certification of same provided to stallion owner within the time specified, the stallion owner has the option either to (a) rebreed the mare the following year, or (b) refund the $ _____ portion of the breeding fee, thereby cancelling this entire contract.

The mare will not receive more than _____ covers during the breeding season, and she will not be
(number)

bred before _____ , 19_____ , or after _____ , 19_____ .

_____   _____   _____
(date)   (signature, mare owner or rep.)   (address)

_____   _____   _____
(date)   (signature, stallion owner or rep.)   (address)

Figure 5.7 Stallion breeding contract.

THE MARE

Characteristics found in the broodmare are likely to be reflected in the offspring. It is fundamental that "like tends to produce like." The broodmare should possess an abundance of femininity in addition to being sound and of good type. She should be of good ancestry, whether purebred or grade. Also, when selecting a broodmare for breeding, it is best to select one that is three or four years old. Where an older mare is selected, make certain that her breeding habits have been regular and normal.

REPRODUCTIVE ORGANS OF THE MARE

The mare's functions in reproduction are to (1) produce the female reproductive cells, the eggs or ova; (2) develop the new individual, the embryo, in the uterus; (3) expel the fully developed young at the time of birth, or parturition; and (4) produce milk for the nourishment of the young.

The part played by the mare in the generative process is much more complicated than that of the stallion. It is imperative, therefore, that the modern horseman have a full understanding of the anatomy of the reproductive organs of the mare and the functions of each part. Figure 5.8 shows the reproductive organs of the mare.

The two ovaries are the primary sex organs of the mare. They are bean-shaped organs 2 to 3 inches long. The ovaries produce eggs. Each egg is contained in a bubble-like sac on the ovary, called a follicle. There are hundreds of follicles on each ovary. Generally, the follicles remain

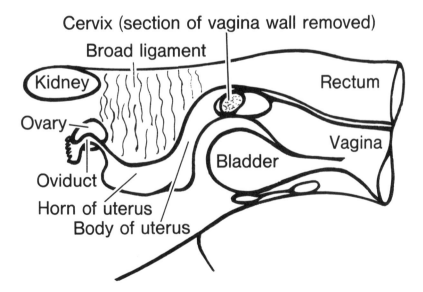

Figure 5.8 Reproductive organs of the mare.

unchanged until puberty when one of them begins to grow because of an increase in the follicular liquid in it; the others remain small. The egg is suspended in the follicular fluid.

When the growing follicle is about an inch in diameter, a hormone causes it to rupture and discharge the egg. This is known as ovulation and is the time when mating should take place. The egg is trapped in a funnel-shaped membrane, called the infundibulum, that surrounds the ovary. The infundibulum narrows into a tube called the oviduct. The oviduct then carries the egg to the uterus, or womb, the largest of the female reproductive organs, where the unborn young, or fetus, will develop.

The lining of the uterus is soft and spongy. It contains a vast network of blood vessels that provide a "bed" for the fertilized egg to settle into and develop. At birth, the heavy layers of muscles of the uterus wall contract with great pressure to force the new animal out through the cervix and vagina.

BREEDING HABITS AND CARE OF THE MARE

A knowledge of the mare's normal breeding habits will help to improve the fertility rate. However, not all mares that conceive give birth to live foals. So, improved care and management of the pregnant mare are important also. The age of puberty (sexual maturity) for mares is 12 to 15 months; the duration of heat ranges from 1 to 37 days, and averages 4 to 6 days; the interval between heat periods ranges from 10 to 37 days, and averages 21; and the gestation period ranges from 310 to 370 days, and averages 336. A handy rule-of-thumb method that may be used to figure the approximate date of foaling is: subtract 1 month and add 2 days to the date the mare was bred. Hence, a mare bred May 20 should foal April 22 the following year.

The following points are pertinent to the care and management of the mare.

1. *Age to breed* — Well-grown fillies may be bred as 2-year-olds, but most fillies are not bred until they are 3 years old.

2. *Normal breeding season and time of foaling* — Spring is the ideal season for both breeding and foaling. At this time of year, the mare is most fertile, the heat cycles are more regular and evident, and the mare is more likely to conceive. Also, a foal conceived in the spring may be dropped on pasture the following spring with a minimum danger of becoming infected with parasites or diseases. Abundant fresh air, sunshine, and exercise contribute to the proper development of the youngster. Persons who race or show horses want foals to be born as soon as possible after January 1.

3. *Conditioning for breeding* — Mares are conditioned by proper feeding and adequate exercise. To achieve high conception rates, mares should not be too thin or too fat. Try to check the natural tendency of barren or maiden mares to become overweight.

Mares may be exercised by riding them under saddle or driving them in harness. When this is not practical, they usually will get enough exercise if allowed to run in a large pasture.

4. *Signs of heat* — In season, mares generally exhibit (a) relaxation of the external genitals, (b) more frequent urination, (c) teasing of the other mares, (d) apparent desire for company, and (e) slight mucus discharge from the vagina.

Mares in foal may have false heat. Breeding such mares may result in abortion. An experienced horseman who is familiar with the peculiarities of the individual animal can detect false heat when the mare is teased and can prevent such an accident.

BREEDING THE MARE

A young, shy mare should be presented to the teaser stallion fairly often as the breeding season approaches. This will acquaint her with the breeding procedure.

Since actual ovulation probably takes place toward the end of the heat period, the mare should be mated every day or every other day beginning with the third day after she first comes into heat.

No phase of horse production has become more unnatural or more complicated with domestication than the actual breeding operation. This is so because breeders try to get mares bred in about 4 months instead of 12 and have arbitrarily limited the breeding season to late winter and early spring. The following facts and pointers are pertinent to the breeding operation.

1. Hand mating, in which the animals are coupled under supervision, is the most common. It guards against injury to both the stallion and the mare. However, corral or pasture breeding may be preferable under certain conditions. For example, corral breeding may be resorted to when only one person is handling the breeding operation, and pasture breeding

Figure 5.9 Teasing mares on pasture, with the teaser taken to the mares. Breeding a mare that is not in season is a wasteful practice. Besides, it may damage future breeding efficiency. (Photo by John C. Wyatt, Lexington, Kentucky; courtesy, Lee Eaton, Lexington, Kentucky)

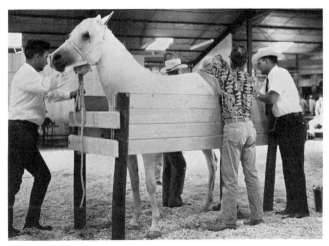

Figure 5.10 Examining a mare prior to breeding. When mares have been barren over an extended period or when there is the slightest suspicion of infection, it is good protection to have the veterinarian ascertain that she is in healthy breeding condition. (Courtesy, *Western Horseman,* Colorado Springs, Colorado)

Figure 5.11 A hobbled mare, with tail properly bandaged, ready for service. Hobbles are used only to protect the stallion as he approaches and dismounts, and not in any way to force the mare into submission to service when not ready.

is sometimes followed on the ranges of the West. In corral breeding, the stallion and the mare are turned together in a corral; in pasture breeding, the stallion is turned to pasture with a band of mares.

2. Breed only healthy mares to a healthy stallion. Require that all mares from the outside be accompanied by a health certificate signed by a veterinarian.

3. Teasing is the best way in which to make certain that a mare is in season.

4. Serve the mare daily or every other day during the heat period, beginning with the third day.

5. After making certain that the mare is in season, wash the reproductive organs of the stallion and the external parts of the mare that are likely to come in contact with the reproductive organs of the stallion; bandage the upper 6 to 8 inches of the mare's tail. Place a twitch and hobbles on the mare and allow the sexual act to be completed. Return the mare for retrial approximately 21 days later.

SIGNS AND TESTS OF PREGNANCY

The signs of pregnancy are (1) cessation of the heat period, and (2) observed movement of the fetus through the abdominal walls. A veterinarian or an experienced horseman can determine pregnancy by making a rectal examination 40 to 60 days after the last service. Also, tests can be made by a laboratory.

CARE OF THE PREGNANT MARE

The pregnant mare is inclined to be inactive. She should be separated from barren mares, which are likely to be playful and frisky.

Pregnant, idle mares should be turned to pasture in which there are shade and water. A simple shelter is all that is needed; an open shed is satisfactory in temperate climates, even in winter. Pregnant mares that are used under saddle or in harness may be given quarters like those of other horses used similarly.

The nutritive requirements of the mare are discussed in chapter 6 of this book; hence, the reader is referred thereto.

Mares that have the run of a large pasture will usually get sufficient exercise. Stabled mares should be exercised moderately for an hour daily under saddle or hitched to a cart. Continue this routine to within a day or two of foaling. During the last couple of days, mares may be led.

CARE OF THE MARE AT FOALING TIME

Keep a written record of the date the mare is due to foal. (Remember that the gestation period can range from 310 to 370 days, with an average of 336 days.) This record enables the caretaker to make plans for foaling.

Giving birth is a critical time in the life of a mare. All the advantages gained by selecting genetically desirable and healthy parent stock and by providing the best environmental and nutritional conditions during the gestation period can be dissipated quickly through carelessness or ignorance at this time.

SIGNS OF APPROACHING PARTURITION

These signs are a distended udder, which may be observed 2 to 6 weeks before foaling; a shrinkage or falling away of the buttocks muscles near the tailhead and a falling of the abdomen 7 to 10 days before foaling; filling out of the teats 4 to 6 days before foaling; and the appearance of wax on the ends of the nipples 4 to 6 days before foaling. As foaling time draws nearer, the vulva becomes full and loose; milk drops from the teats; and the mare becomes restless, may break into a sweat, urinates frequently, and lies down and gets up. But there are times when all signs fail, so be prepared 30 days in advance of the expected time.

FOALING PLACE

Provide a foaling place 7 to 10 days before the event is expected, so that the mare becomes accustomed to the new surroundings. When the weather is warm and it can be arranged, allow the mare to foal in a clean pasture away from other livestock. Avoid foaling in an unsanitary paddock or in a lot filled with droppings, because infections, such as "navel ill," often follow.

During bad weather, use a foaling stall. It should be at least 12 feet square; it should have a smooth, well-packed clay floor; and it should be free of obstructions (such as low mangers or racks) on which the mare and foal might hurt themselves. If possible, it should be located away from other occupied stalls. Before occupancy, the foaling stall should be cleaned and disinfected with 13 ounces of lye in 10 gallons of water; use one-half strength solution in scrubbing mangers and grain boxes. Sprinkle the floor and walls lightly with quick lime or burnt lime. Provide plenty of bedding for the occasion.

FOALING TIME

The following information and procedures may be helpful during foaling:

1. The feed should be decreased and wheat bran should be added. Feed a wet bran mash if the mare is constipated.

2. An attendant should be near but not in sight.

3. Foaling begins with the rupture of the outer fetal membrane, which is followed by the escape of a large amount of fluid. The inner membrane surrounding the foal appears next and labor becomes more marked.

The mare foals rapidly in the normal presentation of her young. The entire birth procedure generally does not take more than 15 to 30 minutes. The mare usually will be down at the height of labor. The foal generally is born while the mare is lying on her side with her legs stretched out.

In normal presentation of the foal, the front feet with heels down appear first (see Figure 5.12), followed by the nose and head, then shoulders, middle (with back up), hips, and finally hind legs and feet.

Figure 5.12 Normal presentation. The back of the fetus is directly toward that of the mother, the forelegs are extended toward the vulva with the heels down, and the nose rests between the forelegs.

Summon a veterinarian at once when the presentation is not normal. There is great danger that the foal will smother if birth is delayed. If the feet are presented with the bottoms up, it is a good indication that they are the hind ones and there is likely to be difficulty.

If the mare does not appear to be making any progress in parturition after reasonable time and effort, make an examination and give her help before she has exhausted her strength in futile efforts at expulsion. Often, the fetus dies when parturition is retarded because of twists or knots in the umbilical cord or is unduly delayed for other reasons.

4. Make certain that the newborn foal is breathing and that the membrane has been removed from its mouth and nostrils. If the foal fails to breathe, give it artificial respiration immediately. This may be done by blowing into its mouth, by working the ribs, by rubbing the body vigorously, and by lifting it up and dropping it gently. Then rub and dry the foal with towels, treat the navel cord with tincture of iodine, and let the mare and foal rest for a time.

Remove the expelled afterbirth from the stall and burn or bury it; it is usually expelled within 1 to 6 hours after foaling. If it is retained longer than 6 hours, or if the mare seems lame, blanket her and call a veterinarian. Clean and rebed the stall after the mare and foal are up. Give the mare small quantities of lukewarm water at intervals and feed considerable wheat bran for the first few days after foaling; take 7 to 10 days to get

Figure 5.13 Newborn foal. (Courtesy, California Thoroughbred Breeders Association, Arcadia, California)

the mare on full feed. Be observant; if the mare has much temperature, call a veterinarian. The normal temperature is 100.5° F. Also, regard with suspicion any discharge from the vulva.

BREEDING AFTER FOALING

Mares usually come back in heat 7 to 11 days after foaling (foal heat), but the time can range from 3 to 13 days. Some horsemen rebreed mares during the first heat after foaling, usually on the eighth or ninth day, providing the birth was normal and the mare suffered no injury or infection. Other horsemen prefer to rebreed mares during the heat period that follows the foal heat (25 to 30 days from foaling), provided there is no discharge or evidence of infection. An increasing number of good horsemen prefer to rebreed on the second heat period after foaling.

Mares with infected genital tracts seldom are settled in service. If they are bred, the infection may spread to the stallion — thence to other mares. If they conceive, there is danger that the foals will be undersized and poorly developed.

DRYING UP THE MARE

Permanently separate the mare and foal at weaning time. Decrease the mare's ration before and during weaning. Rub camphorated oil or a mixture of lard and spirits of camphor on the udder, but do not milk out the udder until 5 to 7 days later when it is soft and flabby. At that time, the little secretion that remains, perhaps not more than half a cup, may be milked out.

MANAGEMENT FOR HIGH FERTILITY

In order to improve the conception rate of mares above the general average, good management of both mares and stallions must go hand in hand with superior nutrition, including added vitamins E and A; and, in addition, the microbiological, surgical, and endocrinological facets of veterinary medicine should be encompassed as necessary. Good management calls for:

1. Keeping broodmares in strong, healthy breeding condition, but avoiding overfeeding and overweight.

2. Controlling parasites.

3. Providing exercise.

4. Flushing mares, beginning 4 to 8 weeks ahead of the breeding season. Flushing refers to having the mares gain in weight. This is best accomplished by more liberal feeding at this time. When properly flushed, mares should start to shed their hair coats at the time breeding begins. Of course, if they are overweight, proper flushing is impossible. When mares are too fat, slim them down well ahead of the breeding season, by (a) cutting down on the quantity of the feed and by using low energy feeds (like cereal straws), and (b) stepping up the exercise.

A combination of proper condition (not overweight), nutritious feed (with added vitamins E and A prior to and during breeding), flushing beginning 4 to 8 weeks ahead of the breeding season, parasite control, and adequate exercise of both the mare and the stallion will result in a higher conception rate, and the mares will breed both earlier and more nearly at the same time.

On a horse-breeding establishment, a barren mare or an infertile stallion make for added costs — and there is no financial return. Moreover, most horses are quite valuable; hence, any mating that fails could have been a valuable horse.

THE FOAL

After the newborn foal starts breathing and has been rubbed dry, put it in one corner of the stall on clean, fresh straw. The mare usually will be less restless if this corner is in the direction of her head.

Protect the eyes of a newborn foal from bright light.

TREATMENT OF THE NAVEL CORD

If left alone, the navel cord of the newborn foal usually breaks within 2 to 4 inches of the belly. If it does not break, cut it about 2 inches from the belly with clean dull shears or scrape it in two with a knife. A torn or broken blood vessel will bleed very little, but one cut directly across may bleed excessively. Treat the severed cord immediately with tincture of iodine, or other reliable antiseptic; then leave the mare and foal alone so they can rest and gain strength.

VALUE OF COLOSTRUM

Colostrum is milk secreted by the dam for the first few days after parturition. It differs from ordinary milk in that it is more concentrated; is higher in protein content, especially in globulin; is richer in vitamin A; contains antibodies that protect the foal temporarily against certain infection; and is a natural purgative that removes fecal matter accumulated in the digestive tract.

Do not dissipate the benefits of colostrum by "milking out" a mare shortly before foaling time.

THE FIRST NURSING

A strong, healthy foal will be on its feet and ready to nurse within $\frac{1}{2}$ to 2 hours after birth. Before allowing the foal to nurse for the first time, wash the mare's udder with a mild disinfectant and rinse thoroughly with clean, warm water.

A big, awkward foal occasionally needs assistance and guidance when it nurses the first time. If the foal is stubborn, forced feeding will be useless. Back the mare onto additional bedding in one corner of the stall and coax the foal to the teats with a bottle and nipple. An attendant may hold the bottle while standing on the opposite side of the mare from the foal.

A very weak foal should be given the mare's first milk even if it is necessary to draw this milk into a bottle and feed the foal one or two times by nipple. An attendant sometimes must steady a foal before it will nurse.

BOWEL MOVEMENT

Regulation of the bowel movement of the foal is very important. Constipation and diarrhea (scours) are common ailments.

Excrement impacted in the bowels during prenatal development — material called meconium — may kill the foal if it is not eliminated promptly. A good feed of colostrum usually will cause natural elimination. This is not always the case, however, especially when foals are from stall-fed mares.

Observe the foal's bowel movement 4 to 12 hours after birth. If there has been no fecal discharge by this time, and the foal seems sluggish and fails to nurse, give it an enema. Use 1 to 2 quarts of water at body heat (101° F) mixed with a little glycerin, or use 1 to 2 quarts of warm, soapy water. Inject the solution with a baby syringe that has about a 3-inch nipple, or use a tube and can. Repeat the treatment until normal yellow feces appear.

If the foal is scouring, reduce the mare's feed and take away part of her milk from the foal at intervals by milking her out.

Diarrhea or scours in foals may result from infectious diseases or dirty surroundings. It is caused by an irritant in the digestive tract that should be removed. Give an astringent only in exceptional cases and on the advice of a veterinarian.

Conditions that may cause diarrhea are contaminated udder or teats, nonremoval of fecal matter from the digestive tract, fretfulness or temperature above normal in the mare, too much feed affecting the quality of the mare's milk, a cold damp bed, or continued exposure to cold rains.

CARE OF THE SUCKLING FOAL

Weather conditions permitting, there is no better place for a mare and foal than on pasture. When the foal is from 10 days to 3 weeks old, it will begin to nibble on a little grain and hay. To promote thrift and early development, and to avoid any setback at weaning time, encourage the foal to eat supplementary feed as early as possible. The foal should be provided with a low-built grain box especially for this purpose or if on pasture, it may be creep fed.

Foals normally reach one-half of their mature weight during the first year. Most breeders of Thoroughbreds and Standardbreds plan to have their two-year-old animals at full height. Such results require liberal feeding from the beginning. A foal stunted in the first year by insufficient

Figure 5.14 A good start in life. When the weather is warm, the most natural and ideal place for the foal is a clean pasture. Abundant fresh air, sunshine, and exercise contribute to the proper development of the youngster. (Courtesy, J. C. Skeets Meadors)

feeding cannot be developed properly later in life. It is well recognized that forced development must be done expertly if the animals are to remain durable and sound.

RAISING THE ORPHAN FOAL

Occasionally, a mare dies during or immediately after parturition, leaving an orphan foal to be raised. At other times, a mare may fail to give sufficient milk, or she may have twins. In such cases, the foal may be (1) shifted to another mare, known as a foster mother or nurse mare, or (2) placed on mare's milk replacer, or synthetic milk, that is mixed and fed according to the manufacturer's directions.

It is important, however, that the orphan foal receive colostrum, preferably for about the first four days of life. For this purpose, colostrum from a mare that produces excess milk or one that has lost her foal should be collected and frozen from time to time; then, as needed, it may be thawed and warmed to 100° to 105° F and fed.

For the first few days, the orphan foal should be fed with a bottle and rubber nipple. Within about two weeks, it may be taught to drink from a pail. All receptacles must be kept sanitary (clean and scald each time they are used) and feeding must be at regular intervals. Dry feeding should be started at the earliest possible time with the orphan foal.

The following formula may be used for feeding the orphan foal if a substitute milk must be used:

1 pint of low fat cow's milk (about 3% fat)
4 ounces of lime water
1 teaspoon of sugar

Two teaspoons of lactose or corn syrup may be used to replace the sugar, and one large can of evaporated cow's milk may be used with one can of water to replace the fresh milk. The foal should be fed about one-half pint every hour. Give large foals slightly more than a pint. After 4 or 5 days increase the interval to 2 hours. After a week, feed every 4 hours and increase the quantity accordingly.

CARE OF THE FOAL'S FEET

Foals may damage their limbs when the weight is not equally distributed because of unshapely hoofs. On the other hand, faulty limbs may be helped or even corrected if the hoofs are trimmed regularly. Also, trimming helps educate the foal and makes shoeing easier at maturity. If the foal is run on pasture, trimming the feet may be necessary long before weaning time. A good practice is to check the feet every month or six weeks and, if necessary, trim a small amount each time rather than a large amount at one time. Tendons should not become strained because of incorrectly trimmed feet. Usually, only the bottom rim of the hoof should be trimmed, although sometimes the heel, frog, or toe of the hoof may need trimming. The hoofs are trimmed with a rasp, farrier's knife, and nippers. A rasp is used more than the other tools.

Before the feet are trimmed, the foal should first be inspected while standing squarely on a hard surface and then inspected at the walk and the trot.

WEANING

Foals usually are weaned at four to six months of age. Thorough preparation facilitates weaning.

It may be advisable to wean the foal at a comparatively early age if either the foal or mare is not doing well, if the mare is being given heavy work, or if the mare was rebred on the ninth day after foaling.

If by using a creep or a separate grain box the foal has become accustomed to eating a considerable amount of hay and about $\frac{3}{4}$ pound of grain daily per 100 pounds of body weight, weaning will cause only a slight disturbance or setback. If the ration of the dam is cut in half a few

days before the separation, her udder usually will dry up without difficulty.

Move the mare to new quarters from the stall she shares with the foal.
Remove anything in the stall on which the foal might hurt itself during the
first unhappy days that it lives alone. Make the separation of the foal
from the mare complete and final. If the foal sees, hears, or smells its dam
again, the separation process must be started all over again.

Turn the foal out on pasture after a day or two. If there are several
weanlings together, some of them might get hurt while running and
frolicking in the pasture. Guard against this by first turning out two or
three less valuable individuals and letting them tire themselves; then turn
out the rest.

At this stage, if numerous weanlings are involved, separate them by
sexes. Put the more timid ones by themselves. Do not run weanlings with
older horses.

CASTRATING

Geldings, or castrated males, are safer and easier to handle than
stallions. Therefore, a colt should be castrated unless he is to be saved for
breeding purposes. Have a veterinarian perform this operation. A colt
may be castrated when only a few days old, but most horsemen prefer to
delay the operation until the animal is about a year old. While there is
less real danger to the animal and much less setback with early altering, it
results in imperfect development of the foreparts. Delaying castration for
a time results in more muscular, bolder features and better carriage of the
foreparts.

Weather and management conditions permitting, the time of altering
should be determined by the development of the individual. Underde-
veloped colts may be left uncastrated six months or even a year longer
than overdeveloped ones.

Breeders of Thoroughbred horses usually prefer to race them first as
uncastrated animals.

There is less danger of infection if colts are castrated in the spring soon
after they are turned out on clean pasture and before hot weather and "fly
time" arrive. This is extremely important in the southern states because of
the danger of screwworm infestation.

BREAKING

A foal will not need "breaking" if it has been trained properly. When
a young horse can be saddled or harnessed with satisfactory ease, it is
because the proper training program has been followed. Saddling and
harnessing are just additional steps. A good time to harness and work the
horse for the first time is during the winter as a rising two-year-old.

ARTIFICIAL INSEMINATION

Artificial insemination is, by definition, the deposition of spermatozoa in the female genitalia by artificial rather than by natural means.

Today, there is renewed interest in artificial insemination of horses, as a result of a successful method of freezing stallion semen. Stallion semen is now being collected, processed, and frozen somewhat like bull semen.

Mares are inseminated by (1) using a syringe and catheter arrangement with a speculum, (2) placing a gelatin capsule, holding 10 to 25 milliliters of extended semen, in the cervix by hand, or (3) introducing a rubber catheter by hand into the cervix and injecting the semen by means of a syringe attached to the opposite end of the tube.

Among the advantages of artificial insemination, in comparison with natural service, are the following:
- It increases the use of outstanding sires.
- It alleviates the danger and bother of keeping a sire.
- It makes it possible to overcome certain physical handicaps to mating.
- It lessens sire costs.
- It reduces the likelihood of costly delays through using infertile sires.
- It makes it feasible to prove more sires.
- It creates large families of animals.
- It increases pride of ownership, when a better stallion can be used.
- It may lessen and control certain diseases.
- It increases profits.

But there are limitations to artificial insemination, among which are the following:
- It must conform to physiological principles.
- It requires skilled technicians.
- It necessitates considerable capital to initiate and operate an A.I. breeding service.
- It is not always possible to obtain the services of a given sire.
- It may accentuate the damage of a poor sire.
- It may restrict the sire market.
- It may increase the spread of disease.
- It may be subject to certain abuses.

Until recently, stallion semen could not be stored for any length of time. It is viable for only one to two days in the liquid state. However, stallion semen has now been frozen successfully, and its use will grow. This development may write a new chapter in horse breeding, especially in breeding grade mares.

But before wide-scale use can be made of artificial insemination of horses, solutions to additional problems must be found. These include the following needs:
- The ability to breed more mares per stallion.

- The ability to detect when mares are ready for breeding.
- The ability to bring mares in heat at will.

REGISTRATION OF FOALS PRODUCED
THROUGH ARTIFICIAL INSEMINATION

Although artificial insemination was first practiced with horses, many American registry associations now frown upon or forbid the practice. Moreover, there is little unanimity of opinion among them concerning the rules and regulations they apply to the practice. Table 5.1 summarizes the current horse association rules relative to registering young produced artificially.

Table 5.1 Horse Association Rules Relative to Registering Young Produced Artificially

Breed	Present Rules or Attitude of Registry Association Relative to Artificial Insemination
LIGHT HORSES:	
American Bashkir Curly	No rules relative to A.I. to date.
American Creme	A.I. discouraged, but accepted.
American Gotland Horse	No rules.
American Mustang..................	Acceptable. Association to be contacted for specifics.
American Saddle Horse	Accepted provided A.I. takes place (1) on premises where stallion is standing, and (2) in presence of owner or party authorized to sign certificate of breeding.
American Shetland Pony............	Accepted only if (1) sire and/or dam incapable of natural service, (2) sire and dam owned by same person, and (3) owner retains dam until she foals.
American Walking Pony	Accepted only if (1) stallion and mare are on same premises and insemination is done by licensed veterinarian, or (2) same veterinarian collects, transports, and inseminates if sire and dam are on different premises.
American White.....................	A.I. discouraged, but accepted.
Andalusian..........................	The breed registry reports: "not practiced."
Anglo-Arabian and Half-Arabian..	Accepted provided (1) stallion licensed by Arabian Horse Registry for A.I., and (2) registration certificate is stamped to show animal was A.I.-produced.

(Cont.)

Table 5.1 Horse Association Rules Relative to Registering
Young Produced Artificially (*Cont.*)

Breed	Present Rules or Attitude of Registry Association Relative to Artificial Insemination
Appaloosa...........................	Accepted provided (1) accompanied by natural service in same heat period, and (2) semen used only where stallion is standing.
Arabian..............................	Accepted provided (1) stallion licensed by Arabian Horse Registry of America for A.I., (2) both collection and insemination take place on same premises, and (3) semen not stored longer than 48 hours.
Buckskin	*International Buckskin Horse Association, Inc.:* Accepted provided (1) registry is notified in advance of intent to use A.I., (2) collecting, storing, and inseminating performed by approved practitioner, and (3) letters "A.I." incorporated in Stud Book and on certificate. *American Buckskin Registry Association, Inc.:* Accepted provided (1) prior notice of intent to use the stallion A.I. is given the Association, and (2) semen is used on premises of collection immediately following collection.
Chickasaw...........................	No A.I. used.
Connemara	Accepted provided (1) fresh semen is used, and (2) signed letters are on file from stallion owner, mare owner, and veterinarian who collected the semen and did the inseminating.
Galiceno.............................	Accepted if veterinarian (1) is present, and (2) signs certification to accompany registration application.
Lipizzan.............................	A.I. frowned upon, but no rules made.
Missouri Fox Trotting	No rules, no horses registered by A.I. to date.
Morab...............................	Accepted provided (1) stallion owner notifies the registry annually of intent to use A.I., and (2) insemination is done immediately following collection.
Morgan..............................	Accepted only if (1) collection and insemination by licensed veterinarian, (2) insemination immediately following collection, and (3) both collection and insemination are on same premises.
Paint Horse	Accepted only if A.I. used (1) within 24 hours of collection, and (2) on premises of collection.

(*Cont.*)

Table 5.1 Horse Association Rules Relative to Registering
Young Produced Artificially (*Cont.*)

Breed	Present Rules or Attitude of Registry Association Relative to Artificial Insemination
Palomino............................	*Palomino Horse Breeders of America:* Accepted, but do not advocate. *Palomino Horse Association, Inc.:* Accepted only if semen used at time and place of collection.
Paso Fino	No rules.
Peruvian Paso	*Peruvian Paso Horse Registry of N.A.:* Accepted only if (1) deemed necessary (in writing) by veterinarian, (2) stallion and mare are at same location, and (3) stallion serves mare naturally once each heat period. *American Association of Owners & Breeders of Peruvian Paso Horses:* A.I. accepted only (1) in case of injury to stallion, and (2) if stallion and mare are on same premises.
Pinto.................................	Accepted provided (1) intent of each A.I. breeding requested in letter to registrar, (2) a veterinarian (not necessarily the same one for each step) certifies to collection of semen, insemination of mare, and birth of foal, and (3) blood type evidence of parentage, along with foaling date, is furnished.
Pony of the Americas	A.I. on the farm where the stallion is located is approved. But mailing of semen is not allowed.
Quarter Horse........................	A.I. not permitted unless insemination (1) immediately follows collection, and (2) is at the place or premises of collection.
Rangerbred	No rules. No request to use A.I.
Spanish-Barb	No rules at present.
Spanish Mustang.....................	No official ruling at this time.
Standardbred	Accepted provided (1) fresh semen is used (frozen or dessicated not permitted), and (2) insemination takes place on same day and same premises where semen was produced.
Tennessee Walking Horse...........	Accepted provided insemination (1) is done on premises where stallion is standing, and (2) takes place in presence of owner or party authorized to sign certificate of breeding for the stallion used.

(Cont.)

Table 5.1 Horse Association Rules Relative to Registering
Young Produced Artificially (*Cont.*)

Breed	Present Rules or Attitude of Registry Association Relative to Artificial Insemination
Thoroughbred	Natural service only. But the immediate A.I. reinforcement of the stallion's service with a portion of the ejaculate produced by the stallion during such cover is permitted.
Welsh Pony...........................	No requests for A.I. received. Directors would have to decide.
JACKS AND DONKEYS:	
Donkeys..............................	*American Donkey and Mule Society, Inc.:* No rules. *Miniature Donkey Registry of the U.S.:* Would accept; no rules against A.I.
Jacks and Jennets....................	Eligible for registration. No stipulations.

SUMMARY OF ARTIFICIAL INSEMINATION

Today, artificial insemination is taking on a new look. Stallion semen is being frozen and stored, with the result that these "King Tuts" may be in production long after death.

Without doubt, from a technical standpoint, the wide-scale use of artificial insemination of horses only awaits the time when a few of the remaining problems are overcome. To be sure, there is and will continue to be resistance on the part of some horse registry associations and some breeders, with the result that research in the area of artificial insemination of horses will continue to lag. But progress cannot be stopped! Artificial insemination will expand among horses, especially with grade mares, just as it has in the dairy industry, as soon as the remaining barriers are removed.

Who would not like to use a valuable stallion as widely as possible, and long after death? Imagine being able to increase substantially the number of offspring per year from a syndicated stallion whose stud fee is $5000 or $20,000! Also, through the wide-scale use of artificial insemination of horses, many stallions could be eliminated (one stallion is now kept for each 7.3 foals produced), thereby affecting a considerable saving in keep.

The knowledge of the reproductive processes gained from artificial insemination can contribute materially to the increased efficiency of horse breeding. Perhaps, among its virtues, therefore, artificial insemination does offer some promise of assuring a higher conception rate in horses.

BLOOD TYPING HORSES

Blood typing was developed at the University of Wisconsin during the decade 1940–50. It involves a study of the components of the blood, which are inherited according to strict genetic rules that have been established in the research laboratory. By determining the genetic "markers" in each sample and then applying the rules of inheritance, parentage can be determined. To qualify as the offspring of a given mare and stallion, an animal must not possess any genetic markers not present in its alleged parents. If it does, it constitutes ground for illegitimacy.

Blood typing is used for the following purposes.

■ *To verify parentage* — The test is used in instances where the offspring may bear some unusual color or markings or carry some undesirable recessive characteristic. It may also be used to verify a registration certificate. There is need to use blood typing much more extensively as a bulwark of breed integrity. Through blood typing, parentage can be verified with 90 percent accuracy.[1]

Although this means that 10 percent of the cases cannot be settled, it's not possible to do any better than that in human blood typing.

■ *To determine which of two stallions* — When a mare has been served by two or more stallions during one breeding season, blood typing can identify the sire.

■ *To provide a permanent blood type record for identification purposes* — Two samples of blood are required for each animal to be studied; and the samples must be taken in tubes and in keeping with detailed instructions provided by the laboratory. In parentage cases, this calls for blood samples from the foal and both parents; in paternity cases, samples must be taken from the foal, the mare, and all the stallions.

■ *To substitute for fingerprinting* — Much attention is now being given to the idea of utilizing blood typing as a positive means of identification of stolen animals, through proving their parentage.

The following laboratories are capable of determining parentage.

1. Department of Reproduction, School of Veterinary Medicine, University of California, Davis, California 95612.

2. Immunogenetics Laboratory, Department of Animal Science, Texas A & M University, College Station, Texas 77843.

3. Cattle Blood Typing Laboratory, Department of Dairy Science, 625 Stadium Drive, Columbus, Ohio 43210.

4. Animal Disease Research Institute (E), Health of Animals Branch, Agriculture Canada, P.O. Box 11300, Postal Station "H," Ottawa, Ontario, Canada K2H 8P9.

---

[1]In a personal communication to the author, Dr. Clyde Stormont, Professor of Immunogenetics, Department of Reproduction, School of Veterinary Medicine, University of California, Davis, reported that in the California laboratory they have been able to solve approximately 91 percent of all the parentage cases.

6. Feeding Horses

Feed is the most important influence in the environment of the horse. Unless properly fed, the horse's maximum potential in reproduction, growth, body form, speed, endurance, style, and attractiveness cannot be achieved. Also, feed constitutes the greatest single cost item in the horse business.

Feeding practices vary from one locality to another — and among horsemen. The size of individual horses, the use to which they are put, and the size of the enterprise also make for differences.

Fundamentally, the nature of horses remains the same. For this reason, successful feeding in one stable is not much different from successful feeding in another stable.

Skill and good judgment are essential in feeding horses. Horsemen may secure widely different results under similar conditions. The horses may be in the best of condition in one stable — and have animation, nerve, speed, and endurance. In another stable, listless animals with dull eyes and rough coats testify to lack of judgment in their feeding and management. The unsatisfactory condition in the latter stable may not mean that the owner tried to economize on feed; horsemen who feed their animals the most economically may have the best horses.

Unfortunately, altogether too many horse feeds are based on fads, foibles, and trade secrets, rather than on sound, scientific facts. Worse yet, some concoctions contain ingredients that aren't needed or that are in excess; some of them actually produce harmful imbalances, and all of them cost money.

HORSE FEEDS AND FEEDING FACTS

The following facts relative to horse feeds and feeding are noteworthy:

■ *Grass hay and farm grains are inadequate* in quantity and quality proteins, in certain minerals and vitamins, and in unidentified factors; this is especially so during the critical periods (growth, reproduction, lactation, and when under stress) of the horse. It is also noteworthy that in the country of its origin the Arabian never had oats or timothy hay.

■ *Horses differ* from other farm animals because (1) they are kept for recreation, sport, and work, instead of for meat, milk, or wool production; (2) they are fed for a longer life of usefulness than meat animals — the latter are usually marketed for slaughter at an early age; (3) they have a smaller digestive tract, which does not permit as much use of bulk as is possible with ruminants; (4) they should not carry surplus body weight; and (5) they are fed for nerve, mettle, animation, and character of muscle, rather than tenderness and flavor.

■ *Artificial conditions have been created* for horses, more so than for any other class of livestock. In the wild state, they roamed the plains in bands, with plenty of outdoor exercise on natural footing, feed derived from unleached soils, and unforced production. Today, many horses are stall-fed all or a large part of the year (some horses spend up to 95 percent of their time in a stall); feeds are often produced on depleted soils; and young stock are forced for early growth and use (as in racing two-year-olds). Under these unnatural conditions, (1) unsoundnesses, (2) breeding problems, and (3) nutritional diseases and ailments have become increasingly common.

■ *Feed storage and labor costs have spiraled,* with the result that, for reasons of economy, storage space for feed, and labor for feeding and cleanup, should be held to a minimum — factors which favor the use of pelleted feeds.

THE DIGESTIVE SYSTEM

The alimentary canal includes the entire tube extending from the mouth to the rectum. Table 6.1 and Figure 6.1 show the comparative structures and sizes of the digestive tracts of farm animals. As noted, the digestive tract of the horse is anatomically and physiologically quite different from that of the ruminant; and it is much smaller, with the result that horses cannot eat as much roughage as cattle. Also, the primary seats

Table 6.1 Capacities of Digestive Tracts of Horse, Cow, and Pig[1]

Parts of Digestive Tract	Horse (quarts)	Cow (quarts)	Pig (quarts)
Stomach	8 to 16		6 to 8
Rumen (paunch)		160	
Reticulum (honeycomb)		10	
Omasum (manyplies)		15	
Abomasum (true stomach of cow)		15	
Small intestine	48	62	9
Cecum	28 to 32		
Large intestine	80	40	10

[1] Values are for average size horses of 1000 to 1200 lb.

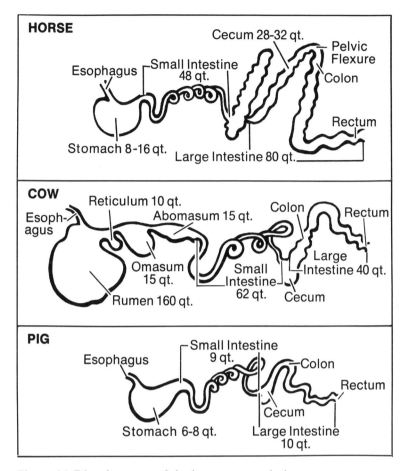

Figure 6.1 Digestive tracts of the horse, cow, and pig.

of microbial activity in ruminants and horses occupy different locations in the digestive system in relation to the small intestine. In cows and sheep, the rumen precedes the small intestine; in horses, the cecum follows it.

Both the amount of bacterial synthesis and the efficiency of absorption of nutrients synthesized by the microorganisms are likely to be lower in a horse than in a ruminant. In comparison to a cow, therefore, a horse should be fed less roughage, more and higher quality protein (no urea), and added B vitamins. Actually, the nutrient requirements of a horse appear more nearly parallel to those of a pig than a cow.

STOMACH OF HORSE VS STOMACH OF COW

Some basic differences between the stomach of the horse and the stomach of the cow are:

- The cow has four compartments (rumen, reticulum, omasum, and the abomasum or true stomach), whereas the horse has one.

■ The stomach capacity of the horse is smaller — 8 to 16 quarts for the mature horse (but it functions best at two-thirds capacity) as opposed to about 200 quarts for the mature cow. Because of its small stomach, if a horse is fed too much roughage, labored breathing and quick tiring may result. Actually the horse's stomach is designed for almost constant intake of small quantities of feed (such as happens when a horse is out grazing on pasture), rather than large amounts at one time.

■ Without feed, the horse's stomach will empty completely in 24 hours, whereas it takes about 72 hours (3 times as long) for the cow's stomach to empty. At the time of eating, feed passes through the horse's stomach very rapidly — so much so that the feed eaten at the beginning of the meal passes into the intestine before the last part of the meal is completed.

■ There is comparatively little microbial action in the stomach of the horse, but much such action in the stomach (rumen) of the cow.

CECUM SYNTHESIS GIVES ONLY LIMITED ASSIST

In the case of ruminants (cattle and sheep), there is tremendous bacterial action in the paunch. These bacteria build body proteins of high quality from sources of inorganic nitrogen, but nonruminants (humans, rats, chickens, swine, poultry, and dogs) cannot do this. Further on in the digestive tract, the ruminant digests the bacteria and obtains good proteins therefrom. Although the horse is not a ruminant, apparently the same bacterial process occurs to a limited extent in the cecum — that greatly enlarged blind pouch of the large intestine of the horse. However, it is much more limited than in ruminants, and the cecum is located beyond the small intestine, the main area for digestion and absorption of nutrients. This points up the fallacy of relying on cecum synthesis in the horse; above all, it must be remembered that little cecum synthesis exists in young equines.

In recognition of the more limited bacterial action in the horse, most state laws forbid the use of such nonprotein nitrogen sources as urea in horse rations. For such an animal, high quality proteins in the diet are requisite to normal development.

The limited protein synthesis in the horse (limited when compared with ruminants), and the lack of efficiency of absorption due to the cecum being on the lower end of the gut (thereby not giving the small intestine a chance at the ingesta after it leaves the cecum), clearly indicate that horse rations should contain high quality proteins, adequate in amino acids.

FUNCTIONS OF FEEDS

The feed consumed by horses is used for a number of different purposes, the exact usage varying somewhat with the class, age, and productivity of the animal. A certain part of the feed is used for the maintenance of bodily functions aside from any useful production. This is known as the maintenance requirement. In addition, feed is used to take care of the functions for which horses are kept. Thus, young growing equines need nutrients suitable for building muscle tissue and bone; horses being readied for show or sale need a surplus of energy feeds for formation of fat; broodmares require feed for the development of their fetuses, and, following parturition, for the production of milk; whereas work animals (horses in heavy use or training, like racehorses) use feed to supply energy for work.

NUTRIENT REQUIREMENTS AND ALLOWANCES

In ration formulation, two words are commonly used — "requirements" and "allowances." Requirements do not provide for margins of safety. Thus, to feed a horse on the basis of meeting the bare requirements would not be unlike building a bridge without providing margins of safety for heavier than average loads or for floods. No competent engineer would be so foolish as to design such a bridge. Likewise, knowledgeable horse nutritionists provide for margins of safety — they provide for the necessary nutritive allowances. They allow for variations in feed composition; possible losses during storage and processing; day to day, and period to period, differences in needs of animals; age and size of animal; stage of gestation and lactation; the kind and degree of activity; the amount of stress; the system of management; the health, condition and temperament of the animal; and the kind, quality, and amount of feed — all of which exert a powerful influence in determining nutritive needs.

RECOMMENDED NUTRIENT ALLOWANCES

Unfortunately, little experimental work has been done on the minimum nutritional requirements of horses. However, presently available information indicates that the nutrient allowances recommended in Tables 6.2 and 6.3 will meet the minimum requirements for horses and provide a

Table 6.2 Recommended Allowances of Protein, Fiber, and Total Digestible Nutrients (TDN)

Type of Horse	Minimum Crude Protein (%)	Maximum Crude Fiber (%)	Minimum TDN (%)
Most mature horses used for race, show,			
or pleasure	12	25	53 to 70[1]
Broodmares	13	25	50 to 60
Stallions	14	25	50 to 68[2]
Young equines:			
Foals, 2 weeks to 10 months old	21	8	68 to 74
Weanlings to 18 months old	14	20	60
18 months to 3 years old	13	25	50 to 60

[1] The heavier the work, the more energy is required.

[2] Increase the energy immediately before and during the breeding season.

Table 6.3 Recommended Allowances of Minerals and Vitamins

Kind of Mineral or Vitamin	Daily Allowance per 1000-Pound Horse[1]	Allowances per Ton of Finished Feed (Hay and Grain Combined)[2]
MINERALS:		
Salt	2 oz	10 lb
Calcium	70.0 g	12.33 lb
Phosphorus	60.0 g	10.57 lb
Potassium	68.1 g	12 lb
Magnesium	6.4 g	1.3 lb
Iron	640 mg	51.2 g
Zinc	400 mg	32.0 g
Manganese	340 mg	27.2 g
Copper	90 mg	7.2 g
Iodine	2.6 mg	.21 g
Cobalt	1.5 mg	.12 g
VITAMINS:		
Vitamin A (IU)	50,000	4,000,000
Vitamin D_2 (IU)	7000	560,000
Vitamin E (IU)	200	16,000
Choline (mg)	400	32,000
Pantothenic acid (mg)	60	4800
Niacin (mg)	50	4000
Riboflavin (mg)	40	3200
Thiamin (B_1) (mg)	25	2000
Vitamin K (mg)	8	640
Folic acid (mg)	2.5	200
Vitamin B_{12} (mcg)[3]	125	10,000

[1] This is based on an allowance of 25 pounds of feed per 1000-pound horse per day, or 2.5 pounds of feed per 100 pounds of body weight.
[2] Where hay is fed separately, double this amount should be added to the concentrate.
[3] Micrograms.

reasonable margin of safety. A margin of safety is important owing to (1) variations in feed composition because of the soil on which it was grown, stage of maturity when it was harvested, amount of weathering, and losses in processing and storage; and (2) differences in environment and individual animals.

STRESS AND NUTRITIVE REQUIREMENTS

Stress may be caused by excitement, temperament, fatigue, number of horses together, previous nutrition, breed, age, and management. Race and show horses are always under stress; and the more tired they become and the greater the speed, the greater the stress. Thus, the ration for race and show horses should be scientifically formulated, rather than based on fads, foibles, and trade secrets. The greater the stress, the more exacting the nutritive requirements.

SPECIFIC NUTRIENT NEEDS

To supply all the needs — maintenance, growth, fitting (fattening), reproduction, lactation, and work — the different classes of horses must receive sufficient feed to furnish the necessary quantity of energy (carbohydrates and fats), protein, minerals, and vitamins, plus water.

ENERGY NEEDS

The energy needs of horses vary with the individuality and size of animals, and the kind, amount, and severity of work performed. The energy requirements of a horse in strenuous effort are 78 times greater than in walking, and in racing they're up to 100 times greater than at rest.

It is common knowledge that a ration must contain proteins, fats, and carbohydrates. Although each of these has specific functions in maintaining a normal body, they can all be used to provide energy for maintenance, for work, or for fattening. From the standpoint of supplying the normal energy needs of horses, however, the carbohydrates are by far the most important, more of them being consumed than any other compound, whereas the fats are next in importance for energy purposes. In comparison with fats, carbohydrates are usually more abundant and cheaper, and they are very easily digested, absorbed, and transformed into body fat. Besides, carbohydrate feeds may be more easily stored in warm weather and for longer periods of time, whereas feeds high in fat content are likely to become rancid, and rancid feed is unpalatable, if not actually injurious in some instances.

Generally, increased energy for horses is met by increasing the grain and decreasing the roughage. Young equines and working (or running) horses must have rations in which a large part of the carbohydrate content of the ration is low in fiber, and in the form of nitrogen-free extract.

A lack of energy may cause slow and stunted growth in foals, and loss of weight, poor condition, and excessive fatigue in mature horses.

PROTEIN NEEDS

Proteins are complex organic compounds made up chiefly of amino acids, which are present in characteristic proportions for each specific protein. This nutrient always contains carbon, hydrogen, oxygen, and nitrogen; and, in addition, it usually contains sulphur and frequently phosphorus. Proteins are essential in all plant and animal life as components of the active protoplasm of each living cell.

In plants, the protein is largely concentrated in the actively growing portions, especially the leaves and seeds. Legumes also have the ability to synthesize their own proteins from such relatively simple soil and air compounds as carbon dioxide, water, nitrates, and sulfates. Thus, plants, together with some bacteria that are able to synthesize these products, are the original sources of all proteins.

In animals, proteins are much more widely distributed than in plants.

Thus, the proteins of the animal body are primary constituents of many structural and protective tissues — such as bones, ligaments, hair, hoofs, skin, and the soft tissues which include the organs and muscles. The total protein content of a horse's body ranges from about 10 percent in very fat mature horses to 20 percent in thin young foals. By way of further contrast, it is also interesting to note that, except for the limited bacterial action in the cecum, horses lack the ability of the plant to synthesize proteins from simple materials. They must depend upon plants as a source of dietary protein. In brief, except for the proteins built by the bacterial action in the cecum, they must have amino acids or more complete protein compounds in the ration.

Horses of all ages and kinds require adequate amounts of protein of suitable quality, for maintenance, growth, fattening, reproduction, and work. Of course, the protein requirements for growth and reproduction are the greatest and most critical.

A deficiency of proteins in the horse may result in the following deficiency symptoms: depressed appetite, poor growth, loss of weight, reduced milk production, irregular estrus, lowered foal crops, loss of condition, and lack of stamina.

Since the vast majority of protein requirements given in feeding standards meet minimum needs only, the allowances for race, show, breeding, and young animals should be higher.

QUALITY OF PROTEIN

In addition to supplying an adequate quantity of proteins, it is essential that the character of proteins be thoroughly understood. Proteins are very complex compounds with each molecule made up of hundreds of thousands of amino acids combined with each other. The amino acids, of which some 23 are known, are sometimes referred to as the building stones of proteins. Certain of these amino acids can be made by the animal's body to satisfy its needs. Others cannot be formed fast enough to supply the body's needs, and therefore are known as essential (or indispensable) amino acids. These must be supplied in the feed. Thus, rations that furnish an insufficient amount of any of the essential amino acids are said to have proteins of poor quality, whereas those which provide the proper proportions of the various necessary amino acids are said to supply proteins of good quality. In general, proteins of plant origin (linseed meal, cottonseed meal, and soybean meal) are not of as good quality as proteins of animal origin and their by-products.

The necessity of each amino acid in the diet of the experimental rat has been thoroughly tested, but less is known about the requirements of large animals or even the human. According to our present knowledge, based largely on work with the rat, the following division of amino acids as indispensable and dispensable seems proper:

Indispensable (*essential*): Arginine, Histidine, Isoleucine, Leucine, Lysine, Methionine, Phenylalanine, Threonine, Tryptophan, Valine.
Dispensable (*not essential*): Alanine, Aspartic Acid, Citrulline, Cysteine, Glutamic Acid, Glycine, Hydroxyglutamic Acid, Hydroxyproline, Proline, Serine, Tyrosine.

Fortunately, the amino acid content of proteins from various sources varies. Thus, the deficiencies of one protein may be improved by combining it with another, and the mixture of the two proteins often will have a higher feeding value than either one alone. It is for this reason, along with added palatability, that a considerable variety of feeds in the horse ration is desirable.

The feed proteins are broken down into amino acids by digestion. They are then absorbed and distributed by the bloodstream to the body cells, which rebuild these amino acids into body proteins.

PROTEIN POISONING

Some opinions to the contrary, protein poisoning as such has never been documented. There is no proof that heavy feeding of high protein feeds to horses is harmful, provided (1) the ration is balanced out in all other respects, (2) the animal's kidneys are normal and healthy (a large excess of protein in terms of body needs increases the work of the kidneys for the excretion of the urea), (3) any ration change to high protein feed is made gradually, as is recommended in any change in feed, and (4) there is adequate exercise and normal metabolism.

Some horses do appear to be allergic to certain proteins or to excesses of specific amino acids, as a result of which they may develop "protein bumps."

It is recognized that protein in excess of what the body can use tends to be wasted insofar as its specific functions are concerned, since it cannot be stored in any but very limited amounts and must be catabolized. Nevertheless, some wastage of protein in terms of its known functions may be both physiologically and economically desirable in order to (1) maintain the protein reserves, (2) provide an adequate protein-calorie ratio for efficient energy utilization, and (3) assure that protein quality needs are met, despite the marked difference of quality among commonly fed rations. Generally speaking, high protein feeds are more expensive than high energy feeds (feeds high in carbohydrates and fats), with the result that there is the temptation to feed too little of them.

MINERALS

When we think of minerals for the horse, we instinctively think of bones and unsoundnesses. This is so because (1) a horse's skeleton is very large, weighing 100 pounds or more in a full-grown horse, of which more than half consists of organic matter or minerals, and (2) experienced trainers estimate that one-third of the horses in training require treatments for unsoundnesses, in one form or another. But in addition to furnishing structural material for the growth of bones, teeth, and tissues, minerals regulate many of the life processes.

The classical horse ration of grass hay and farm grains is usually deficient in calcium, but adequate in phosphorus. Also, salt is almost always deficient; and many horse rations do not contain sufficient iodine and certain other trace elements. Thus, horses usually need special mineral supplements. But they should not be fed either more or less minerals than needed.

In an amazingly short time after birth, a healthy foal can run almost as fast as its mother — and on legs almost as long. In fact, the cannon bones (the lower leg bones extending from the knees and hocks to the fetlocks) are as long at the time of birth as they ever will be. This indicates that important development of the skeleton takes place in the fetus, before the foal is born. It is evident, therefore, that adequate minerals must be provided the broodmare if the bones of her offspring are to be sound.

Although acute mineral-deficiency diseases and actual death losses are relatively rare, inadequate supplies of any one of the 15 essential mineral elements may result in lack of thrift, poor gains, inefficient feed utilization, lowered reproduction, and decreased performance in racing, showing, riding, or whatnot.

The 15 mineral elements which have been shown to be essential are: calcium, phosphorus, sodium, chlorine, iodine, iron, copper, manganese, magnesium, sulfur, zinc, potassium, cobalt, selenium, and molybdenum. This does not mean that all 15 of these minerals must always be included in horse mineral supplements. Rather, only the specific minerals that are deficient in the ration — and in the quantities necessary — should be supplied. *Excesses and mineral imbalances are to be avoided.*

SALT (Sodium Chloride)

Salt, which serves as both a condiment and a nutrient, is needed by all classes of animals, but more especially by herbivora (grass-eating animals). It may be provided in the form of granulated, rock, or block salt. In general, the form selected is determined by price and availability. It is to be pointed out, however, that it is difficult for horses to eat very hard block and rock salt. This often results in inadequate consumption. Also, if there is much competition for the salt block, the more timid animals may not get their requirements.

Both sodium and chlorine are essential for animal life. They are necessary in maintaining the osmotic pressure of body cells (thereby assisting in the transfer of nutrients to the cells and the removal of waste materials). Also, sodium is important as one of the main body buffers and in making bile, which aids in the digestion of fats and carbohydrates.

Chlorine is required for the formation of the hydrochloric acid in the gastric juice, so vital to protein digestion. The blood contains 0.25% chlorine, 0.22% sodium, and 0.02 to 0.22% potassium; thus, the chlorine content is higher than that of any other mineral in the blood. The salt requirement is greatly increased under conditions which cause heavy sweating, thereby resulting in large losses of this mineral from the body. Unless it is replaced, fatigue will result. For this reason, when engaged in hard work and perspiring profusely, horses should receive liberal allowances of salt.

On the average, a horse needs about 3 ounces of salt daily or $1\frac{1}{3}$ pounds per week, although salt requirements vary with work and temperature. Iodized salt should be used in iodine-deficient areas.

Salt can be fed free-choice to horses, provided they have not been salt-starved. That is, if the animals have not previously been fed salt for a considerable length of time, they may overeat, resulting in digestive disturbances and even death. Salt-starved animals should first be hand-fed salt, and the daily allowance should be increased gradually until they start leaving a little in the mineral box. When this point is reached, self-feeding may be followed. The Indians and the pioneers of this country handed down many legendary stories about the large numbers of buffalo and deer that killed themselves simply by gorging at a newly found salt lick after having been salt-starved for long periods of time.

When added to the concentrate ration, salt should be added at a level of 0.5 to 1.0 percent.

CALCIUM AND PHOSPHORUS

Horses are more apt to suffer from a lack of calcium and phosphorus than from any of the other minerals except salt. These two minerals comprise about $\frac{3}{4}$ the ash of the skeleton and from $\frac{1}{3}$ to $\frac{1}{2}$ of the minerals of milk.

Knowledge of the following general characteristics of feeds in regard to calcium and phosphorus is important in rationing horses.

■ The cereal grains and their by-products and straws, dried mature grasses, and protein supplements of plant origin are low in calcium.

■ The protein supplements of animal origin and legume forage are rich in calcium.

■ The cereal grains and their by-products are fairly high or even rich in phosphorus, but a large portion of the phosphorus is not readily available.

■ Almost all protein-rich supplements are high in phosphorus. But, here again, plant sources of phosphorus contain much of this element in a bound form.

■ Beet by-products and dried, mature nonleguminous forages (such as grass hays and fodders) are likely to be low in phosphorus.

■ The calcium and phosphorus content of plants can be increased through fertilizing the soil upon which they are grown.

In considering the calcium and phosphorus requirements of horses, it is important to realize that the proper utilization of these minerals by the body is dependent upon three factors: (1) an adequate supply of calcium and phosphorus in an available form (growing horses should be provided calcium at a level of approximately 0.6 to 0.7% of the diet, and phosphorus at a level of about 0.5%); (2) a suitable ratio between them — somewhere within the range 1.1 to 1.4:1. (The exact calcium to phosphorus ratio is not known, although it appears to differ according to age. For example, older horses can have a calcium to phosphorus ratio of 2.0 to 1.0. It is important, however, to have slightly more calcium than phosphorus. Excess phosphorus may cause osteomalacia in mature horses. This condition may develop when rations with a Ca:P ratio of 0.8 to 1 are fed 6 to 12 months, and it will progress rapidly when the ration is 0.6 to 1.); and (3) sufficient vitamin D to make possible the assimilation and utilization of the calcium and phosphorus. Many "cure-alls" and commericial mineral mixtures fail to take these factors into consideration.

If plenty of vitamin D is present (as provided either by sunlight or through the ration), the ratio of calcium to phosphorus becomes less important. Also, less vitamin D is needed when there is a desirable calcium-phosphorus ratio.

Where both calcium and phosphorus are needed, the author favors the use of high quality steamed bone meal for horses, because bone meal contains many ingredients in addition to calcium and phosphorus. It is a good source of iron, manganese, and zinc, and it contains such trace minerals as copper and cobalt; but it is felt that the content of the latter is too low to be of much value as a supplement for them. However, it is increasingly difficult to get good bone meal. Some of the imported products are high in fat, rancid, and/or odorous and unpalatable. Where good bone meal is not available, dicalcium phosphate is generally recommended.

When calcium alone is needed, ground limestone or oyster shell flour are commonly used, either free-choice or added to the ration in keeping with nutrient requirements.

Where phosphorus alone is needed, monosodium phosphate or defluorinated phosphate are the minerals of choice.

Earlier experiments cast considerable doubt on the availability of phosphorus when the phosphorus was largely in the form of phytin. Although wheat bran is very high in phosphorus, containing 1.32%, there was some question as to its availability due to the high phytin content of this product. More recent studies, however, indicate that cattle, and perhaps mature swine, can partially utilize phytin phosphorus. Cattle can utilize about 60% of the total phosphorus from most plant sources, whereas swine can utilize only about 50%. The situation relative to horses is unknown. It must be emphasized, however, that phosphorus availability depends to a large extent on phosphorus sources, dietary supplies of calcium, and adequate vitamin D.

For humans, the availability of the calcium of certain leafy materials is impaired by the presence of oxalic acid — the acid precipitating the calcium and preventing its absorption. On the other hand, the deleterious effects of oxalic acid are reduced in the ruminant because of the ruminant's apparent ability to metabolize oxalic acid in the body. The situation relative to horses is unknown.

During World War II, the shortage of phosphorus feed supplements led to the development of defluorinated phosphates for feed purposes. Raw, unprocessed rock phosphate usually contains from 3.25 to 4.0 percent fluorine, whereas steamed bone meal normally contains only 0.05 to 0.10 percent. Fortunately, through heating at high temperatures under conditions suitable for elimination of fluorine, the excess fluorine of raw rock phosphate can be removed. Such a product is known as defluorinated phosphate.

Under the definition of the Association of American Feed Control Officials, to qualify as a defluorinated phosphate, rock phosphate cannot contain more than one part of fluorine to 100 parts of phosphate.

Excess fluorine results in abnormal development of bones; softening, mottling, and irregular wear of the teeth; roughened hair coat; delayed maturity; and less efficient utilization of feed.

TRACE MINERALS

A discussion of each of the trace minerals follows.

Cobalt — Cobalt is required for the synthesis of vitamin B_{12} in the intestinal tract of the horse. A lack of cobalt and/or B_{12} will result in anemia. Since the feeds normally used by horses are deficient in vitamin B_{12}, it is advisable to supply a low level of cobalt in the ration of horses. The addition to the ration of 1.5 mg of cobalt per day will be adequate.

Copper — A copper deficiency has been reported in Australia in horses grazing on pastures low in copper. Also, mare's milk (along with milk from all species) is low in copper.

Copper is of special interest to horsemen because, in addition to its effect on iron metabolism, it is closely associated with normal bone development in young growing animals. In copper-deficient dogs and swine, there is a marked failure of deposition of bone in the cartilage matrix and deformed bones. Cattle and sheep grazing copper-deficient areas develop brittle bones which fracture easily. Abnormal bone development has been reported in foals on low copper diets.

The recommended copper allowance for a 1000-pound horse is 90 mg per day, about half of which should be added to the ration.

Iodine — Pregnant mares are very susceptible to iodine deficiency. Where such a deficiency exists, the foals are usually stillborn or so weak that they cannot stand and suck. There is also some evidence to indicate that navel-ill in foals may be lessened by feeding iodine to broodmares. Iodine deficiency is most prevalent in inland regions of the United States;

it seldom occurs in the coastal areas because of the abundance of iodine from ocean and sea water.

The addition to the daily ration of 2.6 mg of iodine will be ample.

Iron — The National Research Council (NRC) estimates the iron requirement of the horse at 40 ppm. However, it has been reported that horses which are subjected to pressure from racing, showing, or other heavy use require 80 to 100 ppm of iron in their daily ration; which calls for 907 to 1134 mg of iron in the ration of a 1000-pound horse consuming 25 pounds of feed per day. To be on the safe side, approximately one-half of the iron requirement of the horse should be added to the ration; and it should be in a biologically available form (iron oxide should not be used as a source of iron for horses because it is poorly absorbed).

Magnesium — The magnesium requirements of the horse are not known. But perhaps the following guidelines will suffice until specific research data are available:

1. Swine require 400 ppm (180 mg per lb of diet) of magnesium for growth. On this basis, a 1000-lb horse consuming 25 lb of feed per day would require 4535 mg of magnesium per day.

2. It appears that the magnesium requirement of farm animals for growth is of the order of 0.06 percent of the dry ration, provided the calcium and phosphorus intakes are adequate but not excessive. On this basis, a 1000-lb horse consuming 25 lb of feed per day would require 6810 mg of magnesium per day.

Horse rations containing 50 percent forage will likely contain sufficient magnesium for unstressed horses. But horses at hard work (as in racing and showing) consume more grain (which is low in magnesium) and less forage. Also, horses being raced or shown, or otherwise stressed, are frequently keyed up, high-strung, and jumpy, similar to the nervousness that characterizes animals and humans known to be suffering from a magnesium deficiency.

In view of the above, it would appear prudent that $\frac{1}{2}$ to $\frac{2}{3}$ of the recommended daily magnesium allowance of the horse be added to the ration; or about 3200 mg daily per 1000-pound horse.

Manganese — Based on research with other species, it is reasonable to assume that horses should meet their daily requirements on feeds containing 20 ppm and no more than 40 ppm of manganese.

Since most natural feedstuffs are rich in manganese, it can be assumed that part of the requirement for this element will be met by the normal ration.

Thirty ppm calls for 340 mg of manganese in the ration of a 1000-pound horse consuming 25 pounds of feed per day.

Zinc — Swine require 50 ppm zinc on diets properly balanced with calcium. But if excessive levels of calcium are fed (1.0% or more), then the requirement is increased to about 100 ppm. Research with cattle has shown that supplementing the ration with 50 to 100 ppm of zinc will improve the hair coat. Obviously, zinc is necessary for the maintenance and development of skin and hair.

Since beautiful hair coats are important in horses, fortifying the daily ration with 400 mg of zinc per day will prevent any possibility of a deficiency if the zinc in the feed is on the low side.

Chelated Trace Minerals — The word chelate is derived from the Greek chelae, meaning a claw or pincer-like organ. Those selling chelated minerals generally recommend a smaller quantity of them (but at a higher price per pound) and extoll their "fenced-in" properties.

When it comes to synthetic chelating agents, much needs to be learned about their selectivity toward minerals, the kind and quantity most effective, their mode of action, and their behavior with different species of animals and with varying rations.

It is possible that their use may actually create a mineral imbalance. These answers, and more, must be forthcoming through carefully controlled experiments before they can be recommended for valuable horses.

MINERAL IMBALANCES

It has become increasingly evident that there is a delicate relationship between certain mineral elements. Thus, the requirements of any mineral may be modified by another mineral which enhances or interferes with its utilization. For this reason, playing the "minerals numbers game" can be hazardous when it comes to buying horse feeds. By the "minerals numbers game," reference is made to the gimmick of comparing products on the basis of which has the most "numbers," or units, of certain minerals, some of which may not be needed at all. So, beware of the person who extolls brand "X" on the basis that it has more units of certain minerals than brand "Y."

Indeed, excess fortification of the horse's diet with trace elements may prove more detrimental than helpful. Thus, the horseman who knows and cares will avoid harmful imbalances; he will provide minerals on the basis of recommended allowances.

In recommended allowances, reasonable margins of safety are provided to allow for variations in feed composition (due to soils on which grown, stage of maturity, weathering, and processing and storage), environment, stress, and individuality. Also, when fortifying with minerals, consideration should be given to the minerals provided by the ingredients of the normal ration, for it is the total composition of the feed that counts.

SELF-FEED MINERALS

People and horses have many things in common; among them, some individuals require more salt and other minerals than others. The ration should contain a reasonable level of minerals. Then, animal and feed differences (due to stage of maturity at harvest, weathering, length of storage, etc.) should be met by free-choice mineral feeding. Allow free access to a double compartment mineral box, with ground iodized salt in one side, and in the other either (1) a home-mixed mineral of $\frac{1}{3}$ iodized salt and $\frac{2}{3}$ steamed bone meal (or dicalcium phosphate), or (2) a good commercial mineral.

MARE'S SKELETON IS MINERAL BANK

Most mares weighing about 1000 lb will produce an average of 2 gallons, or more, of milk per day throughout the 7-month suckling period. That's a total of 3360 lb of milk. This amount of mare's milk contains as much mineral as the bodies of 3 steers weighing 1000 lb each at 18 months of age. This means that 3 steers work 54 months (3 x 18) to produce as much mineral as a mare produces for her foal in a 7-month suckling period.

Here's how this phenomenon works: the mare's skeleton is like a bank — people deposit money in a bank, then draw out or write checks on their reserves as needed. So, when properly fed before breeding, in early pregnancy, and when barren, mineral deposits are made in the mare's skeleton. Then at those times when the mineral demands are greater than can be obtained from the feed — the last of pregnancy, and during lactation — the mare draws from the stored reserves in her skeleton.

Of course, if there hasn't been proper storage in the mare's skeleton, something must "give" — and that something is the mother. Nature has ordained that growth of the fetus, and the lactation that follows, shall take priority over the maternal requirements. Hence, when there is a mineral deficiency, the mare's body will be deprived, or even stunted if she is young, before the developing fetus or milk production will be materially affected.

This points up the importance of good mineral nutrition throughout the lifetime of the mare.

VITAMINS

Certain vitamins are necessary for the growth, development, health, and reproduction of horses. Deficiencies of vitamins A and D are sometimes encountered. Also, indications are that vitamin E and some of the B vitamins are required by horses. Further, it is recognized that single, uncomplicated vitamin deficiencies are the exception rather than the rule.

High quality, leafy, green forages plus plenty of sunshine generally give horses most of the vitamins they need. Horses get carotene (which they can convert to vitamin A) and riboflavin from green pasture and green hay not over a year old, and they get vitamin D from sunlight and sun-cured hay. If plenty of green forage and sunlight are not available, the horseman should get the advice of a nutritionist or veterinarian on the use of vitamin additives to the feed.

Vitamin A

Vitamin A is not synthesized in the cecum; thus, it must be provided in the feed, either (1) as vitamin A, or (2) as carotene, the precursor of vitamin A. Severe deficiency of vitamin A may cause night blindness, lachrymation (tears), keratinization of the cornea, reproductive difficulties, poor or uneven hoof development, difficulty in breathing, incoordination, progressive weakness, and poor appetite. There is also some evidence that deficiency of this vitamin may cause or contribute to certain leg bone weaknesses. When vitamin A deficiency symptoms appear, the horseman should add a stabilized vitamin A product to the ration.

It is wasteful to feed more vitamin A than is needed. Also, there are some indications that too high levels of vitamin A over an extended period of time may actually be harmful to man and to some animal species. When fed as directed, the vast majority of horse feeds won't provide excesses of vitamin A. But where higher product levels than needed are used as a sales gimmick, there is hazard that the horseman will administer the "stuff" like the Irishman's medicine — "If a little will do some good, a larger dose will do more good." Then, too, there may be a doubling up if both the mixed feed and the "conditioner" contain vitamin A. Finally it must be remembered that, unlike meat animals that are produced for slaughter, horses are fed for a long life of usefulness.

For a 1000-pound horse, 50,000 USP of vitamin A per day are recommended.

The vitamin A potency (whether due to the vitamin itself, to carotene, or to both) of feeds is usually reported in terms of IU or USP units. These two units of measurement are the same. They are based on the growth response of rats, in which several different levels of the test product are fed to different groups of rats, as a supplement to a vitamin A-free diet which has caused growth to cease. A USP or IU is the vitamin A value for rats of 0.30 microgram of pure vitamin A alcohol, or of 0.60 microgram of pure beta-carotene. The carotene or vitamin A content of feeds is commonly determined by colorimetric or spectroscopic methods.

Vitamin D

For horses, both D_2 (the plant form) and D_3 (the animal form) are equally effective, so there is no need to use some of each.

Foals sometimes develop rickets because of insufficient vitamin D, calcium, or phosphorus. This can be prevented by exposing the animal to direct sunlight as much as possible, by allowing it free access to a suitable mineral mixture, or by providing it with good quality sun-cured hay or luxuriant pasture grown on well-fertilized soil. In northern areas that do not have adequate sunshine, many horsemen provide the foal with a vitamin D supplement.

With vitamin D, as with vitamin A, there is need for adequacy without harmful excesses. Too much vitamin D may harm a horse. In 1964, Dr. Robert E. Cooke, Director of Pediatrics at Johns Hopkins Hospital

Figure 6.2 Osteomalacia of the facial bones in a Hackney. This deficiency disease in mature horses may be caused by (1) a lack of vitamin D, (2) a lack of calcium or phosphorus, or (3) an incorrect ratio of calcium to phosphorus. (Courtesy, College of Veterinary Medicine, University of Illinois, Urbana, Illinois)

reported evidence that the consumption of high levels of vitamin D by pregnant mothers may cause mental retardation, changes in the bony structure of the face, and effects upon the aortic valve of the hearts of babies. Admittedly, research on the subject with horses is needed.

The vitamin D requirement is less when a proper balance of calcium and phosphorus exists in the ration. A vitamin D level for horses of about one-seventh the level of vitamin A appears to be about right — or about 7000 USP daily.

VITAMIN E

There is experimental evidence that vitamin E improves the fertility of both mares and stallions, and that it prevents and corrects anhidrosis (dry, dull hair coat).

Most practical rations contain liberal quantities of vitamin E, perhaps enough except under conditions of work stress or reproduction, or where there is interference with its utilization. Rather than buy and use costly vitamin E concentrates indiscriminately, the horseman should add them to the ration only on the advice of a nutritionist or veterinarian.

Stowe, of the University of Kentucky, reported that daily doses per mare of 100,000 USP units of vitamin A and 100 IU of vitamin E, beginning 1 month prior to the breeding season and continuing for 3 months, improved conception rate by 64 percent.

Anhidrosis (dry coat) in horses — a condition showing dull hair coat, elevated temperature, high blood pressure, and labored breathing — has been successfully treated by the oral administration or 1000 to 3000 IU of vitamin E daily for 1 month.

The requirements for vitamin E are influenced by interrelationships with other essential nutrients — increased by the presence of interfering substances, and spared by the presence of other substances that may be protective or that may assume part of its functions. The addition of approximately 200 IU of vitamin E per day to most rations should be adequate.

B Complex Vitamins

Vitamins of the B complex (thiamine, riboflavin, B_{12}, choline, niacin, pantothenic acid, and folic acid) may be essential, especially for horses that are under stress, as in racing or showing. However, it is not clear which ones are needed, in what quantities they are needed, and their status from the standpoints of synthesis and absorption in the horse. Healthy horses usually get enough of them either in natural rations or by synthesis in the intestinal tract. However, when neither green pasture nor high-quality dry roughage is available, it may be in the nature of good insurance to provide them, especially for horses that are under stress, by adding to the ration distillers' dried solubles, dried brewer's yeast, animal liver meal, or dried fish solubles.

There is no evidence that deficiencies of the following B complex vitamins occur in horses on normal rations: B_6 (pyridoxine), biotin, and para-aminobenzoic acid.

Vitamin B_1 (Thiamine) — Vitamin B_1 is synthesized in the lower gut of the horse by bacterial action, but there is some doubt as to its sufficiency and as to the amount absorbed always meeting the full requirements. A thiamine deficiency has been observed in horses fed on poor-quality hay and grain.

Vitamin B_1 is required for normal carbohydrate metabolism. Since carbohydrate metabolism is increased during physical exertion, it is important that B_1 be available in quantity at such times. Hence, the addition to the ration of 25 mg of B_1 per horse per day is the recommended allowance.

Vitamin B_2 (Riboflavin) — A deficiency of riboflavin may cause periodic ophthalmia (moon blindness), but it is known that lack of this vitamin is not the only factor causing this condition. Sometimes moon blindness follows leptospirosis in horses, and it may be caused by a localized hypersensitivity or allergic reaction. Periodic ophthalmia caused by lack of riboflavin may be prevented by feeding green hay and green pasture, supplying feeds high in riboflavin, or by adding crystalline riboflavin to the ration at the rate of 40 mg per horse per day.

Vitamin B_{12} — It has been reported that horses in poor nutritional conditon showing anemia respond to the administration of vitamin B_{12}. An allowance of 125 micrograms of B_{12} per day is recommended. The addition of enough B_{12} to supply half of this total will probably be adequate insurance in most horse rations.

Choline Chloride — Choline is a metabolic essential for building and maintaining cell structure and in the transmission of nerve impulses. Choline deficiency has been produced in rats, dogs, chickens, pigs, and other species. Slow growth is a nonspecific symptom.

The dietary requirement for choline depends on the level of methionine (an amino acid) in the ration. Also, it is noteworthy that all naturally occurring fats contain some choline; however, normal horse feeds are low in fat. Hence, the addition to the ration of about two-thirds of the recommended choline allowance (400 mg per day is the recommended allowance for a 1000-lb horse) is indicated.

Niacin (Nicotinic Acid) — Some evidence indicates that niacin is synthesized by the horse. Also, the horse can convert the essential amino acid tryptophan into niacin. Hence, it is important to make certain that the ration is adequate in niacin; otherwise, the horse will use tryptophan to supply niacin needs. Niacin is widely distributed in feeds; fermentation solubles and certain oil meals are especially good sources. Only a modest addition of niacin to the ration is indicated.

Pantothenic Acid — Intestinal synthesis of pantothenic acid has been found to occur in all species studied. In the case of the horse, such synthesis appears to be sufficiently extensive to meet body needs, at least in part. As indicated in Table 6.3, a daily allowance of 60 mg of pantothenic acid is recommended for a 1000-pound horse.

Folic Acid — Folic acid is widely distributed in horse feeds. Hence, it is unlikely that a dietary source is required, although a small amount may be in the nature of cheap insurance.

Vitamin B$_6$ (Pyridoxine) — There is no evidence that deficiencies of vitamin B$_6$ occur in horses on commonly fed rations; and it is not expected that deficiencies should occur in view of the widespread distribution of vitamin B$_6$ in feedstuffs.

Biotin — There is substantial intestinal synthesis of biotin in all animal species studied, including man. Also, biotin is widely distributed in all feeds. Hence, there is no present evidence that it should be added to horse feeds.

Para-aminobenzoic Acid — Evidence that it performs essential functions on otherwise complete rations is lacking.

Vitamin K

When vitamin K is deficient, the coagulation time of the blood is increased and the prothrombin level is decreased. This is the main justification in adding this vitamin to the ration of the horse.

Ascorbic Acid (Vitamin C)

A dietary need for ascorbic acid is limited to man, the guinea pig, and the monkey. Hence, there is no need to add this vitamin to horse rations.

Vitamin Imbalances

Experiments have shown that the amounts needed of certain vitamins may be affected by the supply of another vitamin or of some other nutritive essential. Also, it is known that excess fortification of the horse's diet with certain vitamins may prove more detrimental than helpful. Thus, the horseman should avoid harmful imbalances; he should provide vitamins on the basis of recommended allowances. Also, when fortifying with vitamins, consideration should be given to the vitamins provided by the ingredients of the normal ration, for it is the total composition of the feed that counts.

Unidentified Factors

Since the U.S. foal crop is only around 50 percent, and since horses under stress (racing, showing, etc.) frequently become temperamental in their eating habits, it is obvious that there is room for improvement in the ration somewhere along the line. Perhaps unidentified factors are involved.

Unidentified factors include those vitamins which the chemist has not yet isolated and identified. For this reason, they are sometimes referred to as the vitamins of the future. There is mounting evidence of the importance of unidentified factors for animals, including man. Among other things, they lower the incidence of ulcers in man and swine. For horses, they appear to increase growth and improve feeding efficiency and breeding performance when added to rations thought to be complete with regard to known nutrients. The anatomical and physiological mechanism of the digestive system of the horse, plus the stresses and strains to which modern horses are subjected, would indicate the wisdom of adding unidentified factor sources to the ration of the horse. Unidentified factors appear to be of special importance during breeding, gestation, lactation, and growth.

Three highly regarded unidentified factor sources are: dried whey product, corn fermentation solubles, and dehydrated alfalfa meal.

WATER

Water is essential for the various physiological processes of the horse, such as the production of saliva. Hence, horses should have access to ample quantities of clean, fresh, water at all times. They will drink 10 to 12 gallons daily; the amount depends on weather, amount of work done (sweating), rations fed, and size of horse.

Free access to water is desirable. When this is not possible, horses should be watered at approximately the same times daily. Opinions vary among horsemen as to the proper times and method of watering horses. All agree, however, that regularity and frequency are desirable. Most horsemen agree that water may be given before, during, or after feeding.

Frequent small waterings between feedings are desirable during warm weather or when the animal is being put to hard use. Do not allow a horse to drink heavily when he is hot, because he may founder; and do not allow a horse to drink heavily just before being put to work.

Water should be available in both stalls and corrals. All waterers should have drains for easy cleaning, and should be heated to 40° to 45° F during the winter months in cold regions.

FEEDS

More than one kind of hay makes for appetite appeal. In season, any good pasture can replace part or all of the hay unless work or training conditions make substitution impractical.

Good quality oats and timothy hay always have been considered standard feeds for light horses. However, feeds of similar nutritive properties can be interchanged in the ration as price relationships warrant. Some of these feeds are grains (oats, corn, barley, wheat, and sorghum), protein supplements (linseed meal, soybean meal, and cottonseed meal), and hays of many varieties. Feed substitution makes it possible to obtain a balanced ration at lowest cost.

During winter months, it is well to add a few sliced carrots to the ration, an occasional bran mash, or a small amount of linseed meal. Also, use bran mash or linseed meal to regulate the bowels.

The propertion of concentrates must be increased and the roughages decreased as energy needs rise with the greater amount, severity, or speed of work. A horse that works at a trot needs considerably more feed than one that works at a walk. For this reason, riding horses in medium to light use require somewhat less grain and more hay in proportion to body weight than light horses that are racing. Also, from an esthetic standpoint, large, paunchy stomachs are objectionable on horses that are used for recreation and sport.

HAY

Through mistaken kindness or carelessness, horses are often fed too much hay or other roughage, with the result that they breathe laboriously and tire quickly. With cattle and sheep, on the other hand, it is usually well to feed considerable roughage. This difference between horses and ruminants is due primarily to the relatively small size of the simple stomach of the horse in comparison with the four-fold stomach of the ruminant.

When limiting the allowance of roughage, it is sometimes necessary to muzzle greedy horses (gluttons) to prevent them from eating the bedding.

Usually, young horses and idle horses can be provided with an unlimited allowance of hay. In fact, much good will result from feeding young and idle horses more roughage and less grain. But one should gradually increase the grain and decrease the hay as work or training begins.

The hay should be early cut, leafy, green, well cured, and free from dust and mold. Hay native to the locality is usually fed. However, horsemen everywhere prefer good quality timothy. With young stock and breeding animals especially, it is desirable that a sweet grass–legume mixture of alfalfa hay be fed. The legume provides a source of high quality proteins and certain minerals and vitamins.

Horses like variety. Therefore, if at all possible, it is wise to have more than one kind of hay in the stable. For example, timothy may be provided at one feeding and a grass-legume mixed hay at the other feeding. Good horsemen often vary the amount of alfalfa fed, for increased amounts of alfalfa in the ration will increase urination and give a softer consistency to the bowel movements. This means that elimination from kidneys and bowels can be carefully regulated by the amount and frequency of alfalfa feedings. Naturally, such regulation becomes more necessary with irregular use and idleness. On the other hand, in some areas alfalfa is fed as the sole roughage with good results.

Timothy

Timothy is the hay preferred by most horsemen. Although it may be grown alone, it is commonly seeded in mixtures with medium red or alsike clover.

Timothy is easy to harvest and cure. However, in comparison with hay made from the legumes, it is low in crude protein and minerals, particularly calcium.

As with all other forages, the feeding value of timothy is affected by the stage of growth of the plants at the time of cutting. With increasing maturity, (1) the percentage of crude protein decreases, (2) the percentage of crude fiber increases, (3) the hay becomes less palatable, and (4) the digestibility decreases. However, delaying cutting until timothy has reached the full bloom stage, or later, usually results in the highest yields. When both yield and quality are considered, the best results are obtained when timothy is cut for hay at the early bloom stage.

Alfalfa (Lucerne)

Alfalfa is an important, perennial, leguminous forage plant with trifoliate leaves and bluish-purple flowers. It is grown widely, principally for hay. Alfalfa is capable of surviving dry periods because of its extraordinarily long root system, and it is adapted to widely varying conditions of climate and soil. It yields the highest tonnage per acre and has the highest protein content of the legume hays.

Good quality alfalfa hay is excellent for horses. It averages 15.3 percent protein, which is of high quality; and it is a good source of certain minerals and vitamins. In addition to being used as a hay, alfalfa is an ingredient of most all-pelleted feeds.

Hay Quality

The easily recognizable characteristics of hay of high quality are:
1. It is made from plants cut at an early stage of maturity, thus assuring

the maximum content of protein, minerals, and vitamins, and the highest digestibility.

2. It is leafy, thus giving assurance of high protein content.

3. It is bright green in color, thus indicating proper curing, a high carotene or provitamin A content (provided it is not over a year old), and palatability.

4. It is free from foreign material, such as weeds and stubble.

5. It is free from must or mold and dust.

6. It is fine-stemmed and pliable — not coarse, stiff, and woody.

7. It has a pleasing, fragrant aroma; it "smells good enough to eat."

FORAGE SUBSTITUTIONS

Forages of similar nutritive properties may be interchanged in the ration as availability and price relationships warrant, thereby making it possible at all times to obtain a balanced ration at the lowest cost. Table 6.4 presents, in summary form, some roughage substitution guidelines.

Table 6.4 Forage Substitution Table

Forage	Value Compared to Timothy Hay, Which Is Designated As Equal to 100	Maximum Percentage of Timothy Hay Which It Can Replace
Timothy hay	100	100
Alfalfa hay	$133\frac{1}{3}$	100
Corn silage	45–55 (wet basis)	$33\frac{1}{3}$–50
Oat hay	100	100
Prairie hay	100	100
Sorghum fodder	100	50

CONCENTRATES

Of all the concentrates, heavy oats most nearly meet the need of horses; and, because of the uniformly good results obtained from their use, they have always been recognized as the leading grain for horses. Corn is also widely used as a horse feed, particularly in the central states. Despite occasional prejudice to the contrary, barley is a good horse feed. As proof of the latter assertion, it is noteworthy that the Arab — who was a good horseman — fed barley almost exclusively. Also, wheat, wheat bran, and commercial mixed feeds are extensively used. It is to be emphasized, therefore, that careful attention should be given to the prevailing price of feeds available locally, for many feeds are well suited to horses. Often substitutions can be made that will result in a marked saving without affecting the nutritive value of the ration. When corn or other heavy grains are fed, it is important that a little linseed meal or wheat bran be used, in order to regulate the bowels.

Oats

Oats are the leading U.S. horse feed. They normally weigh 32 pounds per bushel, but the best horse oats are heavier. The feeding value varies according to the hull content and test weight per bushel.

Because of their bulky nature, oats form a desirable loose mass in the stomach, which prevents impaction.

Oats may be rolled, crimped, or fed whole. Hulled oats are particularly valuable in the ration for young foals.

Barley

Barley is the leading horse grain in western United States.

Compared with corn, barley contains somewhat more protein (crude protein: barley 13%; corn 10%) and fiber (due to the hulls) and somewhat less carbohydrate and fat. Like oats, the feeding value of barley is quite variable, due to the wide spread in test weight per bushel. Most horsemen feel that it is preferable to feed barley along with more bulky feeds; for example, 25% oats or 15% wheat bran.

When fed to horses, barley should always be steam rolled or ground coarsely.

Corn (Maize)

Corn ranks second to oats as a horse feed. It is palatable, nutritious, and rich in energy-producing carbohydrate and fat, but it has certain very definite limitations. It lacks quality (being especially low in the amino acids, lysine and tryptophan) and quantity of proteins (it runs about 9%), and it is deficient in minerals, particularly calcium.

Corn may be fed to horses on the cob, shelled, cracked, as corn-and-cob meal, or flaked.

Wheat Bran

Wheat bran is the coarse outer covering of the wheat kernel. It contains a fair amount of protein (averaging about 16%), a good amount of phosphorus, and is laxative in action. Bran is valuable for horses because of its bulky nature and laxative properties. Also, it is very palatable.

Bran Mash — Feeding a bran mash is the traditional way of regulating the bowels of horses on idle days and at such other times as required.

The mash is prepared by filling a 2- to 2½-gallon bucket with wheat bran, pouring enough boiling hot water over it to make it the consistency of breakfast oatmeal, covering the bucket with a blanket and allowing it to steam until cool, then feeding it to the horse.

Occasionally, when a horse is offered a bran mash for the first time, he may refuse to eat it. When this occurs, the animal may be enticed to eat the mash by either (1) introducing him to a little of it by hand, or (2) sprinkling some sugar, or some other well-liked feed, over it.

MOLASSES (Cane or Beet)

Molasses is a by-product of sugar factories, with cane molasses coming from sugarcane and beet molasses coming from sugar beets. Cane molasses is slightly preferred to beet molasses for horses, although either is satisfactory.

For horses, molasses is 80 to 95 percent as valuable as oats, pound for pound. However, molasses is used primarily as an appetizer.

In hot, humid areas, molasses should be limited to 5 percent of the ration; otherwise, mold may develop. Where mustiness is a problem, add calcium propionate to the feed according to the manufacturer's directions.

MILK BY-PRODUCTS

The superior nutritive values of milk by-products are due to their high quality proteins, vitamins, a good mineral balance, and the beneficial effect of the milk sugar, lactose. In addition, these products are palatable and highly digestible. They are an ideal feed for young equines and for balancing out the deficiencies of the cereal grains. Most foal rations contain one or more milk by-products, primarily dried skim milk, with some dried whey and dried buttermilk included at times. The chief limitation to their wider use is price.

MILK REPLACER

As indicated by the name, a milk replacer is a replacement for milk. Such replacers generally contain the following composition: animal or vegetable fat, 17–20%; crude soybean lecithin, 1–2%; skimmed milk solids, 78–82% (10–15% dried whey powder can be included in place of an equivalent amount of skimmed milk solids); plus fortification with minerals and vitamins.

Foals suckling their dams generally develop very satisfactorily up to weaning time. But the most critical period in the entire life of a horse is that space from weaning time (about six months of age) until one year of

Table 6.5 Grain Substitution Table

Energy Feeds	Relative Value Compared to Oats, Which is Designated As Equal to 100	Maximum Percentage of Oats Which It Can Replace
Oats	100	100
Barley	110	100
Corn	115	100
Milo (sorghum)	110–115	85
Molasses	80–95	10
Wheat	115	50

age. This is especially so in the case of young horses being fitted for shows or sales, where condition is so important. Thus, where valuable weanlings or yearlings are to be shown or sold, the use of a milk replacer may be practical.

GRAIN SUBSTITUTIONS

Table 6.5, Grain Substitution Table, shows the value for horses of certain cereal grains compared to oats.

PROTEIN SUPPLEMENTS

Grass hays and farm grains are low in quality and quantity proteins. Hence, they must be supplemented with other sources of protein.

In practical horse feeding, foals should be provided with some protein feeds of animal origin in order to supplement the proteins found in grains and forages. In feeding mature horses, a safe plan to follow is to provide plant protein from several sources.

In general, feeds of high protein content are more expensive than those high in carbohydrates or fats. Accordingly, there is a temptation to feed too little protein. On the other hand, when protein feeds are the cheapest — as is often true of cull peas in certain sections of the West — excess quantities of them may be fed as energy feeds without harm, provided the ration is balanced in all other respects. Any amino acids that are left over, after the protein requirements have been met, are deaminated or broken down in the body. In this process, a part of each amino acid is turned into energy, and the remainder is excreted via the kidneys.

LINSEED MEAL

Linseed meal is a by-product of flaxseed following oil extraction by either of two processes: (1) the mechanical process (or what is known as the "old process"); or (2) the solvent process (or "new process"). If solvent-extracted, it must be so designated. Horsemen prefer the mechanical process, for the remaining meal is more palatable, has a higher fat content, and imparts more gloss to the hair coat.

Linseed meal averages about 35 percent protein content. For horses, the proteins of linseed meal do not effectively make good the deficiencies of the cereal grains — linseed meal being low in the amino acids, lysine and tryptophan. Also, linseed meal is lacking in carotene and vitamin D, and is only fair in calcium and the B vitamins. Because of its deficiencies, linseed meal should not be fed to horses as the sole protein supplement.

Because of its laxative nature, linseed meal in limited quantities is a valuable addition to the ration of horses. Also, it imparts a desirable "bloom" to the hair of show and sale animals.

SOYBEAN MEAL

Soybean meal, processed from the soybean, is the most widely used protein supplement in the United States. It is the ground residue (soybean oil cake or soybean oil chips) remaining after the removal of most of the oil from soybeans. The oil is extracted by either of three processes: (1) the expeller process; (2) the hydraulic process; or (3) the solvent process. Although a name descriptive of the extraction process must be used in the brand name, well-cooked soybean meal produced by each of the extraction processes is of approximately the same feeding value.

Soybean meal normally contains 41, 44, or 50 percent protein, according to the amount of hull removed; and the proteins are of better quality than the other protein-rich supplements of plant origin. It is low in calcium, phosphorus, carotene, and vitamin D.

Soybean meal is satisfactory as the only protein supplement to grain for mature horses, providing a high quality ground legume is incorporated in the ration and adequate sources of calcium and phosphorus are provided. For foals, it is best that a dried milk by-product be included.

Cottonseed Meal

Among the oilseed meals, cottonseed meal ranks second to soybean meal in tonnage used in the U.S.

The protein content of cottonseed meal can vary from about 22% in meal made from undecorticated (unhulled) seed to 60% in flour made from seed from which the hulls have been removed completely. Thus, in screening out the residual hulls, which are low in protein and high in fiber, the processor is able to make a cottonseed meal of the protein content desired — usually 41, 44, or 50%.

Cottonseed meal is low in lysine and tryptophan and deficient in vitamin D, carotene (vitamin A value), and calcium. Also, unless glandless seed is used, it contains a toxic substance known as gossypol, varying in amounts with the seed and the processing. But it is rich in phosphorus.

Some prejudices to the contrary, good grade cottonseed meal is satisfactory for horses. It may be fed in the amounts necessary to balance ordinary rations.

Sunflower Meal

The development of high oil-yielding varieties by Russian scientists has stirred worldwide interest in the use of sunflowers as an oilseed crop. Some of these varieties yield over 50 percent oil.

Sunflower meal (41% protein or better) can be used as a protein supplement for horses provided (1) it is good quality, and (2) care is taken to supply adequate lysine, for sunflower meal is low in this amino acid. When incorporated in well-balanced rations, properly processed sunflower meal of good quality may supply up to one-third of the protein supplement of horses.

Urea for the Horse

It is recognized that horses frequently consume urea-containing cubes and blocks intended for cattle and sheep, particularly on the western range. Moreover, it appears that mature horses are able to do so without untoward effects. The latter observation was confirmed in one limited experiment[1] in which 4 horses consumed an average of 4.57 lb per day of a urea-containing supplement, or 0.55 lb/head/day of feed urea (262%), for 5 months. Also, the Louisiana Station[2] did not find urea detrimental or toxic to horses when it constituted up to 5 percent of the grain ration, with up to 0.5 lb per day of urea consumed. There are reports, however, of urea toxicity in foals, in which bacterial action is more limited than in older horses. Also, most state feed control laws limit the sale of urea-containing feeds to ruminants.

SPECIAL FEEDS AND ADDITIVES
Special feeds may be needed from time to time for imparting bloom or gloss to the hair, and for promoting growth of young stock.

FEEDS THAT IMPART BLOOM OR GLOSS
Bloom or gloss is important in horses. But sometimes they lack this desired quality — their hair is dull and dry. Feeding a well-balanced ration will usually rectify this situation. Also, feeding either of the following products will make for an attractive, shiny coat:
1. *Corn oil* — Feed at the rate of one tablespoon per horse per day.
2. *Whole flaxseed soaked* — Put a handful of whole flaxseed in a teacup, cover it with water, let it stand overnight, then pour it over the morning feed. Repeat twice each week.
Unless the horse is afflicted with lice, mange, or some other ailment, either of the above treatments will impart bloom or gloss to the coat.

LYSINE
Protein quality is important for horses. Because of more limited amino acid synthesis in the horse than in ruminants, plus the fact that the cecum is located beyond the small intestine — the main area for digestion and absorption of nutrients — it is generally recommended that high quality protein rations, adequate in amino acids, be fed to equines. This is especially important for young equines, because cecal synthesis is very limited in early life.

Fortunately, the amino acid content of proteins from various sources varies. Thus, the deficiencies of one protein may be improved by combining it with another, and the mixture of the two proteins often will have a higher feeding value than either one alone. It is for this reason, along with added palatability, that a considerable variety of feeds in the horse ration is desirable.

Cornell University reported that the addition of lysine to the diet of growing horses increased weight gains, feed consumption, and feed efficiency. But, this experimental diet contained linseed meal as the major

[1] *Veterinary Medicine,* vol. 58, no. 12, Dec. 1963.
[2] "Non-Toxicity of Urea Feeding to Horses," *Veterinary Medicine/Small Animal Clinician,* Nov. 1965.

source of protein. Normally, it is much more practical to supply a source of good quality protein, such as milk protein or soybean meal (perhaps along with some linseed meal), rather than add lysine to linseed meal.

It is not recommended that horsemen spend money on lysine for horses. Instead, a well-balanced ration should be fed to horses of all ages, and especially high quality proteins should be incorporated in the ration of young equines. There is no experimental evidence that the addition of lysine will improve a good ration.

ANTIBIOTICS

Antibiotics are not nutrients; they're drugs. They are a chemical substance, produced by molds or bacteria, which has the ability to inhibit the growth of or to destroy other microorganisms.

Certain antibiotics, at stipulated levels, are approved by FDA for growth promotion and for the improvement of feed efficiency of young equines up to one year of age. Unless there is a disease level, however, there is no evidence to warrant the continuous feeding of antibiotics to mature horses. Such practice may even be harmful. Hence, where antibiotics are needed for therapeutic purposes, it is best to seek the advice of a veterinarian.

TREATS FOR THE HORSE

Horses are fed a great variety of treats. On a government horse-breeding establishment in Brazil, the author saw a large and well-mani-cured vegetable garden, growing everything from carrots to melons, just for horses. Also, trainers recognize that most racehorses, which are the prima donnas of the equine world, don't "eat like a horse"; they eat like people — and sometimes they're just as finicky. Their menus may include a choice of carrots or other roots, fruit, pumpkins, squashes, melons, molasses, sugar, honey, or innumerable other goodies.

Ask the average horseman why he feeds treats to his horse and you'll get a variety of answers. However, high on the list of reasons will be (1) as appetizers, (2) as a source of nutrients and conditioners, (3) as rewards, (4) as a means of alleviating obesity (dieting the horse), or (5) folklore.

TREATS AS APPETIZERS

If a horse doesn't eat his feed, it won't do him any good. Hence, feed consumption is important.

Sooner or later, a horseman is bound to get one of those exasperating equines that just refuses to clean up his feed. Perhaps he'll eat a few bites, then stop; or maybe he won't even touch the "stuff." Sometimes this happens to race and show horses that started training in great physical shape, only to lose appetite and have to be taken out of training for rest.

Lots of things can cause finicky eaters; among them, (1) stress and nervousness, (2) an unpalatable and monotonous ration, (3) nutritional deficiencies, (4) poor health, and (5) lack of exercise. Whatever the cause,

the condition(s) making for poor feed consumption should be rectified — if it can be determined, and if it is within the power of the caretaker
to correct it. Additionally, there should be incorporated in the ration
something that the horse really likes — such as carrots or other roots;
molasses, sugar or honey; or sliced fruit.

But treats can be overdone. Hence a horse should not be permitted to
eat too much of any treat simply because he likes it. In this respect,
horses are like boys and girls. If given a choice between candy and a
well-balanced diet, most youngsters will take the candy. Yet, few parents
or doctors would be so foolish as to permit a child to eat unlimited candy.

TREATS AS A SOURCE OF NUTRIENTS

Sometimes folks, and even nutritionists, overlook the fact that, when
evaluated on a dry matter basis, high-water-content tubers, fruits, and
melons have almost the same nutrient value as the cereal grains. This
becomes apparent in Table 6.6, which gives the energy value on a moisture-free basis of several horse treats compared with barley, corn, oats,
and timothy.

Generally speaking, horse treats are not fed because they're considered
to be a good buy when evaluated on a cost per unit of nutrient content
(protein, energy, etc.) basis. This becomes obvious when it is realized that
it takes nearly 7 pounds of carrots to equal 1 pound of oats in energy
value. Occasionally, such products as carrots are in surplus or of low
quality. At such times, they may be available for as little as $3 to $4 per
ton, in which case they are a good buy in comparison with grains. Even
then, it is best that they not replace more than 10 to 20 percent of the
normal grain ration. For the most part, however, treats are fed to horses
because they possess qualities not revealed by a chemical analysis —
because of their values as appetizers, in aiding digestion, and as conditioners.

Table 6.6 Comparative Energy Value, Dry Basis, of Some
Common Horse Feeds and Treats

Feed	Water (%)	Energy Value (TDN)		Dry Matter Basis (%)
		Dry Matter (%)	As Fed (%)	
Barley	10	90	77	85
Corn	10	90	80	90
Oats	11	89	68	76
Timothy hay, mature	14	86	41	48
Apples	82	18	13	74
Carrots	88	12	10	82
Melons	94	6	5	80
Potatoes	79	21	18	85
Sugar beets	87	13	10	77

TREATS AS REWARDS

The training of horses is based on a system of rewards and punishment. This doesn't mean that the horse is fed a tidbit each time he obeys, or that he is beaten when he refuses or does something wrong.

But horses are big and strong; hence, it's best that they want to do something, rather than have to be forced. Also, too frequent or improper use of such artificial aids as whips, spurs, reins, and bits makes them less effective; worse yet, it will likely make for a mean horse.

Horses appreciate a pat on the shoulder or a word of praise. However, better results may be obtained by working on an equine's greediness — his fondness for such things as carrots or a sugar cube. Also, treats may be used effectively as rewards to teach some specific thing such as posing, or to cure a vice like moving while the rider is mounting; but this should not be overdone.

TREATS TO ALLEVIATE OBESITY

Horses are equine athletes; hence, they should be lean and hard rather than fat and soft. Obese horses should be avoided because (1) they lack agility, (2) excessive weight puts a strain on the musculoskeletal system, (3) fertility is lowered in broodmares and stallions, (4) fat horses are prone to founder, and (5) overweight horses are more susceptible to azoturia.

Such watery feeds as carrots and melons are filling, but low in calories. This becomes obvious when it's realized that (1) it takes more than 8 lb of fresh carrots to produce 1 lb of dried product, and (2) it takes nearly 7 lb of carrots or over 13 lb of melons to furnish as much energy as 1 lb of oats. Thus, when used as a "salad" for the horse, carrots or melons are as effective as slenderizers for equines as they are for humans.

TREATS FOR FOLKLORE REASONS

Among the bagful of horsemen's secrets, sometimes the claim is made that apple cider will prolong life, increase vigor, and improve sex drive, fertility, and reproduction. However, there isn't a shred of evidence, based on studies conducted by a reputable experiment station, to substantiate such claims. Of course, it's good to have faith in something; and, too, nature is a wonderful thing. It is estimated that 70 to 80 percent of all horses with afflictions would recover even without treatment.

CARROTS AND OTHER ROOTS

Carrots are relished by horses. Additionally, they're succulent, and high in carotene and minerals. Carotene, known as the precursor of vitamin A because the animal body can convert it into the vitamin, derives its name from the carrot, from which it was first isolated over 100 years ago. Carotene is the yellow-colored substance that imparts the characteristic yellow color to carrots. Each pound of fresh carrots contains 48 milligrams of carotene, which can be converted into 26,640 IU of vitamin A by the young equine, sufficient vitamin A to meet the daily requirement of a 1000-lb horse. By contrast, 1 lb of timothy hay (mature) provides only 2.1 milligrams of carotene, or 1165 IU, which is only $\frac{1}{26}$th of the daily vitamin A requirement for a 1000-lb horse. Also, carrots are a good source of minerals; on a dry basis one pound contains 0.42% calcium and 0.34% phosphorus, whereas mature timothy hay as fed contains 0.17% and 0.15% of these elements, respectively. Additionally, carrots are high in sugar; on a dry basis they contain 40% sugar (invert), which explains their sweetness.

Horsemen have long fed carrots, especially during the winter months when green feeds are not available and to horses that are stabled much of the time. They report that one to two pounds of carrots per horse per day will stimulate the appetite, increase growth, assist in reproduction, make for normal vision, and improve the health, coat, and attractiveness of the animal.

Carrots should be cleaned, sliced from end to end in small strips, so as to avoid choking, then mixed with the grain.

Other roots such as parsnips, rutabagas, turnips, potatoes, and sugar beets may be fed to horses in small amounts, provided they are first cut finely enough to avoid choking.

PUMPKINS, SQUASHES, AND MELONS
Pumpkins, squashes, and melons are sometimes used as relish for horses. They contain only 6 to 10 percent dry matter; hence, their nutritive value on a wet basis is low in comparison with cereal grains. When fed in the usual amounts, their seeds are not harmful to horses, some opinions to the contrary. However, an entire ration of seeds alone is apt to cause indigestion, because of their high fat content.

APPLES AND OTHER FRUITS
An apple a day is good for a horse, especially when used as a tidbit or reward. They are very palatable because of their sugar content. However, the feeding of apples can be overdone; many a case of colic, or even death, has resulted from old dobbin's stolen visit to the orchard.

Also, peaches, plums, and pears are occasionally used as treats for the horse. The seeds of stone fruits should always be removed prior to feeding.

MOLASSES, SUGAR, AND HONEY
The horse has a "sweet tooth"; or at least he readily cultivates a taste for sweets. Hence, when added to the ration, molasses, sugar, and honey make for a "sweet feed," or appetizer. For this reason, small amounts (usually about 5%) of molasses, sugar, or honey are sometimes added to the concentrate mixtures of racehorses, show horses, and other finicky

eaters. Once a horse becomes accustomed to a sweet feed, it is difficult to eliminate it from the ration; in fact, if the sweets are suddenly deleted, the horse may refuse to eat altogether. Thus, if for any reason sweets must be taken out of the ration, the change should be very gradual.

Also, sugar cubes are a good and convenient reward, provided too many of them are not used and the tendency of nipping or biting is avoided.

PALATABILITY OF FEED

Palatability is important, for horses must eat their feed if it's to do them any good. But many horses are finicky simply because they're spoiled. For the latter, stepping up the exercise and halving the ration will usually effect a miraculous cure.

Also, it seems possible that well-liked feeds are digested somewhat better than those which are equally nutritious, but less palatable.

Palatability is particularly important when feeding horses that are being used hard, as in racing or showing. Unless the ration is consumed, such horses will not obtain sufficient nutrients to permit maximum performance. For this reason, lower-quality feeds, such as straw or stemmy hay, should be fed to idle horses.

Familiarity and habit are important factors concerned with the palatability of horse feeds. For example, horses have to learn to eat pellets, and very frequently they will back away from feeds with new and unfamiliar odors. For this reason, any change in feeds should be made gradually.

Occasionally, the failure of horses to eat a normal amount of feed is due to a serious nutritive deficiency. For example, if horses are fed a ration made up of palatable feeds, but deficient in one or more required vitamins or minerals, they may eat normal amounts for a time. Then when the body reserves of the lacking nutrient(s) are exhausted, they will usually consume much less feed, due to an impairment of their health and consequent lack of appetite. If the deficiency is not continued so long that the horses are injured permanently, they will usually recover their appetites if some feed is added which supplies the nutritive lack and makes the ration complete.

PALATABILITY OF THE PROTEIN SUPPLEMENT

Where a protein supplement lacks palatability, the situation can usually be corrected by increasing the salt content of the supplement to 3.0%. The reasoning back of increasing the salt is this: whatever the cause of the unpalatability in a supplement may be (particularly if it is one of the ingredients), it's apt to show up more in the supplement than in other feeds, simply because it is more concentrated. The high salt content usually overcomes the unpalatability and adequate consumption follows. Of course, one should not go higher than 2.0% in a concentrate or in an all-pelleted ration because higher levels of salt are unpalatable, but up to 3.0% salt in a supplement fed at a level of 1 to 2 pounds per horse per day will usually work wonders.

Here is a checklist, along with the author's comments, where there appears to be a palatability problem with a horse feed:

☐ 1. *Quality of feeds* — Make very certain on this point. It's almost impossible to detect through a chemical analysis many factors that may lower quality, such as "heated grain" and poor-quality hay.

☐ 2. *Mustiness* — Again, check with care. Remember that horses can detect mustiness more quickly and easily than people.

☐ 3. *Hard pellets* — If pellets are too hard, horses will spit them out.

☐ 4. *Flavors* — In some cases, flavors will help in overcoming the lack of palatability due to poor quality feeds, but they will do little to enhance good quality feeds.

☐ 5. *Your premix* — Check on the "carrier" and premix ingredients which your feed manufacturer is using in his horse feeds. The author recalls one incident where dried fish meal was being used in a premix as a source of unidentified factors; and an unpalatable ration resulted because of the poor quality of the fish meal in the premix.

☐ 6. *The formulation* — Of course, some feeds are more palatable to horses than others. Among the well-liked feeds are wheat bran and molasses, both of which are usually incorporated in horse rations.

DISTANCE LENDS ENCHANTMENT TO FEEDS
Distance lends enchantment! Many horsemen not only believe that there is something magical about certain horse feeds, but they think that they must be grown in a specific area. For example, timothy hay and oats are frequently extolled on the basis that they are grown in certain "name" areas; they are even referred to as "racehorse oats" or "racehorse timothy hay." Such specialty areas may produce superior products, but their feeding value is generally exaggerated far beyond their price, with much of their added cost going for hundreds of miles of transportation and for middlemen.

RATIONS
Correctly speaking, a ration is the amount of feed given to a horse in a day, or a 24-hour period. To most horsemen, however, the word implies the feeds fed to an animal without limitation of the time in which they are consumed.

To supply all the needs — maintenance, growth, reproduction and lactation, and work (running) — horses must receive feeds in quality and quantity to furnish the necessary energy (carbohydrates and fats), proteins, minerals, vitamins, and perhaps unknown factors and additives. Such rations are said to be balanced. Moreover, the feed must be palatable — horses must like it. The rations listed in Table 6.7 meet these standards. Also, liberal margins of safety have been provided to compensate for variations in feed composition, environment, possible losses of nutrients during storage, and differences in individual animals.

HOME-MIXED FEEDS

A horse feeding guide is given in Table 6.7. In selecting rations, compare them with commercial feeds. If only small quantities are required or little storage space is available, it may be more satisfactory to buy ready-mixed feeds.

When home-mixed feeds are used, feeds of similar nutritive properties can be interchanged in the ration as price relationships warrant. This makes it possible to obtain a balanced ration at lowest cost.

The quantites of feeds recommended in Table 6.7 are intended as guides only. Increase the feed, especially the concentrates, when the horse is too thin and decrease the feed if he gets too fat.

Avoid sudden changes in diet, especially when changing from a less concentrated ration to a more concentrated one. When this rule of feeding is ignored, digestive disturbances result and the horse goes "off feed." In either adding or omitting one or more ingredients, the change should be made gradually. Likewise, caution should be exercised in turning horses to pasture or in transferring them to more lush grazing.

In general, horses may be given as much nonlegume roughage as they will eat. But they must be accustomed gradually to legumes because legumes may be laxative.

In feeding horses, as with other classes of livestock, it is recognized that nutritional deficiencies (especially deficiencies of certain vitamins and minerals) may not be of sufficient proportions to cause clear-cut deficiency symptoms. Yet, such deficiencies without outward signs may cause great economic losses because they go unnoticed and unrectified. Accordingly, sufficient additives (especially minerals and vitamins) should always be present, but care should be taken to avoid imbalances.

SUGGESTED RATIONS

Several suggested rations are given in Table 6.7.

Table 6.7 Light Horse Feeding Guide

Age, Sex, and Use	Daily Allowance	Kind of Hay	Suggested Grain Rations		
			Rations No. 1 (lb)	Rations No. 2 (lb)	Rations No. 3 (lb)
Stallions in breeding season (weighing 900 to 1400 lb)	¾ to 1½ lb grain per 100 lb body weight, together with a quantity of hay within same range.	Grass-legume mixed; or ⅓ to ½ legume hay, with remainder grass hay.	Oats-55 Wheat-20 Wheat bran-20 Linseed meal-5	Corn-35 Oats-35 Wheat-15 Wheat bran-15	Oats-100
Pregnant mares (weighing 900 to 1400 lb)	¾ to 1½ lb grain per 100 lb body weight, together with a quantity of hay within same range.	Grass-legume mixed; or ⅓ to ½ legume hay, with remainder grass hay. (Straight grass hay may be used first half of pregnancy.)	Oats-80 Wheat bran-20	Barley-45 Oats-45 Wheat bran-10	Oats-95 Linseed meal-5
Foals before weaning (weighing 100 to 350 lb with projected mature weights of 900 to 1400 lb)	½ to ¾ lb grain per 100 lb body weight, together with a quantity of hay within same range.	Legume hay.	Oats-50 Wheat bran-40 Linseed meal-10	Oats-30 Barley-30 Wheat bran-30 Linseed meal-10	Oats-80 Wheat bran-20
			Rations balanced on basis of following assumption: Mares of mature weights of 600, 800, 1000, and 1200 lb may produce 36, 42, 44, and 49 lb of milk daily.		
Weanlings (weighing 350 to 450 lb)	1 to 1½ lb grain and 1½ to 2 lb hay per 100 lb body weight.	Grass-legume mixed; or ½ legume hay, with remainder grass hay.	Oats-30 Barley-30 Wheat bran-30 Linseed meal-10	Oats-70 Wheat bran-15 Linseed meal-15	Oats-80 Linseed meal-20

(Cont.)

Table 6.7 Light Horse Feeding Guide (*Cont.*)

Age, Sex and Use	Daily Allowance	Kind of Hay	Suggested Grain Rations		
			Rations No. 1 (lb)	Rations No. 2 (lb)	Rations No. 3 (lb)
Yearlings, second summer (weighing 450 to 700 lb)	Good, luxuriant pasture. (If in training or for other reasons without access to pasture, the ration should be intermediate between the adjacent upper and lower groups.)				
Yearlings, or rising 2-year-olds, second winter (weighing 700 to 1000 lb)	½ to 1 lb grain and 1 to 1½ lb hay per 100 lb body weight.	Grass-legume mixed; or ⅓ to ½ legume hay, with remainder grass hay.	Oats-80 Wheat bran-20	Barley-35 Oats-35 Bran-15 Linseed meal-15	Oats-100
Light horses at work; riding, driving, and racing (weighing 900 to 1400 lb)	Hard use — 1¼ to 1⅓ lb grain and 1 to 1¼ lb hay per 100 lb body weight. Medium use — ¾ to 1 lb grain and 1 to 1¼ lb hay per 100 lb body weight. Light use — ⅔ to ½ lb grain and 1¼ to 1½ lb hay per 100 lb body weight.	Grass hay.	Oats-100	Oats-70 Corn-30	Oats-70 Barley-30
Mature idle horses; stallions, mares, and geldings (weighing 900 to 1400 lb)	1½ to 1¾ lb hay per 100 lb body weight.	Pasture in season; or grass-legume mixed hay.	(With grass hay, add ¾ lb of a high protein supplement daily.)		

Note — With all rations and for all classes and ages of horses, provide free access to separate containers of (1) iodized salt, and (2) a mixture of 1 part salt and 2 parts steamed

Actually, a horse does not have to have any hay. Also, more horses receive too much roughage rather than not enough, as evidenced by hay bellies (distended digestive tracts), quick tiring, and labored breathing.

Under most conditions, the roughage requirement of horses ranges from 0.5 percent to 1.0 percent of body weight, or from 5 to 10 pounds of roughage daily for a 1000-pound horse.

Racehorses should receive a minimum of roughage, since they need a maximum of energy. Sometimes it is necessary to muzzle greedy horses to keep them from eating bedding when their roughage allowance is limited.

COMMERCIAL FEEDS

Commercial feeds are feeds mixed by manufacturers who specialize in the feed business. Today, about 60 million tons of commercial feeds are marketed each year.

Commercial feed manufacturers are able to purchase feed in quantity lots, making possible price advantages and the scientific control of quality. Many horsemen have found that because of the small quantities of feed usually involved, and the complexities of horse rations, they have more reason to rely on good commercial feeds than do owners of other classes of farm animals.

Table 6.8 Commercial Horse Feeds and Needs

Needed Horse Feeds	Prevailing Conditions	Crude Protein (%)	Used for
Complete (hay and grain combined in a pellet)	For the horseman who must buy all feeds.	13	All horses 10 mo. or older.
Concentrate	For the horseman who has satisfactory hay and /or pasture.	14	All horses 10 mo. or older.
Protein supplement	For supplementing available hay and grain.	25	All horses 10 mo. or older.
Foal ration	For creep feeding.	21	2 wk. to 10 mo. of age.
Protein-salt block	For free-choice feeding in corral or on pasture.	20	All horses 10 mo. of age or older.
Enriched vitamin-trace mineral-unidentified factor supplement	For the horseman who has hay and grain that meet all needs except vitamin-trace mineral-unidentified factors.	. . .	All horses not receiving any of the above feeds.

The nutritive requirements of horses vary according to age, weight, use or demands, growth, stage of gestation or lactation, and environment. Also, part of the horse ration may be homegrown. It would appear, therefore, that the commercial feeds shown in Table 6.8 are necessary if one is to meet most horse needs.

"Sweet feed" refers to a feed to which has been added one or more ingredients that are sweet. Most commonly, it contains considerable molasses (approximately 10%); although brown sugar (about 5%) is sometimes used, and occasionally honey.

The horse has a "sweet tooth"; hence, it's not easy to switch him from a sweet feed to what may be a more nutritious ration. Of course, the manufacturer of the sweet feed would have it that way. Also, it must be remembered that sweet feeds are a way in which a feed manufacturer may make poor-quality feed ingredients more appetizing. Remember, too, that most boys and girls would rather eat candy than foods that are more nutritious. But doctors and mothers know best!

How to Evaluate a Commercial Feed

There is a difference in commercial feeds! That is, there is a difference from the standpoint of what a horseman can purchase with his feed dollars. The smart horseman will know how to determine what constitutes the best in commercial feeds for his specific needs. He will not rely solely on how the feed looks and smells. The most important factors to consider or look for in buying a commercial feed are:

1. *The reputation of the manufacturer* — This may be determined by conferring with other horsemen who have used the particular product and checking on whether or not the commercial feed under consideration has consistently met its guarantees. The latter can be determined by reading the bulletins or reports published by the respective state departments in charge of enforcing feed laws.

2. *The specific needs* — Feed needs vary according to (a) the class, age, and productivity of horses, and (b) whether animals are fed primarily for maintenance, growth, fattening (or show-ring fitting), reproduction, lactation, or work (running). The wise operator will buy different formula feeds for different needs.

3. *Flexible formulas* — Feeds with flexible formulas are usually the best buy. This is because the price of feed ingredients in different source feeds varies considerably from time to time. Thus, a good feed manufacturer will shift his formulas as prices change, in order to give the horseman the most for his money. This is as it should be, for (a) there is no one best ingredient, and (b) if substitutions are made wisely, the price of the feed can be kept down, and the horseman will continue to get equally good results.

4. *What's on the tag?* — Horsemen should be able to study and interpret what's on the feed tag. The information that follows was taken from a foal ration:

GUARANTEED ANALYSIS

Crude Protein, not less than 21.00%
Crude Fat, not less than 2.00%
Crude Fiber, not more than 9.00%
Ash, not more than 9.00%
Added Mineral, not more than 3.00%
Calcium, not less than 1.00%
Phosphorus, not less than 75%
Salt, not more than 50%
Iodine, not less than 00035%
TDN, not less than 68.00%

Ingredients: Rolled Oats, Dried Whey, Soybean Meal, Cottonseed Meal, Linseed Meal, Dehydrated Alfalfa Meal, Wheat Bran, Wheat Shorts, Wheat Flour, Cane Molasses, Bone Meal, Iodized Salt, Distiller's Dried Grains with Solubles, Alfalfa Leaf Meal, Condensed Fish Solubles (Dried), Brewer's Dried Yeast, Streptomycin Mycelia Meal, Vitamin A Palmitate with Increased Stability, Fleischmann's Irradiated Dry Yeast (source of Vitamin D_2), d-Alpha-Tocopherol Acetate (source of Vitamin E), Choline Chloride, Ferrous Carbonate, Niacin, Calcium Pantothenate (source of d-Pantothenic Acid), Ribo-flavin Supplement, Copper Oxide, Manganous Oxide, Thiamine, Sulphur, Menadione Sodium Bisulfate (source of Vitamin K), Calcium Iodate, Folic Acid, Cobalt Carbonate, Vitamin B_{12} Supplement. Preserved with Ethoxyquin (1, 2-dihydro-6-ethoxy-2, 2, 4-trimethyl-quinoline), Anise.

An analysis of the above tag reveals the following:

a. The guaranteed analysis, each stated in percent, in minimum crude protein and crude fat; maximum crude fiber, ash, and mineral; minimum calcium and phosphorus; maximum salt; and minimum iodine and TDN. But guaranteed analysis, within itself, will not suffice. For example, on the basis of chemical composition, soft coal (9.06% crude protein) and coffee grounds (11.23% crude protein) are comparable in protein content to many commonly used grains.

b. The ingredients (the constituent material making up the feed) listed in descending order of amounts, by weight. This type of listing aids in making decisions as to the possible quality of the feed. For example, if feather meal, which contains 85% protein by analysis, were listed (which it is not in the above feed), you could conclude that the horse would obtain little nutritional advantage from this type of ration component. All ingredients listed in the above ration are good, and each one appears to contribute needed nutrients.

Many states differ slightly in feed labeling requirements from the tag just analyzed. Some require both the minimum and maximum percentage of calcium and salt.

By studying the feed tag, a knowledgeable user can readily and easily see what's in the feed and determine if it will meet the requirements of the horse to which it is to be fed.

RATION FORMULATION BY IMITATION

Sometimes horse trainers pattern their ration after what some great horse is getting — they get some of the same "stuff."

Of course, it is difficult to argue with success. Also, it is well known that horsemen as a whole are great imitators. The author has known them to pay $50 for a gallon of a mysterious concoction, in a green jug, made in a little hamlet in Kentucky. Of course, the fallacy of such imitation — of feeding what the "great horse" got — is that the "name" horse might have been even greater had he been fed properly, and that there must be a reason why there are so few truly great horses. Also, the following searching question might well be asked: Why do many horses start training in great physical shape, only to slow down and lose appetite, and be taken out of training for some rest?

RESULTS MORE IMPORTANT THAN COST PER BAG

As is true when buying anything — whether it be a suit of clothes, a dinner, or whatnot — horse feed should be bought on a quality basis, rather than what is cheapest. Results are more important than cost per bag. If this were not so, one might well buy and feed many cheap products, including sawdust.

Consideration should be given to meeting the specific needs of the horse, with special attention given to providing adequate quantity and quality proteins, minerals, vitamins, unidentified factors, and palatability.

FEED PREPARATION

The physical preparation of cereal grains for horses has been practiced by horsemen for a very long time. Basically, grain is either soaked, cooked, ground, or rolled (wet or dry), and hay is either fed long, pelleted, or cubed.

A summary relative to each of the common methods of feed preparation for horses follows.

FLAKING

Flaking, which is the modification of steam rolling in which the grain is subjected to steam for a longer period of time, is the preferred method of processing grains for horses. It produces light, fluffy particles, which result in fewer digestive disturbances than any other method of feed preparation.

The flaking process varies according to the grain. For example, corn is usually steamed for approximately 20 minutes at a temperature of 200° F, to a moisture content of about 18 percent. The grain that responds the most to flaking is milo, which is generally flaked as follows: the grain is subjected to 20 pounds of steam pressure for 20 to 25 minutes, at approximately 205° F; then, at 18 to 20 percent moisture content, it is run through large rollers operated at $\frac{1}{3}$ to $\frac{1}{2}$ capacity and rolled to thin flakes. The end product has a distinct and pleasant aroma, resembling cooked cereal.

STEAM ROLLING

If properly done, steam rolling of grains is preferred to grinding for horses. However, there is great variation in steam rolling. Altogether too much steam rolling consists of exposing the grain to steam for 3 to 5 minutes, using a temperature of about 180° F, and adding an unknown amount of moisture. Such processing is little better than dry rolling.

DRY ROLLING, CRIMPING, AND GRINDING

These methods can be and are used in preparing horse feeds. The important thing is to keep the grain as coarse as possible and to avoid fines.

PELLETING

Currently, horsemen are much interested in complete, all-pelleted feed, in which the hay and grain are combined. Pelleted feeds may be prepared from concentrates alone, forage alone, or concentrates and roughage combined in a complete ration.

Compared to conventional long hay and grain concentrate fed separately, all-pelleted feed has the following advantages:

1. It is less bulky and easier to store and handle, thus lessening transportation, building, and labor costs. Pelleted roughage requires $\frac{1}{5}$ to $\frac{1}{3}$ as much space as is required by the same roughage in loose or chopped form.

2. Pelleting prevents horses from selectively refusing ingredients likely to be high in certain dietary essentials; each bite is a balanced feed.

3. Pelleting practically eliminates waste; therefore, less pelleted feed is required. Horses may waste up to 20 percent of long hay. Waste of conventional feed is highest where low-quality hay is fed or feed containers are poorly designed.

4. Pelleting eliminates dustiness and lessens the likelihood of heaves.

5. Pellet-fed horses are trimmer in the middle and more attractive because they consume less bulk.

6. Pellets lessen pollution. Pelleting lessens the manure by about 25 percent, simply because of less wastage and lower feed consumption; hence, it lessens pollution. Since a 1000-pound horse normally produces about 8 tons of manure, free of bedding, per year, this is an important consideration in the present environment-conscious era. Thus, an all-pelleted ration will result in about 2 tons less manure per horse per year.

The following points are pertinent to the proper understanding and use of all-pelleted rations.

1. One-half inch pellets are preferred for mature horses, and $\frac{1}{4}$-inch pellets for weanlings and short yearlings. Also, very hard pellets should be avoided; if horses cannot chew them, they will not eat them.

2. The ratio of roughage to concentrates should be higher in all-pelleted rations than when long hay is fed. For most horses, the ratio may range from 60.5% roughage to 39.5% concentrate up to 69% roughage to 31% concentrate.

3. Any horse feed should form a loose mass in the stomach to assure ease of digestion, fewer digestive disturbances, and less impaction. To this end, in a complete all-pelleted ration, such feeds as oats and barley should be crimped or steam rolled but not finely ground. The roughage should be $\frac{1}{4}$-inch chop or coarser. Otherwise, a couple of pounds of long hay may be fed daily to each horse.

4. Young horses and horses at heavy work need more energy. They should be fed less roughage and more concentrate.

5. When less roughage and more concentrate is fed, horses are likely to be overfed and get too fat if they are idle or at light to medium work. But if the total feed consumption is limited too severely to keep the weight down, the problem of wood chewing is increased because of a lack of physical filling of the digestive tract.

6. When the roughage consists of high quality legume hay, a higher percentage of roughage may be used than when all or part of the roughage is grass or other nonlegumes.

7. If more energy is needed for racing or young stock on an all-pelleted ration, it can be provided either by increasing the daily allowance of the all-pelleted ration, and/or replacing a portion of the all-pelleted ration with a suitable concentrate or supplement.

8. Because waste is eliminated, less all-pelleted feed is required than conventional feed. For a horse at light work, give 14 to 18 pounds of all-pelleted feed daily per 1000 pounds of body weight. Use a feed that contains 51 to 58 percent total digestible nutrients (TDN). Increase the feed allowance with the severity of work.

9. As with any change in feed, the switch to an all-pelleted ration should be made gradually; otherwise, such vices as wood chewing and bolting (eating feed too rapidly) may be induced. At first, continue to offer all the long hay the horse wants and slowly replace the grain portion of the conventional ration with the complete pelleted feed. Increase the pelleted feed by 1 to 2 pounds daily and begin gradually lessening the hay. After a few days, the horse usually will stop eating the hay and it can be removed completely from the ration.

10. The feces of pellet-fed horses are softer than the feces of those not fed pellets.

Among many horsemen, the feeling persists that horses fed all-pelleted rations are more likely to chew wood than those fed long hay. This may be true to some degree. But some horses will chew wood regardless of what they are fed. (See section on "Pica; Wood Chewing" at the end of this chapter.)

HAY CUBES

This refers to the practice of compressing long or coarsely cut hay in cubes or wafers, which are larger and coarser than pellets. Most cubes are about $1\frac{1}{4}$ inch square and 2 inches long, with a bulk density of 30 to 32 pounds per cubic foot. Cubing costs about $5.00 per ton more than baling.

This method of haymaking is increasing, because it (1) simplifies haymaking, (2) facilitates automation, (3) lessens transportation costs and storage space — cubed roughages require about one-third as much space as when the forage is baled and stacked — and (4) decreases nutrient losses.

From a nutrition standpoint, hay cubes are as satisfactory as hay in any other form (long or baled). However, some horsemen report occasional choking from feeding cubes.

HOW TO FEED

Feeding horses is both an art and a science. The art is knowing how to feed and how to take care of each horse's individual requirements. The science is meeting the nutritive requirements with the right combination of ingredients.

AMOUNT TO FEED

Because the horse has a limited digestive capacity, the amount of concentrates must be increased and the roughages decreased when the energy needs rise with more work. The following general guides may be used for the daily ration of horses under usual conditions.

Horses at light work (1 to 3 hours per day of riding or driving) — Allow $\frac{2}{5}$ to $\frac{1}{2}$ lb of grain and $1\frac{1}{4}$ to $1\frac{1}{2}$ lb of hay per day per 100 lb of body weight.

Horses at medium work (3 to 5 hours per day of riding or driving) — Allow about $\frac{3}{4}$ lb of grain and 1 to $1\frac{1}{4}$ lb of hay per 100 lb of body weight.

Horses at hard work (5 to 8 hours per day of riding or driving) — Allow about $1\frac{1}{4}$ to $1\frac{1}{3}$ lb of grain and 1 to $1\frac{1}{4}$ lb of hay per 100 lb of body weight.

As will be noted from these recommendations, the total allowance of both concentrates and hay should be about 2 to $2\frac{1}{2}$ lb daily per 100 lb of body weight.

The recommended feed allowances on the basis of animal weight are equally applicable to equines of all sizes, including ponies and donkeys; simply vary as necessary according to the work performed and the individuality of the animal.

About 6 to 12 lb of grain daily is an average grain ration for a light horse at medium or light work. Racehorses in training usually consume 10 to 16 lb of grain per day; the exact amount varies with the individual requirements and the amount of work. The hay allowance averages about 1 to $1\frac{1}{4}$ lb daily per 100 lb of body weight, but it is restricted as the grain allowance is increased. Light feeders should not be overworked.

Horses differ just as people do, in feed required and tendency to put on weight. Moreover, the age and degree of activity of horses are quite important factors; the amount of feed should be increased in keeping with the amount, severity, and speed of work; and feed requirements are influenced by weather — for example, under ideal fall weather conditions, a horse may require 14 lb of 60 percent TDN feed daily, whereas in the same area the same horse may require 16 lb daily of the same feed in July and August, and 20 lb in the winter.

The quantities of feeds recommended are intended as guides only. The allowance, especially the concentrates, should be increased when the horse is too thin and decreased when the horse is too fat.

OVERFEEDING

Overfeeding may result in two consequences: if done suddenly it may cause founder (laminitis); if prolonged it will likely result in obesity (too fat). Both are bad.

The main qualities desired in horses are trimness, action, spirit, and endurance. These qualities cannot be obtained in horses that are overfed and fat. The latter is especially true with horses used for racing, where the carrying of any surplus body weight must be avoided.

SELF-FEEDING

A few caretakers do self-feed high energy rations, but, sooner or later, those who do usually founder a valuable horse. Except for the use of reasonably hard salt-protein blocks, salt-feed mixes in meal form (never in pellet form), or high roughage rations, the self-feeding of horses is not recommended.

STARTING HORSES ON FEED

Horses must be accustomed to changes in feed gradually. In general, they may be given as much nonlegume roughage as they will consume. But they must be accustomed gradually to high-quality legumes, which may be very laxative. This can be done by slowly replacing the non-legume roughage with greater quantities of legumes. Also, as the grain ration is increased, the roughage is decreased.

Starting horses on grain requires care and good judgment. Usually it is advisable first to accustom them to a bulky type of ration; a starting ration with considerable rolled oats is excellent for this purpose.

The keenness of the appetite and the consistency of the droppings are an excellent index of a horse's capacity to take more feed. In all instances, scouring should be avoided.

FREQUENCY, REGULARITY, AND ORDER OF FEEDING

The grain ration usually is divided into 3 equal feeds given morning, noon, and night. Because a digestive tract distended with hay is a hindrance in hard work, most of the hay should be fed at night. The common practice is to feed $\frac{1}{4}$ of the daily hay allowance at both the morning and noon feedings and the remaining $\frac{1}{2}$ at night when the animals have plenty of time to eat leisurely.

Usually the grain ration is fed first and then the roughage. This way, the animals can eat the bulky roughages more leisurely.

Horses learn to anticipate their feed. Accordingly, they should be fed at the same time each day. During warm weather, they will eat better if the feeding hours are early and late, in the cool of the day.

AVOID SUDDEN CHANGES

Sudden changes in diet should be avoided, especially when changing from a less concentrated ration to a more concentrated one. If this rule of feeding is ignored, horses have digestive disturbances and go "off feed." When ingredients are added or omitted, the change should be made gradually. Likewise, caution should be exercised in turning horses to pasture or in transferring them to more lush grazing.

ATTENTION TO DETAILS

A successful horseman pays great attention to details. In addition to maintaining the health and comfort of his animals, he also considers their individual likes and temperaments. Nervousness and inefficient use of feed are caused by excessive exercise to the point of undue fatigue and stress, rough treatment, noise, and excitement.

GENERAL FEEDING RULES

Observance of the following rules will help avoid some of the common difficulties that result from poor feeding practices.

1. Know the approximate weight and age of each animal.
2. Never feed moldy, musty, dusty, or frozen feed.
3. Inspect the feed box frequently to see if the horse goes off feed.
4. Keep the feed and water containers clean.
5. Make certain that the horse's teeth are sound.
6. Do not feed concentrates to a hot horse; allow time for his feed to digest before he is worked.

7. Feed horses as individuals. Learn the peculiarities and desires of each animal because each one is different.

8. See that horses get enough exercise. It improves their appetite, digestion, and overall well-being.

9. Do not feed from the hand; this can lead to "nibbling."

10. Gradually decrease the condition of horses that have been fitted for show or sale. Many horsemen accomplish this difficult task, and yet retain strong vigorous animals, by cutting down gradually on the feed and increasing the exercise.

BOLTING FEED

Horses that eat too rapidly are said to be bolting their feed. It can be lessened by spreading the concentrate thinly over the bottom of a large grain box, so that the horse cannot get a large mouthful; or by placing in the grain box a few smooth stones about the size of baseballs, so that the horse has to work to get feed.

SIGNS OF A WELL-FED HEALTHY HORSE

The signs of a well-fed, healthy horse are:

Contentment — The horse looks completely unworried when resting.

Alertness — The horse is "bright eyed and bushy tailed," and he will perk up his ears at the slightest provocation.

Good appetite — The appetite is good, as indicated by neighing and pawing before he is fed and attacking the feed with relish.

Sleek coat and pliable, elastic skin — A sleek coat and a pliable, elastic skin characterize a healthy horse. When the hair loses its luster and the skin becomes dry, scurfy, and hidebound, usually trouble is ahead.

Pink eye membranes — The eye membranes, which can be seen when lower lid is pulled down, should be pink and moist.

Normal feces and urine — The consistency of the feces varies with the diet. For example, lush pasture usually causes looseness, and pellets generally cause moist feces. Neither extreme dryness nor scouring should exist. Both the feces and urine should be passed without effort and free of blood, mucus, or pus.

Normal temperature, pulse, and breathing — The average rectal temperature of horses is 100.5° F, with a range of 99 to 100.8° F. The normal pulse rate is 32 to 44 beats per minute, and the normal breathing rate is 8 to 16 breaths per minute. In general, any marked and persistent deviations from these normals are signs of ill health.

FEEDING PLEASURE HORSES

Keeping pleasure horses — horses used for recreation and sport — in peak condition makes for greater satisfaction when they're used.

It is difficult to feed pleasure horses properly because their use is often irregular. Sometimes they're used moderately; at other times they're idle; at still other times they're worked hard over the weekend or on a trail ride.

Most horses used for pleasure are worked lightly, perhaps 1 to 3 hours of riding per day. Others are worked medium hard, as when ridden 3 to 5 hours per day. Still others are worked very hard, as when raced or when ridden 5 to 8 hours per day. The recommended daily feed allowance per 100 pounds body weight of pleasure horses in light, medium, and hard use follows:

Lb Daily/100 Lb Weight of Horse	Light Use	Medium Use	Hard Use
Hay	$1\frac{1}{4}-1\frac{1}{2}$	$1-1\frac{1}{4}$	$1-1\frac{1}{4}$
Grain	$\frac{2}{5}-\frac{1}{2}$	$\frac{3}{4}-1$	$1\frac{1}{4}-1\frac{1}{3}$

As shown above, the roughage content of the ration decreases and the concentrate content increases as the amount of work increases. This is because the digestibility and the efficiency of conversion are greater for high energy concentrates than for roughages.

Of course, horses differ in temperament and in ease of keeping. Also, no two horses will perform the same amount of work with an equal expenditure of energy, and no two horsemen will get the same amount of work out of the same horse. So, the feed allowance should be increased if the horse fails to maintain condition, and it should be decreased if the animal becomes too fat.

In season, pasture may replace hay, all or in part, according to the quality of the pasture. But the concentrate allowance of the working horse should remain about the same on pasture as in the stable or dry corral. There is a tendency of the pastured working horse to sweat and tire more easily (be "soft"), probably due to the high water content of green forage.

In addition to forage and grain, pleasure horses should have access to salt and a suitable mineral mix, free-choice. The mineral requirements of the working horse differ from the idle horse mainly in the salt requirements, due to the loss of salt in perspiration.

The vitamin requirements of working horses are approximately the same as those of idle horses, except for the increase in the B complex requirements due to the greater carbohydrate metabolism of the working horse.

FEEDING HORSES IN TRAINING

Horses in heavy training for specific purposes — such as training for racing, cutting, roping, jumping, or hunting — have a higher nutritional requirement than most pleasure horses. And the younger the animal in training, the higher the level of nutrition needed in order to develop and maintain sound legs and build a strong frame and body. Therefore, the level of work, the temperament of the individual, and the age of the horse determine the nutritional needs. For this reason, horses in training should be fed as individuals.

Horses in training will eat about $1\frac{1}{2}$ lb of grain and 1 lb of hay per 100 lb liveweight.

FEEDING RACEHORSES

Racehorses are equine athletes whose nutritive requirements are the most exacting, but the most poorly met, of all animals. This statement may be shocking to some, but it's true because racehorses are commonly:

■ Started in training very shortly past 12 months of age, which is comparable to an adolescent boy or girl doing sweatshop labor.

■ Moved from track to track under all sorts of conditions.

■ Trained the year around, raced innumerable times each year, and forced to run when fatigued.

■ Outdoors only a short time each day — usually before sunup, with the result that the sun's rays have little chance to produce vitamin D from the cholesterol in the skin.

■ Without opportunity for even a few mouthfuls of grass — a rich, natural source of the B vitamins and unidentified factors.

■ Fed oats, grass hay, and possibly bran produced in unknown areas and on soils of unknown composition. Such an oats-grass hay-bran ration is almost always deficient in vitamins A and D and the B vitamins, and lopsided and low in calcium and phosphorus.

■ Given a potion of some concoction of questionable value — if not downright harmful.

By contrast, human athletes — college football teams and participants in the Olympics, for example — are usually required to eat at a special training table, supervised by nutrition experts. They are fed the best diet that science can formulate and technology can prepare. It's high in protein, rich in readily available energy, and fortified and balanced in vitamins and minerals.

It's small wonder, therefore, that so many equine athletes go unsound, whereas most human athletes compete year after year until overtaken by age.

Indeed, high-strung and highly stressed racehorses need special rations just as human athletes do — and for the same reasons; and the younger the age, the more acute the need. This calls for rations high in protein, rich in readily available energy, fortified with vitamins, minerals, and unidentified factors — and with all nutrients in proper balance.

A racehorse is asked to develop a large amount of horsepower in a period of 1 to 3 minutes. The oxidations that occur in a racehorse's body are at a higher pitch than in an idle horse, and, therefore, more vitamins are required. In this connection, it is noteworthy that the late Clyde Beatty, great animal trainer of the circus, sweated off a pound under the stress of every 18-minute performance.

Also, racehorses are the prima donnas of the equine world; most of them are temperamental, and no two of them can be fed alike. They vary in rapidity of eating, in the quantity of feed that they will consume, in the proportion of concentrate to roughage that they will take, and in response to different caretakers. Thus, for best results, they must be fed as individuals.

Most racehorse rations are deplorably deficient in protein, simply because they are based on the minimum requirements of little-stressed, slow, plodding horses.

During the racing season, the hay of a racehorse should be limited to 7 or 8 pounds, whereas the concentrate allowance may range up to 16 pounds. Heavy roughage eaters may have to be muzzled, to keep them from eating their bedding. A bran mash is commonly fed once a week.

FEEDING BROODMARES

Regular and normal reproduction is the basis for profit on any horse breeding establishment. However, only 40 to 60 percent of mares bred produce foals. There are many causes of reproductive failure, but inadequate nutrition is a major one. The following pointers are pertinent to feeding a broodmare properly.

1. Condition the mare for breeding by providing adequate and proper feed and the right amount of exercise prior to the breeding season.

2. See that adequate proteins, minerals, and vitamins are available during the last third of pregnancy when the fetus grows most rapidly.

3. Feed and water with care immediately before and after foaling. For the first 24 hours after parturition, the mare may have a little hay and a limited amount of water from which the chill has been taken. A light feed of bran or a wet bran mash is suitable for the first feed and the following meal may consist of oats or a mixture of oats and bran. A reasonably generous allowance of good-quality hay is permissible after the first day. If confined to the stable, as may be necessary in inclement weather, the mare should be kept on a limited and light grain and hay ration for about 10 days after foaling. Feeding too much grain at this time is likely to produce digestive disturbances in the mare and, even more hazardous, it may produce too much milk, which may cause indigestion in the foal. If weather conditions are favorable and it is possible to allow the mare to foal on a clean, lush pasture, she will regulate her own feed needs most admirably.

4. Provide adequate nutrition during lactation, because the requirements during this period are more rigorous than the requirements during pregnancy.

5. Make sure that young growing mares receive adequate nutrients; otherwise, the fetus will not develop properly or the dam will not produce milk except at the expense of her body tissues.

FEEDING STALLIONS

The ration exerts a powerful effect on sperm production and semen quality. Successful breeders adhere to the following stallion feeding rules.

1. Feed a balanced ration, giving particular attention to proteins, minerals, and vitamins.

2. Regulate the feed allowance because the stallion can become infertile if he gets too fat. Also, increase the exercise when the stallion is not a sure breeder.

3. Provide pasture in season as a source of both nutrients and exercise.

FEEDING FOALS

Growth is the very foundation of horse production. This is so because horses cannot perform properly, or possess the necessary speed and endurance if their growth has been stunted or their skeletons have been injured by inadequate rations during early age. Naturally, these requirements become increasingly acute when horses are forced for early use, such as the training and racing of the two-year-old. Also, unless foals are rather liberally fed when young, they never attain the much-desired body form, even if they are well fed later in life; this point is especially important where young stock is sold or shown.

The foal should be provided with a low-built grain box, or with a creep (a separate enclosure away from the dam) if on pasture.

The following pointers are pertinent to proper feeding of foals.

1. Start on feed early, which means at 10 days to 3 weeks of age. Rolled oats and wheat bran, to which a little brown sugar has been added, is especially palatable as a starting ration. Crushed or ground oats, cracked or ground corn, wheat bran, and a little linseed meal may be provided later with good results. Or a good commercial ration may be fed if desired and available.

2. Use a scientifically formulated ration even though it seems expensive, for usually it will represent a wise investment. Supplemental feeding

Figure 6.3 A foal creep. With this arrangement the foal can be fed separately from the dam.

also affords a convenient way in which to improve upon milk, by reinforcing it with certain minerals (for example, milk is low in iron and copper), vitamins, and additives.

Provide a good hay, preferably a legume, or pasture, in addition to its grain ration.

3. Allow about $\frac{1}{2}$ lb of grain daily per 100 lb of body weight at 4 to 5 weeks of age. This ration should be increased by weaning time to about $\frac{3}{4}$ lb or more per 100 lb of body weight. The exact amount of the ration will vary with the individual, the type of feed, and the development desired.

4. Obtain growth with durability and soundness, which calls for expert care and particular emphasis on the kind of ration, feed allowance, and exercise.

5. Simplify weaning and setback by feeding foals so that they rely less upon their mothers.

FEEDING WEANLINGS

The most critical period in the entire life of a horse is that interval from weaning time (about six months of age) until one year of age. Foals suckling their dams and receiving no grain may develop very satisfactorily up to weaning time. However, lack of preparation prior to weaning and neglect following the separation from the dam may prevent the animal from gaining proper size and shape. The primary objective in the breeding of horses is the economical production of a well-developed, sound individual at maturity. To achieve this result requires good care and management of weanlings.

Figure 6.4 Young stock wintering in an open shed and eating hay from a rack along the wall. (Photo by John C. Wyatt, Lexington, Kentucky; courtesy, Lee Eaton, Lexington, Kentucky)

No great setback or disturbances will be encountered at weaning time provided that the foals have developed a certain independence from proper grain feedings during the suckling period. Generally, weanlings should receive 1 to $1\frac{1}{2}$ lb of grain and $1\frac{1}{2}$ to 2 lb of hay daily per each 100 lb of liveweight. The amount of feed will vary somewhat with the individuality of the animal, the quality of roughage, available pastures, the price of feeds, and whether the weanling is being developed for show, race, or sale. Naturally, animals being developed for early use or sale should be fed more liberally, although it is equally important to retain clean, sound joints, legs, and feet — a condition which cannot be obtained so easily in heavily fitted animals.

Because of the rapid development of bone and muscle in weanlings, it is important that, in addition to ample quantity of feed, the ration also provide quality of proteins, and adequate minerals and vitamins.

FEEDING YEARLINGS

If young animals have been fed and cared for so that they are well grown and thrifty as yearlings, usually little difficulty will be experienced at any later date.

When on pasture, yearlings that are being grown for show or sale should receive grain in addition to grass. They should be confined to their stalls in the daytime during the hot days and turned out at night (because of not being exposed to sunshine, adequate vitamin D must be provided). This point needs to be emphasized when forced development is desired; for, good as pastures may be, they are roughages rather than concentrates.

The winter feeding program for the rising 2-year-olds should be such as to produce plenty of bone and muscle rather than fat. From $\frac{1}{2}$ to 1 lb of grain and 1 to $1\frac{1}{2}$ lb of hay should be fed for each 100 lb of liveweight. The quantity will vary with the quality of the roughage, the individuality of the animal, and the use for which the animal is produced. In producing for sale, more liberal feeding may be economical. Access to salt and to a mineral mixture should be provided at all times; or the minerals should be incorporated in the ration. An abundance of fresh, pure water must be available.

FEEDING TWO- AND THREE-YEAR-OLDS

Except for the fact that the two- and three-year-olds will be larger, and, therefore, will require more feed, a description of their proper care and management would be merely a repetition of the principles that have already been discussed for the yearling.

FITTING FOR SHOW OR SALE

Each year, many horses are fitted for shows or sales. In both cases, a fattening process is involved, but exercise is doubly essential.

For horses that are being fitted for shows, the conditioning process is also a matter of hardening, and the horses are used daily in harness or under saddle. Regardless of whether a sale or a show is the major objective, fleshing should be obtained without sacrificing action or soundness and without causing filling of the legs and hocks.

In fattening horses, the animals should be brought to full feed rather gradually, until the ration reaches a maximum of about 2 lb of grain daily for each 100 lb of liveweight. When on full feed, horses make surprising gains. Daily weight gains of 4 to 5 lb are not uncommon. Such animals soon become fat, sleek, and attractive. This is probably the basis for the statement that "fat will cover up a multitude of sins in a horse."

Although exercise is desirable from the standpoint of keeping the animals sound, it is estimated that such activity decreases the daily rate of gains by as much as 20 percent. Because of the greater cost of gains and the expense involved in bringing about forced exercise, most feeders of sale horses limit the exercise to that obtained naturally from running in a paddock.

In comparison with finishing cattle or sheep, there is more risk in fattening horses. Heavily fed horses kept in idleness are likely to become blemished and injured through playfulness, and there are more sicknesses among liberally fed horses than in other classes of stock handled in a similar manner.

In fitting show horses, the finish must remain firm and hard, the action superb, and the soundness unquestioned. Thus, they must be carefully fed, groomed, and exercised to bring them to proper bloom.

Horsemen who fit and sell yearlings or younger animals may feed a palatable milk replacer or commercial feed to advantage.

CHEMICAL ANALYSIS OF FEEDS

Feed composition tables ("book values"), or average analysis, should be considered only as guides, because of wide variations in the composition of feeds. For example, the protein and moisture content of milo and hay are quite variable. Wherever possible, especially with large operations, it is best to take a representative sample of each major feed ingredient and have a chemical analysis made of it for the more common constituents — protein, fat, fiber, nitrogen-free extract, and moisture; and often calcium, phosphorus, and carotene. Such ingredients as oil meals and prepared supplements, which must meet specific standards, need not be analyzed so often, except as quality control measures.

Despite the recognized value of a chemical analysis, it is not the total answer. It does not provide information on the availability of nutrients to the animal; it varies from sample to sample, because feeds vary and a representative sample is not always easily obtained; and it does not tell anything about the associated effect of feedstuffs. Nor does a chemical analysis tell anything about taste, palatability, texture, undesirable physiological effects such as digestive disturbances and laxativeness. Thus, one cannot buy feed for horses on the basis of chemical analysis alone, as is substantiated by the example that follows.

Example: Based on chemical analysis and price, which of the following would you choose?

	#1	#2	#3	#4
Crude protein. . . .%	9.06	11.23	7.4	9.8
Fat . . . .%		13.59		9.1
Sugar . . . .%		0.43	51.2	
Fiber . . . .%		16.5		0.3
Moisture . . . . . .%		0.63		5.9
N.F.E.. . . . .%				72.8
Price/ton . . . . . .$	60.00	100.00	40.00	80.00
Cost/cwt . . . . . .$	3.00	5.00	2.00	4.00
Cost/lb protein . . .$	0.33	.445	0.27	0.41

Here's the identity of the samples:

Sample #1 . . . . soft coal
Sample #2 . . . . coffee grounds
Sample #3 . . . . candy
Sample #4 . . . . crackers

However, a chemical analysis does give a solid foundation on which to start in evaluating feeds. Also, with chemical analysis at hand, and bearing in mind that it's the composition of the total feed (the finished ration) that counts, the person formulating the ration can more intelligently determine the quantity of protein to buy, and the kind and amounts of minerals and vitamins to add.

TERMS USED IN FEED ANALYSES AND GUARANTEES
Knowledge of the following terms is requisite to understanding feed analyses and guarantees.

Dry matter is found by determining the percentage of water and subtracting the water content from 100 percent.

Crude protein is used to designate the nitrogenous constituents of a feed. The percentage is obtained by multiplying the percentage of total nitrogen by the factor 6.25. The nitrogen is derived chiefly from complex chemical compounds called amino acids.

Crude fat is the material that is extracted from moisture-free feeds by ether. It consists largely of fats and oils with small amounts of waxes, resins, and coloring matter. In calculating the heat and energy value of the feeds, the fat is considered 2.25 times that of either nitrogen-free extract or protein.

Crude fiber is the relatively insoluble carbohydrate portion of a feed consisting chiefly of cellulose. It is determined by its insolubility in dilute acids and alkalies.

Ash is the mineral matter of a feed. It is the residue remaining after complete burning of the organic matter.

Nitrogen-free extract consists principally of sugars, starches, pentoses and nonnitrogenous organic acids. The percentage is determined by subtracting the sum of the percentages of moisture, crude protein, crude fat, crude fiber, and ash from 100.

Carbohydrates represent the sum of the crude fiber and nitrogen-free extract.

Calcium and phosphorus are essential mineral elements that are present in feeds in varying quantities. Mineral feeds are usually high in source materials of these elements.

TDN — The digestible nutrients of any ingredient are obtained by multiplying the percentage of each nutrient by the digestion coefficient. For example, dent corn contains 8.9 percent protein, of which 77 percent is digestible. Therefore, the percent of digestible protein is 6.9.

The TDN is the sum of all the digestible organic nutrients — protein, fiber, nitrogen-free extract, and fat (the latter multiplied by 2.25).

SOIL ANALYSIS

For the horseman who produces his own hay, a soil analysis can be very helpful; for example, (1) the phosphorus content of soils affects plant composition, (2) soils high in molybdenum and selenium affect the composition of the feeds produced, (3) iodine deficiency areas are important in horse nutrition, and (4) other similar soil-plant-animal relationships are important.

No analysis is any better than the sample taken. So, make sure that you get a representative sample of soil. Ask your county agent (farm advisor) how to take the samples and where to send them. Some colleges of agriculture make soil analyses at nominal cost.

NUTRITIONAL DISEASES AND AILMENTS

Nutritional deficiencies may be brought about either by (1) too little feed, or (2) rations that are too low in one or more nutrients. Also, forced

Figure 6.5 Separation of the hoof from the foot of a horse due to selenium poisoning, caused by consuming certain plants grown on soils containing selenium. (Courtesy, A. L. Moxon, South Dakota State University, Brookings, South Dakota)

production (such as racing two-year-olds) and the feeding of forages and grains which are often produced on leached or depleted soils have created many problems in nutrition. This condition has been futher aggravated through the increased confinement of horses, many animals being confined to stalls or lots all or a large part of the year. Under these unnatural conditions, nutritional diseases and ailments have become increasingly common.

Although the cause, prevention, and treatment of most equine nutritional diseases and ailments are known, they continue to reduce profits in the livestock industry simply because the available knowledge is not put into practice. Moreover, those widespread nutritional deficiencies which are not of sufficient proportions to produce clear-cut deficiency symptoms

Table 6.9 Nutritional Diseases and Ailments of Horses

Disease	Species Affected	Cause	Symptoms (and Age or Group Most Affected)	Distribution and Losses Caused by
Anemia, nutritional	All warm-blooded animals, and man.	Commonly an iron deficiency, but may be caused by a deficiency of copper, cobalt, and/or certain vitamins (riboflavin, pyridoxine, pantothenic acid, and/or folic acid).	Loss of appetite, poor performance, progressive emaciation and death.	Worldwide. Losses consist of retarded growth and deaths.
Azoturia (Hemoglobinuria, Monday morning disease, Blackwater)	Horses	Associated with faulty carbohydrate metabolism, and with work following a period of idleness in the stall on full rations.	Profuse sweating, abdominal distress, wine-colored urine, stiff gait, reluctance to move, and lameness. Finally, animal assumes a sitting position, and eventually falls prostrate on the side.	Worldwide, but the disease is seldom seen in horses at pasture and rarely in horses at constant work.
Colic	Horses	Improper feeding, working, or watering.	Excruciating pain; and depending on the type of colic, other symptoms are: distended abdomen, increased intestinal rumbling, violent rolling and kicking, profuse sweating, constipation, and refusal of feed and water.	Worldwide.

cause even greater economic losses because they go unnoticed and unrectified.

Unfortunately, there are no warning signals to tell a caretaker when a horse is not getting enough of a certain nutrient. A continuing inadequate supply of any one of several nutrients can produce illness which is very hard to diagnose until it becomes severe, at which time it is difficult and expensive — if not too late — to treat. The important thing, therefore, is to insure against such deficiencies occurring. But horsemen should not shower a horse with mistaken kindness through using shotgun-type vitamin preparations. Instead, the quantity of each nutrient should be based on available scientific knowledge.

Table 6.9 contains a summary of the important nutritional diseases and ailments affecting horses.

Treatment	Control and Eradication	Prevention	Remarks
Provide dietary sources of the nutrient or nutrients known to cause the condition.	When nutritional anemia is encountered, it can usually be brought under control by supplying dietary sources of the nutrient or nutrients known to cause the condition.	Supply dietary sources of iron, copper, cobalt, and certain vitamins. Keep suckling animals confined to a minimum and provide supplemental feeds at an early age.	Anemia is a condition in which the blood is either deficient in quality or quantity (a deficient quality refers to a deficiency in hemoglobin and/or red cells). Levels of iron in most feeds believed to be ample, since most feeds contain 40 to 400 milligrams/lb.
Absolute rest and quiet. While awaiting the veterinarian, apply heated cloths or blankets, or hot-water bottles to the swollen and hardened muscles.	Azoturia is noncontagious. When trouble is encountered, decrease the ration and increase the exercise on idle days.	Restrict the ration and provide daily exercise when the animal is idle. Give a wet bran mash the evening before an idle day or turn the idle horses to pasture.	
Call a veterinarian. To avoid danger of inflicting self-injury, (1) place the animal in a large, well-bedded stable, or (2) take it for a slow walk. Most veterinarians use the stomach tube in the treatment of colic.	Proper feeding, working, and watering.		

(Cont.)

Table 6.9 Nutritional Diseases and Ailments of Horses (*Cont.*)

Disease	Species Affected	Cause	Symptoms (and Age or Group Most Affected)	Distribution and Losses Caused by
Fluorine poisoning (Fluorosis)	All farm animals, poultry, and man.	Ingesting excessive quantities of fluorine through either the feed or water.	Abnormal teeth (especially mottled enamel) and bones, stiffness of joints, loss of appetite, emaciation, reduction in milk flow, diarrhea, and salt hunger.	The water in parts of Arkansas, California, South Carolina, and Texas has been reported to contain excess fluorine. Occasionally throughout th U.S. high fluorine phosphates are used i mineral mixtures.
Founder (Laminitis)	Horses Cattle Sheep Goats	Overeating (grain; or lush legume or grass, known as "grass founder"), overdrinking, or inflammation of the uterus following parturition. Also intestinal inflammation.	Extreme pain, fever (103° to 106°F) and reluctance to move. If neglected, chronic laminitis will develop, resulting in a dropping of the hoof soles and a turning up of the toe walls.	Worldwide. Actual death losses from founder are not very great.
Heaves	Horses Mules	Exact cause unknown, but it is known that the condition is often associated with the feeding of damaged, dusty, or moldy hay. It often follows severe respiratory infections such as strangles.	Difficulty in forcing air out of the lungs, resulting in a jerking of flanks (double flank action) and coughing. The nostrils are often slightly dilated and there is a nasal discharge.	Worldwide. Losses are negligible.

reatment	Control and Eradication	Prevention	Remarks
ny damage may e permanent, but nimals which have ot developed se- ere symptoms may e helped to some xtent, if the ources of excess uorine are elimi- ated.	Discontinue the use of feeds, water, or mineral supple- ments containing excessive fluorine.	Avoid the use of feeds, water, or mineral sup- plements containing ex- cessive fluorine. Not more than 65 to 100 ppm fluorine should be present in dry matter of rations when rock phosphate is fed. Phosphorus sources should not contain more than 0.1% F.	Fluorine is a cumulative poi- son.
ending arrival of ne veterinarian, the ttendant should and the animal's eet in a cold-water ath. ntihistamines, re- tricting the diet, se of diuretics, and nti-inflammatory gents, such as cor- icosteroids or henylbutazone, nay speed up re- overy and alleviate erious aftereffects.	Alleviate the causes; namely, (1) overeat- ing, (2) overdrink- ing, and/or (3) inflammation of the uterus following parturition.	Avoid overeating and overdrinking (especially when hot).	Unless foundered animals are quite valuable, it is usually desirable to dispose of them following a case of severe founder.
No satisfactory reatment, although ffected animals are ess bothered if urned to pasture, if sed only at light work, or if the hay s sprinkled lightly with water at feed- ng.	(See Prevention.)	Avoid the use of dam- aged feeds. Feed an all-pelleted ra- tion, thereby alleviating dust.	

(Cont.)

Table 6.9 Nutritional Diseases and Ailments of Horses (*Cont.*)

Disease	Species Affected	Cause	Symptoms (and Age or Group Most Affected)	Distribution and Losses Caused by
Iodine Deficiency (Goiter)	All farm animals, and man.	A failure of the body to obtain sufficient iodine from which the thyroid gland can form thyroxine (an iodine-containing compound).	Foals may be weak.	Northwestern U.S. an the Great Lakes regic
Osteomalacia	All farm animals.	Lack of vitamin D. Inadequate intake of calcium or phosphorus. Incorrect ratio of calcium and phosphorus.	Phosphorus deficiency symptoms are: depraved appetite (gnawing on bones, wood, or other objects, or eating dirt); lack of appetite, stiffness of joints, failure to breed regularly, decreased milk production, and an emaciated appearance. Calcium deficiency symptoms are fragile bones, reproductive failures, and lowered lactations. Mature animals most affected. Most of the acute cases occur during pregnancy and lactation.	Southwestern U.S. is classed as a phosphorus-deficient area, whereas calcium-deficient areas have been reported in parts of Florida, Louisiana, N braska, Virginia, and W. Virginia.
Periodic Ophthalmia (Moonblindness)	Horses Mules Asses	It may be due to deficiency of riboflavin in the ration. However, leptospiral microorganisms may play a role, also.	Periods of cloudy vision, in one or both eyes, which may last for a few days to a week or two and then clear up; but it recurs at intervals, eventually culminating in blindness in one or both eyes.	In many parts of the world. In the U.S., it occurs most frequently in th states east of the Missouri River.

reatment	Control and Eradication	Prevention	Remarks
nce the iodine-eficiency symptoms ppear in farm ani-als, no treatment very effective.	At the first signs of iodine deficiency, an iodized salt should be fed to all farm animals.	In iodine-deficient areas, feed iodized salt to all farm animals throughout the year. Salt containing 0.01% potassium iodide is recommended.	The enlarged thyroid gland (goiter) is nature's way of attempting to make sufficient thyroxine under conditions where a deficiency exists.
ncrease the calicum nd phosphorus ontent of feeds hrough fertilizing he soils. elect natural feeds hat contain suffi-ient quantities of alicum and phos-horus. eed a special min-ral supplement or upplements. f the disease is far dvanced, treatment ill not be success-ul.	(See Treatment)	Feed balanced rations, and allow animals free access to a suitable phosphorus and cal-cium supplement.	Calcium deficiencies are much more rare than phosphorous deficiencies in horses.
ntibiotics adminis-red promptly are elpful.	If symptoms of moonblindness are observed, immedi-ately (1) change to greener hay or grass, or (2) add ri-boflavin to the ra-tion at the rate of 40 mg per horse per day.	Feed high riboflavin green grass or well-cured green leafy hays; or Add riboflavin to the ration at the rate of 40 mg per horse per day.	Lack of riboflavin is not the only factor causing periodic ophthalmia. Sometimes it fol-lows leptospirosis in horses, and it may be caused by a localized hypersensitivity or allergic reaction. This disease has been known to exist for at least 2000 years.

(Cont.)

Table 6.9 Nutritional Diseases and Ailments of Horses (*Cont.*)

Disease	Species Affected	Cause	Symptoms (and Age or Group Most Affected)	Distribution and Losses Caused by
Rickets	All farm animals, and man.	Lack of calcium, phosphorus, or vitamin D; or An incorrect ratio of the two minerals.	Enlargement of the knee and hock joints, and the animal may exhibit great pain when moving about. Irregular bulges (beaded ribs) at juncture of ribs with breast-bone, and bowed legs. Rickets is a disease of young animals.	Worldwide. It is seldom fatal.
Salt Deficiency	All farm animals, and man.	Lack of salt (sodium chloride).	Loss of appetite, retarded growth, loss of weight, a rough coat, lowered production of milk, and a ravenous appetite for salt.	Worldwide, especially among grass-eating animals and the pig.
Selenium Poisoning (Alkali disease)	All farm animals, and man.	Consumption of plants grown on soils containing selenium.	Loss of hair from the mane and tail in horses. In severe cases, the hoofs slough off, lameness occurs, food consumption decreases, and death may occur by starvation.	In certain regions of western U.S. — especially certain areas in South Dakota, Montana, Wyoming, Nebraska, Kansas, and perhaps areas in other states in the Great Plains and Rocky Mountains. Also in Canada.
Urinary Calculi (Gravel, Stones, Water belly)	Horses Cattle Sheep Man	Unknown, but there is a higher incidence when there is: A higher P than Ca intake. A high potassium intake. A high proportion of beet pulp or grain sorghum in the ration.	Frequent attempts to urinate, dribbling or stoppage of the urine, pain and renal colic. Usually only males affected, the females being able to pass the concretions. Bladder may rupture, with death following. Otherwise, uremic poisoning may set in.	Worldwide. Affected animals seldom recover completely.

reatment	Control and Eradication	Prevention	Remarks
the disease has ot advanced too r, treatment may e successful by pplying adequate nounts of vitamin , calcium, and hosphorus, and/or ljusting the ratio f calcium to phoshorus.	(See Prevention.)	Provide (1) sufficient calcium, phosphorus, and vitamin D, and (2) a correct ratio of the two minerals. Expose the animal to direct sunlight as much as possible, allow it free access to a suitable mineral mixture, and provide good quality sun-cured hay or pasture grown on well-fertilized soil.	Rickets is characterized by a failure of growing bone to ossify or harden properly.
alt-starved animals ould be gradually ccustomed to salt; owly increase the and-fed allowance ntil the animals ay be safely alowed free access to .	(See Treatment and Prevention.)	Provide plenty of salt at all times, preferably by free-choice feeding.	Common salt is one of the most essential minerals for grass-eating animals and one of the easiest and cheapest to provide. Excess salt intake can result in toxicity.
lthough arsenic as been shown to ounteract the efects of selenium oxicity, there apears to be no pracical method of reating other than emoval of animals rom affected areas.	(See Prevention.)	Abandon areas where soils contain selenium, because crops produced on such soils constitute a menace to both animals and man.	Chronic cases of selenium poisoning occur when animals consume feeds containing 8.5 ppm of selenium over an extended period; acute cases occur on 500 to 1000 ppm. The toxic levels of selenium are in the range of 2.27–4.54 mg/lb of feed.
nce calculi deelop, dietary treatent appears to be f little value. mooth muscle reaxants may allow assage of calculi if sed before rupture f bladder.		Good feed and management appear to lessen the incidence, but no sure preventive is known. 1 to 3% salt in the concentrate ration may help (using the higher levels in the winter when water consumption is normally lower).	Calculi are stone-like concretions in the urinary tract which almost always originate in the kidneys. These stones block the passage of urine.

(Cont.)

Table 6.9 Nutritional Diseases and Ailments of Horses (*Cont.*)

Disease	Species Affected	Cause	Symptoms (and Age or Group Most Affected)	Distribution and Losses Caused by
Vitamin A Deficiency (Night Blindness and Xerophthalmia)	All farm animals, and man.	Vitamin A deficiency.	Night blindness, the first symptom of vitamin A deficiency, is characterized by faulty vision, especially noticeable when the affected animal is forced to move about in twilight in strange surroundings. Xerophthalmia develops in the advanced stages of vitamin A deficiency. The eyes become severely affected, and blindness may follow. Also, a severe deficiency of vitamin A may cause reproductive difficulties, poor or uneven hoof development, certain leg bone weaknesses, difficulty in breathing, incoordination, and poor appetite.	Worldwide.

EATING BEDDING

Sometimes gluttonous animals eat their bedding. This is undesirable because (1) most bedding materials are low in nutritional value, and (2) feces-soiled bedding adds to the parasite problem. The problem can be alleviated by muzzling the horse.

PICA; WOOD CHEWING

Horses, particularly those confined to stalls or lots, sometimes consume such materials as dirt, hair, bones, or feces. Such depraved appetites are known as "pica." This condition is usually caused by one or more of the following conditions:

1. *Boredom,* because they have nothing to do. The more limited the exercise, and the more quickly they consume their feed, the greater the unoccupied time available and the consequent boredom.

reatment	Control and Eradication	Prevention	Remarks
dd stabilized vitamin A to the ration.	(See Treatment and Prevention.)	Provide good sources of carotene (vitamin A) through green, leafy hays; silage; lush, green pastures; yellow corn or green and yellow peas; whole milk; fish oil; or add stabilized vitamin A to the ration.	

By contrast, little *Eohippus* (the dawn horse of 58 million years ago) was a denizen of the swamp. Later, through evolution, he became a creature of the prairies. Although his natural habitat shifted during this long predomestication period, until man confined him he gleaned the feeds provided by nature. Inevitably, this occupied his time and provided exercise.

2. *Nutritional inadequacies,* which may be due to (a) a deficiency of one or more nutrients, (b) an imbalance between certain nutrients, or (c) objection to the physical form of the ration — for example, it may be ground too finely.

3. *Psychological stress and habit,* which contribute to the behavior of horses, and which have been accentuated by the unnatural environment to which man has subjected them.

Whatever the reason(s) for pica, the suspected causative factor(s) should first be rectified. When and where needed, the exercise should be stepped up; the eating time should be prolonged, and the interval between feedings shortened; nutritional deficiencies, imbalances, and physical form of ration should be corrected; and stress should be minimized. Even after these conditions have been rectified, it may be disconcerting to find that wood chewing, and perhaps various other forms of pica, persist among certain horses — perhaps due to habit. Thus, in the final analysis, there is only one foolproof way in which to prevent wood chewing, namely, to have no wood on which they can chew — to use metal, of other similar materials, for fences and barns. Of course, this isn't always practical. So you can lessen, although you cannot entirely prevent, wood chewing through one or more of the following practices:

1. Stepping up the exercise.

2. Feeding three times a day, rather than twice a day, even though the total daily feed allowance remains the same.

3. Spreading out the feed in a larger feed container, and/or placing a few large stones about the size of a baseball in the feed container, thereby making the horse work harder and longer to obtain his feed.

4. Providing two to four pounds of straw or coarse grass hay per animal per day, thereby giving the horse something to nibble on during his spare time.

7. Pastures

The great horse-breeding centers of the world — Kentucky, Ireland, and New Zealand, to name three of them — are characterized by good pastures. Yet, it is becoming difficult to provide good pasture for horses, especially in suburban areas. Also, it is recognized that many horsemen are prone to overrate the quality of their grass.

In season and when available, good pastures — pastures that are more than mere gymnasiums for horses — should be provided, especially for idle horses, broodmares, and young stock. In fact, pastures have a very definite place for all horses, with the possible exception of animals at heavy work or in training. Even with the latter, pastures may be used with discretion. Horses in heavy use may be turned to pasture at night or over the weekend. Certainly, the total benefits derived from pasture are to the good, although pasturing may have some laxative effects and produce a greater tendency to sweat.

Figure 7.1 Good horsemen, good pastures, and good horses go hand in hand. Standardbred mares and foals on pasture at Hanover Shoe Farm, Hanover, Pennsylvania. (Courtesy, *Hoof Beats,* Columbus, Ohio)

The use of a temporary or seeded pasture grown in regular crop rotation is recommended instead of a permanent pasture that may become infested with parasites. Legume pasture is excellent for horses because they are less subject to bloat than cattle or sheep.

Horse pastures should be well drained and not too rough or stony. All dangerous places such as pits, stumps, poles, and tanks should be guarded. Shade, water, and suitable minerals should be available in all pastures.

Most horse pastures can be improved by seeding new and better varieties of grasses and legumes and by fertilizing and management. Also, horsemen need to give attention to supplementing some pastures with additional feed. Pastures early in the season have a high water content and lack energy. Mature, weathered grass is almost always deficient in protein, with as little as three percent or less, and low in carotene, the precursor of vitamin A. However, these deficiencies can be corrected by proper supplemental feeding.

In addition to the nutritive value of the grass, pasture provides invaluable exercise on natural footing — with plenty of sunshine, fresh air, and lowered feeding costs as added benefits. Feeding on pasture is the ideal existence for young stock and breeding animals.

But pastures should not be taken for granted. Again and again, scientists and practical horsemen have demonstrated that the following desired goals in pasture production are well within the realm of possibility:

- To produce higher yields of palatable and nutritious forage.
- To extend the grazing season from as early in the spring to as late in the fall as possible.
- To provide a fairly uniform supply of feed throughout the entire season.

KINDS OF PASTURE

Broadly speaking, all horse pastures may be classified as either (1) permanent pastures, or (2) seeded or temporary pastures.

1. *Permanent pastures* — Those which, with proper care, last for many years. They are most commonly found on land that cannot be used profitably for cultivated crops, mainly because of topography, moisture, or fertility. The vast majority of U.S. farms have one or more permanent pastures, and most range areas come under this classification.

2. *Seeded or temporary pastures* — Seeded pastures are used as part of the established crop rotation. They are generally used for two to seven years before plowing.

Temporary pastures are those that are used for a short period — like rye, wheat, or oat pasture. They are seeded for the purpose of providing supplemental grazing during the season when the regular permanent or seeded pastures are relatively unproductive.

ADAPTED VARIETIES AND SUITABLE MIXTURES

The specific grass or grass-legume mixture will vary from area to area, according to differences in soil, temperature, and rainfall. A complete listing of all adapted and recommended grasses and legumes for horse pastures would be too lengthy for this book. However, Table 7.1 shows the

Table 7.1 Grasses and Legumes Adapted to the 10 Areas (see Figure 7.2) of the 48 Contiguous States[1]

Grasses	Regions of Adaption									
	1	2	3	4	5	6	7	8	9	10
Bahia Grass	...	...	x	x	...	...	...	...	...	...
Bermuda Grass	...	x	x	x	...	...	...	x	...	x
Big Bluestem	x	...	...	...	x	x	...	x	...	...
Blue Grama	...	...	...	...	...	x	...	...	...	...
Blue Panicum	...	...	...	...	...	x	...	...	...	...
Buffalo Grass	...	...	...	...	x	x	...	...	...	...
Carpet Grass	...	...	x	x	...	...	...	...	...	...
Chewings Fescue	...	...	...	...	...	...	...	...	x	...
Common Ryegrass	x	x	x	x	...	...	...	x	x	x
Creeping Red Fescue	...	...	...	...	...	...	...	...	x	...
Dallis Grass	...	...	x	x	...	...	...	x	...	x
Harding Grass	...	...	...	...	...	...	...	x	...	x
Indian Grass	...	...	...	...	x	x	...	...	...	...
Kentucky Bluegrass	x	x	...	...	...	...	...	...	x	...
Little Bluestem	x	...	...	...	x	x	...	...	...	...
Lovegrasses	...	...	...	...	x	x	...	x	...	...
Meadow Fescue	x	x	...	...	...	...	x	...	x	...
Meadow Foxtail	x	...	...	...	...	...	x	...	x	...
Millets	x	...	...	...	x	x	...	...	...	...
Mountain Bromegrass	...	...	...	...	...	...	x	...	...	...
Orchardgrass	x	x	x	x	...	...	x	x	x	x
Pangola	...	...	...	x	...	...	...	...	...	...
Perennial Ryegrass	x	x	x	x	...	...	...	x	x	x
Redtop	x	x	x	...	...	...	...	...	x	...
Reed Canary Grass	x	x	...	...	...	...	...	...	x	x
Rescuegrass	...	...	x	...	...	x	...	x	...	x
Rhodes Grass	...	...	...	...	...	x	...	x	...	x
Sand Dropseed	...	...	...	...	x	x	...	...	...	...
Side Oats Grama	...	...	...	...	x	x	...	...	...	...
Smooth Bromegrass	x	...	...	...	x	...	x	x	...	x
Soft Chess	...	...	...	...	...	...	...	...	...	x
Tall Fescue	x	x	x	x	...	...	x	x	x	x
Tall Oatgrass	x	x	...	...	...	...	x	x	x	...
Timothy	x	x	...	...	x	...	x	...	x	...
Veldt Grass	...	...	...	...	...	...	...	...	...	x
Wheatgrasses	...	...	...	...	x	...	x	x	...	...
Yellow Bluestem	...	...	...	...	...	x	...	...	...	...

Table 7.1 Grasses and Legumes Adapted to the 10 Areas (see Figure 7.2) of the 48 Contiguous States[1] (*Cont.*)

Legumes	Regions of Adaption									
	1	**2**	**3**	**4**	**5**	**6**	**7**	**8**	**9**	**10**
Alfalfa	x	x	x	x	x	x	x	x	x	x
Alsike Clover	x	x	...	...	x	...	x	...	x	...
Birdsfoot Trefoil	x	x	...	...	...	...	x	x	x	...
Bur Clover	...	...	x	x	...	x	...	...	x	x
Crimson Clover	...	x	x	x	...	...	...	...	...	x
Hop Clover	...	...	x	...	...	...	...	...	...	...
Kudzu	...	x	x	x	...	...	...	...	...	...
Ladino Clover	x	x	x	x	x	x	x	x	x	x
Lespedeza	...	x	x	x	...	...	...	...	...	...
Lupine	...	...	x	...	...	...	...	...	...	...
Persian Clover	...	...	x	...	...	...	...	...	...	...
Red Clover	x	x	x	...	x	x	x	x	x	x
Sweet Clover	x	x	x	...	x	x	x	x	x	x
Vetches	x	x	x	x	x	x	x	x	x	...
White Clover	x	x	x	x	x	x	x	x	x	x

[1]Adapted by the author from *Pasture — How to Reduce Feed Costs,* Keystone Steel and Wire, Peoria, Ill., 1958, p. 17.

LEGUMES AND GRASSES ADAPTED TO 10 AREAS OF THE 48 CONTIGUOUS STATES

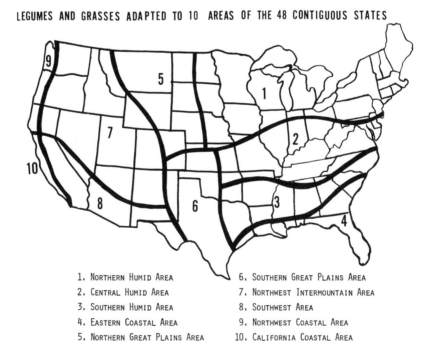

1. Northern Humid Area
2. Central Humid Area
3. Southern Humid Area
4. Eastern Coastal Area
5. Northern Great Plains Area
6. Southern Great Plains Area
7. Northwest Intermountain Area
8. Southwest Area
9. Northwest Coastal Area
10. California Coastal Area

Figure 7.2 The 10 generally recognized U.S. pasture areas.

most important ones for each of the 10 generally recognized U.S. pasture areas (Figure 7.2). In using Table 7.1, bear in mind that many species of forages have wide geographic adaption, but subspecies or varieties often have rather specific adaptation. Thus, alfalfa, for example, is represented by many varieties, which give this species adaptation to nearly all states. Variety then, within species, makes many forages adapted to widely varying climate and geographic areas. The county agricultural agent or state agricultural college can furnish recommendations for the area that they serve.

Five grass species — orchardgrass, reed canary grass, fescue, smooth bromegrass, and Bermuda grass — account for the major portion of seeded grasses in the United States. The leading legumes are alfalfa, trefoil, lupine, sweet clover, Kudzu, and clover.

Sudan and hybrid Sudans in the growing stage should never be grazed by horses, because of the hazard of cystitis. This disease, which occurs more frequently in mares than in stallions or geldings, is characterized by continuous urination, mares appearing to be constantly in heat, and incoordination in the gait. Animals seldom recover after either the incoordination or the dribbling of urine becomes evident. Apparently hay from Sudan or from hybrid Sudans will not produce this malady.

SUPPLEMENTING PASTURES

Except for idle horses, it is generally advisable to provide supplemental feed for horses that are on pasture. This is so because (1) horses are usually subjected to considerable stress; (2) show, sale, and pleasure horses should have eye appeal — sleek, bloomy hair coats that attract judges, buyers, and all who see them; and (3) young animals are usually forced for early development. Further, it is important not to jeopardize soundness or lower the reproductive ability of breeding animals. Consequently, the nutritive requirements of horses are generally more critical than can be met by pasture alone.

Figure 7.3 Supplemental feeding of young stock on pasture, using portable feeders. Also, note open shed. (Courtesy, Lee Eaton, Lexington, Kentucky)

SUPPLEMENTING EARLY SPRING GRASS

Turning horses on pasture when the first sprigs of green grass appear will usually make for a temporary deficiency of energy, due to (1) washy (high water content) grasses, and (2) inadequate forage for animals to consume. As a result, owners are often disappointed in the poor condition of horses.

If there is good reason why grazing cannot be delayed until there is adequate spring growth, it is recommended that early pastures be supplemented with grass hay or straw (a legume hay will accentuate looseness, which usually exists under such circumstances), preferably placed in a rack; perhaps with a high energy concentrate provided, also.

SUPPLEMENTING DRY PASTURE

Dry, mature, weathered, bleached grass characterizes (1) drought periods, and (2) fall-winter pastures. Such cured-on-the-stalk grasses are low in energy, in protein (as low as 3% or less), in carotene (the precursor of vitamin A), and in phosphorus and perhaps certain other minerals. These deficiencies become more acute following frost and increase in severity as winter advances. This explains the often severe loss in condition of horses following the first fall freeze.

In addition to the deficiencies which normally characterize whatever plants are available, dry pasture may be plagued by a short supply of feed.

Generally speaking, a concentrate or supplement is best used during droughts or on fall-winter pastures. However, when there is an acute shortage of forage, hay or other roughage should be added, also.

PASTURE SUPPLEMENTS

Horsemen face the question of what pasture supplement to use, when to feed it, and how much of it to feed.

In supplying a supplement to horses on pasture, the following guides should be observed:

- It should balance the diet of the horses to which it is fed, which means that it should supply all the nutrients missing in the forage.
- It should be fed in such a way that each horse gets its proper proportion, which generally means (1) the use of salt blocks, (2) tying up horses during concentrate feeding when more than one animal is fed in a given pasture, or (3) taking them to their stalls at feeding time.
- The daily allowance of the supplement should be determined by (1) the available pasture (quantity and quality), and (2) the condition of the horse.

The results from the use of the supplement, rather than cost per bag, should determine the choice of supplement.

MANAGEMENT OF HORSE PASTURES

Many good horse pastures have been established only to be lost through careless management. Good pasture management involves the practices that follow.

CONTROLLED GRAZING

Nothing contributes more to good pasture management than controlled grazing. At its best, it embraces the following:

1. *Protection of first-year-seedings* — first-year seedings should be grazed lightly or not at all in order that they may get a good start. Where practical, instead of grazing, it is preferable to mow a new first-year seeding about 3 inches above the ground and to utilize it as hay, provided there is sufficient growth to justify this procedure.

2. *Rotation or alternate grazing* — Rotation or alternate grazing is accomplished by dividing a pasture into fields (usually 2 to 4) of approximately equal size, so that one field can be grazed while the others are allowed to make new growth. This results in increased pasture yields, more uniform grazing, and higher-quality forage.

Generally speaking, rotation or alternate grazing is (a) more practical and profitable on seeded and temporary pastures than on permanent pastures, and (b) more beneficial where parasite infestations are heavy than where little or no parasitic problems are involved.

3. *Shifting the location of salt, shade, and water* — Where portable salt containers are used, more uniform grazing and scattering of the droppings may be obtained simply by the practice of shifting the location of the salt to the less-grazed areas of the pasture. Where possible and practical, the shade and the water should be shifted likewise.

4. *Deferred spring grazing* — Allow 6 to 8 inches of growth before turning horses out to pasture in the spring, thereby giving grass a needed start. Anyway, the early spring growth of pastures is high in moisture and washy.

5. *Avoiding close late fall grazing* — Pastures that are grazed closely late in the fall start late in the spring. With most pastures, 3 to 5 inches of growth should be left for winter cover.

6. *Avoiding overgrazing* — Never graze more closely than 2 to 3 inches during the pasture season. Continued close grazing reduces the yield, weakens the plants, allows weeds to invade, and increases soil erosion. The use of temporary and supplemental pastures may "spell off" regular pastures through seasons of drought and other pasture shortages and thus alleviate over-grazing.

7. *Avoiding undergrazing* — Undergrazing seeded pastures should also be avoided, because (a) mature forage is unpalatable and of low nutritive value, (b) tall-growing grasses may drive out low-growing plants due to shading, and (c) weeds, brush, and coarse grasses are more apt to gain a foothold when the pasture is grazed insufficiently. It is a good rule, therefore, to graze the pasture fairly close at least once each year.

CLIPPING PASTURES AND CONTROLLING WEEDS

Pastures should be clipped at such intervals as necessary to control weeds (and brush) and to get rid of uneaten clumps and other unpalatable coarse growth left after incomplete grazing. Pastures that are grazed continuously may be clipped at, or just preceding, the usual haymaking time; rotated pastures may be clipped at the close of the grazing period.

FERTILIZING

Like animals, for best results grasses and legumes must be fed properly throughout a lifetime. It is not sufficient that they be fertilized (and limed if necessary) at or prior to seeding time. In addition, in most areas it is desirable and profitable to topdress pastures with fertilizer annually, and, at less-frequent intervals, with lime (lime to maintain a pH of about 6.5). Such treatments should be based on soil tests, and are usually applied in the spring or fall.

Properly used, inorganic fertilizers will make for more sound horses. Of course, improper fertilization of pasture or hayland can result in an imbalance of the mineral content of the forage, which, in turn, will affect the animal. But when soil samples are properly taken and analyzed, then used as a guide for fertilizer application, the mineral content of the forage will be improved.

Remember that it's the total mineral intake of the horse that counts. This calls for (1) soil testing, with the fertilizer application based thereon, (2) forage testing, and (3) ration testing, with the mineral supplement balancing out the needs of the horse.

SCATTERING DROPPINGS

The droppings should be scattered three or four times each year and at the end of each grazing season in order to prevent animals from leaving ungrazed clumps and to fertilize a larger area. This can best be done by the use of a brush harrow or chain-type tine harrow.

Figure 7.4 Chain-type tine harrow used in horse pasture renovation.

GRAZING BY MORE THAN ONE CLASS OF ANIMALS

Grazing by two or more classes of animals makes for more uniform pasture utilization and fewer weeds and parasites, provided the area is not overstocked. Different kinds of livestock have different habits of grazing; they show preference for different plants and graze to different heights. Also, horse parasites die in cattle. For these reasons, horses and cattle are commonly grazed on the same pastures in the great horse-breeding centers of the world.

IRRIGATING WHERE PRACTICAL AND FEASIBLE

Where irrigation is practical and feasible, it alleviates the necessity of depending on the weather.

SUPPLEMENTING TO PROVIDE NEEDED NUTRIENTS

Although the horse ration should be as economical as possible, condition and results in show, sale, and use are the primary objectives, even at somewhat added expense. Generally, this calls for supplemented feeding on pasture — for providing added energy, protein, minerals, and vitamins.

EXTENDING THE GRAZING SEASON

In the South and in Hawaii, year-round grazing is a reality on many a successful horse establishment. By careful planning and by selecting the proper combination of crops, other areas can approach this desired goal.

In addition to lengthening the grazing season through the selection of species, earlier spring pastures can be secured by avoiding grazing too late in the fall and by the application of a nitrogen fertilizer in the fall or early

Figure 7.5 Mares on a well-cared-for pasture. (Courtesy, *Western Horseman,* Colorado Springs, Colorado)

Table 7.2 Pointers on Caring for Horse Pastures and Recreational Areas

For	When	How to Do It	Comments
Pasture Maintenance	Spring and fall. Scatter droppings in spring and fall, plus 3 to 4 times during the grazing season.	Use a chain-type tine harrow to — 1. Tear out the old, dead material. 2. Stimulate growth through gentle cultivating action. 3. Prevent a sod-bound condition. 4. Increase moisture penetration. 5. Scatter animal droppings to — a. Help control parasites b. Fertilize a larger area. c. Prevent animals from leaving ungrazed clumps.	Altogether too many horse pastures are merely gymnasiums or exercising grounds. This need not be so. Through improved pasture maintenance, horsemen can — 1. Produce higher yields of nutritious forage. 2. Extend the grazing season from early in the spring to late in the fall. 3. Provide a fairly uniform supply of feed throughout the entire season.
Pasture renovation	Spring or fall.	Use a chain-type tine harrow to work the fertilizer and seed into the soil, and yet destroy a minimum of the existing sod.	Run-down pastures can be brought back into production without plowing and reseeding.
Preparing new pasture seedbed	Spring or fall.	Use a chain-type tine harrow to — 1. Level. 2. Smooth down. 3. Pack.	When properly prepared, a seedbed should be so firm that you barely leave a footprint when you walk across it. The firmer the better from the standpoint of moisture conservation and small seeds.
Racetracks; show-rings	Whenever the track or ring becomes bedded. Just before the race or show; and between races or show events.	Set a chain-type tine harrow for maximum or light penetration, depending on the condition of the track or ring. Use a chain-type tine harrow as a drag mat to smooth and fill holes.	Good racetracks and show-rings must be firm, yet resilient. Because it's flexible, this harrow can be pulled at good speed, as is necessary between races or show events, and yet do an excellent job of smoothing and filling holes.
Bridle paths; farm lanes; dirt roads	Whenever they become rough or uneven.	Use maximum penetration of chain-type tine harrow to put in shape; then turn over to level and fill up holes.	

spring. Nitrogen fertilizers will often stimulate the growth of grass so that it will be ready for grazing 10 days to 2 weeks earlier than unfertilized areas.

POINTERS ON HORSE PASTURES
AND RECREATIONAL AREAS

There is a paucity of information on the care of horse pastures and recreational areas. Few college courses even mention them, and precious little authoritative literature has been published on the subject.

The accompanying table tells how successful operators maintain, renovate, and seed horse pastures, and how they care for racetracks, show rings, bridle paths, and other like areas. These areas can no longer be taken for granted. They're big and important — and they'll get bigger. Hence, they merit the combined best recommendations of scientists and practical operators.

8. Management

Horse management practices vary between areas and individual horsemen. In general, however, the principles of good management are the same everywhere, and they apply whether one horse or many horses are involved.

STABLE MANAGEMENT

The following stable management practices are recommended:

1. Remove the top layer of clay floors yearly; replace with fresh clay, then level and tamp. Keep the stable floor higher than the surrounding area so the floor will stay dry.

2. Keep stalls well lighted.

3. Use properly constructed hayracks to lessen waste and contamination of hay. Do not have hayracks in maternity stalls.

4. Scrub concentrate containers as often as necessary and always after feeding a wet mash.

Figure 8.1 The eye of the caretaker watches over his horse, for they are prone to get hurt. Bandages or boots (such as these shipping boots with Velcro closing) will usually prevent a bumped shin or a cut ankle, or protect an old injury — especially when transporting a horse.

Figure 8.2 A box stall. Good horses merit good stalls and good stable management.

5. Remove excrement and wet or soiled material from the bedding daily, and provide fresh bedding.

6. Practice strict stable sanitation to prevent fecal contamination of feed and water.

7. Lead foals when taking them from the stall to the paddock and back as a way to further their training.

8. Restrict the ration when horses are idle, and provide either a wet bran mash the evening before an idle day or turn idle horses to pasture.

9. Provide proper ventilation at all times by means of open doors, windows that open inwardly from the top, or stall partitions slatted at the top.

10. Keep stables in repair at all times to lessen injury hazards.

BEDDING, KIND AND AMOUNT

The term "bedding" refers to materials used to make a bed for animals. The horseman should select bedding material according to availability and price, absorptive capacity, and potential value as a fertilizer. Bedding should not be dusty, too coarse, or too easily kicked aside. Cereal grain straw or wood shavings generally make the best bedding materials for horses.

A soft, comfortable bed will insure proper rest. Also, horses are much easier to groom if their bedding is kept clean. Table 8.1 shows that bedding materials differ considerably in their relative capacities to absorb liquid. Other facts of importance, relative to certain bedding materials and bedding uses, are:

1. *Wood products* [*sawdust, shavings, tree bark, chips, etc.*] — The suspicion that wood products will hurt the land is rather widespread but unfounded. It is true that shavings and sawdust decompose slowly, but this process can be expedited by the addition of nitrogen fertilizers. Also, when plowed under, they increase soil acidity, but the change is both small and temporary.

Softwood (on a weight basis) is about twice as absorptive as hardwood, and green wood has only 50 percent the absorptive capacity of dried wood.

2. *Cut straw* — Cut straw will absorb more liquid than long straw; cut oats or wheat straw will take up about 25 percent more water than long

TABLE 8.1 Water Absorption of Bedding Materials

Material	Lbs. of Water Absorbed per CWT of Air-Dry Bedding
Barley straw	210
Cocoa shells	270
Corn stover (shredded)	250
Corncobs (crushed or ground)	210
Cottonseed hulls	250
Flax straw	260
Hay (mature, chopped)	300
Leaves (broadleaf)	200
Pine needles	100
Oat hulls	200
Oat straw (long)	280
(chopped)	375
Peanut hulls	250
Peat moss	1000
Rye straw	210
Sand	25
Sawdust (top quality pine)	250
(run-of-the-mill hardwood)	150
Sugar cane bagasse	220
Tree bark (dry, fine)	250
(from tanneries)	400
Vermiculite[1]	350
Wheat straw (long)	220
(chopped)	295
Wood chips (top quality pine)	300
(run-of-the-mill hardwood)	150
Wood shavings (top quality pine)	300
(run-of-the-mill hardwood)	150

[1]This is a mica-like mineral mined chiefly in South Carolina and Montana.

straw from comparable material. But there are disadvantages to chopping: chopped straws may be dusty.

From the standpoint of the value of plant food nutrients per ton of air-dry material, peat moss is the most valuable bedding and wood products the least valuable.

The minimum desirable amount of bedding to use is the amount necessary to absorb completely the liquids in manure. For 24-hour confinement, the minimum daily bedding requirements of horses, based on uncut wheat or oat straw, is 10 to 15 pounds. With other bedding materials, these quantities will vary according to their respective absorptive capacities (see Table 8.1). Also, more than minimum quantities of bedding may be desirable where cleanliness and comfort of the horse are important.

In most areas, bedding materials are becoming scarcer and higher in price, primarily because (1) geneticists are breeding plants with shorter straws and stalks, (2) there are more competitive and numerous uses for some of the materials, and (3) the current trend toward more confinement rearing of livestock requires more bedding.

Horsemen may reduce bedding needs and costs as follows:

■ *Chop bedding* — Chopped straw, waste hay, fodder, or cobs will go further and do a better job of keeping horses dry than long materials.

■ *Ventilate quarters properly* — Proper ventilation lowers the humidity and keeps the bedding dry.

■ *Provide exercise area* — Where possible and practical, provide for exercise in well-drained, dry pastures or corrals, without confining horses to stalls more than necessary.

HORSE MANURE

The term manure refers to a mixture of animal excrements (consisting of undigested feeds plus certain body wastes) and bedding.

The rise in light horse numbers, along with the shift of much of the horse population from the nation's farms and ranches to stables and small enclosures in suburban areas, has made for manure disposal problems.

From the standpoint of soils and crops, barnyard manure contains the following valuable ingredients.

■ *Organic matter* — It supplies valuable organic matter which cannot be secured in chemical fertilizers. Organic matter — which constitutes three to six percent, by weight, of most soils — improves soil tilth, increases water-holding capacity, lessens water and wind erosion, improves aeration, and has a beneficial effect on soil microorganisms and plants. It is the "lifeblood" of the land.

■ *Plant food* — It supplies plant food or fertility — especially nitrogen, phosphorus, and potassium. In addition to these three nutrients, manure contains calcium, and trace elements such as boron, manganese, copper, and zinc. A ton of well-preserved horse manure, free of bedding, contains plant food nutrients equal to about 100 pounds of 13-2-12 fertilizer (see Table 8.2). Thus, spreading manure at the rate of 8 tons per acre supplies the same amounts of nutrients as 800 pounds of a 13-2-12 commercial fertilizer.

The quantity, composition, and value of horse manure produced vary according to weight of animal, kind and amount of feed, and kind and amount of bedding. The author's computations in Table 8.2 are on fresh manure (exclusive of bedding) basis and per 1000 pounds liveweight. As indicated, a 1000-pound horse will produce about 8 tons of manure, free of bedding, per year.

The data in Table 8.2 are based on animals confined to stalls the year around. Actually, the manure recovered and available to spread where desired is considerably less than indicated because (1) animals are kept on pasture and along roads and lanes much of the year, where the manure is dropped, and (2) losses in weight often run as high as 60 percent when manure is exposed to the weather for a considerable time.

Table 8.2 Quantity, Composition, and Value of Fresh Horse Manure (Free of Bedding) Excreted Per 1000 Pounds Liveweight

Tons Excreted/ Year/1000 lbs. Liveweight[1]	Excrement	Composition and Value of Manure on a Tonnage Basis[2]					
		Lbs./ Ton[3]	Water (%)	N (lbs)	P[4] (lbs)	K[4] (lbs)	Value Ton[5] ($)
8	Liquid........	400					
	Solid..........	1600					
	Total	2000	60	13.8	2.0	12.0	4.2

[1] *Manure is Worth Money—It Deserves Good Care,* University of Illinois Circ. 595, 1953, p. 4.

[2] Last 5 columns on the right from *Farm Manures,* University of Kentucky Circ. 593, 1964, p. 5, Table 2.

[3] From Reference Material for 1951 Saddle and Sirloin Essay Contest, p. 43, compiled by M. E. Ensminger, data from *Fertilizers and Crop Production,* by Van Slyke, published by Orange Judd Publishing Co.

[4] Phosphorus (P) can be converted to P_2O_5 by multiplying the figure given above by 2.29, and potassium (K) can be converted to K_2O by multiplying by 1.2.

[5] Calculated on the assumption that nitrogen (N) retails at 20 cents, phosphorus (P) at 24 cents, and potassium (K) at 8 cents per pound in commercial fertilizers.

About 75% of the nitrogen, 80% of the phosphorus, and 85% of the potassium contained in horse feeds are returned as manure. In addition, about 40% of the organic matter in feeds is excreted as manure. As a rule of thumb, it is commonly estimated that 80% of the total nutrients in feeds are excreted by horses as manure.

The urine makes up 20% of the total weight of the excrement of horses. Yet the urine, or liquid manure, contains nearly 50% of the nitrogen, 60% of the phosphorus, and 60% of the potassium of average manure; roughly one-half of the total plant food of manure. Also, it is noteworthy that the nutrients in liquid manure are more readily available to plants than the nutrients in the solid excrement. These are the reasons why it is important to conserve the urine.

Horsemen sometimes fail to recognize the value of this barnyard "crop" because (1) it is produced whether or not it is wanted, and (2) it is available without cost.

Clay floors cannot be cleaned by flushing with water, and hard stable floors of concrete, asphalt, or wood require considerable bedding to provide softness and comfort. These conditions make it impractical to handle horse manure as a liquid. But horse manure is relatively dry and well adapted to handling as a solid.

In large horse establishments, the use of automatic gutter cleaners can eliminate much of the hand labor in handling manure as a solid. Automatic gutter cleaners may be (1) located in the alleyway or immediately outside the barn, (2) covered except for trapdoors, and (3) designed to carry the manure from the gutter directly into a spreader.

Some large establishments fork the manure from the stalls into the alley and then load it by means of a scraper or power loader. But this method is more messy and less convenient than an automatic gutter cleaner.

Both small and large horse establishments face the problem of what to do with horse manure after it is removed from the stable. Because the feces of horses are the primary source of infection by internal parasites, fresh horse manure should never be spread on pastures grazed by horses. The alternatives for the disposal of horse manure are as follows:

1. Spread fresh manure on fields that will be plowed and cropped if there is sufficient land and this is feasible.

2. Contract with a nearby vegetable grower to remove the manure.

3. Store the manure in a tightly constructed pit for at least two weeks before spreading it; this allows the spontaneously generated heat to destroy the parasites.

4. Compost the manure in an area where it will neither pollute a stream nor offend the neighbors; then spread it on the land.

Despite the recognized value of horse manure, it does possess the following objectionable features:

1. It may propagate insects.

2. It may spread diseases and parasites.

3. It may produce undesirable odors.

4. It may scatter weed seeds.

GROOMING

Proper grooming is necessary to keep a horse attractive and help maintain his good health and condition. Grooming cleans the hair, helps keep the skin functioning naturally, lessens skin diseases and parasites, and improves the condition and fitness of the muscles.

In the wild state, horses cleaned (groomed) themselves by rolling and taking dust baths. They do the same thing when turned into a corral.

Grooming should be rapid and thorough but not so severe that it makes the horse nervous or irritates his skin. Horses that are kept in stables or small corrals should be groomed thoroughly at least once a day. When horses are worked or exercised, they should be groomed both before and after the work or exercise.

Wet or sweating animals should be handled as follows:

1. Remove the tack as fast as possible, wipe it off, and put it away.

2. Remove excess water from the horse with a sweat scraper and then rub him briskly with a grooming or drying cloth to dry his coat partially.

3. Cover the horse with a blanket and walk him until he is cool.

4. Allow the horse to drink two or three swallows of water every few minutes while he is cooling and drying.

GROOMING EQUIPMENT

The following articles of grooming equipment are commonly used:

1. A hoof pick to clean the feet.

2. A rubber or metal curry comb to groom horses that have long thick coats and to loosen scurf and dirt in the hair.

Curry Comb

Body Brush

Dandy Brush

Mane & Tail Comb

Sweat Scraper

Grooming Cloth

Hoof Pick
(or hook)

Figure 8.3 Grooming equipment.

3. A body brush to brush the body. This is the principal tool used in grooming.

4. A dandy brush to remove light dirt from the skin and to brush the mane and tail. The dandy brush is made of stiff fiber, usually about 2 inches long.

5. A mane and tail comb to comb out a matted mane and tail.

6. A sweat scraper to remove excess water from wet or sweating animals.

7. A grooming cloth to wipe and polish the coat and for other miscellaneous cleaning. The grooming cloth can be made from old towels or blankets. It should be about 18 to 24 inches square.

HOW TO GROOM A HORSE

To assure that the horse is groomed thoroughly and that no body parts are missed, follow a definite order of grooming. This may vary according to individual preference, but the following order is most common.

The feet — Use a hoof pick to clean the feet. Work from the heel toward the toe. Thoroughly clean the depressions between the frog and the bars. Inspect the feet for thrush and loose shoes.

The body — To groom the body, hold the curry comb in the right hand and the brush in the left hand. Start on the left side of the horse and follow this order: neck, breast, withers, shoulders, foreleg down to the knee, back, side, belly, croup, and hindleg down to the hock.

At frequent intervals, clean the dust and hair from the brush with the curry comb. Knock the curry comb against some solid object to free it of dirt.

Curry gently and in small circular strokes, but brush vigorously. Do not use the metal curry comb below the knees or hocks, about the head, or over body prominences. Also, the metal curry comb should not be used on horses that have been clipped recently or that have a thin coat of hair.

Brush the hair in the direction it grows. Brush with care in the regions of the flanks, between the fore and hindlegs, at the point of elbows, and in the fetlocks.

After grooming the left side of the horse, transfer the brush to the right hand and the curry comb to the left hand and groom the right side.

The head, mane, and tail — Brush the head, and comb and brush the mane and tail. Use the body brush on the head. Brush the mane and tail downward, using either the body brush or the dandy brush.

Clean the tail by combing upward with a mane and tail comb, cleaning a few strands of hair at a time, or by picking and separating a few hairs at a time by hand. Wash the mane and tail occasionally with warm water and soap.

Miscellaneous cleaning — Use the grooming cloth to wipe about the ears, face, eyes, nostrils, lips, sheath, and dock; to give a final polish to the coat; and to dry or ruffle the coat before it is brushed.

Checking the grooming — Rub the fingertips against the natural lay of the hair. If the coat and skin are not clean, the fingers will get dirty and gray lines will show on the coat where the fingers passed. Inspect the cleanliness of the ears, face, eyes, nostrils, lips, sheath, and dock.

Cleaning the grooming equipment — Wash the grooming equipment with warm water and soap often enough to keep it clean. Disinfect it as a precaution against the spread of disease.

Clipping and shearing — Besides routine grooming, horses should be clipped as often as needed. Clip the long hairs from the head, the inside of the ears, on the jaw, and around the fetlocks. A wad of cotton may be put in the horse's ears to cut down on noise from the clippers and to prevent hair from falling in his ears.

HOW TO SHAMPOO A HORSE

Shampooing will make the horse look better and feel better. Horses like to be clean.

Figure 8.4 Following strenuous exercise, the horse should receive a welcome and refreshing bath. The caretaker sponges him all over with water, removing the dust and sweat. Next, he is brushed almost to dryness and covered with a blanket (a cooler). Then, he is led around and around, as his tension subsides and he relaxes. This is the cooling out process, designed to prevent stiff muscles. (Courtesy, *From Dawn to Destiny,* by Frank Jennings and Allen F. Brewer, Jr., published by The Thoroughbred Press, Lexington, Kentucky)

Shampooing (1) cleans the animal — it removes the dirt, stains, and sweat that cannot be removed by grooming; (2) makes for a fine hair coat with a good sheen; and (3) keeps the skin smooth and mellow.

Formerly, there was strong prejudice against washing horses; perhaps stemming from the use of old-fashioned, harsh detergents and strong soaps, followed by poor rinsing. But "baths" are good for horses, just as they are good for people; and horses like to be shampooed.

Shampoo the horse as frequently as necessary, as determined by soiling, work, and weather conditions. For example, always wash him following use on a sloppy, muddy ring, trail, or track — when he comes back covered with mud from head to tail; or after using him when it's hot and muggy, and he's all lathered up with sweat.

In preparation for shampooing, (1) groom the horse carefully, (2) secure the animal for washing either by having someone hold him by the shank or by tying, and (3) have shampoo concentrate, warm water, buckets, and sponges available.

Step 1 — Wet the animal thoroughly all over with water alone. For this purpose, fill one bucket with warm water (and refill it as necessary), then apply the water to the horse by means of a large sponge which may be dipped into the bucket as fast and frequently as desired.

To assure that the horse will be washed thoroughly and that no body parts will be missed, follow a definite order. This may differ somewhat according to individual preference, but the following procedure is most common: Start with the head, wetting between the ears and on the foretop (but do not get water in the ears; either hold them down or shut them off with the hand as the head is washed), over the face and cheeks, and all around the eyes, muzzle, and nostrils.

Next, proceed to the left side. While carrying the bucket in your left hand and holding the sponge in your right hand, with long strokes wet the neck, withers, shoulder, back, side, and croup. Return to the front, and with sponge in left hand, wash the chest. Return the sponge to the right hand and wash under the elbow and down the foreleg. Then, take the sponge in the left hand, set the bucket down as near as possible, and sponge the belly thoroughly. Hold onto the hind leg on the outside above the hock (this precaution will keep a restive horse from pawing, kicking, or stepping on your foot) while sponging the sheath (for stallions and geldings) and the inside of the hind leg down to the hoof.

Station yourself to the left of the horse near the hind leg, facing to the rear. Set the bucket nearby. Take the sponge in the right hand and wash behind the hind legs and in the groove between the thighs. Since many horses fuss about this operation, be careful to avoid getting kicked or stepped on.

Hold up the tail with the left hand and wash under it with the right hand. The tail is best washed by sponging with plenty of water at the tailhead, then putting the full length of the tail into the bucket of water, lifting the bucket to the bone and sloshing the tail around in the water. Set the bucket down, grip the tail near the top and draw the squeezed sponge down the full length of the hair; then give the tail a snap from side to side to swish out the water that is left.

After wetting the near (left) side and the rear end, get a bucket of fresh water. Then, while holding the bucket in your right hand and the sponge in your left hand, wet the off (right) side of the horse in the same order as described above, starting with the neck.

Step 2 — Shampoo the horse. Put in a bucket or other suitable container shampoo concentrate and water in the amounts and proportions recommended on the shampoo label, then stir it vigorously with your hand to form suds. Sponge the shampoo solution over the animal, following exactly the same procedure and order as outlined for wetting. Scrub against the hair with the sponge and your hands until a rich, thick lather covers all parts.

Step 3 — Rinse the horse with warm water, using either a bucket and sponge or a hose (if the horse is used to the latter), following the procedure and order given in Step 1. Rinse thoroughly.

Step 4 — Scrape with a "sweat scraper" held snugly against the hair to remove excess water, using long sweeping strokes and following the procedure and order given in Step 1, except do not scrape the head and legs.

Step 5 — Dry with a clean dry sponge or coarse towel, squeezing it out at intervals; following the procedure and order given in Step 1.

Step 6 — Blanket the horse and walk him until he is completely dry.

Step 7 — Apply a coat dressing if desired.

COAT DRESSING

"Trifles make perfection, but perfection is no trifle," is an old and well-known adage among horsemen. This philosophy prompts experienced caretakers to use a good coat dressing to achieve the all-important "bloom" or eye appeal in show, parade, and sale animals. Also, they use a coat dressing because they take pride in the everyday appearance of their charges, for how the horses look is indicative of the kind of caretakers back of them.

A coat dressing will not take the place of the natural conditioning of the horse, which can be achieved only through proper feeding, health, grooming, and shampooing.

Proper grooming should always precede the use of coat dressing. Coat dressing is best applied by means of a heavy cloth (preferably terry cloth). Moisten the rag with the dressing and rub the coat vigorously in the direction of the natural lay of the hair; then brush to bring out the bloom.

Coat dressing should always be used following washing, and for show, parade, or sale. It is best to apply a heavier application of coat dressing 12 to 24 hours ahead of the event, then go over the horse with a lightly dressed rag immediately before the event.

Figure 8.5 Electromatic Portable Walker, a labor-saving device which may be used for exercising and cooling horses. (Courtesy, Dr. T. D. Crews, Gonzales, Texas)

EXERCISE

Horses should exercise as much as possible on pasture. They will develop strong, sound feet and legs from outdoor exercise. If no pasture is available, exercise mature animals for an hour or two a day under saddle or in harness.

Horses with bad feet frequently cannot exercise on roads. Those with faulty tendons may not be able to exercise under saddle. Allow these animals to exercise in a large paddock, or by longeing on a 30- to 40-foot rope, or by leading.

CARE OF THE FEET

Nature didn't intend that the horse be used on hard surfaces and have a person on his back. Thus, when man domesticated the horse, he assumed certain responsibilities for his care in an unnatural environment — including trimming and shoeing his feet.

To the end that sound feet shall prevail, good caretakers (1) keep the feet clean, (2) prevent them from drying out, (3) trim them to retain proper shape and length, and (4) shoe them correctly, when shoes are needed. But they (or their horseshoer) never rasp off the periople, the shiny covering of the hoof, which is nature's means of keeping moisture within the foot.

The feet of horses that are shod, stabled, or worked should be cleaned each day. A hoof pick is used for this purpose. The caretaker should work from the heel toward the toe, making sure to clean out the depressions in the underside of the feet. While cleaning the feet, he should also inspect for loose shoes and thrush.

Thrush is a disease of the foot characterized by a pungent odor. It causes a deterioration of tissue in the cleft of the frog or in the junction between the frog and bars. This disease produces lameness and, if not treated, can be serious.

When it is realized that the horse has been transplanted from his natural roving environment and soft, mother-earth footing to be used in carrying and drawing loads over hard, dry-surfaced topography by day and then stabled on hard, dry floors at night, it is not surprising that foot troubles are commonplace. Nor are these troubles new. The Greeks alluded to them in the age-old axiom, "No foot, no horse."

Figure 8.6 Correct way to examine the front foot. Position the foot on your knee.

Figure 8.7 Correct way to pick up the hind foot. Push against the horse's hip with one hand and pull the leg up toward you with the other hand.

Figure 8.8 Correct way to examine the hind foot. Place the horse's foot on your outside knee (the knee away from the horse).

PARTS OF THE FOOT

In order to lessen foot troubles, and to permit intelligent shoeing, knowledge of the anatomy of the horse's foot is necessary (see Table 8.3 and Figure 8.9.)

Table 8.3 Parts of the Hoof

The Part	What It Is	Its Functions	Comments
The Four Major Parts:			
The bones	They are: Long pastern bone Short pastern bone Coffin bone Navicular bone	To provide framework of the foot and facilitate locomotion.	Long pastern bone lies entirely above the hoof. Only lower end of short pastern bone is within hoof.
The elastic structure	Consists of: Lateral cartilages Planter cushion	To overcome concussion or jar when the foot strikes the ground.	Normally, heel expands about $1/16$ in. on each side of foot.
The sensitive structure called the corium or pododerm	Consists of: Coronary band Perioplic ring Sensitive laminae Sensitive sole Sensitive frog	To furnish nutrition to corresponding part of hoof.	All 5 parts are highly sensitive and vascular.
The horny wall	The outer horny covering.	To enclose and protect the sensitive parts beneath.	
The Exterior of the Hoof:			
The horny wall	The basic shell and wearing surface of the foot.	To protect; there is no feeling in the wall of the foot until the area of the coronary band is reached.	The horny wall extends vertically from the edge of the hair around the front and sides of the foot; then turns in upon itself at the heel, forming the bar which extends forward toward the center.

(*Cont.*)

Table 8.3 Parts of the Hoof (*Cont.*)

The Part	What It Is	Its Functions	Comments
The Exterior of the Hoof (*cont.*)			
The perioplic ring	The seat where periople is produced.	To produce periople, the varnish-like substance that covers the outer surface of the wall and seals it from excess drying.	The wall of a normal foot consists of about $\frac{1}{4}$ water, by weight.
The white line	The juncture of the wall and horny sole. It is about $\frac{1}{8}$ in. wide.	The horseman's "red light," beyond (toward the inside of the foot) which nails should not go.	A nail past the white line may either enter the sensitive structure or produce pressure, with resulting lameness.
The horny frog	The V-shaped pad in the middle of the sole.	Compresses under weight, and transmits pressure to the elastic structures. Aids blood circulation, absorbs concussion, and prevents slippage.	Without this normal pressure, the hoof has a tendency to shrink and become dormant, with contracted feet and unsoundness resulting.
The commissures	The deep grooves on both sides of the frog.	To give elasticity.	Thrush is often found in the commissures.
The horny sole	The bottom of the foot. It is a thick (about $\frac{3}{8}$ in.) plate or horn which grows out from the fleshy sole.	Protects the foot from the bottom. Nature didn't intend that the horny sole should carry weight; for it is convex in shape so that most of the weight rests on the wall and frog area.	The sensitive sole is directly under the horny sole. Pressure on the horny sole area will usually produce lameness.
	The horny protrusions that lie along the frog between the commissures and the sole.	Help support the foot and keep it open at the heels.	
The perimeter sections: Inside and outside toe The quarters The heel			

Figure 8.9 Parts of the foot.

TRIMMING THE HOOF

The hoof grows downward and forward. A complex system of arteries, veins, and nerves inside the outer structure provides for its growth. The average rate of growth of the horny portions of the hoof (wall, sole, and frog) is about ⅜ inch per month.

Before trimming the hoof, a horseman should be able to recognize proper and faulty conformation. Figure 8.10 shows the proper posture of the hoof and incorrect postures caused by hoofs grown too long either in toe or heel. The slope is considered normal when the toe of the hoof and the pastern have the same direction. This angle should be kept in mind and changed only as a corrective measure. If it should become necessary to correct uneven wear of the hoof, correct gradually over a period of several trimmings.

Before the feet are trimmed, the horse should be inspected while standing squarely on a level, hard surface. Then he should be seen at both the walk and the trot.

The hoofs should be trimmed every month or six weeks whether the animal is shod or not. If shoes are left on too long, the hoofs grow out of

Figure 8.10 (a) Properly trimmed hoof with normal foot axis: O, coffin bone; X, short pastern bone; Y, long pastern bone; Z, cannon bone. (b) Toe too long, which breaks the foot axis backward. Horizontal dotted line shows how hoof should be trimmed to restore normal posture. (c) Heel too long, which breaks the foot axis forward. Horizontal dotted line shows how trimming will restore the correct posture.

proportion. This may throw the horse off balance and put extra stress on the tendons. Always keep the hoofs at proper length and correct posture. Trim the hoofs near the level of the sole; otherwise they will split off if the horse remains unshod. Trim the frog carefully and remove only ragged edges that allow filth to accumulate in the crevices. Trim the sole very sparingly, if at all, and never rasp the wall of the hoof.

CORRECTING FAULTS BY TRIMMING

Before trimming the feet or shoeing a horse, it is important to know what constitutes both proper and faulty conformation (see Chapter 3, Figures 3.14 and 3.15).

The following list describes the common faults of the foot and tells how to correct them by proper trimming.

Splayfoot — The front toes are turned out and the heels are turned in. Trim the outer half of the foot.

Pigeon-toe — The front toes are turned in and the heels are turned out, the opposite of splayfoot. Trim the inner half of the foot more heavily; leave the outer half relatively long.

Quarter crack — A vertical crack appears on the side of the hoof. Keep the hoof moist. Shorten the toe of the hoof and use a corrective shoe.

Cocked ankles — The horse stands with the fetlocks bent forward, most frequently the hind ones. Although raising the heels will give the horse immediate comfort, they should be lowered in order to correct the condition.

Contracted heels — The heels are contracted or shrunken. Lower the heels and allow the frog to carry more of the weight. This tends to spread the heels apart.

TREATMENT OF DRY HOOFS

In the wild state, horses roved over the prairies and moistened their hoofs frequently as they drank deep from the streams and lakes. But man changed all this. Today, the vast majority of horses spend much of their time in a dry stall or corral; stand dry-footed as they water from a bucket, fountain, or tank; are shod; and are exercised on a hard, dry surface — conditions which make for dry, brittle hoofs. With the domestication of the horse, therefore, man entered into an unwritten contract with him — to replace nature's way of keeping the hoofs moist.

When hoofs become dry and brittle, they sometimes split and cause lameness. The frogs lose their elasticity and are no longer effective shock absorbers. If the dryness is prolonged, the frogs shrink and the heels contract.

Dry hoofs usually can be prevented by keeping the ground wet around the watering tank, attaching wet burlap sacks around the hoofs, or applying a hoof dressing.

Hoof Dressing — A good hoof dressing will restore and maintain necessary flexibility and elasticity of the hoof. It will (1) penetrate the hoof structure readily, (2) allow the hoof to "breathe," (3) regulate the absorption and evaporation of moisture, and (4) accentuate the natural luster of the hoof; without leaving a sticky residue or sealing off the hoof wall. When applied daily, a hoof dressing will provide added moisture which will penetrate the hoof and prevent evaporation of the moisture that is already within the hoof, thereby imparting suppleness (elasticity).

When it comes to preventing dry hoofs, "an ounce of prevention is worth a pound of cure" — then some. Each day, the feet of shod horses that are confined to a stable (or corral) should be cleaned thoroughly, then treated with hoof dressing. By means of a brush or cloth, apply the hoof dressing to the coronet, the wall, and the bottom surface (including the frog), of freshly cleaned feet. Because most of the moisture within the hoof rises through the sole (like sap rises in a tree), be sure to apply plenty of hoof dressing to the bottom area.

The telltale symptoms of too dry feet are: hardness and drying of the horny frog, contracted heels, corns, brittle hoofs, and sometimes cracks and lameness. When any one of these conditions prevails, good nursing and first-aid treatment are essential. The first step is to correct any errors in shoeing and trimming, and the second is to restore and maintain the normal moisture content of the horn. Treating the wall and bottom of the feet daily with hoof dressing will accomplish the latter.

Hoof dressing is not designed to take the place of proper trimming and shoeing by an experienced farrier; rather, it should go hand in hand with them.

Use of Gelatin — Although it is true that the major protein in the hoofs of horses is gelatin, the author is not aware of any experimental evidence that the feeding of gelatin as such will improve the structure, toughness, and moisture of the hoof.

Hoof tissue is synthesized in the body primarily from the amino acids contained in the bloodstream, and these can be derived from any good source of protein for horses, such as linseed meal and soybean meal. Of course, a deficiency of protein in the horse's ration would tend to produce poor hoofs, but this protein can be furnished from sources other than gelatin and the same results obtained.

From the standpoint of other tissues in the body, gelatin is a rather incomplete protein, notably deficient in the amino acids lysine and tryptophan. From an overall metabolism standpoint, therefore, gelatin would appear to be a poorer source of protein than the oilseed proteins — linseed, soybean, cottonseed, and peanut meal.

For the above reasons, before buying and feeding gelatin instead of one of the oilseed proteins, the horseman is admonished to see research data, conducted by a reputable independent research laboratory, in support of the "gelatin theory."

SHOEING

Horseshoeing is a time-honored profession. In the Golden Age of the horse, which extended from the Gay Nineties to the mechanization of American agriculture, every schoolboy knew and respected the village blacksmith who plied his trade "under the spreading chestnut tree."

Horses should be shod when they are used on hard surfaces for any length of time. Also, shoes may be used to change gaits and action; correct faulty hoof structure or growth; protect the hoof from such conditions as corns, contractions, or cracks; and aid in gripping the track. Shoes should be made to fit the foot and not the foot to fit the shoes. Reshoe or reset at four- to six-week intervals.

A good horseman should be knowledgeable relative to (1) anatomy and nomenclature of the foot, (2) what constitutes proper stance and motions, and how to correct some faults through trimming, (3) kinds of shoes, (4) the basic horseshoeing tools and how to use them, (5) how to recognize good and faulty shoeing, and (6) treatment of dry hoofs.

HORSESHOES

A number of factors should be considered when selecting the shoes for a given horse; among them —

1. *The proper size* — The shoe should fit the foot, rather than any attempt made to trim the hoof to fit the shoe.

Shoes come in sizes. The old and the new sizes, side by each, follow:

The Old Standard Shoe (size)	The New Multi-Product Shoe (size)
00	3
0	4
1	5
Half Size	6
2	7
Half Size	8
3	9

2. *Front vs hind shoes* — Front shoes are more nearly circular and wider at the heels than hind shoes. Thus, when buying shoes, it is important to specify front or hind shoes, because they are different.

3. *The individual horse* — His weight, the shape and texture of his hoof, and the set of his legs.

4. *The use to which the horse is put, and the kind of ground* — A plain shoe or a rim shoe is satisfactory for most horses used for pleasure, cutting, roping, barrel racing, polo, and jumping; whereas racing plates, to aid in gripping the track, are needed on running horses. Also, there are many corrective shoes, a few of which are listed in the accompanying table (see Table 8.4).

Shoes may either be handmade or ready-made (factory-made). The latter are becoming increasingly popular because they (1) require a minimum of work, and (2) are ideal for the do-it-yourselfer. Both steel and aluminum shoes are available.

Some common kinds of shoes are shown in Figures 8.11 through 8.15, and corrective shoes are described in Table 8.4.

Table 8.4 Some Corrective Shoes and Their Use

Kinds of Corrective Shoes	Purpose or Use
The bar shoe	To apply pressure to the frog of the foot, or to relieve pressure on any part of it.
The rocker toe shoe	For use on horses that stumble, forge, or have ringbone or sidebone.
The squared toe shoe with trailer	For cow-hocked horses.
The lateral extension toed shoe	For horses that either toe out or toe in.

Figure 8.11 Ready-made shoes, recommended for use on most riding and driving horses.

Figure 8.12 Rim shoes, recommended for horses used for riding, cutting, roping, barrel racing, polo, and jumping.

Figure 8.13 Hot shoes, recommended for use by professional farriers and experienced horsemen who ply the trade.

Figure 8.14 Training plates, recommended for the purpose implied by the name — training plates.

Figure 8.15 Racing plates, recommended for racehorses. They're lightweight, with a toe grab that is easily shaped.

HORSESHOEING TOOLS AND HOW TO USE THEM

Horses are shod to protect the foot from breaking and wearing away faster than the growth of the horn. When properly done, shoes should interfere as little as possible with the physiological functions of the different structures of the foot or with the gaits of the horse.

Just as do-it-yourself wood workers, mechanics, and whatnot, usually have a shop and some tools, so the horseman should have certain basic horseshoeing tools, and know how to use them. Table 8.5 may be used as a guide in selecting tools.

Table 8.5 Horseshoeing Tools and Their Use

Tools	Use
Figure 8.16 Anvil.	As a block to shape shoes, and as the farrier's work bench.
Figure 8.17 Forge.	Used to heat steel or shoes in preparation for shaping them for the horse's being shod.
Figure 8.18 Vise.	To finish shoes, and to hold metal.
Figure 8.19 Hoof knife.	To remove dirt and trim excess frog and sole from the foot. The hook on the end is used to trim the frog and clean the crevice between the bar and frog.
Figure 8.20 Nippers or parers.	There is hardly any limit to the sizes and descriptions of these items: some are one-sided, others are two-sided. But all of them are used to trim the wall of the hoof and other parts that are too hard for the knife.
Figure 8.21 Hoof level.	This device is used to determine the angle of the hoof relative to the ground surface.

(*Cont.*)

Table 8.5 Horseshoeing Tools and Their Use (*Cont.*)

Tools	Use
Figure 8.22 Clinch cutter.	Used to cut clinches prior to pulling shoes.
Figure 8.23 Rasp.	Used to level the foot after trimming; one side is coarse, and the other side fine.
Figure 8.24 Driving hammer.	Used to drive nails into hoof.
Figure 8.25 Hardy.	As a wedge in the anvil hole, in cutting steel of the desired length, and in cutting off shoes.
Figure 8.26 Hammers.	Various kinds of hammers may be used to shape shoes.

(Cont.)

HOW TO RECOGNIZE GOOD AND FAULTY SHOEING

It is not necessary that horse owners and managers be expert farriers. But they should know how to recognize good and faulty shoeing.

The following checklist may be used as a means through which to evaluate a shoeing job, whether plied by yourself or a professional farrier:

Yes   No

1. *As viewed from the front —*

☐ ☐ Are the front feet the same size, the toes the same length, and the heels the same height?

☐ ☐ Is the foot in balance in relation to the leg?

☐ ☐ Is the foot directly under the leg; is the axis of the foot in prolongation to the axis of the upper leg bones; and is the weight of the body equally distributed over the foot structures?

Table 8.5 Horseshoeing Tools and Their Use (*Cont.*)

Tools	Use
Figure 8.27 Tongs.	Used to hold hot metal.
Figure 8.28 Nails.	Assorted sizes of nails are available for different types of horseshoes. The old and the new nail sizes, side by each, follow:
Figure 8.29 Apron.	Protects the horseshoer from sparks, from cuts that might otherwise be inflicted by slips of the knife or rasp, and from possible nail injury by nervous horses.

The Old Standard Nail (size)	The New Multi-Product Nail (size)
$3\frac{1}{2}$	1
4	2
$4\frac{1}{2}$	3
5	4
Half Size	5
6	6

Yes No

2. *As viewed from the side —*

☐ ☐ Does the axis of the foot coincide with the axis of the pastern?

☐ ☐ Does the slope of the wall from the coronet to the lower border parallel the slope of the pastern?

☐ ☐ Has the lower outer border of the wall been rasped?

☐ ☐ Does the conformation of the foot and the type of shoe used warrant the amount of rasping done?

3. *As the height and strength of nailing are inspected closely —*

☐ ☐ Do the nails come out of the wall at the proper height and in sound horn?

(Cont.)

Yes   No

☐   ☐ Are the nails driven to a greater height in the wall than necessary?

☐   ☐ Is the size of the nail used best suited for the size and condition of the foot and the weight of the shoe?

☐   ☐ Are the clinches of sufficient thickness where the nail comes out of the wall to ensure strength?

☐   ☐ Are the clinches smooth and not projecting above the surface of the wall?

4. *As the outline and size of the shoe are scrutinized —*

☐   ☐ Is the toe of the shoe fitted with sufficient fullness to give lateral support to the foot at the moment of breaking over and leaving the ground?

☐   ☐ Are the branches of the shoe from the bend of the quarter to the heel fitted fuller than the outline of the wall to provide for expansion of the foot and normal growth of horn between shoeing periods?

☐   ☐ Are the heels of the shoe of sufficient length and width to cover the buttresses?

☐   ☐ Are the heels finished without sharp edges?

☐   ☐ Does the shoe rest evenly on the bearing surface of the hoof, covering the lower border of the wall, white line, and buttresses?

☐   ☐ Is the shoe concaved so that it does not rest upon the horny sole?

☐   ☐ Are the nail heads properly seated?

☐   ☐ Is the shoe the correct size for the foot?

☐   ☐ Will the weight of the shoe provide reasonable wear and protection to the foot?

☐   ☐ Have the ragged particles of the horny frog been removed?

MARKING OR IDENTIFYING HORSES

Until the 16th Century (and even later in some parts of England), the ears of horses were cut in various ways as a means of identification. For example, a "bitted" ear was bitten (a piece was cut out) from the inner edge, and a cropped ear was cut straight across halfway down the ear. Eventually, cropped ears became fashionable, much as they are with certain breeds of dogs today, with the result that the practice persisted into the 18th Century. This explains why early paintings of horses frequently showed the animals with tiny ears, scarcely 2 inches long.

In racehorses, an infallible means of identification is necessary to prevent a "ringer" — the name once given to a horse that was falsely identified, with the idea of entering him in a race with slower horses where he was almost certain to win. In the early 1920s, the most common

Figure 8.30 A drawing showing the lip tattoo under the upper lip of a horse. The prefix letter denotes the age of the horse, and the numbers denote the Jockey Club registry number.

camouflage for a ringer was a coat of paint; hence, the terms "dark horse" and "horse of another color." Formerly, the ringer's nemesis was rain; today, it is the lip tattoo system or the photographs of his chestnuts. Through these the public is guaranteed the identity of each and every horse running in major races. The lip tattoo consists of branding, with forgery-proof dye, the registry number under the upper lip of the horse, with a prefix number added to denote age. The process is both simple and painless.

Pinkertons, and others, have "fingerprinted" the horse's chestnuts or night-eyes — the horny growth on the inside of each of the four legs. Studies have revealed that the chestnuts of no two horses are alike, and that, from the yearling stage on, these protrusions retain their distinctive sizes and shapes. The chestnuts are photographed, and then classified according to size and distinctive pattern.

On the western range, hide branding is primarily a method of establishing ownership. Also, it is a powerful deterrent to rustling (stealing).

In purebred horses, identification is necessary as a means of ascertaining ancestry or pedigree. Among the marks used for identifying registered horses are: (1) the lip tattoo, (2) hot iron brands, and (3) cold brands.

Until recently, the hot iron was the preferred method of branding. In this method, the irons are heated to a temperature that will burn sufficiently deep to make a scab peel, but which will not leave deep scar tissue.

Today, a new method of cold branding (freeze marking), developed by Dr. R. Keith Farrell, Washington State University, is becoming popular. The Arabian Horse Registry has adopted this method for permanent identification, using a series of right angles to replace Arabic numerals. This system is illustrated in Figure 8.31.

Figure 8.31 The series of right angles developed by Dr. R. Keith Farrell to replace the present Arabic numerals. The number that each angle represents is written inside the angle. This is a freeze brand as it would actually appear under the mane of a horse. The encircled numbers do not appear in the brand; they are used in this caption merely to enhance readability. The first symbol, the capital A, denotes that the horse is a purebred Arabian. The stacked symbols in the second position indicate that the horse was born in 1957. The remaining symbols are the horse's registration number: 031987.

Figure 8.32 Cold- (freeze-) branded horses. Note numbers on their right shoulders. (Courtesy, Louisiana State University)

Freeze marking is a permanent, painless, unalterable means of identification. On colored horses, it alters the pigment-producing cells so as to leave a mark of white hair. On a grey horse, a depilated, hairless mark is left in the area of contact.

The Arabian Horse Registry has designated the side of the neck under the mane as the official site of application. The mark is applied approximately 2 inches below the eruption of the mane and about midway between the poll and withers. An area approximately 2″ x 7″ is clipped close to the skin, then washed with alcohol. In the meantime, the marking iron is submerged in a bath of dry ice and alcohol until it reaches a temperature of about −80° C. The iron is then removed from the bath, dried, and applied to the clipped area of the neck. The contact time on the horse is dependent upon the color of the animal.

TRANSPORTING HORSES

Horses are transported via trailer, van, truck, rail, boat, and plane. Regardless of the method, the objectives are: to move them safely, with the maximum of comfort, and as economically as possible. To this end, selection of the equipment is the first requisite. But equipment alone, no matter how good, will not suffice.

The trip must be preceded by proper preparation, including conditioning of horses; and horses must receive proper care, including smooth driving en route.

Most horses are transported in trailers which have the distinct advantage of door-to-door transportation.

The requisites of good transportation are:

■ *Provide good footing* — The floor of the vehicle should be covered with heavy coco matting made for the purpose, sand covered with straw or other suitable bedding material, or rubber mats. Clean the floor covering at frequent intervals while in transit to avoid ammonia and heat.

■ *Drive carefully* — Drive at a moderate, constant speed as distinguished from fast or jerky driving, which causes added stress and tiring. If weather conditions make the roads unsafe, the vehicle should be stopped.

■ *Make nurse stops* — Nurse stops should be made at about three-hour intervals when mares and foals are transported together.

■ *Provide proper ventilation* — Provide plenty of fresh air without drafts.

■ *Teach horses to load early in life* — When horses will be transported later in life, they should be accustomed to transportation as youngsters before they get too big and strong. This can be done by moving them from one part of the farm to another.

Figure 8.33 Car and trailer. Today, horses are hauled to horse shows, rodeos, trail rides, and new homes all over the country. (Courtesy, *Western Horseman,* Colorado Springs, Colorado)

■ *Provide health certificate and statement of ownership* — A health certificate signed by a licensed veterinarian is required for most interstate shipments. Foreign shipments must be accompanied by a health certificate that has been approved by a government veterinarian. This takes several days. Branded horses must be accompanied by a brand certificate, and all horses should be accompanied by a statement of ownership.

■ *Schedule properly* — Schedule the transportation so that animals will arrive on time. Show, sale, and race animals should arrive a few days early.

■ *Have the horses relaxed* — Horses ship best if they are relaxed and not overtired before they are moved.

■ *Clean and disinfect public conveyance* — Before using any type of public conveyance, thoroughly clean and disinfect it. Steam is excellent for this purpose. Remove nails or other hazards that might cause injury.

■ *Have a competent caretaker accompany horses* — Valuable horses should not be shipped in the care of an inexperienced person.

■ *Use shanks except on stallions* — When animals are tied, use a $\frac{5}{8}$-inch cotton rope shank that is 5 feet long and has a big swivel snap at the end. Chain shanks are too noisy. Always tie the shank with a knot that can easily and quickly be released in case of an emergency.

■ *Feed lightly* — Allow horses only a half feed of grain before they are loaded for shipment and at the first feed after they reach their destination. In transit, horses should be given all the good quality hay they will eat, preferably alfalfa, to keep the bowels open, but no concentrates should be fed. Commercial hay nets or homemade burlap containers may be used to hold the hay in transit, but they should not be placed too high.

■ *Water liberally* — When transporting horses, give them all the fresh, clean water they will drink at frequent intervals unless the weather is extremely hot and there is danger of gorging. A tiny bit of molasses may be added to each pail of water, beginning about a week before the horses are shipped, and the addition of molasses to the water may be continued in transit. This prevents any taste change in the water.

■ *Pad the stalls* — Many experienced shippers favor padding the inside of the vehicle to lessen the likelihood of injury, especially when a valuable animal is shipped. Coco matting or a sack of straw properly placed may save the horse's hocks from injury.

■ *Take along tools and supplies* — The following tools and supplies should be taken along in a suitable box: pinch bar, hammer, hatchet, saw, nails, pliers, flashlight, extra halters and shanks, twitch, canvas slapper or short piece of hose, pair of gloves, fork and broom, fire extinguisher, and medicine for colic and shipping fever provided by a veterinarian.

■ *Check shoes, blankets, and bandages* — Whenever possible, ship horses barefoot. Never allow them to wear calked shoes during a long shipment. They may wear smooth shoes. In cool weather, horses may be blanketed if an attendant is present in case a horse gets entangled. The

Figure 8.34 Easy does it! This shows an easy way in which to load a "green" horse into a trailer.

legs of racehorses in training should be bandaged to keep the ankles from getting scuffed or the tendons bruised. Bandages are not necessary on breeding stock except for valuable stallions and young animals. When bandages are used, they should be reset often.

▪ *Be calm when loading and unloading* — In loading and unloading horses, always be patient and never show anger. Try kindness first; pat the horse and speak to him to reassure him. If this fails, it may be necessary to use one of the following techniques.

1. Sometimes the use of the twitch at the right time is desirable, especially if the horse is tossing his head about.

2. When a horse must be disciplined, a canvas slapper or a short rubber hose can be used effectively; these make noise without causing much hurt.

3. If a horse gets very excited and is about to break out, dash a bucket of water in his face; usually he will back off and calm down.

4. A nervous, excitable horse may be calmed by a tranquilizer, which should be administered by a veterinarian.

5. If a horse will not move or is kicking, grab his tail and push it over his back. In this position, he cannot kick but can be pushed along.

▪ *Control insects* — In season, flies and other insects molest animals in transit. When necessary, use a reliable insecticide to control insects. Follow directions on the container label.

STRAY HORSES ON HIGHWAYS

Although state, county, and/or township laws vary, and it is not possible to predict with accuracy what damages, if any, may be recovered in particular instances, the following general rules apply:

▪ If a horse owner is negligent in maintaining his fences and allows his horse(s) to get on the road, he can be held liable for damage resulting to persons using the highway.

■ If a horse owner has good fences that are well maintained, but has a horse(s) which he knows is in the habit of breaking out, he may be held liable for damages caused by such horse(s).

■ If a horse(s) gets onto the highway, despite the facts that there are both good fences and the horse(s) is not known habitually to get out, the owner may be held liable for any damage inflicted provided he knew that the horse(s) was out and made no reasonable effort to get him in.

■ If the horse owner is not negligent in any way, he may or may not be judged liable for the damage inflicted by his horse(s), depending on the state law and other circumstances.

■ If a horseman is driving a horse(s) along or across a highway he is not likely to suffer liability for any damage unless it can be proved that he was negligent. Stock-crossing signs usually increase the caution exercised by motorists, but do not excuse a horse owner from exercising due care.

■ In some states, laws provide that a horse owner may, under supervision of and with varying amounts of assistance from highway authorities, construct an underpass for his horse(s) and for general farm use.

BUSINESS ASPECTS

In addition to being able to handle money matters, most horsemen — big and little — need a working knowledge of one or more of the following business aspects: boarding agreement, syndicated horses, incentive basis for the help, and taxes.

BOARDING AGREEMENT

Today's tough zoning laws and antipollution campaigns are making it increasingly difficult to keep horses in towns and suburban areas. As a result, more and more horses are being stabled and cared for in boarding establishments out in the country, to which owners commute. This prompts the need for an agreement.

Boarding agreements should always be in writing, rather than verbal, "gentlemen's agreements." From a legal standpoint, a boarding agreement is binding to the parties whose signatures are affixed thereto. Thus, it is important that the agreement be carefully filled out, read, and fully understood before signing. A sample boarding agreement may be seen in Figure 8.35.

SYNDICATED HORSES

Reduced to simple terms, a syndicated horse is one that is owned by several people. Most commonly, it's a stallion, although an expensive yearling or broodmare is sometimes syndicated. Also, any number of people can form a syndicate. However, there is a tendency to use the term

BOARDING AGREEMENT

(To be executed in duplicate; one copy to be retained by each party.)

This agreement made and entered into by and between _____,
(owner of horse)
_____, hereinafter designated "Horse Owner," and
(address)

_____, _____,
(owner of stable)   (address)
hereinafter designated, "Stable Owner." This agreement covers the horse described as follows:

_____ _____ _____ _____
(Name)   (Sex)   (Age)   (Color)

Stable Owner agrees that—

1. He will keep the horse in a stall and/or paddock described as follows: _____

_____

_____

2. He will feed, water, and care for the horse in a good and husbandlike manner; feeding horse as follows:

Kind of Feed	Amount of Feed		
	Morning	Noon	Night
	(lbs)	(lbs)	(lbs)

3. He will perform the following additional services:

   a. Grooming (specify): _____

   b. Exercising (specify): _____

   c. Parasite treatments (specify): _____

   _____

   _____

   d. Others (list): _____

   _____

   _____

Horse Owner agrees that—

1. He will make all arrangements for the periodic shoeing of the horse, and assume the cost thereof. Any exception to this shoeing arrangement shall be given in the space that follows:

2. He will pay Stable Owner (a) for the foregoing facilities, feed, and services the sum of $_____ per month, payable on the _____ day of each month in advance; and (b) for drugs and medications, at cost, the first of each month following invoicing.

3. Stable Owner shall be entitled to a lien against the boarded horse for the value of services rendered, and shall be entitled to enforce said lien according to the appropriate laws of the state, *provided* (a) Stable Owner performs the services herein specified, and (b) Horse Owner fails to make a scheduled payment.

Horse Owner and Stable Owner mutually agree that—

1. In the event the horse shall require the services of a veterinarian, Stable Owner will immediately contact Horse Owner. In the event Horse Owner cannot be reached, Stable Owner is hereby authorized, as agent for Horse Owner, (a) to call Dr. _____, DVM; and, should he be unavailable, (b) to call any other licensed veterinarian of his choice. All fees charged by said veterinarian shall be the sole and exclusive responsibility of the Horse Owner, with no liability whatsoever on the part of Stable Owner for such fees.

2. This document constitutes the entire agreement between the parties and there are no other agreements between them except as noted below.

_____   _____
(Signature of Horse Owner)   (date)

_____   _____
(Signature of Stable Owner)   (date)

Figure 8.35 Boarding agreement.

"partnership" where two to four owners are involved, and to confine the word "syndicate" to a larger group of owners.

Each member of the syndicate owns a certain number of "shares," depending on how much he purchased or contributed. It's much like a stock market investor, who may own one or several shares in General Electric, IBM, or some other company. Sometimes one person may own as much as half-interest in a horse. Occasionally, half-shares are sold.

Generally speaking, the number of shares in a stallion is limited to the number of mares that may reasonably be bred to him in one season — usually 30 to 35 with Thoroughbred stallions.

Owners of stallions that have raced successfully usually have the opportunity to choose between: (1) continuing as sole owner of the horse, and standing him for service privately or publicly; or (2) syndicating him. In recent years, more and more owners of top stallions have elected to syndicate. The most common reasons given for so doing are:

1. The stallion owner does not have a breeding farm or an extensive band of broodmares.

2. The owner's belief that the stallion under consideration may not nick well with many of his mares, or perhaps because he's closely related to them.

3. The owner's need for immediate income. Moreover, the profit, according to a tax court ruling, is subject to the frequently advantageous capital-gains treatment on income tax. By contrast, if sole ownership is retained, considerable promotional and advertising expenses will be involved for approximately three years until his get make their debut on the tracks; and, in the meantime, practically no income can be expected until about a year from entering stud, at which time the usual "live foal" guarantee is met — a live foal condition is fulfilled, and stud fees that are collected are generally held in escrow, as protection if they should have to be returned.

4. It spreads the risk, should the stallion get injured or die, or prove unsuccessful as a sire.

The owner may arrange the syndication himself, usually with competent legal advice; or, if preferred, the syndication can be turned over to a professional manager, who will generally take a free share as his organization fee.

INCENTIVE BASIS FOR HELP

On horse-breeding establishments there is need for some system which will encourage caretakers to (1) get a high conception rate, (2) be good nursemaids to newborn foals, though it may mean the loss of sleep, and (3) develop and sell surplus animals advantageously.

From the standpoint of the owner of a horse-breeding establishment, production expenses remain practically unchanged regardless of the efficiency of the operation. Thus, the investment in land, buildings and

Table 8.6 A Proposed Incentive Basis for a Breeder Who Sells Yearlings

Yearling Crop Sold Based on 100 Mares Bred to Produce (No. of year- lings sold)	Price of Yearlings ($)	Here's How It Works
30	200	On this particular establishment, 100 mares are bred annually, and each year 15 top fillies are retained as herd replacements. Over and above this, the break-even point is 50 yearlings marketed annually. Thus, if 100 mares were bred in 1975, to break even there would have to be 65 yearlings in 1976, out of which 15 would be kept and 50 marketed.
35	300	
40	400	
45	500	
50 ←—break-even—→600		
55	700	
60	800	
65	900	
70	1000	
75	1100	Moreover, the historical records of this establishment show that $600/head is the break-even point, provided 50 yearlings are sold; or a total gross of $30,000.
80	1200	
		The sale of each yearling in excess of 50 head involves only $300 expense, primarily for added feed.

Thus, if 60 yearlings are marketed at an average of $1000, that's a gross of $60,000. The break-even point is $30,000 (50 yearlings @ $600) plus the added cost of $3000 to produce 10 more yearlings (10 × $300); or a total of $33,000. Hence, the net is $27,000. It is suggested that there be a 80:20 split on a net up to $27,000; a 70:30 split of a net from $27,000 to $40,000; and a 65:35 split of a net in excess of $40,000.

It is further recommended that division among employees be on a prorata of salary basis.

equipment, stallion and broodmares, feed, and labor differs very little with a change (up or down) in the percent foal crop; and income above the break-even point is largely net profit. Yet, it must be remembered that owners take all the risks; hence, they should benefit most from profits.

On a breeding establishment, the author recommends that profits beyond the break-even point (after deducting all expenses, including the salary of the owner) be split on a 80:20 basis. This means that every dollar made above a certain level is split, with the owner taking 80 cents and the employees getting 20 cents. Also, there is merit in an escalator arrangement; with the split changed to 70:30, for example, when a certain plateau of efficiency is reached. Moreover, that which goes to the employees should be divided on the basis of their respective contributions, all the way down the line; for example, 25% of it might go to the manager, 25% might be divided among the foremen, and 50% of it divided among the rest of the help; or that which goes to the employees may be divided on a prorata of salary basis.

Gross income in horse-breeding operations is determined primarily by (1) percent conception on mares bred, (2) percent foal crop, and (3) prices on horses sold. The first two factors can easily be determined. Usually, enough horses are sold to establish prices or values; otherwise, the going price can be used.

The incentive basis proposed in Table 8.6 for horse-breeding operations is simple, direct, and easily applied. As noted, it is based on the number and price of yearlings sold.

BREAK-EVEN POINTS

Whenever possible, the break-even point on a horse establishment — the dollars gross necessary in order to break even — should be arrived at from actual records accumulated by the specific horse establishment, preferably over a period of years. Perhaps, too, they should be moving averages, based on 5 to 10 years, with older years dropped out and more recent years added from time to time; thereby reflecting improvements in efficiency due primarily to changing technology, rather than to the efforts of the caretakers.

With a new horse operation, on which there are no historical records from which to arrive at break-even points, it is recommended that the figures of other similar operations be used at the outset. These can be revised as actual records on the specific enterprise become available. It is important, however, that the new operation start an incentive basis, even though the break-even points must be arbitrarily assumed at the time.

TAXES

The tax information that follows pertains specifically to horsemen, so that they may be aware of the implications involved, and so that they may take steps to avoid certain pitfalls. Also, horsemen are admonished to consult a competent tax advisor before embarking upon any sizable horse operation.

CASH VS ACCRUAL METHOD

There are two standard methods of reporting, the cash basis and the accrual basis. Most horsemen use the cash basis, in which income is reported when it is actually received and expenses are recorded when actually paid. It does not include the value of products sold or services performed for which payment was not actually available during the taxable year. In addition to being simple and easy, the cash basis has the advantage of allowing the horseman partially to control his income for tax purposes by timing year-end payment of expenses.

From a management standpoint, however, the accrual basis is preferred because it more nearly reflects the income of a particular period. Under it, income is accounted for when it is earned and expenses are recorded when incurred rather than when paid. Also, the accrual basis necessitates that complete annual inventories be kept, with taxes paid on increases of inventory, and deductions made for any decrease in inventory.

On large horse establishments, it is recommended that both record systems be used — the cash basis for tax purposes, and the accrual basis for management purposes. A competent accountant can set up such a system with the same set of records by adding a few memo accounts that are removed at the end of the year when closing the books for tax purposes.

HOBBY OR BUSINESS?

The first real hazard, and one which should be avoided like the plague unless it really applies, is that participation in the horse business — whether in breeding, racing, training, and/or showing — may be regarded by the Internal Revenue Service (IRS) as indulgence in a hobby or diversion rather than a true business venture, with the result that any losses accruing therefrom are disallowed in their entirety. This should cause no concern to those who derive their entire living from the horse business or to those successful horsemen who normally operate at a profit. Rather, it is the person of independent means, or one who is profitably engaged in another enterprise or other enterprises, who is likely to be challenged when he or she has an unbroken string of loss years accruing from breeding, racing, and/or showing operations. Also, IRS does not automatically take cognizance of the fact that breeding programs designed to develop a new breed of horses, or even to build up a herd, take many years. It is essential, therefore, that the horseman establish a profit-making motive and a reasonable chance of achieving this aim. Then, he must conduct his operations in a businesslike manner throughout, and refrain from anything that may cause his actions even to be suspicioned as pursuit of a hobby rather than the conducting of a business.

In breeding, racing, training and/or showing horses, a fine line often separates a hobby from a business. Moreover, a hobby sometimes turns out to be a profitable venture to the point that the taxpayer may turn it into a business.

It is important to the taxpayer that the facts and circumstances support the premise that he entered into the activity with the intent of making a profit. The regulations list different factors which are relevant, no one of which is conclusive or exclusive in making a determination. These factors are:

- History of income or losses.
- High ratio of expenses to receipts, or a declining loss ratio.
- Amount of occasional profits or losses, and their relation to the amount of investment and value of the assets used in the activity.
- Cause of the losses.
- Success of the taxpayer in carrying on other activities.
- Financial status of the taxpayer.

- Time and effort expended by taxpayer in the horse activity.
- Expertise of the taxpayer or his consultant.
- Manner in which the taxpayer carries on the activity.
- Reasonableness of the expectation of profit by the taxpayer.
- Expectation of appreciation of value of assets used.
- Elements involved of personal pleasure or recreation.
- Personal pleasure derived is not conclusive of hobby.

In addition to the items listed above, a review of decided cases produces the following additional important elements for consideration:

- Lack of any other occupation.
- Lack of recreational facilities and absence of social functions at the business location.
- Good, complete, accurate, and separate records of the business and finances.
- Membership and active participation in breed organizations.
- Advertising to develop a market for surplus horses.
- Preparation of cost studies and comparison with trade averages to implement changing methods for better financial results.
- Continuous budgets, and income and expense projections, to move toward lower losses and larger profits.
- Culling of undesirable animals.
- Boarding of horses if it will help generate more income.
- Racing or showing in order to earn purses and premiums and to advertise the business.
- Making additional capital investments and improvements if they may be expected to increase income.
- Finally, if you are satisfied that you cannot make a profit, quit.

It is emphasized that the matter of intent is paramount. Generally speaking, taxpayers who meet, to a reasonable degree, the above points can, if necessary, prove to the courts their "intent to show a profit from a business venture."

Proof of intent is especially difficult if (1) the taxpayer is wealthy and over a period of years has sustained heavy losses sufficient to put an average horseman out of business, or (2) there is some interest connected with the horse enterprise of greater importance in the taxpayer's scheme of life than making a profit. Indeed, these two points tend to indicate an expensive hobby, rather than a business.

Profit Two Years Out of a Consecutive Seven Years

Under the tax laws, an activity is presumed not to be a hobby if profits result in two out of seven consecutive years, unless the IRS proves otherwise. To take advantage of this provision, in principal loss years the horseman must file an election on forms provided by the IRS.

Bought Versus Raised Horses

To be eligible for capital gain treatment, purchased (or gift) horses, including race and show horses, must be held 24 months. (Cattle must be held 24 months, also. Swine and sheep need to be held only 12 months.)

Raised horses for cash method taxpayers have a "zero" tax basis. Hence, all proceeds on disposition of eligible animals are a gain to be treated as capital gain.

Capital Gain

Since capital gain is not taxed nearly so heavily as ordinary income, it behooves horsemen to report the maximum thereunder permitted by law. For an individual horseman with up to $50,000 long-term capital gain, the tax rate is 25%; for over $50,000 it is 35%. For corporations, capital gain tax is 30%.

Limitations on Losses

The basic rule that hobby or pleasure losses cannot be deducted from nonfarm income beyond the income generated from the horse business prevails, and the general rule that a person must enter into the horse business "to make a profit" before deductions for his expenses beyond income from the horse business was left intact by the 1976 Tax Reform Law.

Under the prior law, the amount that could be written off was without limitation until the losses exceeded $25,000, and the nonfarm income or nonhorse business income exceeded $50,000. This was referred to as the "farm loss recapture" rule or the "excess deductions account" (EDA). After 1975, no further additions to EDA were required or permitted, but the rules applied to existing accounts.

Under the 1976 Tax Reform Law, the $25,000 limitation was eliminated and the amount of loss that a horseman can deduct from nonhorse income is limited to the amount that he has "at risk." A taxpayer is generally considered "at risk" with respect to an activity to the extent of his cash and the adjusted basis of the property contributed to the activity, plus any amounts borrowed for use in the activity with respect to which the taxpayer has personal liability for payment from his personal assets. Further, his net fair market value of personal assets which secure nonrecourse borrowings is included in the definition of "at risk." "Nonrecourse" means the taxpayer has no personal liability for the payment of a debt.

These "at risk" provisions apply to losses attributable to amounts paid, incurred, depreciated, or amortized in taxable years after December 31, 1975.

In summary, the horseman will be limited to those dollars he has put out of his pocket, plus contracts or loans for monies or property put into the horse business that carries his personal liability or responsibility.

If the loss in any year is less than the amount "at risk," the full amount of the loss is deductible and the "at risk" amount is reduced by the loss deducted. The reduced "at risk" amount is then carried over to the next year to determine any limit deductions lost under that year.

If the loss is greater than the amount "at risk," the deductible loss is limited to the amount "at risk" at the end of the year. The amount "at risk" is reduced to "0." In this case, the nondeductible portion of the loss is carried over to the next year and is available for deduction then, if not prevented by application by the "at risk" rule.

If the risk amount has been reduced to "0," no further losses may be deducted until such time as the taxpayer places additional amounts of investment through borrowings or additional cash investment.

Horses of Different Sexes Cannot Be Exchanged "Tax Free"

Horses of different sexes are not considered "like kind" and cannot be exchanged on a tax-free basis. Neither do geldings qualify as "like kind" for exchange for stallions. However, mares for mares, and stallions for stallions are eligible for "tax-free" exchange.

Stud and Training Fees Deductible

Both stud fees and training fees are tax deductible in the year paid by a cash basis taxpayer.

Depreciation

A horseman can select the period of time over which he can depreciate his horse, from an ADR (asset depreciation ranges) range of 8 to 12 years.

Depreciation on horses bought (horses raised have no depreciation basis for horsemen on a cash basis) for breeding and racing purposes is subject to depreciation recapture as are all other similar business assets. Thus, gain realized on the sale of such horses is taxed at ordinary income rates to the extent of depreciation claimed or allowable on such animals after 1969; and the remainder of the gain, if any, is taxed as capital gain, provided the holding period of two years has been satisfied.

If the "useful" life guidelines issued by the Treasury are followed, the taxpayer will not be challenged. They are:

Buildings..25 years
Machinery and equipment..10 years
Breeding and work horses ....8–12 years

Definitions of "appraisal, salvage, and depreciation" as applied to horses follow.

- *Appraisal* refers to the act of establishing the worth of the horse.
- *Salvage* refers to the remaining value, if any, of an animal after it has served its intended purpose — for example, at the end of usefulness as a breeding animal, or at the end of a racing or showing career.
- *Depreciation* refers to the amortization or write-off of the cost of a horse over the period of its useful life.

In each of the above, the horseman, or the specialist to whom such matters are entrusted, should apply rates which he can justify.

On purchased animals, the price paid establishes value for depreciation purposes. Inherited or gift horses can also be depreciated, with their value established by a qualified appraiser or on the basis of current sales of similar animals. Raised horses cannot be depreciated, for the cost of raising them has been deducted as an annual expense.

Breeding animals have no appreciable salvage value at the end of their reproductive life. On the other hand, the salvage value of a racehorse that is retired to stud is a matter of opinion.

Depreciation figures on horses are difficult to come by, and they vary according to source, use, and breed. Unfortunately, no adequate scientific

Table 8.7 Horse Depreciation Guide[1]

Age When Acquired	Years of Useful Life Remaining		
	Racehorses	Broodmares	Stallions
1	6		
2	5		
3	4		
4	3	10	10
5	3	9	9
6	2	9	9
7	2	8	8
8	2	7	7
9		7	7
10		6	6
11		5	5
12		5	5
13		5	5
14		4	4
15		4	4
16		4	4
17		3	3
18		3	3
19		2	2
20		2	2
21		2	2

[1] *The Blood Horse,* Dec. 2, 1967, p. 3747, with the permission of Mr. John C. Owens and Mr. Rex. B. Potter, of the firm of Owens, Potter and Hisle, Lexington, Kentucky.

study of the actual average useful life of horses for racing, showing, and breeding purposes has been undertaken. Moreover, the Internal Revenue Service has not stipulated any depreciation rates other than suggesting that horses used for breeding or work purposes should have an 8- to 12-year life.

The accounting firm of Owens, Potter and Hisle, Lexington, Kentucky, which specializes in accounting for horse establishments, has developed Table 8.7 as a depreciation guide of the useful lives of race and breeding horses.

The author suggests that the depreciation schedule on show horses be the same as those given for racehorses in Table 8.7.

Horsemen have claimed and been allowed rates widely at variance with the figures given in Table 8.7. For example, some owners claim depreciation on yearlings from date of acquisition, whereas others date it from the time they are placed in training; but such practices might prove difficult to defend in a well-fought tax case. If the return is filed in a district where there are few horsemen, the examiner may fail to challenge the method simply because he is unfamiliar with the peculiarities of the industry. Inconsistent practices are likely to continue unless the horse industry itself takes initiative and accumulates factual studies, made by an independent agency, which horsemen can present. Without doubt, the results of such a research study would more than justify the cost.

Any one of the following three methods may be used in computing depreciation of horses: (1) the straight-line method, (2) the declining balance method, and (3) the sum of the years-digit method.

Before a horseman adopts any method of depreciation, competent tax assistance should be sought. Many factors must be considered.

IN THE EVENT OF A COURT CASE

In the event of a court case, it is usually advisable that the taxpayer appear in person and testify, rather than expect that his attorney and accountant handle the matter entirely. This is especially important from the standpoint of establishing intent, for no one knows the original intent better than the owner. Additionally, it is usually advisable that the testimony of recognized experts in the field be used to substantiate the fact that there was, or is, a reasonable expectation of making a profit. However, whether or not the taxpayer and/or experts testify in a particular case should be left to the decision of the lawyer, for nothing is worse for the taxpayer than not giving the lawyer free rein to develop the case.

WOMEN AND HORSES — WHY NOT?

Recently, the suffragettes crashed into the man's world of jockeys on U.S.-recognized Thoroughbred tracks. Kathy Kusner, of the U.S. Equestrian Team, was the first woman in America to receive her jockey's license.

Then, in rapid succession, Peggy Ann Early, Barbara Jo Rubin, Diane Crump, Tusdee Testa, and a host of others followed suit.

In some cases, the women were temporarily thwarted by male jockeys boycotting the race. But, as usual, the women won out; and the "sex barrier" has been broken.

Horse racing will never be the same!

All this ruckus about female jockeys raises a vitally important question — why not? Haven't women always been among the most ardent and successful contestants in horse shows throughout the land? Aren't there quite a few young women among the equestrian stars in the Olympics?

At the Exhibition of U.S.S.R. Economic Achievements, in Moscow, the author was much impressed with the person in charge of the horse exhibit — a woman of about forty-five years of age. Her well-conditioned charges — the growthiest Thoroughbred and Standardbred yearlings that the author has ever seen — gave ample evidence of her expertise. Why not?

At Newmarket, the most important racing center in England, if not in the world, where 2000 Thoroughbreds are in training the year around, women make up 15 percent of the help. The leading trainers told the author that the women are well accepted and do a fine job. They did add that some of the men accuse the women of spoiling their mounts, but that the women retort that they are merely more patient than men. Why not?

One renowned riding stable with which the author is acquainted has long used an all-woman crew in its operation. They do everything from mucking out stalls to feeding and caring for the mounts. Why not?

Indeed, the time has arrived — at long last — when the question should be not "why" women should work with horses, but rather, "why not?" If women have a love for and interest in horses, they have the first and most important requisite for success in this rapidly expanding field.

The author receives many letters from women asking about college training and job placement in horse work. Generally, these young ladies proudly tell of their love for horses, confide that their parents and friends have discouraged them every step of the way, and earnestly solicit help and advice. Here is the story that the author tells again and again.

A limited, but increasing, number of colleges offer special courses in horses and/or horsemanship. However, they are generally short on horses and facilities, for both teaching and research. Although this is disappointing, the important thing is to get a college education. From the standpoint of undergraduate courses, these young equine lovers are admonished to major in a department of special interest and take such required or elective horse courses as are available; to take the necessary supporting courses in the sciences and arts; to be good scholars; to become proficient in business skills; and to obtain rather broad training. Then if they are real top students, they are urged to give serious consideration to completing a Ph.D. or a veterinary degree.

JOBS FOR WOMEN

But what are the professional opportunities in horse work for women? Among them are the following:

1. In research and public relations with commercial companies that manufacture and distribute products used in the light horse industry.

2. As veterinarians in private practice, with drug manufacturers, and with horse establishments.

3. In the many levels of agri-business.

4. On the staffs of horse magazines and breed registry associations.

5. In college teaching.

6. As riding instructors.

7. In training and exercising horses, in which — because of their love for horses and their light hands — they usually excel.

8. And as jockeys. Why not?

9. Horse Health: Diseases and Parasites

Horses are generally quite valuable, and they must be in good health if they are to perform at their best. Thus, they merit well-informed and ever present friends to guard against a host of perils and ailments, from scratches to sniffles, from colic to worms.[1]

Figure 9.1 While the horse is restrained by attendants, a veterinarian pushes a rubber tube through the nostrils and into the throat. Then worm medicine is poured into the stomach. (Courtesy, *From Dawn to Destiny,* by Frank Jennings and Allen F. Brewer, Jr., published by The Thoroughbred Press, Lexington, Kentucky)

[1] The material presented in this chapter is based on factual information believed to be accurate, but it is not guaranteed. When the instructions and precautions given herein are in disagreement with those of competent local authorities or manufacturers, always follow the latter two.

Table 9.1 Normal Temperature, Pulse Rate, and Breathing
Rate of Horses

Normal Rectal Temperature		Normal Pulse Rate	Normal Breathing Rate
Average	Range		
(degrees F) 100.5	(degrees F) 99–100.8	(rate/minute) 32–44	(rate/minute) 8–16

Today, with more rapid transportation and dense horse centers, the
opportunities for animals to get diseases and parasites are greatly increased compared to a generation ago.

Table 9.1 gives the normal temperature, pulse rate, and breathing rate
of horses. Any marked and persistent deviations from these normals may
be looked upon as a sign of ill health.

Every horseman should provide himself with an animal thermometer,
which is heavier and more rugged than the ordinary human thermometer.
The temperature is measured by inserting a thermometer (with a long
string tied to the outside end) full length in the rectum, where it should be
left three minutes; the pulse rate is taken either at the margin of the jaw
where an artery winds around from the inner side, at the inside of the
elbow, or under the tail; and the breathing rate can be determined by
observing the rise and fall of the flank, or, in cool weather, by watching the
breath condensate as it comes from the nostrils.

In general, infectious diseases are ushered in with a rise in body
temperature, but it must be remembered that body temperature is affected
by stable or outside temperature, exercise, excitement, age, feed, etc. It is
lower in cold weather, in older animals, and at night. Also, the pulse rate
increases with exercise, excitement, digestion, and high outside temperature; and respiration is accelerated by exercise, excitement, hot weather,
and poorly ventilated buildings.

IMMUNITY

When an animal is immune to a certain disease, it means that it is not
susceptible to that disease.

The animal body is remarkably equipped to fight disease. Chief among
this equipment are large white blood cells, called phagocytes, which are
able to overcome many invading organisms.

The body also has the ability, when properly stimulated by a given
organism or toxin, to produce antibodies and/or antitoxins. When an
animal has enough antibodies for overcoming particular disease–producing organisms, it is said to be immune to that disease.

When immunity to a disease is inherited, it is referred to as a natural
immunity.

Acquired immunity or resistance is either active or passive. When the animal is stimulated in such manner as to cause it to produce antibodies, it is said to have acquired active immunity. On the other hand, if an animal is injected with the antibodies (or immune bodies) produced by an actively immunized animal, it is referred to as an acquired passive immunity. Such immunity is usually conferred by the injection of blood serum from immunized animals, the serum carrying with it the substances by which the protection is conferred. Passive immunization confers immunity upon its injection, but the immunity disappears within three to six weeks.

In active immunity, resistance is not developed until after one or two weeks, but it is far more lasting, for the animal apparently keeps on manufacturing antibodies. It can be said, therefore, that active immunity has a great advantage.

It is noteworthy that young suckling mammals secure a passive immunity from the colostrum that they obtain from the mother for the first few days following birth.

A PROGRAM OF HORSE HEALTH, DISEASE PREVENTION, AND PARASITE CONTROL

Although the exact program will and should vary according to the specific conditions existing on each individual horse establishment, the basic principles will remain the same. With this thought in mind, the following program of horse health, disease prevention, and parasite control is presented with the hope that the horseman will use it (1) as a yardstick with which to compare his existing program, and (2) as a guide

Figure 9.2 A horse health program.

so that he and his local veterinarian, and other advisors, may develop a similar and specific program for his own enterprise.

GENERAL HEALTH PROGRAM

The following general, overall health program should be observed:

1. Avoid public feeding and watering facilities.

2. Read the sections in this book that discuss the diseases and parasites of horses; become familiar with symptoms and treatments.

3. When signs of infectious disease appear, isolate affected animals promptly, provide them with separate water and feed containers, and follow the instructions and prescribed treatment of a veterinarian.

4. Prevent or control parasites by adhering to the following program:

a. Provide good sanitation and a high level of nutrition.

b. Have adequate acreage. Use seeded pasture rather than permanent pasture, and practice rotation grazing.

c. Pasture young animals on clean pastures. Never allow them to graze on an infested area unless the area has been either plowed or left idle for a year.

d. Do not spread fresh horse manure on pastures grazed by horses. Either store the manure in a suitable pit for at least two weeks or spread it on fields that are to be plowed and cropped.

e. When small pastures or paddocks must be used, pick up droppings at frequent intervals.

f. Keep pastures mowed and harrowed. Use a chain harrow.

g. Prevent fecal contamination of feed and water.

h. Administer suitable vermifuges when internal parasites are present. Later move horses to a clean area.

i. Apply the proper insecticide when external parasites are present.

j. If cattle are on the farm, alternate the use of pastures between cattle and horses because horse parasites die in cattle.

k. Avoid overgrazing because more parasites are present on the bottom inch of grass.

l. As a disease preventive measure, arrange a scheduled yearly vaccination program with your veterinarian.

HEALTH PROGRAM FOR BREEDING AND FOALING

Reproduction is paramount in a horse-breeding program. To the end that there be superior conception followed by a high percent foal crop born and raised, the following reproductive disease-control program is recommended:

1. Mate only healthy mares to healthy stallions and observe scrupulous cleanliness at the time of service and examination. Never breed a mare that has any kind of discharge.

2. Provide plenty of exercise for the stallion and pregnant mare in harness, under saddle, or by turning them loose in a large pasture where plenty of shade and water are available.

3. During spring and fall when the weather is warm, allow the mare to foal in a clean, open pasture away from other livestock. During bad weather, keep the mare in a roomy, well-lighted, well-ventilated box stall that is provided with clean bedding. Before using the stall, thoroughly disinfect it with a lye solution made by adding 1 can of lye to 12 to 15 gallons of water. After the foal is born, remove all wet, stained, or soiled bedding and dust the floor lightly with lime. Do not use too much lime because it irritates the eyes and nasal passages of foals. When the afterbirth has been completely discharged, it should be buried in lime or burned. The mare should be kept isolated until all discharges have stopped.

4. To lessen the danger of navel infection, promptly treat the navel cord of the newborn foal with tincture of iodine.

5. As a precaution against foaling diseases and other infections, a veterinarian may administer antibiotics to both the mare and foal on the day of foaling.

HEALTH PROGRAM FOR NEW HORSES AND VISITING MARES

New horses and visiting mares may bring in diseases and parasites. In order to minimize this hazard, the following program is recommended.

1. Isolate new animals for three weeks before adding them to the herd. During this period, a veterinarian may administer sleeping sickness vaccine in season and tetanus toxoid, make a thorough general and parasitic examination, make a genital examination of breeding animals, and treat animals when necessary.

2. Make sure that mares brought in for breeding are accompanied by a health certificate issued by a veterinarian. Closely watch mares that have had trouble foaling or have lost foals.

3. If possible, saddle, bridle, or harness visiting mares near their own isolation quarters and use tack and equipment that is not used by mares kept on the establishment.

VACCINATION SCHEDULE

In no case should the vaccination program be used as a crutch for poor management. Likewise, no vaccination program is entirely successful without strict management practices to limit possible spread of infections.

For guidance purposes, a suggested vaccination program and schedule is given in Table 9.2.

Table 9.2 Equine Disease Vaccination Program and Schedule

Disease	Type	Initial Immunization			Booster	Age First Given to Foals
Distemper (strangles)	Intramuscular vaccine. (Distemper bacterin causes some complications.)	1st injection.	2nd injection—7 days after the first.	3rd injection—7 days after the second.	One annually.	3 months.
Encephalomyelitis: 1. Eastern and Western	Intradermal vaccine. (Also, there is a new killed virus vaccine which can be used to vaccinate simultaneously against Eastern, Western, and Venezuelan types.)	1st injection—in spring (April–May).		2nd injection—7–14 days after the first.	Both injections should be repeated annually.	2–3 months
2. Venezuelan (VEE)	Subcutaneous vaccine.	One injection only. (Do not give to pregnant mares.)			One annually.	3 months.
Equine influenza (flu)	Intramuscular vaccine.	1st injection.		2nd injection—4–12 weeks after the first.	One annually.	3–4 months
Rabies	Intramuscular vaccine. (High egg passage or inactivated tissue-culture vaccines only.)	1st injection.		2nd injection—30 days after the first.	One annually.	3 months.
Tetanus (lockjaw)	Toxoid—horse builds immunity lasting for at least 6–18 months after vaccination.	1st injection—intramuscular.		2nd injection—intramuscular, 2–4 weeks after 1st injection.	One annually.	2–3 months
	Antitoxin—only effective for 10–20 days.	Given to injured animals that have not been previously immunized with tetanus toxoid.				

(Con

Table 9.2 Equine Disease Vaccination Program and Schedule (*Cont.*)

Disease	Type	Initial Immunization		Booster	Age First Given to Foals
Viral rhino-pneumonitis (virus abortion)	Intramuscular vaccine.	Pregnant mares: 1st injection—after 2nd month of pregnancy.	Pregnant mares: 2nd injection—during 5th–7th month of pregnancy.	Both injections should be repeated annually.	
		All other horses should be given initial vaccination in 2 doses (2–4 weeks apart), followed by annual vaccination with a single dose.			
	Intranasal vaccine—not allowed in all states.	1st injection—during July.	2nd injection—during October.	Both doses should be repeated annually to all horses on the farm.	July of birth year.

DISEASES OF HORSES

It is intended that the summary of diseases that follows will (1) enhance the services of the veterinarian, (2) make for more rapid detection of trouble and improve nursing of sick horses, and (3) lessen the superstition, myth, and secret formulas so frequently used by horsemen.

ANTHRAX (Splenic Fever, Charbon)

An acute, infectious disease caused by *Bacillus anthracis,* a large, rod-shaped organism. It affects man, as well as horses. For this reason, a veterinarian should be summoned at the first sign of an outbreak.

Symptoms — This disease has a history of sudden deaths. Sick animals are feverish, excitable, and later depressed. They carry the head low, lag behind the herd, and breathe rapidly. Swellings appear over the body and around the neck regions. Milk secretion may turn bloody or stop entirely, and there may be a bloody discharge from all body openings.

Treatment — Isolate all sick animals. At the first sign of any of the above symptoms, a veterinarian should be called at once. The veterinarian may give large quantities of antibiotic (3 to 12 million units of penicillin or streptomycin). In the early stages of the disease, 50 to 100 milliliters (ml) of antianthrax serum may also be helpful. Provide good nursing care.

Control — Quarantine infected herds. All carcasses and contaminated material should be burned completely or buried deeply and covered with quicklime, preferably on the spot. Vaccinate all exposed but healthy animals, rotate pastures, and initiate a rigid sanitation program. Spray sick and healthy animals with an insecticide to avoid fly transmission of the infection.

Prevention — In infected areas, vaccination should be repeated each year, usually in the spring. Provide fly control by spraying animals during the insect season.

Discussion — The disease is general throughout the world in so-called anthrax districts. Cattle are more susceptible to anthrax than horses. A farmer or rancher should never open the carcass of a dead animal suspected of having died from anthrax. Instead, a veterinarian should be summoned at the first sign of an outbreak. Control measures should be carried out under the supervision of a veterinarian. The bacillus that causes anthrax can survive for years in a spore stage, resisting all destructive agents.

DISTEMPER (Strangles)

A widespread contagious disease caused by *Streptococcus equi,* a bacterium.

Symptoms — Sick animals show depression, loss of appetite, high fever, and a discharge from the nose. By the third or fourth day of the disease, the glands under the jaw start to enlarge, become sensitive, and eventually break open and discharge pus. A cough is present.

Treatment — Good nursing is the most important treatment. This includes clean, fresh water, good feed, uniform temperature, and shelter away from drafts. A veterinarian may prescribe one of the sulfas or antibiotics, or both. Early treatment is of the utmost importance in distemper.

Control — Put affected animals in strict quarantine. Clean and disinfect contaminated quarters and premises.

Prevention — Prevention consists of avoiding contact with infected animals or contaminated feeds, premises, and equipment.

Previously unvaccinated horses should receive the vaccine in three 10-milliliter doses at weekly intervals. One "booster" shot is sufficient for horses that are known to have had strangles. Vaccination should be on a yearly basis, with one "booster" dose. The vaccine should not be given to newborn foals.

Discussion — The disease is worldwide and it attacks animals of any age, but it is most common in young stock. Death losses are low. Affected animals are usually immune for the remainder of life.

ENCEPHALOMYELITIS (Sleeping Sickness; or Eastern,
Western, or Venezuelan equine encephalomyelitis)

This virus, epizootic (epidemic) brain disease, which affects both horses and man, is known as equine encephalomyelitis, or sleeping sickness. Both horse and man are "dead-end" hosts, infected only by the mosquito.

Since 1930, the Eastern and Western types of the disease have assumed alarming proportions in the United States. Then, in 1971, Venezuelan equine encephalomyelitis first occurred in the United States, when an outbreak was reported in Texas. The Venezuelan type was first diagnosed in Venezuela in 1936 and was reported in several South and Central American countries prior to appearing in the United States. Equine encephalomyelitis is seasonal in character, extending from early summer until the first sharp frost of fall, when it invariably disappears.

The disease is caused by several distinct viruses. The three most active types in the United States are: Eastern equine encephalomyelitis, Western equine encephalomyelitis, and Venezuelan equine encephalomyelitis. All three viruses may be spread from animals to man, with mosquitoes serving as the primary means of transport. Wild birds, rodents, and wild animals in all areas of the country are reservoirs of the disease, which enters the body of a mosquito when it feeds on infected creatures. While in the mosquito, the virus multiplies and becomes highly concentrated in the salivary glands. The infected mosquito then transmits the virus to a horse or a man, whichever is handy at its next feeding. In the Venezuelan type, horses can spread the disease directly since the virus is present in their saliva and nasal discharges.

Symptoms — In early stages, animals walk aimlessly about, crashing into objects. Later they may appear sleepy and stand with a lowered head. Grinding of the teeth, inability to swallow, paralysis of the lips, and blindness may be noted. Paralysis may cause animals to fall. If affected animals do not recover, death occurs in 2 to 4 days.

In mild cases, the horse may merely yawn a few times; and this may be the only clinical sign of the disease.

Treatment — Treatment is not very effective, because of the rapid course of the disease. Since the Western type progresses more slowly and results in a lower mortality rate than the Eastern and Venezuelan types, it lends itself to more supportive treatment. Good nursing is perhaps the best and most important treatment. The maintenance of fluid and electrolyte balance is recommended. No specific therapeutic agent is known to influence the course of the disease.

Control — Control measures include the isolation of infected animals in screened cages or the application of insect repellent; prompt disposal of all infected carcasses; destruction, if possible, of insect breeding grounds; and discouragement of movement of animals from an epizootic area to a clean one. Fly and mosquito control seems to be very effective, since most outbreaks of the disease do not extend to racetracks and stables where insect control is practiced.

Prevention — Prevention entails vaccination of all horses against the three separate strains. Vaccination against Eastern and Western encephalomyelitis involves two injections, 7 to 14 days apart, given annually in April or May. Protection against Venezuelan equine encephalomyelitis requires one injection only, given annually. Also, there is a new killed virus vaccine which can be used to vaccinate simultaneously against all three types — Eastern, Western, and Venezuelan. A veterinarian should administer the vaccine.

Discussion — The disease is widespread. Since 1930, nearly a million horses and mules have been affected in the United States. Some animals make full recovery but other survivors do not.

Generally speaking, mortality from the Western type does not exceed 50 percent, whereas that from the Eastern and Venezuelan types is 90 percent or higher.

EQUINE ABORTION (Premature Expulsion of the Fetus)

Abortion is the expulsion of the impregnated ovum at any period prior to the time that the foal can survive out of the uterus. If the foal is advanced enough to live, it is known as premature parturition, and in the mare this may occur as early as the tenth month.

Symptoms — Equine abortion symptoms vary according to the cause. The causes of abortion in mares may be grouped into two types: (1) infectious agents, such as viruses, bacteria, and fungi; and (2) noninfectious abortions, such as twinning, hormonal deficiencies, congenital anomalies, and miscellaneous causes. Some of the more common causes are discussed in the sections that follow.

■ *Infectious causes of abortion* — A discussion of each of the infectious abortions follows.

1. *Virus abortion* — The most common cause of abortion in mares is a herpes virus (the herpes class of viruses commonly affect the cells of the skin and mucous membranes), which produces the disease known as rhinopneumonitis in horses. Rhinopneumonitis gained notoriety as "virus abortion" because abortion often results when pregnant mares are affected with the disease.

Rhinopneumonitis is a mild, usually nonfatal disease of the upper respiratory tract, commonly seen in young horses in the fall or winter. It is characterized by a cough, a nasal discharge, a loss of appetite, and a temperature of 102°–105° F. As the disease progresses, the temperature returns to normal, but the nasal discharge and cough may persist for several weeks. In older horses, the disease may be so mild as to go unnoticed. Most abortions due to this virus occur between the eighth and eleventh months of gestation, although they may occur as early as the fifth month. Sometimes the foal is born alive at term, but dies at 2 to 3 days of age due to infection by the virus. The fetal membranes are seldom retained; and the genital tract returns to normal as quickly as it does following normal parturition. The abortion rate may approach 100 percent in a herd of susceptible mares. An effective vaccine will prevent rhinopneumonitis and should be used in areas subject to the disease.

The virus of equine arteritis may also cause abortion. It produces more obvious signs of illness than equine rhinopneumonitis, including discharges from the eyes and nose, fever (102°–106° F), and filling (edema) of the limbs. A laboratory examination is necessary conclusively to establish the presence of the specific virus. Up to 50 percent of affected pregnant mares may abort. The name "arteritis" is derived from the particular type of arterial damage that this disease inflicts; it results in degeneration of the middle layer of arterial walls, especially in the small arteries. Treatment consists in absolute rest and good nursing, augmented by antibiotics to prevent or combat secondary bacterial infections. An effective vaccine is available and should be used in areas where the disease is a problem.

2. *Bacterial abortion* — Bacterial infection is a common cause of abortion in mares. Several species of bacteria have been incriminated. *Salmonella abortus equi,* which was formerly responsible for abortion storms, still occurs sporadically. However, the most common cause of bacterial abortion at the present time is organisms of the *Streptococcus* group. Other bacteria frequently cultured from aborted feti include *E. coli, Klebsiella,* and *Staphylococci.* They may cause abortion at any stage of pregnancy. But, generally *Streptococci* cause abortion during the first five months, whereas *E. coli* are more apt to cause abortion during the last half of

pregnancy. Bacteria gain entrance to the reproductive tract at the time of foaling or breeding, thence travel to the uterus, where they cause infection of the fetal membranes, and result in abortion. Bacterial abortion, which may occur at any stage of pregnancy, is often characterized by retention of the placenta, as well as by metritis or inflammation of the uterus. Treatment of the mare may be necessary before she can be rebred successfully. It is a good practice to swab mares before rebreeding, to determine if harmful bacteria are present in the vagina. The latter precaution is especially important where it is the intent to rebreed mares on the ninth day after foaling.

3. *Fungi* — Abortions may result from infection of the placenta by various types of fungi, which are widespread in nature. Fungi probably enter the uterus during the heat period at which conception occurs, or soon after birth — in the case of foaling mares. Another school of thought is that the fungi are inhaled into the lungs, thence enter the blood and go to the pregnant uterus. Fungi do not attack the fetus directly; rather, they cause degeneration of the placenta so that the fetus has insufficient nourishment. For this reason, the aborted fetus is often small and only a fraction of the normal weight for its gestational age. If abortion does not occur, the foal may be carried to full term and be born in a reasonably vigorous, but undersized and undernourished, state. Most mycotic abortions occur during the second half of pregnancy. There is no vaccine.

■ *Noninfectious causes of abortion* — The common noninfectious causes of abortion are:

1. *Twinning* — The birth of healthy twin foals is unusual. The generally accepted theory relative to the inability of the mare to carry twin foals successfully to term is that it is due to placental insufficiency — meaning that there are not enough fetal membranes to accommodate and provide nutrition for two developing fetuses.

2. *Hormone failure* — The hormone progesterone plays a dominant role in the maintenance of pregnancy, preparing the uterus for reception of the fertilized egg and the attachment of the placenta. It is responsible for the necessary changes in the uterus for the continuance of pregnancy and nourishment of the fetus. Other hormones, such as estrogen and cortisone, are also involved in the process and can contribute to abortion. Thus, the maintenance of pregnancy is a matter of hormone balance. Although there are many gaps in our knowledge of reproductive physiology, it appears that some abortions are caused by failure of the glands that control hormonal balance.

3. *Congenital defects* — Early embryonic deaths, which may be mistaken for failure of conception or silent heats, frequently occur. Some of these are presumed to be due to genetic or chromosomal defects resulting in improper development of the embryo, followed by rejection by the dam.

4. *Miscellaneous causes* — This embraces all cases of abortion that cannot be definitely classified in any of the categories discussed above — it

includes abortions *not* caused by viruses, bacteria, fungi, twinning, hormonal deficiencies, or congenital anomalies. In the category of miscellaneous causes of abortions are nutritional deficiencies, certain drugs, accidents and injury — such as a severe kick that disturbs the uterus, and noninfectious pathological lesions in the uterus of the mare. Causes of this type are so numerous and general that aside from good breeding, feeding, and management practices not much can be done to prevent them; but these three practices are vital in prevention of abortion as well as other diseases. The mare may abort from almost any cause that very profoundly disturbs the system.

Treatment — It is important to recognize an impending abortion as early as possible, for sometimes it may be prevented. When a pregnant mare shows any general indefinable illness, she should be examined closely for abortion indications. Any suggestive indications should prompt the horseman to call the veterinarian immediately. Treatment should be left to the veterinarian.

Control — When a case of abortion is encountered, the following procedure is recommended: (1) Gather up the fetus and afterbirth with great care and arrange through the local veterinarian for a diagnosis by the state diagnostic laboratory; (2) isolate the mare in a place where she can be kept in quarantine; (3) burn or bury the bedding; and (4) thoroughly disinfect the stall with a five percent Lysol solution.

Prevention — Preventive measures embrace avoidance of all possible causes. It begins with mating only healthy mares to healthy stallions, and with being scrupulously clean at the time of breeding. New horses should always be isolated as a preventive measure, and aborting mares should be quarantined. Where abortions have occurred in the broodmare band, the special cause in the matter of feed, water, exposure to injuries, overwork, lack of exercise, and so forth may often be identified and removed. Avoid constipation, diarrhea, indigestion, bloating, violent purgatives or other potent medicines — including administering cortisones in late pregnancy — painful operations, and slippery roads.

The following points are pertinent in controlling abortion in a band of broodmares:

1. Prevent rhinopneumonitis by following a planned immunization program under the direction of a veterinarian.

2. Prevent equine arteritis in areas where the disease is a problem by administering the vaccine.

3. Prevent *Salmonella* abortion on premises known to be contaminated by vaccinating all pregnant mares each year.

4. Control and prevent bacterial abortion by mating only healthy mares to healthy stallions and observing scrupulous cleanliness at the time of service and examination. Suture mares where necessary.

5. Keep broodmares healthy and in good flesh, and feed a ration that contains all the essential elements of nutrition.

One of the most important factors to remember about abortion is that a veterinarian should be called for diagnosis, prevention, treatment, and cure. To forget this is to invite trouble and to pave the way for possible spreading of the infection.

EQUINE INFECTIOUS ANEMIA — E.I.A. (Swamp Fever)

An infectious virus disease.

Symptoms — Symptoms of the disease vary, but usually they include some of the following: high and intermittent fever; depression; stiffness and weakness, especially in the hindquarters; anemia; jaundice; edema and swelling of the lower body and legs; unthriftiness; and loss of condition and weight, even though the appetite is good. Most affected animals die within 2 to 4 weeks.

■ **Coggins Test** — The "Coggins Test" for diagnosing E.I.A. is accurate — if properly used — fairly simple, and rather inexpensive. The test was developed by Dr. Leroy Coggins of the New York State Veterinary College, Cornell University; hence, the common name. Technically, the correct name for the blood test is the agar gel immunodiffusion (AGID) test. It is valid only if the blood sample is drawn by a veterinarian and submitted to a recognized laboratory. The AGID test is approved by the U.S. Department of Agriculture and is conducted in approximately 100 laboratories.

The Coggins Test is based on detection of antibodies (modified globulins) to E.I.A. virus. Infected horses become positive to this test 2 to 4 weeks after the onset of the initial infection and remain test positive the rest of their lives. Since foals receive large quantities of antibodies from their dams by way of colostrum, a nursing foal born of an E.I.A. positive dam may be positive for the first 4 to 6 months of its life but not actively infected. Such foals can be considered free from the disease if they test negative at about 7 months of age.

The test is usually repeated to confirm all positive reactions because horses are often destroyed on the basis of the test.

In 1976, the U.S. Department of Agriculture amended the animal import regulations to require that imported horses pass the Coggins Test to assure that they are free of equine infectious anemia.

Treatment — No successful treatment is known.

Control — Segregate infected animals and have them use separate feeding and watering facilities. Kill sick animals and burn or bury their carcasses.

Prevention — Use disposable hypodermic needles when horses are vaccinated against disease and sterilize all other skin penetrating instruments by boiling them at least 15 minutes after each use. Practice good sanitation and eliminate or reduce biting insects as much as possible. Watch for sick horses and get a diagnosis by a veterinarian if any are observed. Use separate tack equipment on each horse. Keep stalls, starting gates, and other facilities clean at racetracks and shows. This disease has existed in different sections of the United States for at least 50 years but no preventive vaccination is known.

Discussion — Infected horses may be virus carriers for years and are a danger to susceptible horses.

After horse owners test and eliminate all infected animals from their herd, the Coggins Test can be used to protect their stock from reinfection, (1) by buying horses only after they have been tested and found free from the disease, (2) by not allowing untested horses to be stabled or pastured with their own, and (3) by not bringing their horses to any assembly point (show, sale, racetrack, trail ride, etc.) where prior testing is not required.

EQUINE INFLUENZA

An infectious disease caused by a myxovirus that has properties of the Type A influenza viruses.

Symptoms — Young animals, except for very young foals that have immunity from the dam's milk, are particularly susceptible. Older animals are usually immune. Symptoms develop 2 to 10 days after exposure. The onset of the disease is marked by a rapidly rising temperature that may reach 106° F and persist for 2 to 10 days. Other symptoms include loss of appetite, extreme weakness and depression, rapid breathing, a dry cough, and a watery discharge from the eyes and nostrils that is followed by a white to yellow nasal discharge.

Treatment — Treatment should be handled by a veterinarian. Avoid exercising the animals during the period of elevated temperature. The use of antibiotics and/or sulfa drugs may prevent some of the complicated secondary conditions.

Control — Avoid transmission of the virus on contaminated feed, bedding, water, buckets, brooms, clothing and hands of attendants, and transportation facilities.

Prevention — Vaccinate with a killed virus. Use two doses; follow the manufacturer's directions on the time of the second dose. Also, give each animal an annual booster shot, or a booster when animals are exposed or when an epidemic occurs. Quarantine sick animals, and isolate all new animals to the premises for 3 weeks.

Discussion — The disease is widespread throughout the world. It frequently appears where a number of horses are assembled, such as racetracks, sales, and shows. The death rate is low but economic loss is high. The disease interrupts training, racing, and showing schedules, and it may force the withdrawal of animals from sales. Although horses, swine, and humans are subject to influenza and the symptoms are similar for each, there appears to be no transmission of the disease among them.

GLANDERS (Farcy)

In acute or chronic infectious disease caused by *Malleomyces mallei,* a bacterium.

Symptoms — The chronic form most often attacks horses, affecting the lungs, skin, or nasal passages. There may be a nasal discharge that later becomes pus, and nodules and ulcers may appear in the skin. With the lung type, there generally is loss in condition, lack of endurance, bleeding and a mucus discharge from the nose, and coughing. The skin of the extremities may develop ulcers that exude a honeylike tenacious discharge.

The acute form more often attacks mules and donkeys. The symptoms are similar to the chronic form, but more severe. Death usually occurs in a week.

Treatment — Sulfadiazine, given every 20 days has proven fairly effective.

Control — Use the mallein test to detect infected animals or animals suspected of having the disease. Destroy infected animals and clean and disinfect contaminated equipment and premises.

Prevention — Avoid inhalation or ingestion of the causative organism. Do not use public watering places.

No method of immunization is available.

Discussion — Glanders is prevalent in areas where horses still are used for transportation and work. The disease has largely disappeared from the mechanized areas of the world, including the United States, but it is not eradicated. Through the transport of animals, glanders can make its appearance anytime in any area.

NAVEL INFECTION (Joint Ill, Navel Ill,
Actinobacillosis, Streptococcus)

An infectious disease of newborn animals caused by several kinds of bacteria.

Symptoms — Infected animals have loss of appetite; swelling, soreness, and stiffness in the joints; general listlessness; and umbilical swelling and discharge.

Treatment — A veterinarian may give a blood transfusion from the dam to the offspring, or he may administer a sulfa, an antibiotic, a serum, or a bacterin.

Control — See prevention.

Prevention — Practice good sanitation and hygiene at mating and parturition. Feed iodized salt to pregnant mares in iodine-deficient areas. Soon after birth, treat the navel cord of newborn animals with tincture of iodine.

Discussion — The disease appears throughout the United States. About 50 percent of infected foals die and many that survive have deformed joints. Providing clean quarters for the newborn and painting the navel cord with tincture of iodine are the best preventive measures.

TETANUS (Lockjaw)

Chiefly a wound-infection disease caused by a powerful toxin, more than 100 times as toxic as strychnine, that is liberated by the bacterium *Clostridium tetani,* an anaerobe.

Symptoms — This disease usually is associated with a wound. First sign of tetanus is a stiffness about the head. Animals often chew slowly and weakly and swallow awkwardly. The third or inner eyelid protrudes over the forward surface of the eyeball. The slightest noise or movement causes sick animals to have violent spasms. Usually sick animals remain standing until close to death. All ages are susceptible.

Treatment — Place sick animals under the care of a veterinarian and keep them quiet. Good nursing is important. If given early in the disease, massive doses of antitoxin, 100,000 to 200,000 units or more, may be effective. Also, tranquilizers will reduce the extent and severity of muscular spasms, and antibiotics will help.

Control — See prevention.

Prevention — Under the direction of a veterinarian, give tetanus toxoid in 2 doses at 6-week intervals, followed by a booster injection annually. If premises are unsanitary, all surgery should be accompanied with tetanus antitoxin.

Discussion — Tetanus is worldwide, but in the United States it occurs most frequently in the South. Death occurs in over half of the affected cases.

VENEZUELAN EQUINE ENCEPHALOMYELITIS (VEE)
See ENCEPHALOMYELITIS.

VESICULAR STOMATITIS

A contagious disease of the mouth caused by a virus.

Symptoms — Blisters and rawness appear mainly on the tongue but also on the inner surfaces of the lips, angles of the mouth, and the gums. There is considerable salivation. Symptoms appear in 2 to 5 days after exposure.

Treatment — Make the animal as comfortable as possible and provide plenty of water and soft feed.

Control — None.

Prevention — None. No vaccination is available.

Discussion — The disease may affect 50 percent of the animals on the premises.

OTHER AILMENTS

Horses are subject to many other ailments; among them, colds and scouring (foals), a discussion of which follows. (Also, see Chapter 6, Feeding Horses, for section on Nutritional Diseases and Ailments.)

COLDS

Horses are subject to colds very similar to those in man. Colds are caused by a virus and, as in humans, there are various strains of the horse cold virus. The symptoms are: loss of appetite, shivering, a rise in temperature to 103° F or 104° F, and an increased pulse rate to around 50 or 60. Usually, a discharge develops, but the glands are not affected. Afflicted horses often develop a sore throat and a nasty cough.

Colds are highly contagious and can spread rapidly through an entire stable. Therefore, affected animals should be isolated immediately. A veterinarian should be called, who will generally administer an antibiotic to prevent secondary infection. Good nursing will help. The latter includes keeping the horse warm and dry in a well-ventilated but not drafty place and giving him a bran mash.

SCOURING (Foal Diarrhea)

Scouring or diarrhea in foals may be associated with infectious diseases or may be caused by unclean surroundings. Any of the following conditions may bring on diarrhea: contaminated udder or teats; nonremoval of fecal matter from the digestive tract; fretfulness or temperature above normal in the mare; an excess of feed affecting the quality of the mare's milk; cold, damp bed; or continued exposure to cold rains. As treatment is not always successful, the best practice is to avoid the undesirable conditions.

Some foals scour during the foal heat of the mare, which occurs between the seventh and ninth day following foaling.

Diarrhea is caused by an irritant in the digestive tract that should be removed if recovery is to be expected. Only in exceptional cases should an astringent be given with the idea of checking the diarrhea; and such treatment should be prescribed by the veterinarian.

If the foal is scouring, the ration of the mare should be reduced, and a part of her milk should be taken away by milking her out at intervals.

PARASITES OF HORSES[2]

Parasites live in or on the bodies of host animals. Parasites kill some horses but the main damage is lowered efficiency. Attacks are insidious and can easily cause damage before the parasite is noticed.

INTERNAL PARASITES

Some 150 different kinds of internal parasites attack horses throughout the world, and probably no animal is ever entirely free of them.

Parasites may be located in practically every tissue and cavity of the body. However, most of them are in the alimentary tract, lungs, body cavity, or bloodstream. Those in the digestive system usually become localized there, but others travel throughout different parts of the body.

The general symptoms of parasitic infection in horses are weakness, unthriftiness, emaciation, tucked-up flanks, distended abdomen, rough coat, pale membranes in the eyes and mouth, stunted growth in young animals, and in some cases frequent colic and diarrhea. Affected animals usually eat well and the temperature remains normal. But an infected animal always loses some efficiency as a working unit.

Few treatments with only one drug are effective in removing bots and various gastrointestinal worms from horses. Usually, it is necessary to use a combination of drugs. For this purpose, the specific combination is dependent upon the kinds of parasites present in the horses to be treated. It is always wise, therefore, to obtain a definite diagnosis from a veterinarian or veterinary diagnostic laboratory before treatment is given. Also, a veterinarian should always be consulted for safe and effective dosages of the various drugs and treatment schedules.

COMMON INTERNAL PARASITES AND THEIR CONTROL

Parasites are so widespread that no horse escapes all of them. Because there are so many kinds of internal parasites, only the most common and damaging ones are summarized in Table 9.3 and discussed at length in the narrative that follows. Strongyles, ascarids, and bots are generally the most injurious of internal parasites, although other kinds are capable of producing severe injury on occasion and generally contribute to the overall picture of parasitism wherever they occur.

■ *Choice of drug (anthelmintic) and dosage* — Knowing what internal parasites are present within a horse is the first requisite to the choice of the proper drug, or anthelmintic. Since no one drug is appropriate or economical for all conditions, the next requisite is to select the right one: the

---

[2] Trade names of pesticides used to control parasites are mentioned in this book solely to provide specific information. Mention of a trade name does not constitute a guarantee of the product by the author nor does it imply an endorsement by the author over comparable products that are not named. When any trade-named compound is used, the directions for use given on the label should be followed very carefully.

Table 9.3 Internal Parasites of Horses

Parasite	Where found	Damage	Signs
Ascarids (*Parascaris*)	Small intestine.	Irritate intestinal wall; possible obstruction.	Digestive upsets (colic), diarrhea, retarded growth, rough hair coat, potbelly, death (ruptured intestine). More common in young horses.
Bots (*Gastrophilus*)	Stomach, gums.	Inflammation, perforation of stomach wall, gums.	Excitement (caused by flies), digestive upsets (colic), retarded growth, poor condition, death (stomach rupture).
Pinworm (*Oxyuris*)	Large intestine.	Adults feed on gut contents. Larvae feed on mucosa.	Digestive disturbances, retarded growth, anemia, tail rubbing.
Stomach worm (*Habronema* adult) (*Habronema* larvae)	Stomach, injured skin.	Causes tumors on wall and granulomatus ulcers.	Gastritis, digestive disorders, and summer sores—which often heal spontaneously after first frost.
Strongyles, large (Bloodworm)	Large intestine and colon.	Adults suck blood, cause ulcers on mucosa. Larvae cause enlargement and aneurysms of anterior mesenteric artery.	Anemia, rough hair coat, colic, loss of appetite, retarded growth, depression, soft feces with a foul odor. In large infections, legs and abdomen swell.
Strongyles, small (*Triodontophorus, Poteriostomum, Trichonema,* and others)	Large intestine and colon.	Irritate intestinal wall, causing thickening and nodules with larvae in them feeding on blood.	Anemia, loss of appetite, retarded growth, dark or black manure, soft feces with a foul odor. Inlarge infections, legs and abdomen swell.
Tapeworm (*Anoplocephala*)	Small intestine.	Ulceration of ileocecal valve, enteritis.	Unthriftiness.
Threadworm (*Strongyloides*)	Small intestine.	Erosion of intestinal mucosa, enteritis.	Loss of appetite, loss of weight, diarrhea, worms disappear by time foals are 6 months old.

one which, when used according to directions, will be most effective and produce a minimum of side effects on the animal treated. So, coupled with knowledge of the kind of parasites present, an individual assessment of each animal is necessary. Among the factors to consider are age, pregnancy, other illnesses and medications, and the method by which the drug is to be administered. Some drugs characteristically put horses off performance for several days after treatment, whereas others have less tendency to do so. Some drugs are unnecessarily harsh or expensive for the problem at hand, whereas a safe inexpensive alternative would be equally suitable.

Table 9.4 lists the drug selections, along with the trade name, source, and method of administration of each, for the removal of four important internal parasites of horses — ascarids, bots, pinworms, and strongyles.

Table 9.4 Drug Selections for Specific Parasites

Parasite	Active Ingredient	Trade Name	Source	Method of Administration
Ascarids	Piperazine	Several, including Parvex Equizole-A Dizan suspension with piperazine	Several, including Upjohn Merck Elanco	Tube or feed Tube Tube, feed Tube
	Trichlorfon	Dyrex Anthon Combot	Ft. Dodge Bayvet Bayvet	Tube, feed, bolus Feed Tube
	Butonate of trichlorfon	T-113	Thuron	Tube
	Dichlorvos	Equigard Equigel	Shell Shell	Feed Intraoral
	Mebendazole	Telmin Telmin-SF	Pitman-Moore Pitman-Moore	Tube, feed Intraoral
	Carbon disulfide	None	Various	Tube
	Pyrantel	Strongid Strongid T	Pfizer Pfizer	Feed Tube, feed, drench
	Cambendazole	Camvet	Merck	Tube
	Levamisole and piperazine	Ripercol L-piperazine	American Cyanamid	Tube

(Cont.)

Table 9.4 Drug Selections for Specific Parasites (*Cont.*)

Parasite	Active Ingredient	Trade Name	Source	Method of Administration
Bots	Trichlorfon	Dyrex	Ft. Dodge	Tube, feed, bolus
		Anthon	Bayvet	Feed
		Combot	Bayvet	Tube
		Equizole-B	Merck	Tube, feed
	Butonate of trichlorfon	T-113	Thuron	Tube
	Piperazine-carbon disulfide complex	Parvex	Upjohn	Tube
		Parvex Plus	Upjohn	Tube
	Dichlorvos	Equigard	Shell	Feed
		Equigel	Shell	Intraoral
	Carbon disulfide	None	Various	Tube
Pinworms	Dithiazanine iodide and piperazine citrate	Dizan suspension with piperazine	Elanco	Tube
	Thiabendazole	Equizole	Merck	Tube, feed
		Equizole-A	Merck	Tube, feed
		Equizole-B	Merck	Tube, feed
	Trichlorfon	Dyrex	Ft. Dodge	Tube, feed, bolus
		Anthon	Bayvet	Feed
		Combot	Bayvet	Tube
	Piperazine	Several, including	Several, including	Tube, feed
		Parvex	Upjohn	Tube
		Ripercol L-piperazine	American Cyanamid	Tube
	Dichlorvos	Equigard	Shell	Feed
	Pyrantel	Strongid	Pfizer	Feed
		Strongid-T	Pfizer	Tube, feed, drench
	Mebendazole	Telmin	Pitman-Moore	Tube, feed
		Telmin-SF	Pitman-Moore	Intraoral
	Cambendazole	Camvet	Merck	Tube

(*Cont.*)

Table 9.4 Drug Selections for Specific Parasites (*Cont.*)

Parasite	Active Ingredient	Trade Name	Source	Method of Administration
Strongyles	Phenothiazine	Various	Various	Low level in feed
	Phenothiazine and piperazine mixtures	Several, including Parvex Plus Dyrex T.F.	Several, including Upjohn Ft. Dodge	Tube Tube Tube
	Thiabendazole	Equizole Equizole-A Equizole-B	Merck Merck Merck	Tube, feed Tube, feed Tube, feed
	Dichlorvos	Equigard	Shell	Feed
	Dithiazanine iodide and piperazine citrate	Dizan suspension with piperazine	Elanco	Tube
	Pyrantel	Strongid Strongid-T	Pfizer Pfizer	Feed Tube, feed, drench
	Mebendazole	Telmin Telmin-SF	Pitman-Moore Pitman-Moore	Tube, feed Intraoral
	Cambendazole	Camvet	Merck	Tube
	Levamisole and piperazine	Ripercol L-piperazine	American Cyanamid	Tube

Table 9.5 lists the antiparasitic compounds, and gives the recommended dosage level and the efficacy of each, for the removal of ascarids, bots, pinworms, and strongyles.

It is recommended that wormers be rotated — that several different dewormers be used — combined with low-level phenothiazine treatment. Preventive (prophylactic) treatment with phenothiazine does not kill worms rapidly. Rather, it interferes with the parasite's capacity to lay fertile eggs, so reinfestation is reduced. Reinfestation occurs constantly because all stages of the parasites are present at all times.

Anthelmintics are constantly being improved, and new ones are becoming available. So, the horseman should consult his local veterinarian relative to the choice of drug to use on his horse(s) at the time.

Table 9.5 Dosage Level and Efficacy of Antiparasitic Compounds Used in Horses

| Compound | Dose Level[1] | Ascarids (%) | Bots (%) | Pinworms | | Strongyles | | |
				Mature Oxyurids (%)	Immature Oxyurids (%)	S. vulgaris (%)	S. edentatus (%)	Small (%)
Butonate of trichlorfon	2.0 g/cwt	90-100	90-100	N.D.[2]	N.D.[2]	20-60	5-15	N.D.[2]
Carbon disulfide (CS$_2$)	2.4 ml/cwt	50-100	90-100	0	0	0	0	0
CBZ	.9 g/cwt	95-100	0	95-100	85-100	95-100	90-100	70-100
Dichlorvos (pellets)	1.6 g/cwt	95-100	80-100	90-100	90-100	95-100	70-80	85-95
Dichlorvos (gel)	.45-.9 g/cwt	90-100	90-100	90-100	N.D.[2]	0-10	0	N.D.[2]
Dithiazanine iodide + PPZ	2.0 + 2.5 g/cwt	95-100	0	90-100	90-100	60-80	10-30	90-100
FBZ	.23 g/cwt	70-90	0	95-100	50-70	95-100	95-100	90-100
Mebendazole	1 g/250 lb	90-100	0	95-100	95-100	95-100	65-95	80-95
Phenothiazine	low-level	0	0	0	0	95-100	95-100	95-100
Phenothiazine (PTZ)	2.5 g/cwt	0	0	0	25-50	50-75	20-40	85-95
Piperazine (PPZ)	4.0 g/cwt	95-100	0	40-60	0-15	40-60	0-10	90-100
PPZ-CS$_2$ complex	4.0 g/cwt	95-100	78-85	50-70	10-20	40-60	0-10	90-100
PTZ + PPZ	1.25 + 4.0 g/cwt	95-100	0	50-70	20-40	90-100	40-60	90-100
PTZ + PPZ-CS$_2$ complex	.83 + 2.67 g/cwt	95-100	70-80	50-70	20-40	90-100	70-90	90-100
PTZ + PPZ + T	1.25 + 4.0 + 1.8 g/cwt	95-100	90-100	90-100	90-100	95-100	30-50	90-100
Pyrantel	.33 g/cwt	90-100	0	60-70	50-60	95-100	65-75	90-100
TBZ + PPZ	2.0 + 2.5 g/cwt	95-100	0	90-100	30-40	95-100	90-100	90-100
Thiabendazole (TBZ)	2.0 g/cwt	10-30	0	90-100	30-40	95-100	90-100	90-100
Trichlorfon (T)	1.8 g/cwt	95-100	90-100	90-100	N.D.[2]	0-10	0-5	0-30

■ *Program and schedule* — Each horse establishment should, in coop-eration with the local veterinarian and/or other advisors, evolve an internal parasite program and schedule. A general understanding of the life cycles of the various parasites is necessary in order to time the treatments to best advantage. Also, it is recommended that an equine practitioner or parasitology laboratory do periodic fecal examinations to help assess the effectiveness of the parasite control program.

A suggested treatment program for (1) foals, and (2) yearlings, two-year-olds, and mature horses follows.

1. *Foals* — For the control of ascarids, foals should be started on Parvex or piperazine at 8 weeks of age, with treatment repeated at 8-week intervals. This treatment will also control pinworms and small strongyles, but not large strongyles. For large strongyle control, mares should be maintained on one of the strongyle control programs for mature horses. Addition of thiabendazole to piperazine is commonly practiced to control strongyloides infection, a common concurrent infection in foals. Table 9.6 gives two suggested worming programs for foals.

Table 9.6 Sample Worming Programs for Foals

Date	Program "A"	Program "B"
June 1	Parvex	piperazine
Aug. 1	Parvex	piperazine
Oct. 1	Parvex	piperazine
Dec. 1	Parvex, Equigard, or Dyrex T.F.	Parvex, Equigard, or Dyrex T.F.

2. *Yearlings, two-year-olds, and mature horses*[3] — A low-level pheno-thiazine program has been used for several years. Phenothiazine is fed in the ration at the rate of 2 grams per day for the first 21 days of each month on a year-round basis. One of the bot control drugs (carbon disulfide, Anthon, Dyrex, or Equigard) should be given in late fall or winter. Yearlings may require 1 to 3 treatments with piperazine for ascarids during the first part of the year.

Periodic treatment programs, with the number of treatments varying from twice a year to six times a year, and alternating among the various drugs and combinations of drugs, may be used, depending upon the degree of parasitism. Alternating the drugs provides broad spectrum control of strongyles, bots, ascarids, and pinworms. Table 9.7 gives suggested worming programs and schedules for yearlings, two-year-olds, and mature horses.

---

[3]Do not treat mares within one month of foaling.

Table 9.7 Sample Programs of Periodic Treatments

| Date | Number of Treatments per Year | | |
	6X	4X	2X
Feb. 1	Parvex Plus, Equigard, or Dyrex T.F.	......	......
Apr. 1	Equizole, or Equizole-A	Parvex Plus, Equigard, or Dyrex T.F.	Parvex Plus, Equigard, or Dyrex T.F.
June 1	Equizole, or Equizole-A	Equizole, or Equizole-A	......
Aug. 1	Parvex Plus, or Phenothiazine/ piperazine mixture	Equizole, or Equizole-A	......
Oct. 1	Equizole, or Equizole-A	......	......
Dec. 1	Dyrex T.F., Equigard, or Parvex Plus	Dyrex T.F., Equigard, or Parvex Plus	Dyrex T.F., Equigard, or Parvex Plus

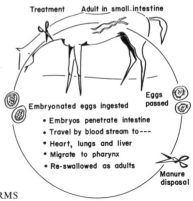

ASCARIDS OR LARGE ROUNDWORMS
(*Parascaris equorum*)

The female varies from 6 to 22 inches long and the male from 5 to 13 inches. When full grown, both are about the diameter of a lead pencil.

Symptoms — The injury caused by ascarids ranges from light infections producing moderate effects to heavy infections that may cause death. Death usually is due to a ruptured intestine. Serious lung damage caused by migrating ascarid larvae may result in pneumonia. More common are retarded growth and development manifested by a potbelly, rough hair coat, and digestive disturbances. Ascarids affect foals and young animals, but rarely affect horses over 5 years old; older animals develop immunity from early infections.

Treatment — Tables 9.4 and 9.5 give the drug selections and recommended dosage levels for the control of ascarids.

Prevention and control — Keep the foaling barn and paddocks clean, store manure in a pit 2 to 3 weeks, provide clean feed and water, and place young foals on clean pasture.

Discussion — Ascarids attack horses throughout the United States. The presence of ascarids results in loss of feed to feeding worms, lowered work efficiency, retarded growth in young animals, lowered breeding efficiency, and death in severe infections.

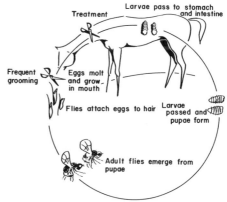

BOTS (*Gasterophilus* spp.)

Four species of bots have been found in the United States but only three are serious pests of horses.

Symptoms — Animals attacked by the botfly may toss their heads in the air, strike the ground with their front feet, and rub their noses on each other or any convenient object. Animals infected with bots may show frequent digestive upsets and even colic, lowered vitality and emaciation, and reduced work output. Bots may penetrate the stomach wall and cause death.

Figure 9.3 Bots attached to the stomach wall of a horse. At this stage they remain attached to the lining of the stomach and intestines for several months, feeding on blood until they are about ¾ inch in length, after which they release their hold and pass out with the feces. (Courtesy, Department of Veterinary Pathology and Hygiene, College of Veterinary Medicine, University of Illinois, Urbana, Illinois)

Figure 9.4 Washing to remove the eggs of adult botflies attached to the hairs of the horse. (Courtesy, USDA)

Treatment — Tables 9.4 and 9.5 give the drug selections and recommended dosage levels for the control of bots.

Prevention and control — Frequent grooming, washing, and clipping help prevent bot attacks. Prevention of reinfection is best assured through community campaigns in which all horses within the area are treated. Fly nets and nose covers offer some relief from the attacks of botflies.

Discussion — Bots are worldwide. The presence of bots results in loss of feed to feeding worms, itching and loss of tail hair from rubbing, lowered work efficiency, retarded growth of young animals, lowered breeding efficiency, and death in severe infections.

EQUINE PIROPLASMOSIS (Babesiasis)

Caused by *Babesia caballi* or *B. equi,* protozoan parasites that invade the red blood cells.

Symptoms — Equine piroplasmosis is similar to equine infectious anemia but a positive diagnosis can be made by determining whether or not protozoa are in the red blood cells. Symptoms include a fever of 103° to 106° F, anemia, jaundice, depression, thirst, a discharge from the eyes, and swelling of the eyelids. Constipation and colic may occur and the urine is a yellow to reddish color. Symptoms appear 1 to 3 weeks after exposure.

Treatment — In the past, a number of treatments were used, each with varying degrees of success. A new and promising treatment developed by the University of Florida, consists of 2 successive treatments of Diamprom, 4 milligrams per pound body weight, given intramuscularly 48 hours apart. This will eliminate the positive carrier state.

Prevention and control — Control the ticks that carry the parasites, especially brown dog ticks and tropical horse ticks, both of which are found in the United States. Methods of tick control are discussed in the section on external parasites. Practice rigid sanitation in the use of all syringes, needles, and medical instruments. Recovered animals remain carriers for 10 months to 4 years and should be isolated.

Discussion — This infection is worldwide. In the United States, it was first diagnosed in Florida in 1961. The death rate is from 10 to 15 percent of infected animals.

LUNGWORMS (*Dictyocaulus arnfieldi*)

The equine lungworm is very rare in the United States.

Symptoms — Donkeys seem to be able to carry large numbers of lungworms without showing any symptoms. They develop a tolerance. However, infected foals may become unthrifty and develop a cough. There is a rise in temperature with lungworm infection.

Prevention and control — Where lungworm infection is suspected, a fecal examination should be made. Infected burros should be kept away from foals.

Discussion — Lungworms may be found in the air passages of the horse and other equines. The male worm reaches a length of about 1 inch and the female may be about 2 inches long. The eggs are laid in the lungs and pass out of the horse's body through the intestine. They hatch into first-stage larvae that develop eventually into the third, or infective, stage. The infective larvae enter the body through the mouth, travel in the lymph vessels to the thoracic duct, then to the heart, and eventually to the lungs.

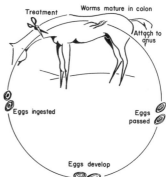

PINWORMS (Rectal Worms; *Oxyuris equi*, *Probstmyria vivipara*)

Two species of pinworms, or rectal worms, frequently are found in horses. *Oxyuris equi* are whitish worms with long, slender tails. *Probstmyria vivipara* are so small they are scarcely visible to the eye.

Symptoms — The symptoms are irritation of the anus and tail rubbing. Heavy infections also may cause digestive disturbances and anemia. Large pinworms are most damaging to horses and may be seen in the feces of heavily infected animals.

Treatment — Tables 9.4 and 9.5 give the drug selections and recommended dosage levels for the control of pinworms.

Prevention and control — Provide good sanitation and keep animals separated from their own excrement.

Discussion — Pinworms attack horses throughout the United States.

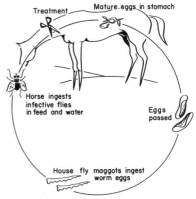

Stomach Worms (*Habronema* spp.,
Trichostrongylus axei)

A group of parasitic worms that produces inflammation of the stomach.

Symptoms — Horses suffer loss of condition and severe gastritis. Sometimes, the larvae of large stomach worms are partially responsible for the skin disease of horses called summer sores.

Treatment — Carbon disulfide and levamisole (Tramisol) are effective treatments, when used according to manufacturer's directions.

Dilute formaldehyde or ronnel are commonly used in the treatment of summer sores.

Prevention and control — Provide good sanitation, proper manure disposal, and fly control.

Discussion — Stomach worms attack horses throughout the United States. Wasted feed and lowered efficiency are the chief losses.

Strongyles, Large and Small
(Bloodworms; *Strongylus* spp. and others)

There are about 40 species of strongyles. Three are large worms that grow up to 2 inches long. The rest are small and some are barely visible to the eye. Large strongyles are variously called bloodworms (*Strongylus vulgaris*), palisade worms, sclerostomes, and red worms.

Symptoms — Infected horses have lack of appetite, anemia, progressive emaciation, a rough hair coat, sunken eyes, digestive disturbances including colic, a tucked-up appearance, and sometimes posterior paralysis

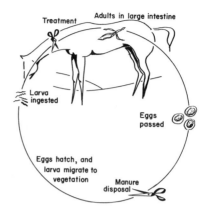

and death. Collectively these symptoms indicate the disease known as strongylosis. Harmful effects are greatest in young animals. One species of large strongyles (*Strongylus vulgaris*) may permanently damage the intestinal blood vessel wall and cause death at any age.

Treatment — Tables 9.4 and 9.5 give the drug selections and recommended dosage levels for the control of strongyles.

Prevention and control — Gather manure daily from pastures and barns and store it in a pit 2 to 3 weeks. Rotate pastures and avoid moist pasture and overstocking.

Discussion — Strongyles attack horses throughout the United States wherever horses are pastured. Attacks of strongyles result in loss of feed to feeding worms, lowered work efficiency, retarded growth of young animals, lowered breeding efficiency, and death in severe infections.

TAPEWORMS (*Anoplocephala magna, A. perfoliata, Paranoplocephala mamillana*)
Anoplocephala perfoliata is the most common and most damaging.

Symptoms — Heavy infections may cause digestive disturbances, loss in weight, and anemia.

Treatment — Treatment is not ordinarily suggested, primarily because only light infections are encountered. Yomesan or lead arsenate (Biforma), used according to manufacturer's directions, are the common treatments.

Prevention and control — Provide good sanitation and husbandry, proper manure disposal, and clean bedding.

Discussion — Tapeworms attack horses throughout the northern part of the United States. Losses are primarily in wasted feed and retarded growth.

THREADWORMS (*Strongyloides westeri*)
Threadworms are also known as strongyloides.

Symptoms — Threadworms attack foals, causing diarrhea. The worms disappear by the time foals are six months old.

Treatment — Thiabendazole (Equizole), thiabendazole-trichlorfon (Equivet-14), and thiabendazole-piperazine (Equizole-A), used according to manufacturer's directions, are effective in removing intestinal threadworms.

Prevention and control — Provide good sanitation and clean, dry bedding.

Discussion — These worms are common where there is a concentration of foals. Losses are primarily in stunted growth and unthriftiness.

EXTERNAL PARASITES

Several kinds of external parasites attack horses. These pests lower the vitality of horses, damage the hair and skin, and produce a generally unthrifty condition.

External parasites also are responsible for the spread of several serious diseases of horses. Equine piroplasmosis (babesiasis) is transmitted by a tick, *Dermacentor nitens.* Mosquitoes (*Culicidae*) are vectors of equine infectious anemia (swamp fever) and equine encephalomyelitis (sleeping sickness).

The common measures used to prevent and control external parasites of horses are practicing good sanitation, good grooming, avoiding a too heavy concentration of horses, and spraying or dusting with insecticides. Flies and lice are the most common external parasites of horses but some of the others can produce more severe injury when they occur.

The common external parasites of horses and recommended control measures follow. *Caution:* The choice of insecticides will vary because of (1) the diversity of environments and management practices under which they are used, (2) the varying restrictions on the use of insecticides from area to area, and (3) the fact that registered uses of insecticides change from time to time. Information about what insecticide is available and registered for use in a specific area can be obtained from the county agent, extension entomologist, agricultural consultant, or veterinarian.

BLOWFLY

The blowfly group consists of several species of flies that breed in animal flesh.

Damage inflicted; symptoms and signs of affected animals — The maggots of blowflies infest wounds and spread over the body, feeding on the skin surface, producing severe irritation, and destroying the ability of the skin to function. Infested animals rapidly become weak, fevered, and unthrifty.

Figure 9.5 Blowfly — the blowfly group consists of a number of species of flies, all of which breed in necrotic animal flesh.

Treatment — Daily dusting of the irritated or infected area with coumaphos (Co-Ral, etc.) or ronnel (Korlan) will control the flies. Puff-bottle applicators containing these insecticides are available and provide an effective means of application.

Prevention and control — To control the blowfly, destroy dead animals by burning or deep burial and by using traps, posioned baits, electrified screens, and repellents.

Discussion — Blowfly attacks are widespread but they present the greatest problem in the Pacific Northwest, the South, and the Southwest. Death losses are not large but work efficiency is lowered.

FLIES AND MOSQUITOES

Flies and mosquitoes are probably the most important insect pests of horses. They lower the vitality of horses, mar the hair coat and skin, produce a general unthrifty condition, lower performance, and make for hazards when riding or using horses. Also, they may temporarily or permanently impair the development of foals and young stock. Even more important, they can be the vector (carrier) of serious diseases. Because of their varying habits, along with different materials and methods required for their control, flies have been classed as either biting or nonbiting in the discussion that follows.

Figure 9.6 Horse fly and mosquito.

Biting Flies and Mosquitoes

Several species of biting (bloodsucking) flies and mosquitoes attack horses, but the following are the most common: horse flies (*Tabanus* spp.), deer flies (*Chrysops* spp.), stable flies (*Stomoxys calcitrans*), horn flies (*Haematobia irritans*), mosquitoes (species of the genera *Aedes, Anopheles, Culex,* and *Psorophora*), black flies (family Simuliidae), and biting midges (genus *Culicoides*). Because these flies suck blood, several of them may transmit such diseases as anthrax, encephalomyelitis (Eastern, Western, and Venezuelan), swamp fever, vesicular stomatitis, and anaplasmosis. All of them are pests — that is, they cause considerable annoyance to horses.

Distribution; losses caused by biting flies and mosquitoes — Biting (bloodsucking) flies and mosquitoes are found wherever there are horses, with the highest population occurring during warm weather and where there is lack of sanitation. They annoy horses — on pastures, in stalls, and in paddocks. They cause pain and discomfort to the animal, and, at times, they make them unmanageable when they are being worked.

Horse and deer flies attack horses pastured in or near areas with a marsh, swamp, creek, or irrigation ditch.

Stable flies are found wherever there are horses, people, or other mammals — their usual victims.

Horn flies are found near cattle. So, horses are attacked when they are pastured with cattle, kept in areas near cattle, or ridden near cattle.

Mosquitoes cause special discomfort to horses, particularly during early spring and wet years.

Life history and habits — Horse flies and deer flies breed in standing water that is fairly shallow and has an abundance of organic matter. Stable flies breed in horse manure, soiled bedding, feed wastes, decomposed fruit and vegetable matter, and compost piles and clippings. Horn flies breed in single, fresh droppings of cow manure. Mosquitoes breed on water, in such places as water-holding low spots in corrals and paddocks, infrequently used drinking troughs, irrigated pastures, drainage ditches, natural flooded meadows, swamps, creeks, tree holes, leaf-choked rain gutters, and poorly covered septic tanks and drains.

Damage inflicted; symptoms and signs of affected animals — Horse flies and deer flies possess sharp, scissorlike mouthparts, which slice into the skin and make for a good flow of blood.

The stable fly sucks blood and is a vicious biter, especially in the early evening hours when the weather is warm and humid. Severe attacks irritate horses and cause restlessness and the stamping of feet. Because stable flies crawl over horse manure and then suck blood from the horse, they readily transmit stomach worms (*Habronema*).

Horn flies feed primarily on the back of the head, the sides of the neck, shoulders, withers, along the back, around the navel, and on the legs. They remain on the horse day and night.

In addition to their vicious biting habits, mosquitoes are of particular concern to horsemen because they transmit the viruses causing encephalomyelitis (Western, Eastern, and Venezuelan).

Figure 9.7 Stable fly (*Stomaxys calcitrans*). (Courtesy, USDA)

Figure 9.8 Horn fly (*Haematobia irritans*).

Treatment — Fly repellents containing pyrethrins which last 4 to 8 hours after application have been developed for the control of horse flies and deer flies on horses.

Prevention and control — Sanitation — the destruction of the breeding areas of the pests — is the key to the control of biting flies and mosquitoes. Do not allow manure or other breeding areas to accumulate. Spread manure in fields (to dry) every day or two. Control horse flies, deer flies, and mosquitoes by filling low spots in corrals or paddocks and draining all water-holding areas.

As a supplement to sanitation, use insecticide (of which there are several) according to manufacturer's directions. Treat manure piles and buildings for fly control; and treat wet areas that harbor mosquitoes.

Nonbiting Flies

Horses may be annoyed by the face fly (*Musca autumnalis*) and the house fly (*M. domestica*), neither of which suck blood.

Distribution; losses caused by nonbiting flies — Face flies are serious pests of horses (and cattle) in the eastern, midwestern, and certain western states.

House flies are widely distributed throughout the world and are one of the principal pests around horse stables.

Life history and habits — The face fly breeds only in single, fresh animal droppings, and only from cattle on rangeland or pasture. The life cycle from egg to adult takes 8 days during warm summer months and up to 2 to 3 weeks in cooler weather.

House flies are attracted to waste materials, where they feed and deposit their eggs. This includes stacked horse manure, soiled bedding, wet feed, and decomposed plant material (grass clippings, vegetable and fruit wastes). House flies do not normally develop in single manure droppings; rather, they use piles of manure or other organic matter. Under favorable conditions — warm weather and plenty of food — the usual life cycle from egg to adult fly is one week.

Damage inflicted; symptoms and signs of affected animals — Face flies congregate about the nose and eyes of horses, where they sponge up liquids. The feeding of face flies causes excessive flow of tears and saliva — and irritation. Infested horses usually stand about restlessly switching their tails and not grazing naturally. Almost complete freedom from face flies can be obtained by keeping horses confined to stables during the daytime.

The house fly, which feeds twice daily, regurgitates liquid through its proboscis while depositing fecal matter as it crawls over its food. In this manner, it can transmit human and animal diseases, and it transmits stomach worms (*Habronema*) to horses. The dark spots on walls, ceilings, corral fences, etc., are the characteristic "fly specks" of vomit or fecal material.

House flies are attracted to the moist areas of the horse's face.

Treatment — Residual sprays will eliminate many house flies. Also, house flies are attracted to baits (insecticides mixed with sugar or other attractive material), which are effective house fly killers.

Prevention and control — Good face fly control is difficult to achieve. Pyrethrin repellents applied to the horse's face and head will repel nonbiting flies for 8 to 12 hours. A mask or net can be made and attached to the halter so that its movements protect the horse's eyes from face flies when on pasture. Residual sprays, when applied to the sunny surfaces of barns, shelters, and fences where face flies congregate reduce populations.

Figure 9.9 Face fly (*Musca autumnalis*).

Sanitation is the most efficient method of reducing populations of house flies. Sanitation may be additionally important if the horses are located near an urban area, in order to avoid complaints from neighbors.

LICE

These are small, flattened, wingless insect parasites. Horses are commonly infested by two species of lice; they are the common horse biting louse, *Damalinia equi,* and the horse sucking louse, *Haematopinas asini.*

Damage inflicted; symptoms and signs of affected animals — Symptoms include intense irritation, restlessness, and loss of condition. There may be severe itching and the animal may be seen scratching, rubbing, and gnawing the skin; scabs may be evident and the hair may be rough, thin, and without luster. Lice are likely to be most plentiful around the root of the tail, on the inside of the thighs, over the fetlock region, and along the neck and shoulders.

Treatment — Lice are easily controlled by periodic applications, according to the directions on the label, of one of the following insecticides: crotoxyphos, coumaphos (Co-Ral), dioxathion, malathion, or rotenone.

Prevention and control — Because of the close contact of horses during the winter, it is practically impossible to keep them from becoming

Figure 9.10 Sucking lice.   FEMALE   MALE

infested with lice. For effective control, all horses should be treated with insecticides simultaneously at intervals as needed, especially in the fall about the time they are placed in winter quarters.

Discussion — Lice are widespread. They retard growth, lower work efficiency, and produce unthriftiness. They show up most commonly on neglected animals in winter.

MITES

These are very small parasites that cause mange (scabies, scab, and itch). The two chief forms of mange are sarcoptic mange caused by burrowing mites and psoroptic mange caused by mites that bite the skin and suck the serum and lymph but do not burrow. Mites also may cause chorioptic mange.

Figure 9.11 Psoroptic mange mite (left) and sarcoptic mange mite (right).

Damage inflicted; symptoms and signs of affected animals — Symptoms are irritation, itching, and scratching. The skin crusts over and becomes thick, tough, and wrinkled. Mange appears to spread most rapidly during the winter months.

Treatment — Any of the following insecticides, used as a spray or dip, will meet the federal regulations for the control of mites on horses: lime-sulfur (2% sulfide sulfur), lindane (0.05–0.06%), or toxaphene (0.5–0.6%); using 2 applications of each insecticide, 10–14 days apart.

Prevention and control — Keep healthy horses away from diseased animals or infested premises. Spray infested animals with insecticides and quarantine affected herds.

Discussion — Mites are widespread. They retard growth, lower work efficiency, and produce unthriftiness. When sarcoptic and psoroptic mange appear, they must be reported to state or federal animal health agencies. Also, in many states, chorioptic mange must be reported.

RINGWORM

This is a contagious infection of the outer layers of skin caused by an infestation of microscopic fungi.

Damage inflicted; symptoms and signs of affected animals — Round, scaly areas almost devoid of hair appear mainly in the vicinity of eyes, ears, side of the neck, or root of the tail. Mild itching usually accompanies the infection.

Figure 9.12   Ringworm.

Treatment — Clip the hair from the infected skin areas. Soften skin crusts with warm soap and water and remove them if desired. Let infected areas dry and then paint them with weak tincture of iodine every 3 days or treat them with a mixture of one part salicylic acid and 10 parts alcohol every 3 days until the infection clears up.

Prevention and control — Isolate infected animals. Disinfect everything that has been in contact with infected animals, including curry combs and brushes. Practice strict sanitation.

Discussion — Ringworm attacks horses throughout the United States, primarily as a stable infection. It is unsightly, and infected animals may have considerable discomfort, but economic losses are low.

SCREWWORM

Maggots of the screwworm fly require living flesh of animals on which to feed.

  SCREWWORM FLY   SCREWWORM LARVA

Figure 9.13 Screwworm — the screwworm fly raises its maggots in the open wounds of animals.

Damage inflicted; symptoms and signs of affected animals — Symptoms include loss of appetite, unthriftiness, and lowered activity.

Treatment — Use ronnel (Korlan) smear. Brush or smear the infected area twice the first week and then weekly until healed. A wash containing 0.25 coumaphos (Co-Ral) also is effective.

Prevention and control — Area-wide screwworm eradication by sterilizing pupal-stage screwworms with X-rays or gamma rays has been most effective. Try to keep animals from wounding themselves and protect any wounds that do occur. Schedule castrations in winter when flies are least numerous and active.

Discussion — Screwworm appears mostly in the South and Southwest where it may cause 50 percent of the normal annual livestock losses. The screwworm has been eradicated from the southern United States east of the Mississippi River.

Figure 9.14 Ticks.   FEMALE   MALE

TICKS

Several kinds may be found on horses. The most common ones are the winter tick, *Dermacentor albipictus;* the lone star tick, *Amblyomma americanum;* and the spinose ear tick, *Otobius megnini.*

Damage inflicted; symptoms and signs of affected animals — The symptoms are lowered vitality and itching; animals rub and scratch infested parts.

Treatment — Recommended insecticides for control of ticks (except ear ticks) are: crotoxyphos, coumaphos (Co-Ra), dioxathion, malathion, and pyrethrins. For the control of ear ticks, use lindane or ronnel (Korlan).

Prevention and control — Treatment with insecticides will control ticks on horses and protect them against reinfestation for several weeks.

Discussion — Ticks appear mostly in the South and West. They reduce vitality of horses and may spread piroplasmosis and African horsesickness.

FIRST AID FOR THE HORSE

Accidents do happen; horses are more injury prone and subject to a more awesome variety of wounds than any other class of domestic animal. They are thin-skinned; and they cut, tear, and bruise easily. For this reason, maximum wound preventative measures should be an integral part of horse management procedure. Such things as loose wire, sticks, sharp rocks, machinery, loose or broken boards, and trash have no place in horse pastures or corrals; and stables and trailers should be periodically examined for loose boards, protruding nails, or any sharp objects.

Despite all possible precautions, however, as long as there are horses, there will be such things as wire cuts, saddle galls, cinch sores, rope burns, and other abrasions. Hence, it is important that the horseman have on hand at all times a good first aid powder, as an aid in (1) stopping bleeding, (2) killing germs, (3) drying the wound (thereby speeding the healing process and discouraging flies and other insects from congregating around it), and (4) lessening proud flesh.

The horse, more than any other species of animal, must receive proper care and treatment of wounds. Mistreatment will result in slow healing, excessive scarring, blemishing, and sometimes unsoundness. Wounds below the knees and hocks are especially sensitive; hence, they require careful treatment, and sometimes bandaging, to prevent complications.

Wounds take a variety of forms, sizes, and severity; and, in turn, these determine the treatment. Generally speaking, there are 5 classes of wounds: (1) *cut wounds* (*incised*) produced by sharp objects, such as glass or sharp metal, where there is a minimum of tissue damage and little bruising; (2) *torn wounds* (*lacerated*) produced by irregular objects, such as barbed wire and horn gores, characterized by extensive damage to underlying tissues; (3) *puncture wounds* (*penetrating*) produced by sharp objects, such as nails and pitchforks, characterized by small punctures and a considerable amount of deep injury; (4) *abrasions* caused by such things as rope burns and rubbing against a door or trailer, characterized by oozing of the serum and little bleeding; and (5) *bruises* (*contusions*) caused by a blow, such as a kick or fall, which do not break the skin but which cause bleeding and fluid loss deep down.

If the wound is serious, such as a deep puncture wound, or where the swelling or irritation persists, a veterinarian should be consulted. With minor wounds, however, the horseman may administer first aid. At the outset, it should be recognized that only nature can produce living cells and heal a wound; hence, man can merely aid the process.

Although wound treatment will vary according to form and severity, the following steps may be involved.

Step 1 — *Stop the bleeding.* If it is severe, pressure may be applied by tight bandaging above and below the wound, or by placing a pad on the wound and bandaging over it. When a large artery is severed, as evidenced by bright red blood spurting with a pulsing action, it may be necessary to control the loss of blood by applying a tourniquet on the side of the wound nearest the heart, until the arrival of the veterinarian. A tourniquet must be released after about 20 minutes for a minute or two, but it can be reapplied.

Step 2 — *Clean the wound* by washing it with cotton swabs soaked in warm saline (salt) solution. Remove all foreign material (objects and dirt), hair, and torn tissue. Cleanliness is of great importance.

Step 3 — *Clip or shave long hair* (it is often best not to remove short hair, because of the danger of contamination) from around the wound, to a distance of about $\frac{1}{2}$ inch.

Step 4 — *Apply first aid powder* according to the directions on the label.

Step 5 — *Suture incised and lacerated wounds if necessary,* with this decision being left to, and the work done by, a veterinarian. Proper wound drainage should always be established.

Step 6 — *Protect against tetanus* by administering (a) tetanus antitoxin if the animal is not already on a toxoid program, or (b) a toxoid booster when the horse has been immunized previously with this product. Also, the veterinarian may inject an antibiotic(s).

Step 7 — *Switch from powder to salve.* As soon as a scab has formed over the wound, switch from first aid powder to first aid salve.

It should be recognized that poor nutrition of the horse will delay healing of a wound. Hence, poorly balanced or inadequate rations, bad teeth, and parasitism may contribute to delayed wound healing.

LINIMENT FOR THE HORSE

A good liniment, properly used, will hasten and assist nature in returning an injured part to normal and relieve fatigue, overexertion, and soreness.

Exercise and work cause greatly increased need for oxygen, carbohydrates, and other nutrients of muscular tissues. When a muscle contracts, certain mechanical, electrical, chemical, and thermal changes take place. It has been shown that during prolonged hard work the expenditure of energy may be 78 times greater than during rest (Chapter 6, Feeding Horses, section on "Energy Needs"); and during very intense muscular use, such as racing, horses may expend 100 times more energy than at rest. Such activity cannot be long maintained because of the onset of fatigue.

Fatigue is produced when wastes accumulate faster than they can be removed by the circulation, and, unless the condition is rectified, aches, pains, and soreness follow. Thus, it is imperative that the circulation of the blood be increased in proportion to the demands of the muscle for energy, food, and removal of waste materials. The application of massage, heat, and counterirritants are methods of providing muscles (and tendons, ligaments, and skin) with better blood circulation.

Liniment is an astringent. Its use, along with massage, stimulates circulation, assists the body in removing waste products of muscle metabolism, and hastens nature in returning an injured part to normal.

The use of liniment is recommended for the following conditions: lameness, stiffness, soreness, strained tendons, sore shins, certain types of arthritis, and swellings, bumps, and bruises. It hastens recovery time and helps to prevent everyday injuries from turning into serious problems.

Also, liniment may be used as a body wash or brace after strenuous workouts or transportation, especially on the horse's legs, to relieve fatigue and overexertion and prevent soreness.

Except when used as a body wash and brace, liniment should be applied (pour on or dab) to the affected area at full strength. Then, the tissue should be massaged vigorously for 3 to 5 minutes to stimulate circulation, and the animal should be allowed to rest. Repeat treatment every 3 to 4 hours until relief is obtained, and as necessary thereafter.

Where the shoulder, back, and loin areas are involved, best results will be obtained by (1) first applying hot (but not scalding), steaming towels to the affected area, so as to stimulate natural circulation, and (2) then following with an application of liniment, rubbing until dry.

Where a "body wash and brace" is desired, use the liniment according to the manufacturer's directions. Such a brace may be used as a leg and body wash after workouts, to relieve fatigue and overexertion and prevent soreness. Sponge generously over the horse's body and legs.

DISINFECTANTS

A disinfectant is a bactericidal or microbicidal agent that frees from infection (usually a chemical agent which destroys disease germs or other microorganisms, or inactivates viruses).

The high concentration of horses and continuous use of horse barns often results in a condition referred to as disease buildup. As disease-producing organisms — viruses, bacteria, fungi, and parasite eggs — accumulate in the environment, disease problems can become more severe and be transmitted to each succeeding group of horses raised on the same premises. Under these circumstances, cleaning and disinfection become extremely important in breaking the life cycle. Also, in the case of a disease outbreak, the premises must be disinfected.

Under ordinary conditions, proper cleaning of barns removes most of the microorganisms, along with the filth, thus eliminating the necessity of disinfection.

Effective disinfection depends on five things:

1. Thorough cleaning before application.

2. The phenol coefficient of the disinfectant, which indicates the killing strength of a disinfectant as compared to phenol (carbolic acid). It is determined by a standard laboratory test in which the typhoid fever germ often is used as the test organism.

3. The dilution at which the disinfectant is used.

4. The temperature; most disinfectants are much more effective if applied hot.

5. Thoroughness of application, and time of exposure.

Disinfection must in all cases be preceded by a very thorough cleaning, for organic matter serves to protect disease germs and otherwise interferes with the activity of the disinfecting agent.

Sunlight possesses disinfecting properties, but it is variable and superficial in its action. Heat and some of the chemical disinfectants are more effective.

The application of heat by steam, by hot water, by burning, or by boiling is an effective method of disinfection. In many cases, however, it may not be practical to use heat.

A good disinfectant should (1) have the power to kill disease-producing organisms, (2) remain stable in the presence of organic matter (manure, hair, soil), (3) dissolve readily in water and remain in solution, (4) be nontoxic to animals and humans, (5) penetrate organic matter rapidly, (6) remove dirt and grease, and (7) be economical to use.

The number of available disinfectants is large because the ideal universally applicable disinfectant does not exist. Table 9.8 gives a summary of the limitations, usefulness, and strength of some common disinfectants. When using a disinfectant, *always read and follow the manufacturer's directions.*

Table 9.8 Handy Disinfectant Guide

Kind of Disinfectant	Usefulness	Strength	Limitations and Comments
Alcohol (Ethyl-ethanol, isopropyl, methanol)	Primarily as skin disinfectants and for emergency purposes on instruments.	70% alcohol—the content usually found in rubbing alcohol.	Too costly for general disinfection. Alcohol is ineffective against bacterial spores.
Boric Acid[1]	As a wash for eyes, and other sensitive parts of the body.	1 oz in 1 pt water (about 6% solution).	It is a weak antiseptic. It may cause harm to the nervous system if absorbed into the body in large amounts. For this and other reasons, antibiotic solutions and saline solutions are fast replacing it.
Chlorines (Sodium hypochlorate, chlormine-T)	Used for dairy equipment and as deodorants. They will kill all kinds of bacteria, fungi, and viruses, providing the concentration is sufficiently high.	Generally used for dairy equipment and as a deodorant at about 200 ppm.	They are corrosive to metals and neutralized by organic materials.
Cresols (Many commercial products available)	A generally reliable class of disinfectant. Effective against brucellosis, shipping fever, swine erysipelas, and tuberculosis.	Cresol is usually used as a 2 to 4% solution (1 cup to 2 gallons of water makes a 4% solution).	Cannot be used where odor may be absorbed, and, therefore, not suited for use around milk and meat.
Formaldehyde (Gaseous disinfectant)	In a 1 to 2% solution, formaldehyde will kill anthrax spores, TB organisms, and animal viruses. It is often used to disinfect buildings following a disease outbreak. A 1 to 2% solution may be used as a foot bath to control foot rot.	As a liquid disinfectant, it is usually used as a 1 to 2% solution. As a gaseous disinfectant (fumigant), use 1½ lb of potassium permanganate plus 3 pt of formaldehyde. Also, gas may be released by heating paraformaldehyde.	It has a disagreeable odor, destroys living tissue, and can be extremely poisonous. The bactericidal effectiveness of the gas is dependent upon having the proper relative humidity (above 75%) and temperature (above 30° C and preferably near 60° C).

(Cont.)

Table 9.8 Handy Disinfectant Guide (*Cont.*)

Kind of Disinfectant	Usefulness	Strength	Limitations and Comments
Heat (By steam, hot water, burning, or boiling)	Very useful in the burning of rubbish or articles of little value, and in disposing of infected body discharges. The steam Jenny is effective for disinfection *if properly employed* (example; poultry equipment), particularly if used in conjunction with a phenolic germicide.	10 minutes exposure to boiling water is usually sufficient.	Exposure to boiling water will destroy all ordinary disease germs but sometimes fails to kill the spores of such disease as anthrax and tetanus. Moist heat is preferred to dry heat, and steam under pressure is the most effective. Heat may be impractical or too expensive.
Iodine[1] (Tincture)	Extensively used as skin disinfectant, for minor cuts and bruises.	Generally used as tincture of iodine, either 2% or 7%.	Never cover with a bandage. Clean skin before applying iodine. It is corrosive to metals.
Idophore (Tamed iodine)	Primarily used for dairy utensils. Effective against all bacteria (both gram-negative and gram-positive), fungi, and most viruses.	Usually used as disinfectants at concentrations of 50–75 ppm titratable iodine, and as sanitizers at levels of 12.5 to 25 ppm. At 12.5 ppm titratable iodine can be used as an antiseptic in drinking water.	Inhibited by organic matter and quite expensive.
Lime (Quicklime; burnt lime; calcium oxide)	Used as a deodorant when sprinkled on manure and animal discharges; as a disinfectant when sprinkled on the floor, as a newly made "milk of lime," or as a whitewash.	Use as a dust, as "milk of lime," or as a whitewash, but use *fresh.*	Not effective against anthrax or tetanus spores. Wear goggles when adding water to quicklime.
Lye (Sodium hydroxide; caustic soda)	Useful on concrete floors, in milk houses (because there is no odor), against the microorganisms of brucellosis and the viruses of foot-and-mouth disease, hog cholera, and vesicular exanthema. In strong solution (5%), effective against anthrax and blackleg.	Lye is usually used as either a 2% or 5% solution. To prepare a 2% solution, add 1 can of lye to 5 gallons of water. To prepare a 5% solution, add 1 can of lye to 2 gallons of water. A 2% solution will destroy the organisms causing foot-and-mouth disease, but a 5% solution is necessary to destroy the spores of anthrax.	Damages fabrics, aluminum and painted surfaces. Be careful, for it will burn the hand and face. Not effective against organism of TB or Johne's disease. Lye solutions are most effective when used hot. **Diluted vinegar can be used neutralize lye.**

(*Cont.*

Table 9.8 Handy Disinfectant Guide (*Cont.*)

Kind of Disinfectant	Usefulness	Strength	Limitations and Comments
Lysol (The brand name of a product of cresol plus soap)	For disinfecting surgical instruments and instruments used in castrating and tattooing. Useful as a skin disinfectant before surgery, and for use on the hands before castrating.	0.5 to 2.0%.	Has a disagreeable odor. Does not mix well with hard water. Less costly than phenol.
Phenols (Carbolic acid): Phenolics-coal tar derivatives Synthetic phenols	They are ideal general-purpose disinfectants. Effective and inexpensive. They're very resistant to the inhibiting effects of organic residue; hence, they are suitable for barn disinfection and foot and wheel dip-baths.	Both phenolics (coal tar) and synthetic phenols vary widely in efficacy from one compound to another. So, note and follow manufacturer's directions. Generally used in a 5% solution.	They are corrosive, and they're toxic to animals and humans. Ineffective on fungi and viruses.
Quaternary ammonium compounds (QAC)	Very water soluble, ultra-rapid kill rate, effective deodorizing properties, and moderately priced. Good detergent characteristics and harmless to the skin.	Follow manufacturer's directions.	They can corrode metal. Not very potent in combating viruses. Adversely affected by organic matter.
Sal Soda	It may be used in place of lye against foot-and-mouth disease and vesicular exanthema.	10½% solution (13½ oz to 1 gal. water).	
Sal Soda and Soda Ash (or sodium carbonate)	May be used in place of lye against foot-and-mouth disease and vesicular exanthema.	4% solution (1 lb to 3 gal. water). Most effective in hot solution.	Commonly used as cleansing agent, but has disinfectant properties, especially when used as a hot solution.
Soap	Its power to kill germs is very limited. Greatest usefulness is in cleansing and dissolving coatings from various surfaces, including the skin, prior to application of a good disinfectant.	As commercially prepared.	Although indispensable for sanitizing surfaces, soaps should not be used as disinfectants. They are not regularly effective; staphylococci and the organisms which cause diarrheal diseases are resistant.

Sometimes loosely classed as a disinfectant but actually an antiseptic and useful practically only on living tissue.

10. Buildings and Equipment

Properly designed, constructed, and arranged horse buildings and equipment give increased animal comfort and performance, greater efficiency in the use of feed, and less expenditure of labor in the care of horses. Also, attractive barns add to the beauty of the landscape. In serving these purposes, buildings and equipment need not be elaborate or expensive.

SPACE REQUIREMENTS

One of the first and frequently one of the most difficult problems confronting the horseman who wishes to construct a building is that of arriving at the proper size or dimensions. Tables 10.1, 10.2, and 10.3 contain some conservative average figures giving the space requirements for (1) horse barns, (2) service passages, and (3) feed and bedding storage, respectively.

Figure 10.1 A two-stable horse barn. (Drawing by Steve Allured, after sketch from Sunset Magazine)

Table 10.1 Space Requirements of Buildings for Horses: Kinds and Plans

Kinds, Uses, and Purposes	Recommended Plan	Box Stalls or Shed Areas				Tie Stalls (Size)
		Size	Height of Ceiling	Height of Doors	Width of Doors	
Smaller Horse Establishments: Horse barns for pleasure horses, ponies, and/or raising a few foals.	12' x 12' stalls in a row; combination tack-feed room for 1- and 2- stall units; separate tack and feed rooms for 3-stall units or more. Generally, not more than a month's supply of feed is stored at a time. Use of all-pelleted rations (hay and grain combined) lessens feed storage space requirements.	Horses: 12' x 12' Ponies:[1] 10' x 10'	8'–9'	8'	4'	5' wide; 10'–12' long
Larger Horse-Breeding Establishments: The following specially designed buildings may be provided for different purposes:						
Broodmare and foaling barn	A rectangular building, either (1) with a central aisle, and a row of stalls along each side, or (2) of the "island" type, with two rows of stalls, back to back, surrounded by an alley or runway. Ample quarters for storage of hay, bedding, and grain. A record or office room, toilet facilities, hot water supply, veterinary supply room, and tack room are usually an integral part of a broodmare barn.	12' x 12' to 16' x 16'	9'	8'	4'	
Stallion barn	Quarters for one or more stallions, with or without feed storage. A small tack and equipment room. Stallion paddocks, at least 300 ft. on a side, adjacent to or in close proximity.	14' x 14'	9'	8'	4'	

(Cont.)

Table 10.1 Space Requirements of Buildings for Horses: Kinds and Plans (*Cont.*)

Kinds, Uses, and Purposes	Recommended Plan	Box Stalls or Shed Areas				Tie Stalls (Size)
		Size	Height of Ceiling	Height of Doors	Width of Doors	
Larger Horse-Breeding Establishments: (*Cont.*)						
Barren mare barn	An open shed or rectangular building, with a combination rack and trough space down the center or along the wall. Storage space for ample hay, grain, and bedding.	150 sq. ft. per animal	9'	8'	4'	
Weanling or yearling quarters	Open shed or stalls. The same type of building is adapted to both weanlings and yearlings; but different ages and sex groups should be kept separate. When stalls are used, two weanlings or two yearlings may be placed together.	10' x 10'	9'	8'	4'	
Breeding shed	A large, roofed enclosure with a high ceiling; should include laboratory for the veterinarian, hot water facilities, and stalls for preparing mares for breeding and holding foals.	24' x 24'	15'-20'	8'	9'	
Isolation (quarantine) quarters	Small barn, with feed and water facilities and adjacent paddock; for occupancy by new or sick animals.	12' x 12'	9'	8'	4'	
For Riding Academies and Training and Boarding Stables	Either (1) stalls constructed back to back in the center of the barn, with an indoor ring around the outside; (2) stalls around the outside and a ring in the center; or (3) stalls on either side of a hallway or alleyway, and an outdoor ring.	12' x 12'	9'	8'	4'	5' wide; 10'-12' long

¹Even for ponies, a 12' x 12' stall is recommended since (1) it costs little more than a 10' x 10', and (2) it affords more flexibility—it can be used for bigger horses when and if the occasion demands.

Table 10.2 Recommended Minimum Width for Service Passages

Kind of Passage	Use	Minimum Width
Feed Alley.........................	For feed cart..	4'
Driveway...........................	For wagon, spreader or truck.....................	9'–12'
Doors and gate...................	Drive-through.......................................	8'–9'

Table 10.3 Storage Space Requirements for Feed and Bedding

Kind of Feed or Bedding	Pounds per Cubic Feet (approx.)	Cubic Feet per Ton (approx.)	Pounds per Bushel of Grain	Cubic Feet per Bushel
Hay[1]—				
Timothy, loose........................	3	625–640		
Wild hay, loose.......................	3–4	450–600		
Alfalfa, loose..........................	4	470–485		
Clover, loose...........................	4	500–512		
Chopped hay	10	210–225		
Baled hay (closely stacked)	10	150–200		
Straw and shavings—				
Straw, baled...........................	10	200		
Straw, loose[1]........................	2–3	600–1000		
Shavings, baled......................	20	100		
Silage—				
Corn or sorghum silage in				
tower silos..........................	40	50		
Corn or sorghum silage in				
trench silos.........................	35	57		
Mill feed—				
Bran..................................	13	154		
Middlings..............................	25	80		
Linseed or soybean meal.............	35	57		
Grain—				
Corn, shelled..........................	45	45	56	1.25
Corn, ear.............................	28	72	70	2.50
Corn, snapped........................	25	81	80	3.25
Oats..................................	26	77	32	1.25
Barley................................	39	51	48	1.25
Wheat................................	48	42	60	1.25
Rye...................................	45	44	56	1.25
Grain sorghum	45	44	56	1.25

[1] Under hay and loose straw, a range is given under the columns for "pounds per cubic feet," and "cubic feet per ton," the higher figures being for hay and loose straw settled 1 to 2 months, and the lower figures for hay or loose straw settled over 3 months.

TYPES AND SIZES OF HORSE BARNS

The primary reasons for having horse buildings are: (1) to provide a place in which to confine horses and store feed and tack; and (2) to modify the environment by controlling temperature, humidity, and other factors.

Needs for housing horses and storage of materials vary according to the intended use of the buildings. Broadly speaking, horse barns are designed to serve either (1) small horse establishments that have one to a few animals, (2) large horse-breeding establishments, or (3) riding, training, and boarding stables.

Various types and sizes of stalls and sheds are used in horse barns. However, in all types except the breeding shed, ceilings should be 9 feet high and doors should be 8 feet high and 4 feet wide. The breeding shed should have a ceiling of 15 to 20 feet high and a door wide enough to permit entrance of vehicles.

The recommended plans for different kinds of horse barns are as follows.

SMALL HORSE ESTABLISHMENTS

These horse barns are for housing pleasure horses or ponies or raising a few foals. Box stalls should be 12 feet square and tie stalls should be 5 feet wide and 10 to 12 feet long.

Build the stalls in a row and provide a combination tack and feed room for units with 1 or 2 stalls. Use separate tack and feed rooms for units with 3 or more stalls. Generally, not more than a 1-month supply of feed is stored at a time. The use of all-pelleted feed lessens storage space requirements.

Building plans for a small horse barn are shown in Figure 10.2.

Figure 10.2 Riding horse barn above and floor plan below. Barn has two box stalls, a feed room, and a tack room.

Complete working drawings of small horse barns may be obtained through county agricultural agents or from extension agricultural engineers at most state agricultural colleges.

LARGE HORSE-BREEDING ESTABLISHMENTS

Large establishments need specially designed buildings for different purposes. They are as follows.

Broodmare and Foaling Barn — This can be a rectangular building either (1) with a central aisle and a row of stalls along each side, or (2) of the "island" type with two rows of stalls back to back surrounded by an alley or runway. Most broodmare stalls are 12 feet square, although they may be up to 16 feet square. A stall 16 feet square is desirable for foaling. A broodmare barn needs the following: (1) an office for records; (2) toilet facilities; (3) hot water supply; (4) veterinary supply room; (5) tack room; and (6) storage space for hay, bedding, and grain.

Stallion Barn — This barn provides quarters for one or more stallions. It should have a small tack and equipment room, and it may or may not have feed storage. The stalls should be 14 feet square.

Provide a paddock near the barn or, if possible, adjacent to it. The paddock can be any shape but each side should be at least 300 feet long.

Barren Mare Barn — Use an open shed or rectangular building that has a combination rack and trough down the center or along the wall. Provide

Figure 10.3 Foaling barn (interior view) of Golden Land Farm, Apple Valley, Calif. Note solid, safe construction and plenty of air vents. (Courtesy, California Thoroughbred Breeders Association, Arcadia, California)

storage space for hay, grain, and bedding. Allow each animal 150 square feet of space.

Weanling and Yearling Quarters — Either an open shed or a barn with stalls may be used. Both weanlings and yearlings may be kept in the same building, but different age and sex groups should be kept apart. When stalls are used, two weanlings or two yearlings may be kept together. Stalls should be 10 feet square.

Breeding Shed — This should be a large, roofed enclosure that has a laboratory for the veterinarian, hot water facilities, and stalls for preparing mares for breeding and for holding foals. The shed should be 24 feet square.

Isolation Quarters — These quarters are for sick animals and animals new to the farm. Use a small barn that has feed and water facilities and an adjacent paddock. Stalls should be 12 feet square.

RIDING, TRAINING AND BOARDING STABLES

For this purpose, the quarters may consist of (1) stalls constructed back to back in the center of the barn with an indoor ring around the stalls, (2) stalls built around the sides of the barn with the ring in the center, or (3) stalls on either side of a hallway or alleyway and the ring outdoors. Box stalls should be 10 to 12 feet square and tie stalls should be 5 feet wide and 10 to 12 feet long.

REQUISITES OF HORSE BARNS

Whether a new horse layout is built or an old one is altered, all buildings, fences, corrals, and trees should be placed according to a master plan, for, once established, they usually are difficult and expensive to move. The arrangement should make the best possible use of land and should require little walking by attendants when caring for horses.

All horse barns should meet the following requisites

1. *Accessibility* — Barns should be on an all-weather roadway or lane to facilitate the use of horses, delivery of feed and bedding, and removal of manure.

2. *Dryness* — Barns should be on high ground so water will drain away from them.

3. *Expandable design* — Barns should be designed so they are easy to expand if and when the time comes. Often a building can be lengthened provided no other structures or utilities interfere.

4. *Water and electricity* — Water and electricity should be available and convenient to use.

5. *Controlled environment* — Barns should be built to modify winter and summer temperatures, maintain acceptable humidity and ventilation, minimize stress on the horses' nerves, and protect horses from rain, snow, sun, and wind.

6. *Reasonable cost* — Initial cost is important but durability and maintenance should be considered, as well as such intangible values as pride and satisfaction in the buildings, and advertising value.

7. *Adequate space* — Too little space may jeopardize the health and well-being of horses, but too much space means unnecessary expense.

8. *Storage areas* — Storage space for feed, bedding, and tack should be provided in the building where they are used.

9. *Attractiveness* — An attractive horse barn increases the sale value of the property. A horse barn will have aesthetic value if it has good proportions and is in harmony with the natural surroundings.

10. *Minimum fire risk* — The use of fire resistant materials gives added protection to horses. Also, fire retarding paints and sprays may be used.

11. *Safety* — Projections that might injure horses should be removed. Feeding and watering equipment should be arranged so attendants need not walk behind horses.

12. *Labor saving construction* — This requisite is a must in any commercial horse establishment. Also, where horses are kept for pleasure, unnecessary labor should be eliminated in feeding, cleaning, and handling.

13. *Healthful living conditions* — Healthy horses are better performers; therefore, barns should be easy to keep clean so they will provide healthful living conditions.

14. *Rodent and bird control* — Feed and tack storage areas should be rodent- and bird-proof.

15. *Suitable corrals and paddocks* — Horse barns should have well-drained, safe, fenced corrals or paddocks adjacent to them. If this is not possible, the corral or paddock should be nearby.

16. *Flexibility* — Possible changes in use make it desirable for horse barns to be as flexible as possible, even to the point that they can be cheaply and easily converted into cabins, garages, storage buildings, or buildings for other uses. Also, for suburbanites and renters, permanent, portable barns are advantageous.

STALLS

Stalls are of two general types: (1) box stalls; and (2) tie stalls. Most horsemen prefer box stalls because they allow the horse more liberty, either when standing or lying down. In addition to space requirement, the following features are important in stalls.

1. *Floors* — A raised clay floor covered with a good absorbent bedding, with proper drainage away from the building, is the most satisfactory flooring for horse stables. Clay floors are noiseless and springy, keep the hoofs moist, and afford firm natural footing unless wet; but they are difficult to keep clean and level. To lessen the latter problems, the top layer should be removed each year, replaced with fresh clay, and leveled.

Figure 10.4 A satisfactory type of box stall for horses.

Also, a semicircular concrete apron extending into each stall at the doorway will prevent horses from digging a hole in a clay floor at this point. This arrangement is particularly desirable in barns for yearlings, as they are likely to fret around the door.

Rough wooden floors furnish good traction for animals and are warm to lie upon; but they are absorbent and unsanitary, they often harbor rats and other rodents, and they lack durability.

Concrete, asphalt, or brick floors are durable, impervious to moisture, easily cleaned, and sanitary; but they are rigid and without resilient qualities, slippery when wet, hazardous to horses, and cold to lie upon. It is noteworthy that concrete and asphalt, generously covered with bedding, are widely used for stable floors throughout Eastern and Western Europe.

2. *Concrete footings* — Concrete footings and foundation walls are recommended as they are both durable and noncorrosive. The foundation should be a minimum of 8 inches high, so as to be above the manure level.

3. *Ceiling height* — A ceiling height of 8 to 9 feet is recommended, although there is no harm if it is higher.

4. *Walls* — The inside of the stall should be boarded up to a height of about 5 feet, using either (a) durable plywood of adequate thickness and strength, or (b) 2-inch, hard lumber, (such as oak) placed horizontally. Hollow concrete blocks encourage stall kicking; hence, when used, they should either be filled with concrete or lined with wood. About 5 feet, and extending up to a minimum of 7 feet (or even to the ceiling), stall partitions or fronts may be slatted, preferably with metal, to allow for air circulation and companionship with other horses.

5. *Doors* — Stall doors may be either (a) full sliding type suspended by

Figure 10.5 Dutch-type stall door, with air vent, at Golden Land Farms, Apple Valley, Calif. Note durable construction. (Courtesy, California Thoroughbred Breeders Association, Arcadia, California)

overhead rollers or rails, or (b) the swinging Dutch type, with the top part swinging down or to the side.

6. *Weather protection over stall doors* — This is important. It can be easily and simply achieved by an overhanging roof.

TACK ROOM

A tack room is an essential part of any barn. With one- and two-stall units, a combination tack and feed room is usually used, for practical reasons. Good horsemen take pride in their tack and its arrangement in the tack room. Tack rooms should be floored, rodent- and bird-proof, and ceiled over.

ENVIRONMENTAL CONTROL

Animals perform better and require less feed if they are raised under ideal conditions of temperature, humidity, and ventilation. Environmental control is of particular importance in horse barn construction because many horses spend most of the time in a stall. The investment in environmental control facilities must be balanced against the expected increased returns because there is a point where further expenditures for environmental control will not increase returns sufficiently to justify added cost.

Before the building is designed, it is necessary to know how much heat and moisture a horse produces. Body heat production varies according to

Figure 10.6 A tack room, featuring a revolving saddle rack. (Photo by John H. Williamson, Arcadia, Calif.; courtesy, *Western Livestock Journal*)

body weight, rate of feeding, environmental conditions, and degree of activity. Under average conditions, a 1000-pound horse produces about 1790 British thermal units (Btu) per hour, and a 1500-pound horse about 2450 Btu per hour.

A horse breathes into the air approximately 17.5 pounds, or 2.1 gallons, of moisture per day. When it's cold and this moisture is not removed, it condenses and forms frost. The latter condition is indicative of lack of ventilation, and it may be indicative of insufficient insulation, also.

Until more experimental information is available, the following environmental control recommendations, based on confinement systems used for other classes of animals, may be followed:

▪ Temperature — A range of 45° to 75° F (7° to 24° C) is satisfactory, with 55° F (13° C) considered best. Until a newborn foal is dry, it should be warmed to 75° to 80° F (24° to 27° C). This can be done with a heat lamp.

▪ Humidity — A range of 50 to 75 percent relative humidity is acceptable, with 60 percent preferred.

▪ Ventilation — The barn should have as little moisture and odor as possible, and it should be free from drafts. In a properly ventilated barn, the ventilation system should provide 60 cubic feet per minute (cfm) for each 1000 pounds of horse (1.7 m^3/454 kg horse) in winter and 160 cfm per 1000 pounds of horse (2.8 m^3/454 kg horse) in summer. In summer, satisfactory ventilation usually can be achieved by opening barn doors and by installing hinged doors or panels near the ceiling that swing open.

▪ Water Temperature — In the winter months, water for horses should be warmed to 40° to 45° (4° to 7° C); in the summer, it should be within the range of 60° to 75° F (16° to 24° C).

MATERIALS

When building materials for horse barns are bought, the factors to be considered are initial cost, durability and maintenance, attractiveness, and fire resistance.

Some of the materials available and being used are wood, including plywood; metal; masonry, including concrete, concrete block, cinder, pumice block, brick, and stone; and plastics. Also, preengineered and prefabricated horse barns are being used more often, especially on smaller horse establishments.

SHEDS

In the wild state (as nature ordained it), the horse augmented his shaggy winter coat by seeking the protection afforded by hills, ravines, and trees. But man changed all this — and not always for the better. Diseases and unsoundnesses began with too close confinement and lack of exercise. Through mistaken kindness, horses are often subjected to lack of ventilation and high humidity.

Figure 10.7 A horse shed; open to the south, away from the direction of the prevailing winds, and toward the sun. (Photo by Ernst Peterson, Hamilton, Mont.; courtesy, Margit Sigray Bessenyey, Hamilton, Montana)

For broodmares and horses not in constant use, an open shed, with access to a pasture or corral, is preferred. Horses kept in an open shed, even in the colder areas, are healthier and suffer fewer respiratory diseases than horses kept in enclosed barns.

Sheds are usually open to the south or east, preferably opposite to the direction of the prevailing winds and toward the sun. They are enclosed on the ends and sides. Sometimes the front is partially closed, and in severe weather drop-doors may be used. The latter arrangement is especially desirable when the ceiling height is sufficient to accommodate a power manure loader.

So that the bedding be kept reasonably dry, it is important that sheds be located on high, well-drained ground; that eave troughs and downspouts drain into suitable tile lines, or surface drains; and that the structures have sufficient width to prevent rain and snow from blowing to the back end. Sheds should be a minimum of 24 feet in depth, front to back, with depths up to 36 feet preferable. As a height of $8\frac{1}{2}$ feet is necessary to accommodate some power-operated manure loaders, when this type of equipment is to be used in the shed a minimum ceiling height of 9 feet is recommended. The extra 6 inches allow for the accumulation of manure. Lower ceiling heights are satisfactory when it is intended to use a blade or pitchfork in cleaning the building.

The length of the shed can be varied according to needed capacity. Likewise, the shape may be either a single long shed or in the form of an L or T. The long arrangement permits more corral space. When an open shed is contemplated, thought should be given to feed storage and feeding problems.

Sometimes hayracks are built along the back wall of sheds, or next to an alley, if the shed is very wide or if there is some hay storage overhead. Most generally, however, hayracks, feed bunks, and watering troughs are placed outside the structure.

SHADE

Shade, either from trees or man-made, should be provided for horses that are in the hot sun.

Figure 10.8 Nature's shade — trees — are excellent for horses. This shows Standardbred mares and foals on pasture. (Courtesy, The United States Trotting Association, Columbus, Ohio)

The most satisfactory man-made horse shades are (1) oriented with a north-south placement, (2) at least 12 to 15 feet in height (in addition to being cooler, high shades allow a mounted rider to pass under), and (3) open all around.

FEED AND WATER EQUIPMENT

The design of feed and water equipment should fill the basic need for simple and effective equipment with which to provide hay, concentrates, minerals, and water without waste or hazard to the horse. Whenever possible, for convenience and safety, feed and water equipment should be located so it can be filled without the caretaker entering the stall or corral.

Feed and water equipment may be built-in or detached. Because specialty feed and water equipment is more sanitary, flexible, and suitable, many horseman favor it over old-style wood mangers and concrete or steel tanks. Bulk-tank feed storage may be used to advantage on large horse establishments to eliminate sacks, lessen rodent and bird problems, and make it possible to obtain feed at lower prices by ordering large amounts.

The kind, size, and location of the most common equipment used to hold concentrates, hay, minerals, and water are described.

CONCENTRATE PAIL, TUB, BOX, OR PORTABLE FEEDER

A pail or tub can be made of metal, plastic, or rubber. Usually it has screw eyes and hooks or snaps so it can be suspended. The capacity should be 16 to 20 quarts for horses and 14 to 16 quarts for ponies.

In a stall, the pail or tub should be at the front. The height should be two-thirds the height of the animal at the withers, or 38 to 42 inches for horses and 28 to 32 inches for ponies.

Figure 10.9 Flat back pails.

In a corral put the tub or pail along a fence line and at the same height as in a stall.

For sanitary reasons, removable concentrate containers are preferable so they can be easily and frequently cleaned. This is especially important after feeding a wet mash.

A wooden box for horses should be 12 to 16 inches wide, 24 to 30 inches long, and 8 to 10 inches deep. A box for ponies should be 10 to 12 inches wide, 20 to 24 inches long, and 6 to 8 inches deep.

The location and height of a box in a stall are the same as for a pail or tub. Do not use a wooden box in a corral.

If desired, a wedge-shaped metal pan set on a wooden shelf can be mounted in a front corner of the stall and pivoted so it can be pulled out for filling and cleaning and then pushed back into the stall and locked in place.

HAYRACK OR MANGER

A stall rack may be made of metal, fiber, or plastic. A rack for horses should hold 25 to 30 pounds of hay and a rack for ponies, 10 to 15

Figure 10.10 Hayrack.

pounds. It should be in a corner of the stall. The bottom of the rack should be the same height as the horse or pony at the withers.

Hayracks lessen hay contamination, parasitic infestation, pawing by horses, and hay waste. Racks should open at the bottom so dirt, chaff, and trash may be removed or allowed to fall out. For stallions and brood-mares, use high racks to lessen injury hazards.

A wooden manger may be used. It should be 30 inches wide and 24 to 30 inches long for horses and 20 inches square for ponies. Put the manger in the front or in a corner of the stall. The height should be 30 to 42 inches for horses and 20 to 24 inches for ponies.

Corral racks are usually made of wood. They should be large enough to hold a one-day supply of hay for the intended number of horses. Put the rack in the fence line of the corral if horses feed from one side only. Put it on high ground if horses feed from both sides.

The top of the rack may be 1 to 2 feet higher than the horses at the withers. Corral hayracks that feed from both sides should be portable.

MINERAL BOX OR SELF-FEEDER

A box may be made of wood and a self-feeder may be made of metal or wood. In a stall, the box or self-feeder should be in a corner of the stall

Figure 10.11 Wooden hay manger — satisfactory type. (Courtesy, *Western Horseman,* Colorado Springs, Colorado)

and should be the same height as the box or pail used for concentrates.

In a corral, mineral containers should be in a fence corner. The height should be two-thirds the height of the horse at the withers. If a mineral container is in the open, it should be protected from wind and rain. Mineral containers should have two compartments; one for the mineral mix, and the other for the salt.

WATERING FACILITIES

Automatic waterers are made of metal. Waterers should be located in a front corner of a stall or in a fence corner of a corral or pasture.

Watering equipment should be designed to facilitate draining and cleaning. Locate waterers a considerable distance from feed containers if possible. Otherwise, horses will carry feed to the waterer or drip water in the concentrate container. A large 20- by 30-inch automatic waterer will accommodate about 25 horses; a 2-cup waterer, about 12.

The daily water requirements for horses are: mature horse, 12 gallons; foal to 2-year-old, and pony, 6 to 8 gallons. In cold areas, waterers should be heated and equipped with thermostatic controls. A satisfactory water temperature range in winter is 40° to 45° F and in summer 60° to 75° F.

Check automatic waterers daily.

A water pail may be made of metal, plastic, or rubber. It should be located in the front of the stall. The height should be two-thirds the height of the horse at the withers, or 38 to 42 inches for horses and 28 to 32 inches for ponies.

A water tank may be concrete or steel. It is used in a corral and should be set in the fence so there are no protruding corners. If it is out in a corral

Figure 10.12 Stall waterer for one stall.

Figure 10.13 Self-filling, steel corral waterer in horse paddock. (Courtesy, California Thoroughbred Breeders Association, Arcadia, California)

or pasture away from a fence, it should be painted white so the horses can see it at night.

A tank should be 30 to 36 inches high. Allow 1 linear foot of tank space to each 5 horses. A tank should be equipped with a float valve that is protected from the horses.

FENCES FOR HORSES

Good fences (1) maintain boundaries, (2) make horse training and other operations possible, (3) reduce losses to both animals and crops, (4) increase property values, (5) promote better relationships between

Figure 10.14 Horse fence.

Figure 10.15 Chain-link horse paddock gate and fence. (Courtesy, California Thoroughbred Breeders Association, Arcadia, California)

neighbors, (6) lessen the likelihood of car accidents from animals getting
on roads, and (7) add to the attractiveness and distinctiveness of the
premises.

Large pastures in which the concentration of horses is not too great may
be fenced with woven wire. The mesh of the woven wire fence should be
small so horses cannot get their feet through it. Corrals, paddocks, and
small pastures require stronger materials. The deficiencies of board and
pole fences are: they must be kept painted; they splinter, break, and rot;
and they are chewed by horses.

Until recently, conventional metal fences of steel, aluminum, wrought
iron, chain link, or cable had one or more deficiencies. But metal fences
have greatly improved in recent years.

Table 10.4 lists the materials and specifications commonly used for
horse fences.

SHOW-RINGS

Show-rings have no standard or required specifications for ring size,
type of construction, or maintenance.

For most purposes, a ring 125′ x 250′ will suffice. However, many good
show-rings are either smaller or larger than this. For example, the ring of
the famous Devon Horse Show, which is often used for jumpers, is
150′ x 300′. But the ring at the Spanish Riding School in Vienna is only
59′ x 180′.

The surface of a show-ring must be resilient and firm to assure proper
footing, and it also must be free of dust. In outdoor rings, proper drainage
and a good tract base are necessary for all-weather use. A ring can be

Table 10.4 Horse Fences

Post and Fencing Material	Post Length and Diameter	Size of Rails, Boards, or Poles and Gauge of Wire	Fence Height (in.)	Number of Rails, Boards, or Poles and Mesh of Wire	Distance Between Posts on Centers (ft.)
Steel or aluminum posts and rails[1]	7½ feet	10 or 20 feet long	60	3 rails	10
	7½ feet	10 or 20 feet long	60	4 rails	10
	8½ feet	10 or 20 feet long	72	4 rails	10
Wooden posts and boards	7½ ft; 4″–8″	2 x 6 or 2 x 8 in. boards	60	4 boards	8
	8½ ft; 4″–8″	2 x 6 or 2 x 8 in. boards	72	5 boards	8
Wooden posts and poles	7½ ft; 4″–8″	4–6 in. diameter	60	4 poles	8
	8½ ft; 4″–8″	4–6 in. diameter	72	5 poles	8
Wooden posts and woven wire[2]	7½ ft; 4″–8″	9- or 11-gauge staywire	55 to 58	12 in. mesh	12

[1] Because of the strength of most metal, fewer rails and posts are necessary than when wood is used.
[2] Use 1 or 2 strands of barbed wire—with barbs 3 to 4 inches apart—on top of the fence.

drained by (1) locating it high enough for water to drain away from it, and (2) installing drainage tile or perforated steel pipe underneath the track, with the perforations on the bottom side of the pipe.

The track usually will be firm if it is covered with a mixture of organic matter and dirt or sand. For example, the ring at the Spanish Riding School is covered with a mixture of $\frac{2}{3}$ sawdust and $\frac{1}{3}$ sand. It is sprinkled with water at intervals to keep down the dust.

In many indoor rings in the United States, 6 to 8 inches of tanbark are used on a dirt base. Unless tanbark is watered frequently, it will pulverize and give poor footing. Some rings are covered 18 to 24 inches deep with shavings or sawdust mixed with dirt or sand. Other rings are covered with approximately 9 inches of wood shavings, 2 inches of sawdust, and 4 inches of sand all mixed together and oiled. Salt may be added because it holds moisture when wetted down and reduces dust.

In outdoor rings, organic matter for resilience is sometimes provided by seeding rye or other small grain on the track during the off-season and disking under the green crop.

No matter how good the construction, a show-ring must be maintained. It must be smoothed and leveled, holes must be filled, and when it gets too hard, the ground must be broken. A flexible, chain-type harrow is recommended for show-ring maintenance.

Besides ring size, construction, and maintenance, other factors to be considered are (1) ring layout to facilitate reversing a performance class in a ring that has turf or other decorative material in the center; (2) attractiveness of the ring; (3) spectator seating capacity, comfort, and visibility; (4) nearby parking; and (5) handling the crowd.

DEPRECIATION ON BUILDINGS AND EQUIPMENT
In 1962, the Treasury issued "useful life" guidelines. If you follow them, you will not be challenged. For buildings, it's 25 years; for machinery and equipment, it's 10 years.

11. Tack

Tack includes all articles of gear, or equipment, used on or attached to riding and driving horses. Each horse should have his own saddle, bridle, halter, and lead shank so they can be adjusted to fit.

Superior quality tack usually is cheaper in the long run. With proper care, it will last for many years. Some common items of tack are discussed in the following sections.

Figure 11.1 Parade horse, showing elaborate tack. (Courtesy, Willard Beanland, Canoga Park, California)

Figure 11.2 Bridles. Three types of bridles. (A) Weymouth bridle — a double-bitted, double-reined bridle used in showing three- and five-gaited horses; (B) Pelham bridle — a single-bitted, double-reined bridle used on hunters, polo ponies, and pleasure horses; (C) one ear, or split ear, bridle — a bridle often used on working stock horses.

BRIDLES AND HACKAMORES

Lightweight bridles and bits usually indicate competent horsemen and well-mannered horses. Bridles may be either single or double. A single bridle is equipped with one bit, whereas a double bridle is ordinarily equipped with both a snaffle bit and a curb bit, two headstalls, and two pairs of reins. Only one rein is used with western bridles.

All bridles should be properly fitted, and the headstall should be located so that it neither slides back on the horse's neck nor pulls up against his ears. The cheek straps should be adjusted in length so the bit rests easily in the mouth without drawing up the corners. And the throatlatch should be buckled loosely enough to permit the hand, when held edgeways, to pass between it and the horse's throat.

The bosal hackamore and the hackamore bit-bridle are used on horses with tender mouths and as training devices for western horses.

The bosal hackamore has a pair of reins and an ordinary headstall that holds in place a braided rawhide or rope noseband knotted under the horse's jaw. It is an excellent device for controlling a young horse without injuring his mouth and is used extensively in training polo and cow ponies.

Figure 11.3 Hackamores. Two types of hackamores. (A) bosal hackamore — a popular hackamore for breaking horses; (B) hackamore bit-bridle — a hackamore with a removable mouthpiece that is used on western cow ponies and on young horses when they are being broken, because it eliminates the possibility of injuring the mouth.

When properly adjusted, the hackamore should rest on the horse's nose about 4 inches from the top of the nostrils, or at the base of the cheek bones. It should also permit the passage of two fingers held edgeways between it and the jaw.

The hackamore bit-bridle is a "fake" bridle; it has the shanks on each side but no mouthpiece.

The kind of bridle or hackamore used will depend on the horse's training and intended use. Figures 11.2 and 11.3 show the most common types of bridles and hackamores.

HOW TO BRIDLE A HORSE

Bridling is made easy by the procedure that follows.

Take the crownpiece of the bridle in the left hand and the reins in the right. Approach the horse from the left side opposite the shoulder. With your right hand slip the reins over his head, allowing them to rest on the crest directly behind the ears. Remove the halter — if there is one. Place yourself just behind the horse's head, facing front. Then, step by step, bridle him as follows:

- *Step 1* — Take the crownpiece of the bridle in your right hand and

Figure 11.4 Steps in bridling a horse:

A. Step 1 — Bridle in position — with the nose between the cheek pieces, the crownpiece in front of the ears, and the bit dangling against the teeth.

B. Step 2 — Mouth open.

C. Step 3 — Bridle on, with bit in mouth and crownpiece over ears.

D. Step 4 — Throatlatch buckled.

slip the horse's nose between the cheek pieces (and in the cavesson or noseband, if the bridle is so equipped). Raise the bridle with the right hand, until the crownpiece or headstall is just in front of the ears and the bit is dangling against the teeth. With your left hand, cup the horse's chin firmly, holding the bar of the bit across the palm and keeping it against the teeth with your thumb.

- *Step 2* — Slip the ends of your fingers between the horse's lips on the far side and into the animal's mouth. Thereupon, he will open his mouth and curl back his lips.
- *Step 3* — With a quick pull on the crownpiece, bring the bridle into position — that is, the bit in his mouth and the crownpiece slipped over his ears.
- *Step 4* — Buckel the throatlatch.

From these steps and the accompanying figure, the novice should not get the impression that in bridling a horse each step is so distinct and different as to be marked by intermittent pauses. Rather, when properly executed, bridling is a series of rhythmic movements, and the entire operation is done so smoothly and gracefully that it is difficult to discern where one stage ends and the next one begins.

BITS

The bit is the most important part of the bridle. In fact, the chief use of the other parts of the bridle are to hold the bit in place in the horse's mouth. The bit provides communication between the rider or driver and the horse.

Figures 11.5, 11.6, and 11.7 show the most common types of bits. There are many variations on each of these types.

The proper fit and adjustment of the bit is very important. It should rest easily in the mouth and be wide enough so it will not pinch the cheeks or cause wrinkles in the corners of the mouth. As a rule, a curb-type bit rests lower in the mouth than a snaffle. All bits should have large rings or other devices to prevent them from passing through the mouth when either rein is drawn in turning the horse.

The following points about bits should be remembered:

- Usually, the snaffle bit is used when a horse is started in training.
- The hunting, or egg butt, snaffle is used on hunters and jumpers.
- The curb bit is a more severe bit than the snaffle and it may be used either alone or with the snaffle.
- The Pelham bit is one bit that is used with two reins and a curb chain. It is a combination of a snaffle and a curb bit and is used in park or pleasure riding and hunting.
- The Weymouth bit combined with a snaffle bit is known as a bit and bradoon.
- Western bits are similar to the curb bit but they have longer shanks and are larger. Usually, they are used with a solid leather curb strap but

Figure 11.5 Five common types of English riding bits. (A) Weymouth curb bit — a bit used along with a snaffle bit in a Weymouth bridle for three- and five-gaited horses; (B) Pelham curb bit — a bit used in a Pelham bridle for hunters, polo ponies, and pleasure horses; (C) Walking Horse bit — a bit often used on Walking Horses; (D) Snaffle bit — the most widely used of all bits; (E) Dee race bit — a bit often used on Thoroughbred racehorses.

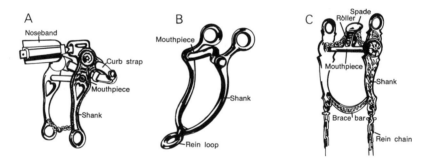

Figure 11.6 Three common types of Western riding bits. (A) Hackamore bit — a bit used on most cow ponies; (B) Roper curved cheek bit — a bit used on many roping horses, (C) Spade mouth bit — a bit used on many stock horses.

sometimes they have a small amount of chain in the middle of the leather curb strap.

SADDLES

The English and Western saddles are the two most common types, but individual styling within the types may vary considerably.

Figure 11.7 Three common types of driving bits. (A) Liverpool bit — a curb bit used on heavy harness horses; (B) Bar bit — a bit used on trotting harness horses that carry checkreins and are driven with a strong hand; (C) Half-cheek snaffle bit — a bit used on harness racehorses, roadsters, and fine harness horses.

Figure 11.8 Two ornate saddles of the Ching dynasty (1644–1911), made of leather covered with gold and inlaid with precious stones. These saddles are on display in the Palace Museum (formerly called the Forbidden City), in Peking, People's Republic of China. (Photo by A. H. Ensminger)

ENGLISH SADDLE

English saddles include the flat types that are modified specifically for pleasure riding, training, racing, jumping, or polo. The English saddle (Figure 11.9) is characterized by its relatively flat seat and its generally light weight.

The following points are pertinent to the use of English saddles:

■ When an English saddle is used on a show horse, use a white web or linen girth.

■ A saddle blanket usually is not necessary with an English saddle.

■ For English pleasure riding or showing, use an English saddle and a double bit or Pelham bridle.

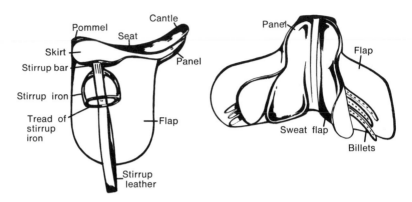

Figure 11.9 An English saddle: Left, upright position; right, the underside.

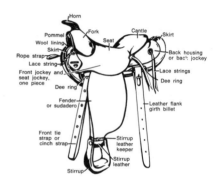

Figure 11.10 A Western saddle.

■ For hunting and jumping, use a forward seat English saddle and a hunting snaffle or Pelham bit.

WESTERN SADDLE

A Western saddle (Figure 11.10) is the common saddle used by cowboys and western stockmen. The essential features are a steel, light metal, or wooden tree; a pommel, topped by a horn for roping, and a cantle (the height of the pommel and cantle vary according to the uses to which the saddle is to be put and the personal preference of the rider); a comparatively deep seat; heavy square or round skirts; a double cinch, usually, but a single cinch may be used; and heavy stirrups that may be hooded or open.

A Western saddle is designed to give comfort for all-day riding and provide enough strength to stand up under the strain of calf roping. The average Western saddle weighs 35 to 40 pounds.

HOW TO SADDLE THE MOUNT

Regardless of the type of saddle — English or Western — it should be placed on the horse's back so that the girth (in English saddles, it's a girth;

Figure 11.11 Girth.

in Western saddles, it's a cinch) will come about 4 inches to the rear of the point of the horse's elbow.

When first adjusted, the girth should be loose enough to admit a finger between it and the horse's belly. After tightening the saddle, it is always good practice to "untrack" the horse — that is, to lead him ahead several paces before mounting. This procedure serves two purposes: first, if the horse is the kind that "blows up" so that he cannot be cinched snugly, the "untracking" will usually cause him to relax; and second, if a horse has any bad habits, he will often get them out of his system before the rider mounts.

After the horse has been ridden a few minutes, the girth should always be re-examined and tightened if necessary. The saddle should always be cinched tightly enough so that it will not turn when the horse is being mounted, but not so tight as to cause discomfort to the horse.

The length of stirrups will depend upon the type of riding. It may vary, from very short on running horses to quite long on stock horses. The stirrup leather on English saddles should always be turned so that the flat side of the leather comes against the leg of the rider.

For correct posting, in English riding, the stirrup straps or stirrup leathers must be adjusted to the right length. If stirrups are too short, posting will be high and exaggerated. For English riding, the stirrups can be adjusted to the approximate correct length before mounting by making them about one inch shorter than the length of the rider's arm with fingers extended. When the rider is sitting in the saddle, with the legs extended downward and the feet out of the stirrups, the bottom of the stirrup iron should touch just below the ankle bone. For Western riding, the length of stirrups may be considered as about right when there is approximately a 3-inch clearance between the saddle tree and the crotch of the mounted rider standing in the stirrups.

HARNESS

It is not within the scope of this book to cover all types and parts of harness. But some conception of the subject can be obtained by studying Figures 11.12 and 11.13.

OTHER TACK

It is beyond the scope of this book to list and describe all of the many articles of horse tack. Nevertheless, the most generally used items, in addition to those already described, follow.

HEAD NUMBER
OPEN BRIDLE
CHECK BIT
TONGUE TIE
MARTINGALE
ELBOW BOOTS-SUSPENDERS
BREAST COLLAR
ELBOW BOOT
QUARTER BOOT
TOE WEIGHT

CHECK REIN
HEAD POLE
THIMBLE
SADDLE PAD
REINS
HAND HOLD
GIRTH
ELBOW BOOT
SHIN BOOTS
SPEEDY CUT
SCALPER
SHAFT
SULKY
WHEEL
DISC

-MIKE GALEGO-USTA

Figure 11.12 Trotter's harness and rigging. (Courtesy, The United States Trotting Association, Columbus, Ohio)

HEAD NUMBER
BLIND BRIDLE
SHADOW ROLL
RING MARTINGALE
KNEE BOOT-SUSPENDERS
BREAST COLLAR
KNEE BOOTS
SHIN & ANKLE BOOTS
BELL BOOTS

CHECK REIN
THIMBLE
HOBBLE HANGERS
SADDLE PAD
REINS
CRUPPER
HAND HOLD
HOBBLES
BRACE BANDAGES
CORONET BOOTS
TRAINING CART

-MIKE GALEGO-USTA

Figure 11.13 Pacer's harness and rigging. (Courtesy, The United States Trotting Association, Columbus, Ohio)

Figure 11.14 Racing blinkers — a hood with leather cups.

Figure 11.15 Ankle boot.

BLINKERS (Blinders or Winkers)

Blinkers are an attachment to the bridle or hood, designed to restrict the vision of the horse from the sides and rear and to focus the vision forward. Driving blinkers (or winkers) are made of leather, often with a crest or embellishment on the outside. Racing blinkers are in the form of a hood with leather cups that act as shields.

BOOTS (for Horses)

Boots are used to protect the legs or feet against injuries. The most common injuries requiring such protection are those caused (1) by brushing when the inside of the leg, usually on, or in the region of, the fetlock joint, is knocked by the opposite foot; (2) by overreaching when the hind toes strike into the rear of the foreleg; or (3) by speedy cutting when the inside of the leg is struck high above the joint, usually under the hock. The shins (either front or hind) may also be endangered as a result of striking an obstacle when jumping.

Various types of boots are available to protect the horse from the different kinds of injuries listed above; among them, the quarter boots to prevent bruising of a front heel from a hind toe, worn by five-gaited Saddle Horses, Tennessee Walking Horses, and harness horses; the shin boots worn by the polo pony to guard cannons from injury by the mallet; and many others.

QUARTER BOOT

This is a flexible boot attached above the coronet which extends down over the hoof. It is designed to protect the quarter of the front heel from the hind toe.

Figure 11.16 Quarter boot on a 5-gaited horse. Because of the speed at which 5-gaited horses are expected to perform at the trot and the rack, they are permitted to wear quarter boots to protect the heels of the front feet, a practice which is forbidden in 3-gaited classes.

BREASTPLATE; BREAST COLLAR

The breastplate usually consists of a short, wide strap that passes over the neck in front of the withers, two adjustable straps that run from each end of the short strap back to the saddle, two adjustable straps that run down the shoulders to a ring on the breastplate, and another adjustable strap that runs from this ring and attaches to the girth after passing between the forelegs. Sometimes this type is equipped with a strap that runs from the ring on the breastplate to the neckband, and acts as a martingale.

The breast collar serves the same purpose as the breastplate. Figure 11.17 shows a breast collar.

Either the breastplate or the breast collar is frequently used on slender-bodied horses and on horses which require some special security to prevent the saddle from slipping to the rear (such as racehorses). With both articles, it is important that they be adjusted as loosely as possible consistent with holding the saddle in place, with proper allowance made for motion and for movement of the horse's neck.

HALTER (Head Collar)

A halter is used for leading a horse or tying him. There are many types of halters made from a number of different materials. The rope halter (formerly made of cotton, now made of nylon) is very strong and inexpensive. It will outlast most leather halters, and it is easy to put on and take off. But care must be taken to fit it loosely, otherwise it will rub the cheek bones.

Leather halters are also widely used. The better ones are mounted with brass. Show halters are of finer, lighter leather than the ordinary stable halter, and usually they have brow bands.

Sometimes the novice has difficulty in figuring out how to put a halter on. The following procedure will alleviate this problem: take the buckle in the left hand and the strap in the right hand, making sure that the three short parallel straps are on the bottom; slip the horse's nose through the noseband; swing the strap over from the far side, place it behind the ears, catch it with the left hand, bring the right hand back, and buckle the strap snugly enough to prevent the horse from getting it over his head.

Never leave a halter on a horse in the pasture. Although a haltered horse may be easier to catch, there is risk of the halter getting caught on some object and the animal not being able to free himself.

LONGE (Lunge)

The longe is a strong light strap (usually made of webbing or leather) about 30 feet long, one end of which is attached by a swiveled snap to the noseband of the cavesson. The young horse can begin training at an early age by means of the longe line. He can be circled to the left and to the

Figure 11.17 The breast collar.

Figure 11.18 A leather halter.

Figure 11.19 Nylon lunging line.

right; made to walk, trot, canter, and halt; and trained to get used to and obey words of command. The longe is especially useful for urban-raised foals, who are limited in space for exercising on natural footing.

Although a young horse can do all kinds of gymnastics without injury when running loose in a corral or pasture, he can be injured by improper use of the longe line. If his head is pulled at the wrong time, or too quickly or too severely, his balance will be destroyed and he may injure a foreleg or foot, throw a curb, or be stifled.

Figure 11.20 Correct method of longeing a horse, with a longeing cavesson and long web tape longe line in use. (Courtesy, *From Dawn to Destiny,* by Frank Jennings and Allen F. Brewer, Jr., published by The Thoroughbred Press, Lexington, Kentucky)

Figure 11.21 The two types of martingales: left, standing martingale; also called a tie-down. It is sometimes used on saddle horses that rear and on polo ponies and stock horses that endanger their riders by throwing their heads up in response to a severe curb when pulled up sharply. Right, a running martingale. It is used for the same purposes as the standing martingale, but permits more freedom of movement; thus it may be used on jumpers. (Drawings by Steve Allured)

MARTINGALES

Martingales are of two types: standing (or sometimes called a tie-down) and running (or ring). The standing martingale consists of a strap which extends from around the girth, between the forelegs, to the nose-band and a light neck strap to keep the martingale from getting under the horse's feet when the head is lowered. When properly adjusted, it has the effect of preventing the elevation of the head beyond a certain level without cramping the horse. The standing martingale is most generally employed on saddle horses that rear and on polo ponies and stock horses that endanger their riders by throwing their heads up in response to a severe curb when pulled up sharply. On the other hand, some competent horsemen prefer to use the running martingale on horses that habitually rear. They feel that the standing martingale sets the head too high.

The running martingale is not attached to the horse's head but terminates in two rings through which the reins pass. It is used for the same purpose as the standing martingale but permits more freedom of movement. Thus, it is better adapted to and more frequently used for jumping than the standing martingale.

Proper adjustment of the running martingale is obtained when, with the horse's head in a normal position, the snaffle reins stretched from the pommel form a straight line from bit to pommel.

SADDLE BLANKET (Numnah, Pad, or Corona)

With English saddles, saddle blankets are usually not necessary when the saddle is thoroughly cleaned after each ride, when the rider uses a balanced seat, and when the mount is properly groomed. When kept clean and when properly used, however, a blanket will usually prevent a sore back. For this reason, even with English saddles, many good horsemen always insist on the use of a saddle blanket.

A saddle blanket or corona is almost always used with western saddle.

Felt, mohair, or pad blankets that are adapted to the various types of saddles may be secured. Many good horsemen even prefer a folded Navajo blanket, with a hair pad inside. The corona is a blanket cut to the shape of the saddle and has a large colorful roll around the edge that is quite showy for use with a stock saddle.

The saddle pad or blanket should be placed well forward on the horse's neck and then slid back into position so as to smooth down the hair. It should come to rest smoothly and in such manner that $2\frac{1}{2}$ to 4 inches of it will show in front of the saddle. After being used, the blanket or pad should be hung up to dry. It then should be brushed thoroughly to eliminate hair and dried sweat.

Figure 11.22 Felt pad.

Figure 11.23 Twitch.

TWITCH

A twitch is a rope run through the end of a stick, used on the horse's upper lip; it is tightened by twisting in order to attract the horse's attention so it will stand still.

CARING FOR TACK

Good tack is expensive and should have good care. If it is properly cared for, it will last for years.

Ideally, each article should be cleaned thoroughly every time it is used on a horse. However, the owner or caretaker of pleasure horses may not have time to do this. A busy person, therefore, should clean the vital parts after each use and then thoroughly clean all tack once a week. After each use, the underside of the saddle and the inside of the bridle should be cleaned; the bit should be washed; and the pad or blanket, if used, should be brushed after it has dried out and before it is reused.

All tack used on race and show horses should be thoroughly cleaned after each use. Proper cleaning of tack will:

- Extend the life of leather and metal
- Make leather soft and pliable
- Help keep the horse comfortable. He will get fewer saddle and harness sores than he will from dirty, crusty, or stiff leather and less irritation and infection than he will from a rusty, moldy, or dirty bit.
- Assure that minor tack defects are noticed and repaired before they

become serious. This lessens the likelihood of breaking a rein or line, girth, girth strap, stirrup leather, or other vital part.

■ Take pride and pleasure in the ownership and use of tack; the horse, rider or driver, and tack will all look good.

EQUIPMENT FOR CLEANING TACK

The following items of cleaning equipment are commonly used:

1. A saddle rack on which to clean the saddle. Preferably, the rack should be designed to hold the saddle with either the seat up or the bottom up so both sides can be easily cleaned.

2. A bridle rack, peg, or hook on which to hang the bridle for cleaning.

3. A rack for cleaning harness, if harness is used.

4. A bucket for warm water.

5. Three sponges, preferably, although one sponge is enough if it is rinsed properly — one sponge for washing off sweat and dirt, another for applying leather preservative or glycerine soap, and a third for occasional application of neat's-foot or similar oil.

6. A chamois cloth for drying off leather.

7. About a yard of cheese cloth for applying metal polish.

8. A flannel rag for polishing.

9. Saddle soap or castile soap for cleaning.

10. A leather preservative or glycerine soap for finishing.

11. Neat's-foot or similar oil.

12. Metal polish.

13. Petroleum jelly.

HOW TO CLEAN TACK

To assure that all parts of all articles of tack are properly cleaned, some practical order of cleaning should be followed. Any order that works is satisfactory.

Once a week all leather should be washed with saddle soap or castile soap as described in the section on washing the saddle, and then neat's-foot oil or other leather dressing should be lightly applied. Do not use too much oil; it will darken new leather and soil clothing.

Wooden parts of equipment may be sanded, varnished, and waxed whenever necessary.

The following order of cleaning is suggested for the saddle, bridle, and saddle pad or blanket.

The saddle — Clean the saddle as follows:

1. Remove the girth and clean it first, the same way the rest of the saddle is cleaned.

2. Turn the saddle upside down and wash the panel (the part of the saddle that touches the horse's back) and the gullet (the underside center of the saddle). Use a sponge that has been wetted in warm water and wrung out to apply saddle soap to the leather. Rub the leather well to

work up a stiff lather that will remove sweat and dirt before it hardens. Wash until clean.

3. Turn the saddle over and wash the rest of it the same way.

4. Dry the saddle with a chamois.

5. Dampen a clean sponge slightly and apply leather preservative or glycerine soap without suds to all parts of the saddle.

The bridle — Clean the bridle as follows:

1. Wash the bit in warm water.

2. Clean the leather parts the same way the saddle was cleaned.

3. Use a cheesecloth to apply metal polish to all metal parts of the bridle and then use a flannel cloth to polish them. If the bridle is not to be used for several days, clean and dry the bit and then apply a light coat of petroleum jelly to keep it from pitting or rusting.

The blanket or pad — Clean blankets and pads as follows:

1. Hang up or spread out blankets and pads to dry.

2. When dry, brush off hair and dried sweat.

STORING TACK

After cleaning — Handle tack as follows after cleaning:

1. Store all tack in a cool, dry place.

2. Hang the bridle on its rack so all parts drape naturally without bending.

3. Put the saddle on its rack.

4. Cover the saddle, bridle, and harness (if harness is used).

CAPARISONED HORSE WITH BOOTS IN REVERSE POSITION

In the funeral processions of both President Dwight (Ike) Eisenhower and President John (Jack) Kennedy there was a riderless horse, led by a man in uniform. The horse was properly saddled, but the stirrups held in reverse position a pair of polished cavalry boots with spurs. Also, a glittering saber was hanging to the right side of the saddle. The significance of this follows.

A riderless horse, decked out with the ornamental trappings described above, accompanies the bodies of general officers and former cavalry officers. Also, this consideration may be accorded to a U.S. President, as Commander-in-Chief.

The practice of having the caparisoned (or decked out) charger of the deceased military officer led in the funeral procession stems from an ancient custom surrounding the burial of warriors. The horse bore a saddle with the stirrups reversed and a sword through them to symbolize that the warrior had fallen and would ride no more. Also, the horse was sacrificed at the time, because it was believed that the equine spirit would find his master in the hereafter; otherwise, the departed warrior would have to walk. Horses are no longer sacrificed. But a riderless horse, with the boots and spurs reversed, is still led in the funeral procession to symbolize that the warrior has fallen.

12. Horse-Drawn Vehicles

Man made much use of saddle horses and packhorses before the carriage came into general use. Also, primitive sliding vehicles preceded the use of wheels. The coming of the wheel made as big an impact on civilization as did the internal combustion engine years later. The Egyptians are believed to have been the original makers of wheels; the first vehicles were probably the wagons and chariots referred to in the Old Testament.

Figure 12.1 Bronze horse-drawn cart, with umbrella over man, taken from a tomb of the late Eastern Han dynasty (25 A.D.–220 A.D.) now on display in Peking, People's Republic of China. (Photo by A. H. Ensminger)

The earliest carriage still in perfect condition to be found today is the State Chariot of Tutankhamen (1361–1352 B.C.) in the Cairo Museum, in Egypt. The first known carriage to be built in Great Britain was made by William Rippon for the second Earl of Rutland in 1555.

Originally, horse-drawn vehicles evolved to meet practical needs, following which they were embellished to meet individual tastes. There was the dignified family carriage with fringe on top; the buckboard with its jump seat — the pickup truck of grandfather's time; the governess cart, with its door at the rear and two seats facing each other; the high two-wheeled dog cart, for transporting hounds to the hunt; the high-seated rig of the society matron; the old-fashioned top buggy of the country doctor; and the roadster of the young gallant.

The golden age of the carriage arrived in the 18th Century. Many different styles of vehicles were built. The high phaeton was a popular vehicle of the period. Later, it was succeeded by the pony phaeton — a long, low vehicle. The names of different types of carriages often came from the name of the builder or the place in which they were made. Although carriages were built throughout the world, it was generally accepted that French and British carriage builders were the masters of their craft.

Even hitches evolved for practical reasons. Tandem driving, for example, was originated by the hunting men of Old England. Wishing to spare their hunting mount as they traveled to and from the meet, these ingenious huntsmen devised the method of driving him ahead, where he trotted between slack traces, while the horse to the rear did all the work.

Today, most horse-drawn vehicles either are used for recreation and sport, drawn by heavy harness horses, fine harness horses, roadsters, or ponies, or are of historical significance only — they are reminiscent of the horse and buggy era.

Figure 12.2 Buckboard wagon — the pickup truck of grandfather's time. In olden times, it was usually a one-seater with a bed behind.

KINDS OF VEHICLES

Drawings and descriptions of some different types of horse-drawn vehicles follow. Figures 12.3, 12.4, and 12.5 are embellished with the Ensminger coat of arms — the coat of arms of the author — as was the custom of the day.

Figure 12.3 Four-wheeled dog cart. Dog carts were so named because they were used for carrying sporting dogs under the seat. They carried four passengers, back to back, plus the hounds. At first they were two-wheeled. Later, they were built with four wheels. Usually, they were pulled by one horse, but the bigger four-wheeled dog carts sometimes required two horses.

Figure 12.4. Landau, the convertible of great-grandfather's time. It was named after Landau, Germany, where it was first manufactured about 1790. It was a four-wheeled covered carriage with the top divided into two sections. The back section could be let down or thrown back while the front section could be removed or left stationary. Landaus held four people and were usually drawn by two horses. This vehicle was very popular in England from Mid-Victorian times onward.

Figure 12.5 The Park Phaeton. The phaeton was a four-wheeled vehicle of which there were many varieties. The early phaetons were built very high. But those of the 19th Century were considerably lower and were made in many different shapes and sizes. There was the Pony Phaeton made in 1824 for King George IV. Then in 1828 came the Massive Male Phaeton driven exclusively by men. Elegant Ladies' Phaetons followed.

Figure 12.6 Stagecoach, a heavy, enclosed, four-wheeled vehicle, usually drawn by four horses, formerly used for making regular trips between stations and carrying passengers and goods.

Figure 12.7 Sulky or bike. These pneumatic tire, bicycle-type wheel racing vehicles, which were first introduced in 1892, are used in harness races. Sulkies weigh from 29 to 37 pounds, and usually have hardwood shafts, although aluminum and steel sulkies have been introduced recently.

ORIGIN OF SOME DRIVING CUSTOMS
The history of some driving customs follows.

SHOWING ROADSTERS
The sport of showing roadsters originated in the horse and buggy era, to satisfy the desire to own an attractive horse that possessed the necessary speed to pass any of his rivals. In the show-ring, roadsters may be shown hitched (1) to a sulky, or (2) to buggy or road wagon; the latter may be singly or in pairs. Roadster vehicles must be attractive and light, but strong. Roadster horses are also known under saddle.

HANDSOME AND HEAVY
Heavy harness horses (Hackneys) in horse shows are harnessed with heavy leather and hitched to heavy vehicles. The heavy leather used on these animals was first decreed by fashion in England, where it stemmed from the idea that to drive handsomely one had to drive heavily. In this country, heavy harness horses are reminiscent of the Gay Nineties, when bobtailed hackneys hitched to high-seated rigs made a dashing picture as they pranced down the avenue.

Figure 12.8 Handsome and heavy. A Hackney heavy harness horse in action. (Courtesy, Mrs. Dean J. Briggs, Garden Plain, Kansas)

Vehicles for hackneys must be of heavy construction, elegant design, and devoid of shiny parts (the latter tends to blind spectators).

WHY DRIVE TO THE RIGHT?

The American custom of driving to the right on the road instead of to the left, as is the practice in some parts of the world, originated among the Conestoga (named after the Conestoga Valley, a German settlement in Pennsylvania) wagon drivers of the 1750s, who transported freight overland to and from river flatboats and barges along the Ohio, Cumberland, Tennessee, and Mississippi Rivers. The drivers of these four- and six-horse teams either sat on the left-wheel horse or on the left side of the seat, the better to wield their whip hand (the right hand) over the other horses in the team. Also, when two Conestoga drivers met, they pulled over to the right so that, sitting on the left-wheel horse or on the left side of the seat, they could see that the left wheels of their wagons cleared each other. Lighter vehicles naturally followed the tracks of the big Conestoga wagons. Even with the development of highways and automobiles, the American custom of driving to the right persisted.

13. Clothes for Riders

Figure 13.1 Western rider in handsome attire, in trail horse class — riding through water. (Courtesy, American Buckskin Registry Assn., Inc., Anderson, California)

In general, riding clothes seldom change in style. Moreover, they are utilitarian. Close fitting legs eliminate wrinkles that might cause chafing. Chamois leather linings inside the knees and calves keep the muscles of the legs from pinching under the stirrup leathers and increase the firmness of the leg grip. Boots or jodhpurs protect the ankles from the stirrup irons. And high boots also keep the breeches from snaring on objects along the trail, shield the trouser legs from the saddle straps and the horse's sides, and protect the legs from rain and cold.

The time of day, the kind of riding horse, and the class in which shown at horse shows determine the riding attire. In addition to selecting proper clothes, well-groomed and experienced riders place emphasis on fine tailoring, good materials, and proper fit. Also, when riding a gaited show horse, do not wear gaudy colors, excess jewelry, or sequins, except in parade classes.

For information on clothes for riders for specific show classes see the official rule book of the American Horse Shows Association.

Appropriate riding clothes for the most common occasions are herewith described.

CLOTHES FOR WESTERN RIDING

Coat — Coats and jackets usually not worn except in bad weather; tailored equitation suits may be worn (matching shirt and pants).

Pants — Western cut, bell-bottom pants of gabardine, cotton twill, cavalry twill, or wool worn with chaps, shotgun chaps, or chinks; a conservative color and well tailored.

Vest — Optional; leather or cloth.

Shirt — Western type; color to match or contrast with western pants; solid or patterned fabric acceptable; long sleeved.

Neckwear — Knotted kerchief, dogger type tie, choker, or silk scarf tied ascot style and tucked into open neck of shirt.

Hat — Western hat, wide brimmed, felt or straw.

Boots — Western cowboy boots. Western boots are more than a handsome trademark of the range. They're practical, too. The high heel is designed to give the wearer protection against losing his stirrups at critical moments; it prevents the foot from slipping through when pressure is applied for quick stops and turns. The top protects the ankles and calves of the legs against inclement weather, brush, insects, and snakes.

Modern Western boots possess two added features; namely, (1) comfort, and (2) adaptation for walking, so that the wearer can walk without it being a painful experience.

Gloves — Optional; leather.

Jewelry and other accessories — Hand carved belt and Western belt buckle; carry a rope or riata; if closed reins are used in trail and pleasure horse classes, carry hobbles; spurs optional.

Figure 13.2 Clothes for rider. Note that there is considerable difference in the riding attire for (1) Western riding, (2) pleasure riding, (3) riding gaited show horses, and (4) riding in a hunt.

Figure 13.3 Handsome Western dress boots.

CLOTHES FOR PLEASURE CLASSES

1. Informal park or school riding, morning or afternoon classes:

Coat — Any conservative color, tweeds or checks, usually light in weight.

Jodhpurs or breeches — Jodhpurs of stretch gabardine, whipcord, corduroy, or stretch twill in colors to match or to contrast with the coat; Kentucky-style breeches with bell bottoms and no flare at the hips.

Vest — Optional; light, solid color or tattersall check.

Shirt — Man's shirt, white or colored, broadcloth or oxford cloth, or a long-sleeved sweater.

Neckwear — Four-in-hand tie or bow tie.

Hat — A soft Panama hat.

Boots — Black or brown strap or elastic jodhpur boots, casual style.

Gloves — Optional; leather gloves to blend with habit.

Jewelry and other accessories — Cuff links, tie pin, belt; spurs of unroweled type and whip or crop optional.

2. Semiformal, afternoon or evening classes:

Coat — Gabardine, wool gabardine, dress worsted, or other men's wear materials; inverted pleats in back; dark colors preferred; in summer, linen or tropical worsted.

Jodhpurs or breeches — Jodhpurs of same material as coat to make a matching riding habit; Kentucky-style breeches with bell bottoms, no flare at the hips, and no cuff.

Vest — Solid color or tattersall check, to match outfit or to contrast.

Shirt — Man's shirt in white or light color to match suit.

Neckwear — Man's four-in-hand tie to match or contrast with the coat.

Hat — Saddle derby to match suit.

Boots — Black or brown jodhpur boots.

Gloves — Optional; leather in a natural shade or to match suit.

Jewelry and other accessories — Tie clasp, cuff links, belt; spurs and riding whip optional.

CLOTHES FOR GAITED SHOW HORSE CLASSES

1. Five-gaited horse; formal evening riding:
Coat — Black or midnight blue tuxedo style riding coat with one button in front and inverted pleats; men usually wear a dark suit instead of a tuxedo. Conservative colors are required; in addition to black and midnight blue, may wear gray, green, beige, or brown.

Jodhpurs or breeches — Material and color to match coat.

Vest — Any solid color to match habit.

Shirt — Man's shirt.

Neckwear — Four-in-hand or bow tie.

Hat — Saddle derby or soft hat.

Boots — Black patent jodhpur boots with tuxedo; brown or black with a suit.

Gloves — Leather gloves to match habit.

Jewelry and other accessories — Cuff links and tie pin; gaited riding whip, crop, and spurs optional.

2. Three-gaited horse; formal evening riding:

Coat — Tuxedo model in black, dark gray, dark brown, or midnight blue; shawl collar with satin lapels; soft pastel colored coats also can be worn; white coat in summer. Equitation classes must wear a dark tuxedo style coat with a silk top hat in the evening and a matched suit with a derby in the daytime.

Jodhpurs or breeches — Material and color to match coat; satin stripe down outside of jodhpurs.

Vest — Optional; white piqué vest or cummerbund.

Shirt — Formal style, white, stiff-front tuxedo; shirt with wing collar and pleated front.

Neckwear — Black, white, or midnight blue bow tie.

Hat — Silk top hat.

Boots — Black leather or patent leather jodhpur boots.

Gloves — Leather gloves to match habit.

Jewelry and other accessories — Formal shirt studs; walk-trot stick optional.

CLOTHES FOR HUNTING AND JUMPING

1. Hunting (*informal*):

Coat — Black oxford or English tweed.

Jodhpurs or breeches — Jodhpurs with peg and cuff or breeches; colors of brick, tan, beige, or canary.

Vest — Optional; hunting yellow or tattersall.

Shirt — Stock shirt or ratcatcher in white, light blue, maize, mint, pink, gray, or rust.

Neckwear — Choker, stock, or ratcatcher tie.

Hat (hard) — Brown or black hunting derby (hunting cap if 18 years old or less), with head harness and sponge rubber head cushion.

Boots — Black or brown boots; high or jodhpur.

Gloves — Brown leather gloves or rain gloves of string.

Jewelry and other accessories — Stock or choker pin, hunting crop, and spurs with straps that match boots.

2. Hunt seat equitation:

Coat — Oxford or tweed hunt coat; black or other conservative color. Conservative wash jacket in season.

Jodhpurs or breeches — Buff, brick, or canary breeches.

Vest — Optional; canary with black coat.

Shirt — Stock shirt.

Neckwear — Optional; white stock or choker.

Hat — Hunting derby; hunting cap if 18 years old or under.

Boots — Black or brown hunt boots.

Gloves — Optional.

Jewelry and other accessories — Stock pin worn straight across on a stock tie or choker; spurs of unroweled type and crop or bat optional.

3. Member of a hunt (*formal*):

Coat — Black or navy hunt coat of melton or English cavalry twill; may wear a black or midnight blue coat of shadbelly or other cutaway-type scarlet hunt livery; collar should be same material and color as the coat unless the rider has been invited to wear hunt-club colors, in which case the collar should conform to hunt livery.

Jodhpurs or breeches — No-flair, in beige, brick, white, or canary with black coat; men wear white breeches if they wear a scarlet coat.

Vest — Buff or yellow; hunt colors if hunt-club members.

Shirt — White stock shirt.

Neckwear — White stock fastened with a plain gold safety pin worn straight across stock.

Hat (hard) — Silk or velveteen hunting hat; hat guard required with scarlet coat or black shadbelly; staff members and juniors wear hunt caps; adults wear a derby with a hat guard when a black coat is worn.

Boots — Regular hunting boots of black calf with tabs; black patent leather tops permissable for women; brown tops for men on the staff.

Gloves — White or yellow string rain gloves or brown leather gloves.

Jewelry and other accessories — Sandwich case, flask, and regulation hunting whip; spurs of heavy pattern with a moderately short neck, preferably without rowels and worn high on the heels.

Boot garters — Plain black or black patent leather with patent leather boot tops; brown with brown boot tops; white with white breeches.

4. Jumping:

Coat — Any color of hunt coat in solid or check; jumping coat may be of any informal forward-seat type.

Jodhpurs or breeches — No-flair breeches of a color contrasting to coat.

Vest — Checkered or solid color.

Shirt — Man's shirt; ratcatcher shirt when stock is worn.

Neckwear — Stock or four-in-hand tie.

Hat (hard) — Hunting derby or hunt cap, black velvet.

Boots — Black or brown hunting boots.

Gloves — Optional.

Jewelry and other accessories — Stock pin and belt; jumping bat and spurs optional.

CLOTHES FOR OTHER RIDING OCCASIONS

Clothes for special riding occasions follow.

SIDE SADDLE FORWARD SEAT FOR HUNTING

Silk hunting hat, hat guard required; dark melton habit with matching skirt; black boots without tops, spurs are optional; white or colored rain gloves. Neckwear, coat collar, vest, sandwich case, and flask are the same as for a member of a formal hunt.

SIDE SADDLE SHOW SEAT

Habit of dark blue, black, or oxford gray with matching or contrasting skirt; black jodhpur boots; four-in-hand or bow tie; white shirt; hard derby; white or pigskin gloves.

WALKING HORSE

Clothes should be the same as those worn for riding three- or five-gaited horses; men can wear a soft felt hat; women seldom wear a hat.

14. Riding the Horse

Riding has become increasingly popular in recent years. It adds zest, balance, understanding, appreciation, and pleasure to the workaday world for many (the outside of a horse is good for the inside of a man). Children build character through riding — automatically acquiring pride, confidence, self-control, and patience — all through companionship with their good friend and stout companion, the horse.

For greatest enjoyment, one should learn to ride correctly; riders should acquire the art of horsemanship, as opposed merely to "pulling leather" or sticking on. A few of the basics of equitation are herewith presented. These should be supplemented by lessons from a competent instructor and much practice.

MOUNTING AND DISMOUNTING, ENGLISH
Before mounting, two precautions should be taken: always check the saddle girth for tightness and the stirrup straps or leathers for length. A loose girth may let the saddle slip down on the horse's side or belly, especially when one is mounting and dismounting. When the girth is adjusted properly, one should be able to get only the first half of the fingers under it without considerable forcing.

When all precautions have been taken, the steps in mounting and dismounting a horse are as shown in Figure 14.2.

From the accompanying figures the novice should not gain the impression that in mounting and dismounting each step is so distinct and different as to be marked by intermittent pauses. Rather, when properly executed, mounting or dismounting is a series of rhythmic movements, and the entire operation is done so smoothly and gracefully that it is difficult to discern where one stage ends and the next one begins.

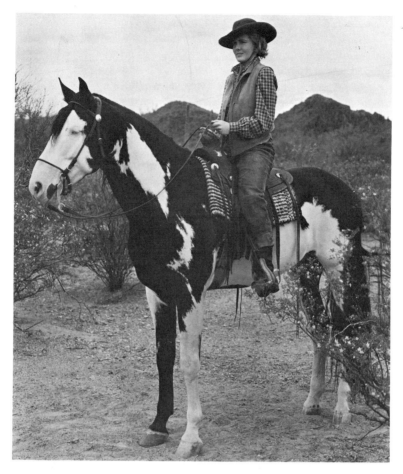

Figure 14.1 "Dice," popular horse of the screen. (Courtesy, *The Horse Lover's Magazine*)

Dismounting is just the reverse of mounting. In succession, the rider should carefully gather the reins in the left hand, place the left hand on the horse's withers and the right hand on the pommel of the saddle, stand up in the stirrups, kick the right foot free from the stirrup, transfer the weight to the left foot as the right leg is swung backward across the horse's back and croup, shift the right hand to the cantle of the saddle, descend to the ground, and remove the left foot from the stirrup.

Another accepted way of dismounting from the English saddle consists in removing the left foot from the stirrup and sliding down the left side with relaxed knees. The rider will never get hung in the stirrups when dismounting in this manner and small children can get off a horse easily and without assistance.

MOUNT FROM "NEAR" OR LEFT SIDE   GATHER REINS IN LEFT HAND

STEADY STIRRUP WITH RIGHT HAND   PAUSE MOMENTARILY IN STANDING POSITION

Figure 14.2 Diagrams showing the steps in mounting and dismounting, English. (From *Horsemanship,* Wash. St. Univ. Ext. Bull. 536, by M. E. Ensminger)

SWING RIGHT LEG OVER HORSE'S BACK

EASE DOWN INTO THE SADDLE

SECURE RIGHT STIRRUP
WITHOUT LOOKING DOWN

SIT EASILY, ALERT, HEAD
UP AND HEELS DOWN

Figure 14.2 (*Cont.*)

Figure 14.3 Mounting, Western.

MOUNTING AND DISMOUNTING, WESTERN

The steps in mounting a horse in Western riding are: (1) take the reins in the left hand and place the left hand on the horse's neck in front of the withers; (2) keep the romal or end of the reins on the near side; (3) grasp the stirrup with the right hand and place the left foot in the stirrup with the ball of the foot resting securely on the tread; (4) brace the left knee against the horse, grasp the saddle horn with the right hand, and spring upward and over; and (5) settle into the saddle and slip the right foot into the off stirrup.

HOLDING THE REINS

The rider may hold the reins either in the left hand alone or in both hands. In Western riding, only one hand, usually the left, holds the reins.

When holding the reins with both hands — as is usual in show-ring riding and training — toss the "bight" (ends) of the reins to the right (off) side of the horse's neck; in hunting and jumping, toss the bight to the left.

When holding the reins in one hand, the left for example — as in English style, cross country riding, or in Western riding—the bight should fall to the left side of the horse's neck and the right hand should be dropped loosely down the side or placed comfortably on the thigh of the right leg. The free hand should never be placed on the pommel of an English saddle or on the pommel or horn of a Western saddle.

Figures 14.4 and 14.5 illustrate better than words the correct methods of holding the reins.

In no case should the rein pressure be more vigorous than absolutely necessary, nor should the reins be used as a means of staying on the horse. A horse's mouth is tender, but it can be toughened by unnecessary roughness. Good hands appear to be in proper rhythm with the head of the horse. Beginners are likely to let the hands bob too much, thus jerking the horse's mouth unnecessarily and using the reins as a means of hanging on the horse. The desired light hands exist when a light feeling extends to the horse's mouth via the reins.

Figure 14.4 Holding the reins English style: Top, double-rein bridle; bottom, single-rein bridle.

Figure 14.5 Holding the reins Western style: (a) only one hand can be used and hands cannot be changed; (b) the hand must be around the reins with no fingers between reins unless split reins are used; (c) when using split reins, one finger between reins is permitted.

SEAT

As in any type of sport, correct riding must include rhythm and balance. The rider's movements must be in complete harmony with the horse's movements, for this assures greater security of the rider and freedom of action by the horse.

Figures 14.6 through 14.10 show the correct riding seats for a three-gaited horse, a five-gaited horse, a plantation walking horse, a Western horse, and a hunter.

Figure 14.6 Correct saddle seat and riding attire for a three-gaited horse.

Figure 14.7 Correct saddle seat and riding attire for a five-gaited horse.

Figure 14.8 Correct saddle seat and riding attire at the running walk.

Figure 14.9 Correct Western seat and riding attire.

Figure 14.10 Correct hunt seat. The eyes should be up and the shoulders back. The toes should be out at an angle best suited to the rider's comfort; ankles flexed in, heels down, calf of leg in contact with horse and slightly behind girth. Iron may be either on toe, ball of foot, or "home."

BALANCED SEAT

The balanced seat may be defined as that position of the mounted rider that requires the minimum of muscular effort to remain in the saddle and which interferes least with the horse's movements and equilibrium. In essence, it means that the rider must be "with the horse," rather than ahead of or behind him. When a balanced seat is maintained, the center of gravity of the rider is directly over the center of gravity of the horse. With the proper seat, the minimum use of aids will be necessary to get immediate and correct response from the horse at any gait.

The balanced seat is obtained largely through shifting the point of balance of the upper body from the hips up; the knees, legs, ankles, and to a great extent the thighs remain in fixed position. Thus, the degree of forward inclination of the upper body will vary according to the speed and gait of the horse; but always the rider should remain in balance over his base of support. The eyes, chin, and chest are lifted, thus permitting clear vision ahead and normal posture of the back. It must also be remembered

Line of body

(a) Walk   **(b) Trot**   **(c) Gallop**   **(d) Extended Gallop**

Figure 14.11 Balanced seat. Note the position for (a) the walk, (b) the trot, (c) the gallop, and (d) the extended gallop. Note, too, that the degree of forward inclination of the upper body will vary according to the speed and gait of the horse; but always the rider should remain in balance over his base of support.

that the greater the speed and the inclination of the body forward, the shorter the stirrups. The jockey, therefore, rides his mount with very short stirrups and reins and a pronounced forward position. He rises out of his saddle and supports himself almost entirely with the stirrups, knees, and legs. In steeplechasing, the position of the rider is less extreme than in flat racing, for in this type of riding it is necessary to combine speed with security.

From what has been said, it can be readily understood that there are different seats or positions for different styles of riding. Fashion, particularly in the show-ring, also decrees that certain form be followed.

Each style of riding differs in appearance, but the end result is the same — balanced riding. An accomplished rider can and does change the seat to meet the style of riding.

RULES OF GOOD HORSEMANSHIP

Horsemen should always practice safety and show consideration for other riders. The following are some of the rules of good horsemanship.

■ Approach a horse on his left. Never walk or stand behind a horse unannounced; let him know you are there by speaking to him and placing your hand on him. Otherwise, you may get kicked.

■ Pet a horse by first placing your hand on his shoulder or neck. Do not dab at the end of his nose.

■ When leading a horse, grasp the reins close to the bit on his left side.

■ Walk a horse to and from the stable; this prevents him from running to the stable and from refusing to leave the stable.

- To prevent a sore back, make sure the saddle blanket or pad is clean and free of any rough places.

- Check the saddle and bridle, or hackamore, before mounting. The saddle should fit just back of the withers; it should not bear down or rub the withers, but also it should not be placed too far back. The girth should be fastened snugly and should not be too close to the forelegs. Be sure that the bridle, or hackamore, fits comfortably and that the curb chain, or strap, is flat in the chin groove and fastened correctly.

- Mount and dismount from the left side. The horse must be made to stand still until the rider is properly seated in the saddle or has dismounted.

- Sit in the correct position for the style of riding.

- Keep the proper tension on the reins; avoid either tight or dangling reins.

- Keep the hand and voice quiet when handling a horse. Never scream, laugh loudly, or make other noises that will upset the horse. Do not slap a horse with the ends of the reins when he is excited.

- Warm up a horse gradually; walk him first and then jog him slowly.

- Keep to the right side of the road except when passing. Yield the right-of-way courteously.

- Walk a horse across bridges, through underpasses, on pavements and slippery roads, and when going up or down a hill. Do not race a horse; he will form bad habits and may get out of control.

Figure 14.12 Riders on a bridle path (or in any group riding) should know and observe the rules of good horsemanship. (Courtesy, J. F. Abernathy)

- Slow down when making a sharp turn.
- Keep a horse moving when a car passes. If he stops, he may back into the passing vehicle.
- Anticipate such distractions as cars, stones, paper, trees, bridges, noises, dogs, and children.
- Vary the gaits; do not force a horse to take a rapid gait such as a canter, rack, or trot for more than a half mile without allowing a breathing spell.
- Keep a horse under control at all times if possible. Try to stop a runaway horse by sawing the bit back and forth to break his stride and his hold on the bit; in an open space, pull one rein hard enough to force the horse to circle.
- Be firm with a horse and make him obey. At the same time, love and understand him and he will be a good friend.
- Never become angry and jerk a horse; a bad-tempered person can make a bad-tempered horse.
- Lean forward and loosen the reins if a horse rears. Do not lean back and pull because the horse might fall over backward.
- Pull up the reins of a bucking horse and keep his head up. Loosen the reins and urge a horse forward with your legs if he starts backing. Do not hold the reins too tightly when a horse is standing still.
- Walk a horse at the end of a ride to let him get cool.
- Do not allow a horse to gorge on water when he is hot; allow a warm horse to drink only a few swallows at a time.
- Do not turn a horse loose at the stall entrance. Walk into the stall with him and turn him around so that he is facing the door. In a tie stall, make certain that the horse is tied securely with a proper length rope.
- Groom a horse thoroughly after each ride.
- Wash the bit thoroughly before it is hung in the tack room. Remove hair and sweat from the saddle and girth before putting them on the rack.
- When riding in a group, keep about 5 feet apart when abreast or a full horse's length behind other mounts when in line, to prevent kicking.
- Never rush past other riders; this may startle the horses and riders and cause an accident. Instead, approach slowly and pass cautiously on the left side.
- Never dash up to another horse or group of horses at a gallop; this can injure riders or horses.
- Wait quietly when a rider must dismount. Do not start moving again until he has remounted and is ready to go.
- Never chase a mounted runaway horse because this will only make him run faster; if possible, another rider should circle and come up in front of him. In case a rider is thrown, stop the other horses and keep quiet; generally the loose horse will return to the group where he can be caught.
- Do not trespass on private property.
- Leave gates closed; otherwise, livestock may get out.

HORSE ACCIDENTS

A horse accident is a sudden event or change occurring without intent, usually through carelessness, unawareness, lack of information, or a combination of causes, and resulting in a person, horse, or object getting hurt. In most horse accidents, the rider is to blame. Either he has been reckless or uninformed, or he is not a good enough horseman for the mount that he is using.

Most accidents result from a failure of the horseman to communicate with the horse. The aids are mutual language between horse and horseman; hence, they should be understood and used properly. But an accomplished horseman does more — he communicates with the horse so that each understands and anticipates the other. A horseman understands the sight and sound of the horse that he is leading; he has a feel for the horse that he is riding or driving; and he interprets the stance of the horse or the movement of his ears, eyes, and/or muscles. Until such time as communication of this type exists, accidents can best be avoided by the horseman entrusting himself only to a well-trained, mature horse.

15. Showing Horses

Horse shows provide spectator entertainment, and recreation, sport, and competition for the exhibitors. Also, the show-ring has been, and will continue to be, an important medium for getting horses and people together in one place and at one time to compare, design, and engineer the most desirable models. But the educational value of horse shows has not been exploited. Many people who attend a horse show for the first time

Figure 15.1 Horse shows are more popular than ever. (Courtesy, Polaris Farm, Charlottesville, Virginia)

are bewildered by the procedure and the many breeds and classes that they see. Others have never gone to a horse show because they feel that their lack of knowledge would prevent them from enjoying it. It is the author's fond hope that this book will result in more people enjoying more horse shows with informed appraisal.

HORSE SHOWS

Horse shows have increased in recent years, on all levels — local, state, and national. Also, they have grown in terms of quality and prize money as is evidenced in Table 15.1, based on figures provided by the American Horse Shows Association.

In addition to spectator entertainment, horse shows stimulate improved breeding, for winning horses (and their relatives) bring good prices.

The American Horse Shows Association (A.H.S.A.) regulates the rules and schedules of all the big shows. Recognized shows include all regular shows, local shows, combined training events, and dressage competitions which are members of the A.H.S.A.

Table 15.1 Growth of Horse Shows

Year	AHSA Sanctioned Shows (no.)	Major Shows (over 50% of Divisions with "A" Rating) (no.)	Prize Money ($)
1959	425	142	1,453,322
1970	945	315	3,297,650
1971	958	325	3,615,550
1972	1090	341	4,212,504
1973	1178	375	4,458,659
1974	1258	405	4,987,649

CLIPPING AND SHEARING

Custom decrees that some breeds be clipped and sheared according to certain haircuts and hairstyles. These are illustrated in Figure 15.2.

SHOWING THE HORSE

The successful showman knows the rules of the classes and follows the correct showing techniques. Broadly speaking, this calls for knowledge of

The natural appearing mane and tail of the Arabian.

The tightly braided mane and the docked and set tail of the Hackney.

Typical mane and tail treatment of the Tennessee Walking Horse.

The clipped or roached mane and the cut, set and shaved tail of the 3-gaited American Saddle Horse.

The shortened, pulled mane and the tightly braided tail of the polo pony. This type of mane treatment is also often seen on Quarter Horses.

The full mane with braided foretop and first lock and the full water spout tail of the 5-gaited American Saddle Horse.

The usual mane and tail treatment of the Quarter Horse. The mane is clipped with the foretop and a tuft of hair at the withers left. The tail is shortened and shaped by pulling.

The braided mane and the thinned tail and braided dock of the hunter.

Figure 15.2 Common haircuts and hairstyles for different breeds and uses of horses.

Figure 15.3 A Western performance class. (Courtesy, *Western Horseman, Colorado Springs, Colorado*)

both performance and breeding (in hand) divisions, as well as of the several classes within each division.

PERFORMANCE CLASSES

Performance classes for horses are so numerous and varied that it is not practical to describe them here. Instead, the showman should refer to the official rule book of the American Horse Shows Association and to the rules printed in the programs of local horse shows.

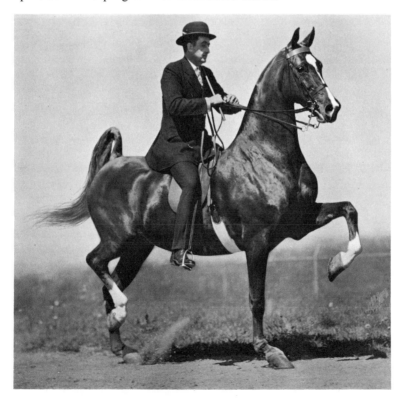

Figure 15.4 A three-gaited Saddle Horse in a performance class. (Courtesy, *The National Horseman, Louisville, Kentucky*)

Figure 15.5 A five-gaited horse in action. (Courtesy, *The National Horseman,* Louisville, Kentucky)

IN HAND (Halter, or Breeding Classes)

Breeding classes are discussed here. They are shown "in hand," which means the horses are exhibited wearing a halter, preferably, or a bridle. The halter should be clean, properly adjusted, and fitted with a fresh-looking leather or rope lead. If the horse is shown wearing a bridle, the exhibitor should not jerk on the reins hard enough to injure the mouth.

The following practices are recommended for showing in hand, or at halter.

1. Train the horse early.

2. Groom the horse thoroughly.

3. Dress neatly for the show.

4. Enter the ring promptly and in tandem when the class is called. Line up at the location indicated by the ringmaster or judge unless directed to continue around the ring in tandem.

5. Stand the horse squarely on all 4 feet with the forefeet on higher ground than the hind feet if possible. The standing position of the horse should vary according to the breed. For example, Arabians are not stretched, but American Saddlers are trained to stand with their front legs straight under them and their hindlegs stretched out behind them. Other

Figure 15.6 Appaloosa mare shown in hand. (Courtesy, Appaloosa Horse Club, Inc., Moscow, Idaho)

Figure 15.7 Correct method of leading when showing "in hand."

breeds generally stand in a slightly stretched position, somewhat intermediate between these 2 examples. When standing and facing the horse, hold the lead strap or rope in the left hand 10 to 12 inches from the halter ring. Try to make the horse keep his head up.

6. Unless the judge directs otherwise, the horse should first be shown at the walk and then at the trot. Move the horse as follows:

a. Reduce the length of the lead strap or rope by a series of "figure 8" folds or by coils held in the left hand. Hold the upper part of the lead strap or rope in the right hand and lead from the left side of the horse. If the horse is well mannered, give him 2 to 3 feet of lead so he can keep his head, neck, and body in a straight line as he moves forward. But keep the lead taut so the horse is always under control. Do not look back.

b. The exhibitor should keep the horse's head up and briskly move him forward in a straight line for 50 to 100 feet as directed.

c. At the end of the walk, turn to the right. That is, the exhibitor should turn the horse away from himself and walk around the horse. If the horse is turned toward the exhibitor, the horse is more likely to step on the exhibitor. Make the turn in as small a space as practical, and as effortless as possible. When showing at the trot, bring the horse to a walk and move him slightly in the direction of the exhibitor before turning.

d. The exhibitor should lift his knees a little higher than usual when he is showing in the ring.

e. Trail the horse with a whip if it is permitted and desired. Most light horses are given early training by trailing with the whip but usually they are shown without this aid. If a "trailer" is used, he should follow at a proper distance. The distance should not be so near he might get kicked but not so far he would be ineffective. The trailer should keep the animal moving in a straight line, avoid getting between the judge and the horse, and always cross in front of the horse at the turn.

7. Walk the horse down about 50 feet and walk back; then trot down about 100 feet and trot back. To save time, the judge may direct that horses be walked down and trotted back, which is a proper procedure. After the horse has been walked and trotted, stand him promptly in front of the judge. After the judge has made a quick inspection, move to the location in the line indicated by the ringmaster or judge.

8. Keep the horse posed at all times; keep one eye on the judge and the other on the horse.

9. When the judge signals to change positions, the exhibitor should back the horse out of line, or if there is room, turn him to the rear of the line and approach the new position from behind.

10. Try to keep the horses from kicking when he is close to other horses.

11. Keep calm; a nervous showman creates an unfavorable impression.

12. Work in close partnership with the horse.

13. Be courteous and respect the rights of other exhibitors.

14. Do not stand between the judge and the horse.

15. Be a good sport; win without bragging and lose without complaining.

Glossary of Horse Terms

A mark of distinction of a knowledgeable horseman is that he "speaks the language" — he uses the correct terms and knows what they mean. Even though horse terms are used glibly by old-timers, often they are baffling to the newcomer.

Some terms that are defined or explained elsewhere in this book are repeated in this chapter. Thus, if a particular term is not listed herein, the reader should look in the index or in the particular chapter and section where it is discussed.

A

ACROSS THE BOARD	A combination pari-mutual (race) ticket on a horse is known as "across the board," meaning that you collect something if your horse runs first, second, or third.
ACTINOBACILLOSIS	See NAVEL INFECTION.
ACTION	Movement of the feet and legs — it should be straight and true.
AFICIONADO	Ardent follower, supporter, or enthusiast; a fan.
AGE	The age of a horse is computed from the first of January.
AGED HORSE	Correctly speaking, a horse 8 years of age or over; but the term is often used to indicate a horse that is smooth mouthed — that is, 12 years of age, or older. Since 1 year of a horse's life corresponds to approximately 3 of man's, it follows that at age 7 a horse "comes of age," or attains maturity.

AIDS	The legs, hands, weight, and voice used in controlling a horse.
ALTER	To castrate a horse; to geld.
ANATOMY	The science of the structure of the animal body and the relation of its parts.
ANTHRAX (Splenic Fever, Charbon)	An acute, infectious disease caused by *Bacillus anthracis,* a large, rod-shaped organism.
ANTIHISTAMINES	A drug used to neutralize and treat allergic conditions in the body.
APPOINTMENTS	Equipment and clothing used in showing.
ARAB	Used interchangeably with Arabian; hence, a breed of horses.
ASCARIDS	See ROUNDWORMS, LARGE.
ASEPTIC	Refers to something being free from the living germs of disease.
ASTERISK	Used in front of a horse's name, an asterisk (*) indicates "imported." Used in front of a jockey's name, it indicates that he is an apprentice rider.
ASTRINGENT	A drug, such as tannic acid, alum, and zinc oxide or sulphate, that causes contraction of tissues.
AT THE END OF THE HALTER	Sold with no guarantee except title.

B

BABESIASIS	See EQUINE PIROPLASMOSIS.
BACK	The command to move backward.
BALANCED SEAT	That position of the mounted rider that requires the minimum of muscular effort to remain in the saddle and which interferes least with the horse's movements and equilibrium.
BALD FACE	A white face, including the eyes and the nostrils, or a portion thereof.
BALKY HORSE	Balking refers to any horse that stands still — refuses to go. This vice was not uncommon in the draft horse and horse-and-buggy era. The causes of balking are numerous; among them, too severe punishment when overloaded, and

Figure G.1 Don't you believe it! The "fire cure" won't work. The singed horse will move forward just far enough to burn up the load of hay.

sore shoulders. The legendary cures (none recommended by the author) included (1) pounding on one shoe to divert the balky horse's attention, (2) pouring sand in one ear, which was supposed to shake the idea of balking out of his head, and (3) building a fire under him. The author recalls the incident of a neighboring farmer who tried the "fire cure" only to have the singed horse move forward just enough to burn up the load of hay which it was pulling.

In the old days, when selling a balky horse at auction, it was generally announced that he "sells at halter." Belatedly, some uninformed buyer learned that this meant that the horse was prone to balk, and that he wouldn't pull the hat off your head.

BANGED Hair of the tail cut off in a straight line.

BANGTAIL Slang term for a racehorse, as in the old days running horses usually had banged tails, often banged close to the dock, or docked and banged. Also, a wild horse.

BAREFOOT Unshod.

BARREN A mare that is not in foal.

BARS May refer either to the bars of the mouth, or of the hoof.

BASE NARROW Standing with front or rear feet close together, yet standing with legs vertical.

BASE WIDE Standing with front or rear feet wide apart, yet with legs vertical.

BEAN-SHOOTER

A horse that throws its front feet violently forward at the trot, with a little flexion, "landing" about 12 inches above the ground. A very undesirable trait.

BEEFY HOCKS

Thick, meaty hocks, lacking in quality.

BELL BOOTS

Rubber protective boots that are bell-shaped, fitting over the coronet bands and down on the hoof.

BELLEROPHON

The Prince of Corinth in Greek mythology who tamed the winged horse, Pegasus. According to legend, Bellerophon used a golden bridle to coax the curious animal from his favorite meadow, then made him captive and rode him off to destroy the dragonlike monster, the Chimera. Success encouraged him to try to fly to Olympia to live with the gods. However, Zeus, angered by this mortal's ambition, sent a gadfly to sting Pegasus, causing him to unseat his venerable and conceited master, who fell to earth crippled and blinded.

BIG HITCH

A hitch of draft horses in fours, sixes, eights, or even more.

BIGHT OF THE REINS

The part of the reins passing between thumb and fingers and out the top of the hand.

BISHOPING

The practice of artificially altering the teeth of older horses in an attempt to make them sell as young horses.

BLAZE

A broad white marking covering almost all of the forehead, but not including the eyes or nostrils.

BLEMISHES

Those abnormalities that do not affect the serviceability of the horse, including such things as wire cuts, rope burns, nail punctures, shoe boils, and capped hocks.

BLINDNESS

Partial or complete loss of vision.

BLINKER

An attachment to the bridle or hood, designed to restrict the vision of the horse from the sides and rear and to focus the vision forward.

BLISTERING

Blistering consists of applying an irritating substance such as Spanish fly and iodide of mercury (one common preparation consists of 15 parts

Spanish fly, 8 parts iodide of mercury, and 120 parts of lard) as treatment for a blemish or unsoundness. Before applying a blister, the hair should be closely clipped from the affected area, the scurf brushed from the skin, and the animal tied so that it cannot rub, lick, or bite the treated area. The blistering agent is then applied by rubbing it into the pores of the skin with the palm of the hand. Three days later the blistered area should be bathed with warm water and soap, dried, and treated with sweet oil or Vaseline to prevent cracking of the skin.

BLOOD-HORSE
A pedigreed horse. To most horsemen, the term is synonymous with the Thoroughbred breed.

BLOOD SPAVIN
A varicose vein enlargement which appears on the inside of the hock but immediately above the location of bog spavin.

BLOOD WORMS
See STRONGYLES, LARGE AND SMALL.

BLOOM
Hair that is clean and of a healthy texture.

BLOW
To blow wind after strenuous exercise.

BLOWFLY
The blowfly group consists of several species of flies that breed in animal flesh.

BLOW OUT
To walk or exercise a horse either to loosen its muscles by further exercise, or to prevent chilling and stiffening after a hard workout.

BLUE EYE
An unsound eye with a blue appearance; the sight may or may not be entirely gone.

BOG SPAVIN
A filling of the natural depression on the inside and front of the hock. A bog spavin is much larger than a blood spavin.

BOLTING
1. The name given to the habit that ravenous horses have of eating too fast. This condition may be controlled by adding chopped hay to the grain ration or by placing some large, round stones, as big or bigger than baseballs, in the feed box.
2. An animal breaking out of control or trying to run away is said to be bolting.

BONE
The measurement of the circumference around the cannon bone about halfway between the

knee and fetlock joints. Eight inches of bone is average for the Thoroughbred. "Flat bone" indicates that the cannon and the back tendon are parallel, with the tendon clean-cut and standing well away from the cannon bone. The word "flat" refers to the appearance of the cannon, which is wide and flat when viewed from the side although narrow from the front; it does not mean that the bone itself is flat.

BONE SPAVIN
(or Jack Spavin)

Bone spavin (or Jack Spavin) is a bony enlargement that appears on the inside and front of the hind leg(s) below the hock at the point where the base of the hock tapers into the cannon part of the leg.

BOOTS

Protective covering for the legs or feet, generally used when exercising. Some types of boots are used for balance and perfection in gait.

BOSAL

The braided rawhide or rope noseband of a bosal hackamore. The bosal is knotted under the horse's jaw.

BOTS
(*Gasterophilus* ssp.)

Four species of bots have been found in the United States. But only three are serious pests of horses.

BOWED TENDONS

Enlarged tendons behind the cannon bones, in both the front and hind legs. Descriptive terms of "high" or "low" bow are used by horsemen to denote the location of the injury; the high bow appears just under the knee and the low bow just above the fetlock. This condition is often brought about by severe strains, such as heavy training or racing. When bowed tendons are pronounced, more or less swelling, soreness, and lameness are present. Treatment consists of blistering or firing. The object of blistering and firing is to convert a chronic into an acute inflammation. This hastens nature's processes by bringing more blood to the part, thus inducing a reparative process which renders the animal suitable for work sooner than would otherwise be the case.

BOWLEGGED

Wide at the knees, close at the feet.

BRACE BANDAGES

Resilient bandages on the legs of horses worn in some cases in an effort to support lame legs, and worn in other cases to protect a horse from cutting and skinning its legs while racing.

BRAND — A mark used as means of identification.

BREAK — To teach a young horse to obey commands, and accept direction and control.

BREAKING — The act of leaving gait (trot or pace) and "breaking" into a gallop. A trotter or pacer must remain on gait in a race. If it makes a break, the driver must immediately pull it back to its gait.

BREEDER — Owner of the dam at the time of service who was responsible for the selection of the sire to which she was mated.

BREEDING — An attempt to regulate the progeny through intensive selection of the parents.

BREEDY — Smart and trim about the head and front part of the body.

BREEZING — A race workout in which a horse is running at a controlled speed.

BRIDOON — The correct name for the little snaffle bit in the full bridle.

BRITTLE HOOFS — Hoofs that are abnormally dry and fragile.

BROKE — 1. Tamed and trained to a particular function, as halter-broke.
2. To leave or alter gait; e.g., the trotter broke stride.

BROKEN CREST — A heavy neck which breaks over and falls to one side.

BROKEN KNEES — Knees with scars on them, indicating that the horse has fallen. Often scars are an indication that the horse is awkward and inclined to stumble.

BRONCHITIS — A condition of the respiratory system, characterized by the inflammation of the bronchial tubes, with signs similar to heaves.

BROODMARE — A mare kept for breeding or reproductive purposes.

BROOMTAIL — A wild and untrained western range horse of inferior quality.

BROTHERS
(or Sisters)

Full brothers — By the same sire and out of the same dam.

Half brothers — Out of the same dam, by different sires. This is one of the most frequently misused terms. Horses by the same sire and out of different dams are referred to as "by the same sire," or else the name of the sire is used, as "by Man O' War." This distinction is for a definite purpose, for only a few horses can be half brothers (or half sisters) to a famous horse, but hundreds can be by the same sire. This restricted definition tends to give a little of the credit to good broodmares instead of leaving the meaning ambiguous.

Brothers in blood — By the same sire out of full sisters; or by full brothers out of the same dam, or any combination of exactly the same blood.

Three-quarter brothers — For example, horses having the same dam and whose sires have identical sires but different dams.

Seven-eights brothers — The progeny of a horse and his son produced by the same mare, or similar combinations of lineage.

BRUSH

To force a horse to top speed over a short distance.

BRUSHING

Striking the fetlock with the other hoof, which results in just roughing the hair of the fetlock, or in an actual injury.

BUCKED SHINS

A temporary racing unsoundness characterized by a very painful inflammation of the periosteum (bone covering) along the greater part of the front surface of the cannon bone, caused by constant pressure from concussion during fast works or races.

BUCKING

Springing with a quick leap, arching the back, and descending with the forelegs rigid and the head held as low as possible.

BUCK-KNEED

See KNEE-SPRUNG.

BUG BOY

An apprentice jockey.

BULL PEN

Auction ring.

C

CALF-KNEED
Standing with knees too far back, directly opposite to buck-kneed or knee-sprung.

CALICO-PINTO
A multicolored or spotted pony.

CALK
Grips on the heels and the outside of the front shoes of horses, designed to give the horse better footing and prevent slipping.

CALKING
Injury to the coronary band by the shoe of the horse. Usually incurred by horses whose shoes have calks, or by horses that are "rough-shod," as for ice.

CANTER
The canter is a slow, restrained, three-beat gait in which the two diagonal legs are paired, thereby producing a single beat which falls between the successive beats of the other unpaired legs.

CAPPED ELBOW
See SHOE-BOIL.

CAPPED HOCK
An enlargement at the point of the hock; it is usually caused by bruising.

CAPRIOLE
An intricate movement performed by the Lipizzan horses in the Spanish Riding School in Vienna. It is considered the ultimate of all high-school and classical training. The horse leaps into the air, and, while in the air, kicks out with the hind feet. The Capriole also, like so many other forms of high-school work, belongs to the medieval methods of combat, in which, by means of such jumps by the horse, the surrounded rider could rid himself of adversaries. By kicking out the hind legs, the horse prevented the enemy from getting within striking distance with sword and lance.

CAST
Refers to a horse's falling or lying down close to a wall or fence so that it cannot get up without assistance.

CAT-HAMMED
Having long, relatively thin thighs and legs.

CAVESSON
Headstall with a noseband (often quite large) used for exercising and training horses.

CENTAURS
The centaurs were an ancient mythical Greek race dwelling in the mountains of Thessalay.

They were imagined as men with the bodies of horses and half-bestial natures.

CHAMPING A term that describes the horse's playing with the bit. Its development is encouraged in bitting a young horse by using a bit with "keys" attached to the mouthpiece, which tends to make the saliva flow and keep the mouth moist — an aid in producing a "soft" mouth.

CHARBON See ANTHRAX.

CHECK Short for checkrein.

CHECKREIN A strap coupling a bit of a bridle to the harness backband to keep the head up and in position.

CHEEK A cheek strap, a part of the bridle.

CHESTNUT The horny growth on the inside of the horse's legs, above the knees and below the hocks.

CHUKKER A seven-and-one-half-minute period in a polo game. (From the Hindi language, meaning "a circle.")

CINCH Girth of a Western saddle.

CLAIMING RACE A race in which all the horses are entered at stated prices and may be claimed (purchased) by any other owner of a starter in the race. In effect, all horses in a claiming race are offered for sale.

CLEAN A term indicating that there are no blemishes or unsoundnesses on the legs.

CLICKING Striking the forefoot with the toe of the hind foot on the same side. Also known as forging.

CLUCK To move the tongue in such a way as to produce clucks. The command to go, proceed; the signal to increase speed.

COARSE Lacking in quality — shown in texture of hair, hairy fetlocks, all-over lack of refinement, common head; flat and shelly feet, and gummy legs.

COB A close-knit horse, heavy-boned, short-coupled and muscular, but with quality, and not so heavy or coarse as to be a draft animal. A cob is usually small, standing under 15 hands.

COBBY	Close-coupled, stoutly built. Like a cob.
COCKED ANKLES	Bent forward on the fetlocks in a cocked position.
COCK HORSE	An extra horse used with English stagecoaches, ridden behind the coach in ordinary going, but hitched before the team for added draft when approaching steep hills or heavy going. The cock horse was usually of a flashy color.
COFFIN BONE	The bone of the foot of a horse, enclosed within the hoof.
COLD-BACKED	Describes a horse that humps his back and does not settle down until the saddle has been on a few minutes. Some "cold-backed" horses will merely tuck their tails and arch their backs when first mounted, but others will take a few crow hops until warmed up.
COLD-BLOOD	A horse of draft horse breeding.
COLD-JAWED	Tough-mouthed.
COLIC	A severe indigestion, which causes abdominal discomfort.
COLLECTED	The term applied to a horse when ridden well up to its bit with its neck flexed, jaw relaxed, and hocks well under it. A collected horse has full control over its limbs at all gaits and is ready and able to respond to the signals or aids of its rider.
COLT	A young stallion under three years of age; in Thoroughbreds, the age is extended to include four-year-olds.
COMBINATION HORSE	One used for saddle and driving.
CONDITION	The state of health, as evidenced by the coat, state of flesh, and general appearance.
CONFORMATION	Body shape or form.
CONGENITAL	Acquired during development in the uterus and not through heredity.
CONTRACTED FEET	A condition characterized by a drawing in or contracting at the heels.

COOL OUT	To cause a horse to move quietly after heavy exercise.
COON-FOOTED	Having long, low pasterns and shallow heels.
CORN	Injury to the sensitive laminae of the sole, frog, bars, or posterior quarters of the hoof.
CORNS	A bruise to the soft tissue underlying the horny sole of the foot which manifests itself in a reddish discoloration of the sole immediately below the affected area.
COUPLING	The section between the point of the hip and the last rib. A short-coupled horse is considered to be an easy keeper, while a long-coupled horse is said to "take a bale of hay a day." The width of four fingers is considered to constitute a short coupling.
COW HOCKS (COW-HOCKED)	Standing with the joints of the hocks bent inward, with the toes pointing outward.
CRAB BIT	Bit with prongs extending at the horse's nose. Purpose is to tip the horse's head up and help prevent him from ducking his head, bowing his neck, and pulling hard on the rein.
CRADLE	A device made of wood or aluminum worn around the neck of the horse which prevents the horse from chewing at sores, blankets, bandages, etc.
CREST	The top part of the neck. This is very well developed in stallions.
CRIBBER (Wind Sucking, or Stump Sucking)	A horse that has the vice of biting or setting the teeth against some object, such as the manger, while sucking air.
CROP	A riding whip with a short, straight stock and a loop.
CROP-EARED	Refers to an animal which has had the tips of its ears either cut off or frozen off.
CROSSBRED	Produced by a sire and a dam of differing breeds.
CROSS-FIRING	A defect in the way of going, generally confined to pacers, which consists of a scuffing on the inside of the diagonal forefeet and hind feet.

CROW HOPS	Mild or playful bucking motions.
CRUPPER	A leather strap with a packed semicircular loop. The loop end goes under the tail and the strap end is affixed at the center of the back band of a harness or the cantle of a saddle to prevent the saddle from slipping over the withers.
CRYPTORCHID	A stallion with one or both testicles retained in the abdomen.
CURB	1. An enlargement at the rear of the leg and below the point of the hock. 2. Also, a bit mouthpiece, designed to bring pressure to bear on the horse's bars.
CURRY	Cleaning (grooming) with a currycomb, dandy brush, body brush, sponge, rub rag, hoof pick, etc.
CUTBACK SADDLE	A long, flat saddle that rests low on the horse's back and is designed to place the rider's weight toward the rear. The name is derived from the U-shaped cutaway slot for the withers. It is used primarily for showing.
CUT-OUT	The cutting out of certain animals in a herd.
CUTTING HORSE	A cow horse used in cutting cattle from the herd. To promote the cutting horse and establish uniform rules for his exhibition, cutting horse enthusiasts are banded together in the following association:

National Cutting Horse Assn.
P.O. Box 12155
Fort Worth, Texas 76116

D

DAISY-CUTTER	A horse that seems to skim the surface of the ground at the trot. Such horses are often predisposed to stumbling.
DAM	The female parent of a horse.
DAPPLE	Small spots, patches, or dots contrasting in color or shade with the background, such as dapple-gray.
DASH	Race decided in a single trial.

DEAD HEAT	A racing term referring to two or more horses that arrive simultaneously at the finish line.
DEERFLY	A biting insect that inflicts a painful bite.
DENERVING	The removal of part of the nerve trunk and/or nerves in certain areas.
DENTAL STAR	A marking on the incisor teeth of horses, used in judging their age. It first appears on the lower central and intermediate incisors when the horse is about eight years of age.
DERBY	A word that stems from a classic race exclusively for three-year-olds which was initiated at Epsom Downs, in England, in 1780, by the twelfth Earl of Derby. This race became so famous that today, the word "derby" is considered synonymous with any well-known race; hence, there is the Kentucky Derby, the Japan Derby, etc. In England, the word is pronounced "darby," whereas in the United States it is pronounced "derby."
DIAGONAL	Refers to the forefoot moving in unison with its opposite hind foot at the trot. If it is the left forefoot, it is called the left diagonal.
DISH-FACED	A term used if the face is concave below the eyes, and, especially in Arabians, if the profile shows a definite depression below the level of the eyes. This term is also applied to some horses and many ponies that have flat or concave foreheads with prominent temples, but this type is the absolute opposite to the "dish" of the Arab, which has a prominent forehead.
DISHING	Carrying the foot forward in a lateral arc in a trot, but advancing the knee in a straight line.
DISQUALIFICATION	A fault so serious that it disqualifies a horse for registry or show.
DISTAFF SIDE	The female side, as in a pedigree.
DISTEMPER (Strangles)	A widespread contagious disease of horses, especially among young animals, caused by *Streptococcus equi,* a bacterium.
DOCK	The solid portion of the tail.

DOCKED	A tail in which part of the dock has been removed.
DOCKING AND SETTING	Removing part of the dock of the tail, cutting the tendons, and "setting" the tail to make the horse carry it high.
DOPING	The administering of a drug to a horse to increase or decrease his speed in a race. Race course officials run saliva tests, urine tests (urinalyses), etc., in order to try to detect any horses that have been doped. Usually such tests are conducted on the winners of every race and on the first three to finish in stakes races. Where doping is proved, the horse may be banned from the track for a period of time, the owner may have his entire stable banned from racing for a period of time, and/or the trainer or jockey may lose his license; with the penalty determined by the circumstances.
DOUBLE-GAITED	A term applied to a horse that can both trot and pace with good speed.
DRAFTY	Having the characteristics of a draft horse. Heavy and lacking in quality.
DRAG HUNT	A hunt staged on horseback with hounds following a laid trail, made by dragging a bag containing anise seed or litter from a fox's den.
DRESSAGE	The guiding of a horse through natural maneuvers without emphasis on the use of reins, hands, and feet.
DROVER	A word reminiscent of one of the most thrilling chapters in American history. Prior to the advent of railroads and improved highways, great herds of cattle, sheep, and hogs were driven on horseback over famous trails, often many hundreds of miles long. The crew of "drovers" usually consisted of the boss (often the owner of the herd), a man to ride along each side, and a fourth man to lead.
	The "drovers" — those who did the driving — were rugged, and their lives were filled with adventure. The work was accompanied by an almost ceaseless battle with the elements,

clashes with thieves, and no small amount of bloodshed.

DUTCHMAN'S TEAM

It is customary to hitch the smaller horse of a team on the left side. When a careless horseman hitches his larger horse on the near side, he is said to be driving a "Dutchman's team."

DWELLING

A noticeable pause in the flight of the foot, as though the stride were completed before the foot reaches the ground. It is most noticeable in trick-trained horses.

E

EAR DOWN

To restrain an animal by biting or twisting its ear.

EASTERN
(Oriental)

Applied to horses of Arab, Barb, or similar breeding.

ENCEPHALOMYELITIS
(or Sleeping Sickness)

A virus, epizootic (epidemic) disease that may be carried by birds and mosquitos. It is caused by four different viruses. The two most common ones are known as the Eastern type and the Western type.

ENDURANCE RIDES

Trials of speed and endurance. Eleven 300-mile endurance rides used to be held, seven in New England and four in Colorado, but these were discontinued in 1926. Today, there are several well-known 50- to 100-mile competitive trail rides in the United States. The time for the different courses varies according to the topography, elevation, and footing, but it is approximately 17 hours for 100 miles and 6 hours for 50 miles.

ENTIRE

An ungelded male.

EQUESTRIAN

One who rides horseback.

EQUESTRIENNE

A female equestrian.

EQUINE

A horse. Correctly speaking, the term includes all the members of the family Equidae — horses, zebras, and asses.

EQUINE ABORTION

The premature expulsion of the fetus.

EQUINE INFECTIOUS ANEMIA (or Swamp Fever)	An infectious virus disease.
EQUINE INFLUENZA	An infectious disease caused by a myxovirus that has properties of the Type A influenza viruses.
EQUINE PIROPLASMOSIS (Babesiasis)	Caused by *Babesia caballi* or *B. equi,* protozoan parasites that invade the red blood cells.
EQUITATION	The act or art of riding horseback.
ERGOT	The horny growth at the back of the fetlock joint; the spurs of a horse's hoofs.
ESTRUS	The estrus period is commonly called "heat."
EWE NECK	A neck like that of a sheep, with a dip between the poll and the withers. Also termed a "turkey-neck" and "upside-down neck."
EXTENDED TROT	Moving the horse at a very rapid, but collected, gait at the trot. To achieve this, the rider applies pressure with the calves of legs as he or she comes down into the saddle while posting.
EXUDATE	Refers to the discharge of fluid and tissue material from an oozing sore or wound. This is usually characterized by a dry, crusty state of scablike sores.

F

FACE FLY	Face flies gather in large numbers on the faces of horses, especially around the eyes and nose.
FALLEN NECK	See BROKEN CREST.
FAMILY	The lineage of an animal as traced through either the males or females, depending upon the breed.
FARCY	See GLANDERS.
FARRIER	A horseshoer.
FAR SIDE	The right side of a horse.
FAVOR	To favor one leg; to limp slightly.
FEATHER IN EYE (or Speck in Eye)	A mark across the eyeball, not touching the pupil; often caused by an injury, it may be a blemish or some other defect.

FERAL	Describes a wild horse — one that has escaped from domestication and become wild, as contrasted to one originating in the wild.
FETLOCK JOINT	The connection between the cannon and the pastern bones.
FETUS	The unborn animal as it develops in the uterus.
FIGURE-EIGHT BANDAGE	A style of bandaging, applied in a figure-eight fashion, which allows for expansion at the flexing of hocks and knees.
FILLY	A young female horse under three years of age; in Thoroughbreds, it includes four-year-olds.
FILM PATROL	The practice of recording a race on film.
FIRING	Applying a hot iron or needle to a blemish or unsoundness as a treatment.
FIRST LOCK	The first lock of the mane on or in back of the poll (when the poll is clipped). The first lock is sometimes braided with a ribbon, as is the foretop.
FISTULOUS WITHERS	An inflamed condition in the region of the withers, commonly thought to be caused by bruising.
FLAT BONE	See BONE.
FLAT FOOT	A foot the angle of which is less than 45°, or one in which the sole is not concave, or one with a low, weak heel.
FLAT RACE	A race without jumps.
FLAT-SIDED	Lacking spring in ribs.
FLAXEN	A light-colored mane or tail.
FLEA-BITTEN	1. A white horse covered with small, brown marks.
	2. Any "mangy-looking" animal.
FLOATING	Filing off the sharp edges of a horse's teeth.
FOAL	A young, unweaned horse of either sex.
FOALING	Giving birth to a foal.
FOLLICLE	A bubblelike structure on the ovary which contains an egg.

FOOT-LOCK OR FEATHER	Long hair which grows back of the fetlock.
FORAGE	Vegetable material in a fresh, dried, or ensiled state which is fed to livestock (pasture, hay, silage).
FOREHAND	The "front" of the horse, including head, neck, shoulders, and forelegs — in other words, that portion of the horse in front of the center of gravity.
FORETOP (Forelock)	The lock of hair falling forward over the face.
FORGING	See CLICKING.
FORM	The past performance of a racehorse; often a table giving details relating to a horse's past performance.
FOUNDER	See LAMINITIS.
FOUR-IN-HAND	A hitch of four horses, consisting of two pairs, with one pair in front of the other.
FOX HUNT	A hunt with hounds, staged on horseback, after a live fox. The fox may have been released from captivity or tracked and flushed out of hiding by the hounds.
FOX TROT	A slow, short, broken type of trot in which the head usually nods. In executing the fox trot, the horse brings each hind foot to the ground an instant before the diagonal forefoot.
FROG	A triangular-shaped, elasticlike formation in the sole of the horse's foot.
FULL BRIDLE	Just another term for either a Weymouth or show bridle.
FULL BROTHERS (or Sisters)	Horses having the same sire and the same dam.
FURLONG	A racing distance of one-eighth mile.
FUTURITY	A race in which the animals entered were nominated before birth.

G

GAIT	A particular way of going, either natural or acquired, which is characterized by a distinctive rhythmic movement of the feet and legs.
GALLOP	See RUN.
GALTON'S LAW	The theory of inheritance expounded by Sir Francis Galton (1822–1911). According to this genetic theory, the individual's inheritance is determined as follows: $\frac{1}{4}$ by its sire and $\frac{1}{4}$ by its dam; $\frac{1}{16}$ by each of the four grandparents; $\frac{1}{64}$ by each of the 8 great grandparents; and on and on, with each ancestor contributing just $\frac{1}{4}$ as much to the total inheritance as did the one a generation nearer to the individual. "Galton's law" is correct in the sense that the relationship between ancestor and descendant is halved with each additional generation which intervenes between them. It is not correct in the sense that the individual's heredity is completely determined by the heredity of its ancestors. Rather, in a random-bred population, the individual is $\frac{1}{4}$ determined by each parent and $\frac{1}{2}$ determined by chance in Mendelian segregation. Determination by more remote ancestors is included in the determination by the parent. Galton's law is often used as a stamina index by Thoroughbred breeders.
GAMETE	A mature sex cell (sperm or egg).
GAUCHO	The South American cowboy. In particular, the term is used in the pampas area of Argentina. The gaucho is considered by many to be the world's finest roughrider.
GEAR	The equipment and accessories used in harness driving (except the vehicle) and in polo playing (except the bridles and saddles). (See TACK.)
GEE	The teamster's term signaling a turn to the right.
GELD	To cut or castrate a male horse.
GELDING	A male horse that was castrated before reaching maturity.
GENOTYPE SELECTION	Selection of breeding stock not necessarily from

the best-appearing animals but from the best-breeding animals, according to genetic makeup.

GERM PLASM
Germ cells and their precursors, bearers of hereditary characters.

GET
Progeny or offspring.

GET-UP
The command to go; proceed; move forward. When repeated, it means to increase speed, "Giddap," slang.

GIRTH
The strap or webbing that holds the saddle or backband in place.

GIRTH-PLACE
The place for the girth, as the name implies, is marked by a depression in the underline just in back of the front legs.

GLANDERS
(or Farcy)
An acute or chronic infectious disease caused by *Malleomyces mallei,* a bacterium.

GLASS-EYED
The term applied to an eye that is devoid of pigment.

GOOD MOUTH
Said of an animal 6 to 10 years of age.

GOOSE-RUMPED
An animal having a short, steep croup that narrows at the point of the buttocks.

GRADE
An animal of unknown ancestry. If it shows some specific breed characteristics, it may be suffixed with the name of that breed; e.g., grade Shetland.

GRAIN
Harvested cereals or other edible seeds, including oats, corn, milo, barley, etc.

GRANULATION
The formation of excess or scar tissue in early wound healing and repair.

GRAVEL
A condition which is usually caused by penetration of the protective covering of the hoof by small bits of gravel or dirt. Access to the sensitive tissue is usually gained by the "white line" or junction of the sole and wall, where the horn is somewhat softer. Once in the soft tissue inside the wall or sole, bacterial infection carried by the foreign material develops rapidly, producing pus and gas which create pressure and intense pain in the foot. In the untreated cases, it breaks out

at the top of the coronary band and the pus and gas are forced out through this opening.

GREASE HEEL
(or Scratches)

A low grade infection affecting the hair follicles and skin at the base of the fetlock joint, most frequently the hind legs. It is similar to scratches, but in a more advanced stage.

GREEN BROKE

A term applied to a horse that has been hitched or ridden only one or two times.

GUMMY-LEGGED

Having legs in which the tendons lack definition, or do not stand out clearly.

GYMKHANA

A program of games on horseback.

H

HACK

A horse used for riding at an ordinary gait over roads, trails, etc.

HAIR

A slender outgrowth of the epidermis which performs a thermoregulatory function, to protect the animal from cold or heat. It becomes long and shaggy during the winter months in cold areas, especially if the horse is left outside. Then, during the warm season, or when the animal is blanketed, the horse sheds and the coat becomes short.

HAIR COLORS

The five basic horse coat colors are bay, black, brown, chestnut, and white. Additionally, there are five major variations of these colors: dun (buckskin), gray, palomino, pinto (calico or paint), and roan.

HALF-BRED

When capitalized, this denotes a horse sired by a Thoroughbred and registered in the Half-Bred Stud Book.

HALF-STOCKING

White extends from the coronet to the middle of the cannon.

HALTER PULLER

A horse that pulls back on the halter rope.

HALTER PULLING

Pulling back on the halter rope when tied in the stable.

HAMMER-HEAD

A coarse-headed animal.

HAMSTRUNG

Disabled by an injury to the tendon above the hock.

HAND	A 4-inch unit of measurement.
HAND-CANTER	A semiextended canter, midway between a promenade canter and a gallop.
HAND GALLOP	An extended canter, but the horse remains collected, unlike the flat-out run when the horse's gait almost returns to a four-beat status.
HANDICAP	A race in which chances of winning are equalized by assigned weights; heaviest weights are given to the best horses, and lightest weights to the poorest.
HARD-MOUTHED	Term used when the membrane of the bars of the mouth where the bit rests have become toughened and the nerves deadened because of the continued pressure of the bit.
HAT-RACK	An emaciated animal.
HAUTE ECOLE	See HIGH SCHOOL.
HAW	The teamster's term signaling a turn to the left.
HAY BELLY	Having a distended barrel due to the excessive feeding of bulky rations, such as hay, straw, or grass. Also called "grass belly."
HEAT	1. One trip in a race that will be decided by winning two or more trials. 2. A common term for the estrus period.
HEAVES	Difficulty in forcing air out of the lungs. It is characterized by a jerking of the flanks (double-flank action) and coughing after drinking cold water.
HEIGHT	Tallness of a horse as measured from the withers to the ground. It is expressed in hands (each hand being 4 inches).
HEREDITY	Characteristics transmitted to offspring from parents and other ancestors.
HERNIA (or Rupture)	The protrusion of any internal organ through the wall of its containing cavity, but it usually means the passage of a portion of the intestine through an opening in the abdominal muscle.
HERRING-GUTTED (or Shadbelly)	Lacking depth of flank, which is also termed "single-gutted."

HETEROZYGOUS	Having unlike genes, which can be present for any of the characteristics such as coat color, size, etc.
HIDEBOUND	Having a hide that is tight over the body.
HIGH SCHOOL (or Haute Ecole)	The highest form of specialized training of riding horses.
HIPPOLOGY	The study of the horse.
HITCH	1. To fasten a horse; e.g., when hitched to a rail. 2. Connection between a vehicle and a horse. 3. A defect in gait noted in the hind legs, which seem to skip at the trot.
HITCHING	1. Having a shorter stride in one hind leg than in the other. 2. Fastening a horse to an object or vehicle.
HIVES	Small swellings under or within the skin similar to human hives. They appear suddenly over large portions of the body and can be caused by a change in feed.
HOBBLES	Straps which encircle the pasterns or fetlock joints on the front legs of the horse and are connected with a short strap or chain to prevent the horse from roaming too far when turned out to graze. Another type of hobble is used on the hind legs (often around the hocks) of a mare in breeding, to prevent her kicking the stallion.
HOGGED MANE	A hogged mane is one that has been clipped short.
HOMOZYGOUS	Having like genes, which can be present for any of the characteristics of the animal such as coat color, size, etc.
HOMOZYGOUS DOMINANT	A dominant character that produces only one kind of gamete.
HOMOZYGOUS RECESSIVE	A recessive character that produces two kinds of gametes; one carries the dominant gene and the other carries the recessive gene.
HONDA	A ring of rope, rawhide, or metal on a lasso through which the loop slides.
HOPPLES	The term applied to hobbles (leather or plastic

straps with semicircular loops) used in harness racing, which are placed on the gaskin and forearm, connecting the fore and hind legs of the same side in pacers, and running diagonally in trotters, connecting the diagonal fore and hind legs. Such hopples, which were invented by a railroad conductor named John Browning in 1885, are used to keep a horse on gait; i.e., to prevent trotters from pacing and pacers from trotting.

HORMONE — A body-regulating chemical secreted by a gland into the bloodstream.

HORN FLY — Primarily pests of cattle, but they sometimes seriously annoy horses.

HORSE — In the restricted sense this applies to an entire, not a gelding or mare.

HORSEFLY — A biting insect that inflicts a painful bite.

HORSEMANSHIP — The art of riding horseback.

HORSE MEAT — In France and Belgium, and other parts of the world, horse meat is considered a delicacy for human consumption. In this country, many horses that have outlived their usefulness or that are less valuable for other purposes are processed in modern sanitary slaughtering plants for pet food.

HORSEPOWER — The historical importance of horses is attested to by the continued use of the term "horsepower." Originally, it was a measure of the power that a horse exerts in pulling. Technically speaking, a horsepower is the rate at which work is accomplished when a resistance (weight) of 33,000 pounds is moved 1 foot in 1 minute, or 550 pounds is moved 1 foot in 1 second. Despite their sophistication, modern motors are rated in horsepower, based on tests made on a machine known as the dynamometer.

Figure G.2 Riding sulky plow about 1881.

HOT-BLOODED   Of Eastern or Oriental blood.

HOT-WALKER   One employed to cool out horses.

HOUSE FLY   Nonbiting, nuisance insect.

HUNT   Pursuit of game. As used by horsemen, the term usually implies a hunt on horseback with hounds.

HUNT SEAT SADDLE   Much like the jump saddle, but with less incline to the cantle.

HYBRIDS   Crosses of species, not breeds. The mule is a hybrid — a cross between the horse family and the ass family. Most mules are infertile.

Figure G.3 One of nature's rarest whims — a colt, sired by a stallion, dropped by a mare mule. (Courtesy, Dr. George P. Broussard, DVM, New Iberia, Louisiana)

I

IMPORT

To bring horses from another country.

IMPORTING

In registering horses from another country in the registry's stud book of their breeds, the certificates of registration issued bear the abbreviation Imp. and the country of export: e.g., Imp. Hydroplane (Eng.). When a name, such as Hydroplane has been previously granted to a horse foaled (born) in this country, a symbol is added; e.g., Imp. Hydroplane — II (Eng.) Imported is also denoted by an asterisk in front of the name; e.g., *Hydroplane II (Eng.)

INDIAN BROKE

Horses trained to allow mounting from the off side.

INDIAN PONY

A pinto.

INFLUENZA

A contagious virus disease, characterized by respiratory inflammation, fever, muscle soreness, and often a loss of appetite.

IN-HAND

Refers to horses shown in halter classes.

INTERFERING

The striking of the fetlock or cannon by the opposite foot that is in motion is known as interfering. This condition is predisposed in horses with base-narrow, toe-wide, or splay-footed standing positions.

ITCH

See MANGE.

J

JACK

1. A bone spavin.
2. The male of the ass family.

JACK SPAVIN

See BONE SPAVIN.

JENNET

Female of the ass family.

JERK LINE

A single rein, originally used in western U.S. It was fastened to the brake handle and ran through the driver's hand to the bit of the lead animal.

JOCKEY CLUB

Probably the most exclusive club in America, limited to about 75 members. The Jockey Club

Figure G.4 They're off! At the starting gate the bell rings, the little doors fly open, the jockey yells, hunches forward, and urges with all his might, and the horse plunges forward — all in a split second. (Courtesy, *From Dawn to Destiny,* by Frank Jennings and Allen F. Brewer, Jr., published by The Thoroughbred Press, Lexington, Kentucky)

is custodian of the American Stud Book, registry of Thoroughbred horses.

JOCKEYS

Professional riders of horses in races. Jockeys are both born and made. They were born to be small people; and they are made as jockeys if they possess courage and intelligence. Jockeys weigh anywhere from 94 to 116 pounds, with an average of about 105 pounds. A famous observation, which the author once overheard in a jockey's room before a race, was, "What would we all be if it weren't for racing? We'd all be bellhops." But, the jockey might well have added that they would be bellhops anyway if they don't have the courage to ride down a track at 40 miles an hour, delicately balanced in a pair of short stirrups, amid 48 flying steel plates (shoes) and six thundering tons of horseflesh — calmly, but in a split second, planning every move as they ride.

JOCKEY STICK

A stick fastened to the hame of the near horse

and the bit of the off horse for use in driving with a single rein to prevent crowding.

JOG CART — A cart longer and heavier than a racing sulky, used in warm-up miles because it's more comfortable for the driver than a sulky.

JOGGING — A slow warm-up exercise of several miles with the horse going the wrong way of the track.

JOINT ILL — See NAVEL INFECTION.

JUGHEAD — A stupid horse. Also one with a large, ugly head.

JUMP SEAT SADDLE — A saddle with a high cantle (back) which inclines the rider's weight forward to keep in balance with the horse when going over jumps. It usually has knee rolls to help maintain balance.

K

KICK — Movement by a horse of the back legs, with intent to hit a person or other object.

KNEE-SPRUNG
(or Buck-kneed) — A condition of over in the knees, or with the knees protruding too far forward.

L

LAMENESS — A defect that can be detected when the affected foot is favored when standing. In action, the load on the ailing foot is eased, and there is a characteristic bobbing of the head of the horse as the affected foot strikes the ground.

LAMINAE — The flat tissue in the sole or base of the hoof.

LAMINITIS
(or Founder) — An inflammation of the sensitive laminae of the hoof. All feet may be affected, but the front feet are most susceptible.

LEAD — The leading foot (leg) of a horse under saddle. When cantering circularly, the foot to the inner arc of the circle — clockwise, a right foot lead; and counter clockwise, a left foot lead.

LEAD LINE — A chain, rope, or strap, or combination thereof, used for leading a horse.

LEADERS — The head team in a 4-, 6-, or 8-horse hitch.

LEATHERS — The straps running from the saddle to the irons on an English saddle.

LEFT LEAD	Left front foot and left rear foot lead on the canter.
LEG BRACER	A solution, lotion, or liniment containing a large amount of alcohol used as a stimulant for the legs, causing increased blood circulation to the applied area.
LEGS OUT OF THE SAME HOLE	Very narrow-fronted. Such horses usually stand basewide; i.e., the feet stand wider apart than the distance across the legs at the chest.
LEVADE	An exercise of the haute ecole, especially as performed in the Spanish Riding School at Vienna. In the Levade the horse is in a half rearing position, with the forelegs well bent and the hind legs in a crouching position.
LICE	Small, flattened, wingless insect parasites.
LINEBACK	An animal having a stripe of distinctive color along the spine.
LINES (or Reins)	A leather strap, webbing, or rope attached to the bit or bits for control and direction. In driving, lines are sometimes called reins. In riding, reins are never called lines.
LIP STRAP	The small strap running through the curb chain from one side of the bit shank to the other. Its primary function is to keep the horse from taking the shank or the bit in its teeth.
LOCKJAW	See TETANUS.
LONG-COUPLED	Too much space between the last rib and the point of the hip.
LONGE	See LUNGE.
LOPE	The Western adaptation of a very slow canter. It is a smooth, slow gait in which the head is carried low.
LOP-NECK	See BROKEN CREST.
LUGGER	A horse that pulls at the bit.
LUGGING AND PULLING	Some horses pull on the reins, "lug" on one rein, or bear out or in with the driver, making it hard to drive them and to rate the mile at an even clip.

LUNGE (Longe)	The act of exercising a horse on the end of a long rope, usually in a circle.
LUNGWORMS (*Dictyocaulus arnfieldi*)	Lungworms may be found in the air passages of the horse and other equines. The male worm reaches a length of about 1 inch and the female may be about 2 inches long. The equine lungworm is very rare in the United States.

M

MAIDEN	1. A mare that has never been bred. 2. On the racetrack, it refers to a horse (stallion, mare, or gelding) that has not won a race on a recognized track; and in the show-ring, it refers to a horse that has not won a first ribbon in a recognized show in the division in which it is showing.
MANE	Long hair on the top of the neck.
MANGE (or Scabies, Scab, or Itch)	A specific contagious disease caused by mites.
MANNERS	A way of behaving.
MARE	A mature female four years or older; in Thoroughbreds, five years or older.
MASCOT	A companion for a horse. The most common mascots are ponies, goats, dogs, cats, and chickens.
MATRON	A mare that has produced a foal.
MITES	Very small parasites that cause mange (scabies, scab, and itch).
MIXED-GAITED	Said of a horse that will not adhere to any one true gait at a time.
MOHAMMED'S TEN HORSES	In the days of Mohammed, intelligence and obedience were the main requisites of the Arab's horse. For war purposes, only the most obedient horses were used, and they were trained to follow the bugle. Legend has it that the Prophet himself had need for some very obedient horses, so he inspected a certain herd to make personal selections.

The horses from which he wished to make selections were pastured in a large area bordering on a river. The Prophet gave orders that the animals should be fenced off from the river until their thirst became very great. Then, he ordered the fence removed, and the horses rushed for the water. When they were just about to dash into the river to quench their thirst, a bugle was sounded.

All but 10 of the horses ignored the call of the bugle. The obedient 10 turned and answered the call of duty, despite their great thirst. The whimsical story goes on to say that these 10 head constituted the foundation of the "Prophet Strain."

Moon Blindness
(or Periodic Ophthalmia)

A cloudy or inflamed condition of the eye which disappears and returns in cycles that are often completed in about a month.

Morning Glory

A horse that works out in record time in the morning but does not live up to its promise in an actual race.

Mosquito

A biting insect.

Mottled

Marked with spots of different colors; dappled, spotted.

Mounting

The act of getting on a horse.

Mouthing

Determining the approximate age of a horse by examining the teeth.

Mudder

A horse that runs well on a track that is wet, sloppy, or heavy.

Mustang

Native horse of the Western Plains.

Mutation

A sudden variation which is later passed on through inheritance and which results from changes in a gene or genes.

Mutton-withered

Low in the withers, with heavy shoulder muscling.

Muzzle

The lower end of the nose, which includes the nostrils, lips, and chin.

N

NARRAGANSETT
PACER

A fast type of pacer, descended from the indigenous horse of Narragansett Bay area of Rhode Island and evolved during the time of the Revolutionary War (1775–1781). During this period, racing was illegal except in Rhode Island.

NAVEL ILL

See NAVEL INFECTION.

NAVEL INFECTION
(or Joint Ill, Navel Ill,
Actinobacillosis)

An infectious disease of newborn animals caused by several kinds of bacteria.

NAVICULAR DISEASE

An inflammation of the small navicular bone and bursa of the front foot. It is often impossible to determine the exact cause of the disease. Affected animals go lame; have a short stubby stride; and usually point the affected foot when standing. Few animals completely recover from the disease. Treatment consists of special shoeing. In cases of persistent and severe lameness, unnerving may be performed by a veterinarian to destroy the sensation in the foot.

NEAR SIDE

The left side of a horse.

The custom of working from the left side of the horse evolved quite logically in two ways:

1. In the days when horsemen wore swords, they hung to the left. Hence, the sword would have interfered with the rider by hanging between his legs had he tried mounting from the right.

2. In England, traffic keeps to the left. Therefore, when working around horses the coachman stood on the left side if possible in order to be on the side of the road and out of the line of traffic.

In both the above situations horsemen were most often on the left side of horses: hence, logically it became known as the "near side," and the right side became the "off" side. With a team of horses, the one on the left is the "near" horse, the one on the right is the "off" horse.

NECK REIN

To guide or direct a horse by pressure of the rein on the neck.

NEIGH	The loud, prolonged call of a horse.

O

OFF SIDE	The right side of a horse.
OPEN BRIDLE	Bridle without blinds or blinkers covering the eyes. Some bridles are rigged with blinds that shut off vision to the rear and side and a few horses are raced with goggles or "peekaboo" blinds.
OPEN-HOCKED	Wide apart at the hocks with the feet close together.
ORIENTAL	See EASTERN.
ORLOFF TROTTER	A breed of horses originating in the U.S.S.R. in the 18th Century, principally through the interest of Count Alexis Gregory Orloff Chesminski. Used in the Soviet Union for light work, pleasure driving and riding, exhibition at fairs in various forms of competition including dressage, and extensively in harness racing.
OSSELETS	A rather inclusive term used to refer to a number of inflammatory conditions around the ankle joints. Generally it denotes a swelling that is fairly well defined and located slightly above or below the actual center of the joint, and, ordinarily, a little to the inside or outside of the exact front of the leg. When touched, it imparts the feeling of putty or mush, and it may be warm to hot. The pain will be in keeping with the degree of inflammation as evidenced by swelling and fever. Afflicted horses travel with a short choppy stride and show evidence of pain when the ankle is flexed.
OUTLAW	A horse that cannot be broken.
OVARY	The female organ that produces eggs. There are two ovaries.
OVERREACH	The hitting of the forefoot with the hind foot.
OVERSHOT JAW (or Parrot Mouth)	The upper jaw protruding beyond the lower jaw.
OVULATION	The time when the follicle bursts and the egg is released.

OVUM	Scientific name for egg.

P

PACE	A fast, two-beat gait in which the front and hind feet on the same side start and stop simultaneously.
PADDLING	Throwing the front feet outward as they are picked up. This condition is predisposed in horses with toe-narrow or pigeon-toed standing positions.
PAIR	1. Two horses hitched abreast. 2. Used in reference to two horses ridden side by side, as in pair classes.
PALISADE WORMS	See STRONGYLES, LARGE AND SMALL.
PARI-MUTUELS	Machine-controlled pool betting, invented in France in 1865, by a perfume-shop proprietor named Pierre Oller, who, embittered by a losing streak with the bookies, worked out the idea of the betting pool and began selling tickets over his store counter. His take was five percent; the rest was divided equally among the winners.
PARROT MOUTH	See OVERSHOT JAW.
PASSAGE	1. A movement of the haute ecole. This is a slow, cadenced, rather high trot with a fairly long period of suspension, giving the impression that the horse is on springs, or "trotting on air." 2. A term for diagonal movement of the horse while facing straight forward, at the walk or trot.
PASTERN	That part of the leg between the fetlock joint and the coronary band of the hoof.
PEDIGREE	A record of the ancestry of an animal.
PEDIGREE BREEDING	Selection on the combined bases of the merits of the individual and the average merits of its ancestry.
PEGASUS	A word of Greek origin, meaning strong. Legend has it that the winged horse, Pegasus, was fashioned from the body of Medusa, daughter of a sea-god who, in her youth, was as mortal as she was beautiful. At his birth, the frisky colt flew to Mount Helicon, where he created a fountain

(Horsewell) with one swift blow of his hoof. Using a golden bridle, Bellerophon coaxed the curious animal from his favorite meadow, made him captive, and rode him off. Later, Pegasus unceremoniously dumped his venerable and conceited master and flew into outer space where he became the constellation that bears his name.

PELHAM BIT

A one-piece bit equipped to handle four reins. Two are snaffle reins, used for guiding the horse and lifting the head; and two are curb reins, used for control and for setting the head. Snaffle reins are always heavier than curb reins.

PERIODIC OPHTHALMIA

See MOON BLINDNESS.

PIAFFE

A dressage movement in which the horse does a cadenced trot in place, without moving from the spot. It is the foundation of all high-school movements.

PIEBALD

Refers to black-and-white coat color.

PIGEON-TOED

Pointing toes inward and heels outward.

PIG-EYED

Having small, narrow, squinty eyes, set back in the head; also, having thick eyelids.

PIN-FIRING

A method of inserting an electric needle into an injured area. This induces healing at the site.

PINTO

A multicolored, spotted horse.

PINWORMS
(*Oxyuris equi, Probstmyria vivipara*)

Two species of pinworms, or rectal worms, frequently are found in horses. *Oxyuris equi* are whitish worms with long, slender tails. *Probstmyria vivipara* are so small they are scarcely visible to the eye.

PIROUETTE

A dressage exercise in which the horse holds its forelegs more or less in place while it moves its hindquarters around them.

PIVOT

A movement in dressage in which the horse pivots around its hindquarters, holding one hind leg more or less in place and sidestepping with the other hind foot.

PLACE

To finish second in a race.

PLACENTA	The membrane by which the fetus is attached to the uterus. Nutrients from the mother pass into the placenta and then through the navel cord to the fetus. When the animal is born, the placenta is expelled. It is commonly called the "after-birth."
PLUG	A horse of common breeding and poor conformation.
POINT	The team in back of the leaders in an eight-horse hitch.
POINTING	1. Perceptible extension of the stride with little flexion is called pointing. This condition is likely to occur in the Thoroughbred and Standardbred breeds — animals bred and trained for great speed with a long stride. 2. Referring to a standing position when one of the front legs is extended ahead of the other. This occurs when a horse with a sore foot places the ailing foot ahead in order to take the weight off it.
POINTS	Black coloration from the knees and hocks down, as in most bays and browns, and in some buckskins, roans, and grays.
POLL EVIL	An inflamed condition in the region of the poll (the area on top of the neck and immediately behind the ears), usually caused by bruising the top of the head.
POLO PONY	A "pony" used for playing polo. Polo ponies of today are mostly of Thoroughbred breeding. They must be fast, and tough and courageous enough to stand the bumping, riding-off, and the many quick stops and turns.
POP-EYED	Refers to a horse whose eyes are generally more prominent or bulge out a little more than normal; also to a horse that is "spooky" or attempts to see everything that goes on.
POPPED KNEE	A general term describing inflammatory conditions affecting the knees, so named because of the sudden swelling that accompanies it.

POST	The starting point of a race.
POSTING	The rising and descending of the rider with the rhythm of the trot.
POST POSITION	Refers to race starting position. Beginning with position number 1 nearest the rail, horses line up at the starting gate according to number.
POULTICE	A moist, mealy mass, applied hot to a sore or inflamed part of the body.
POUNDING	A "heavy foot" contact with the ground, common in high-going horses.
PREPOTENCY	Refers to breeding power, as measured by the degree in which parent likeness is transmitted to offspring.
PRODUCE	Offspring.
PROGENITOR	One that originates or precedes.
PROGENY	Refers to offspring or descendants of one or both parents.
PUFFS	Wind galls, bog spavins, or thoroughpins.
PULLED TAIL	A tail thinned by hairs being pulled.
PULLING RECORD, WORLD	The world's record in pulling contest was established in the 1965 Hillsdale County Fair, in Michigan. It is held jointly by Frank Vurckio, Sun Down, New York; Fowler Bros., Montgomery, Michigan. It was made on a dynamometer with a tractive pull of 4350 pounds (equal to 56,493 pounds, over 28 tons, on a wagon).
PUREBRED	An animal descended from a line of ancestors of the same breed but not necessarily registered. This should not be confused with "Thoroughbred," a breed of horse.
PURSE	Race prize money to which the owners of horses in the race do not contribute.

Q

QUALITY	Refinement, as shown in a neat and well-chiseled head, fine texture of hair with little or no fetlock, clean bone, good texture of hoof, etc.

QUARTER CRACK (or Sand Crack)	A vertical split in the horny wall of the inside of the hoof (in the region of the quarter), which extends from the coronet or hoof head downward.
QUITTOR	A deep-seated running sore which occurs on the coronet band or hoof head. It is caused initially by an injury or puncture wound in the area of the sole of the foot.

R

RACK (or Single-foot)	A fast, flashy, unnatural, four-beat gait in which each foot meets the ground separately at equal intervals; hence, it was originally known as the "single-foot," a designation now largely discarded.
RANDOM	Three horses hitched in single file, usually to a dogcart.
RANGY	Elongated, lean, muscular, of slight build.
RAT TAIL	A tail with a short hair coat.
RATTLERS	Rattlers (wooden, rubber, or plastic balls) or links of light chain fastened about the pasterns of high-going harness and saddle horses and ponies. Weighted boots are also used to enhance action.
REATA	Spanish for lariat.
RECESSIVE CHARACTER	A characteristic which appears only when both members of a pair of genes are alike. Opposite of dominant.
RED WORMS	See STRONGYLES, LARGE AND SMALL.
REINS	See LINES.
REMUDA	A collection of riding horses at a roundup from which are chosen those used for the day. A relay of mounts.
RIBBED-UP	Said of a horse on which the back ribs are well arched and incline well backwards, bringing the ends closer to the point of the hip and making the horse shorter in coupling.

RIDGELING

A horse with at least one testicle in the abdomen. A ridgeling is difficult to geld, and often retains the characteristic of a stallion.

RIGHT LEAD

Right front foot and right rear lead on the canter.

RINGBONE

A bony growth on the pastern bone in the area of the coronet. It is generally on the forefoot, although occasionally the hind foot is affected.

RINGER

A horse passed off under false identity, with the idea of entering it in a race below its class where it is almost certain to win. With today's lip tattoo system of identification, ringers are a thing of the past.

RINGWORM

This is a contagious infection of the outer layers of skin caused by an infestation of microscopic fungi.

ROACH BACKED

Arched-backed, razorbacked.

ROACHED MANE

A mane that has been cut short and tapered so that it stands upright. It is not so short as a clipped mane.

ROARER

A wind-broken animal that makes a loud noise in drawing air into the lungs, especially when respiration is speeded up with exercise.

ROLLERS
(Rattlers)

Wooden balls on a cord, encircling a horse's pastern to give more action.

ROLLING

Excessive lateral shoulder motion, characteristic of horses with protruding shoulders, is known as rolling.

ROMAN-NOSED

Refers to a horse having a profile that is convex from poll to muzzle.

ROPE-WALKING

See WINDING.

ROUNDWORMS, LARGE
(or Ascarids) (*Parascaris equorum*)

The female varies from 6 to 22 inches long and the male from 5 to 13 inches. When full grown, both are about the diameter of a lead pencil.

RUBDOWN

A rubbing of the body with a rough towel, usually given after exercise, to promote circulation and remove fatigue.

RUN
(Gallop)

The run, or gallop, is a fast, four-beat gait where the feet strike the ground separately; first one

	hind foot, then the other hind foot, then the front foot on the same side as the first hind foot, then the other front foot, which decides the lead.
RUNNING WALK	A slow, four-beat gait, intermediate in speed between the walk and rack. The hind foot oversteps the front foot from a few to as many as 18 inches, giving the motion a smooth gliding effect. It is characterized by a bobbing or nodding of the head, a flopping of the ears, and a snapping of the teeth in rhythm with the movement of the legs.
RUPTURE	See HERNIA.

S

SALINE	Consisting of or containing salt.
SALIVA TEST	The testing of saliva for the presence of drugs or narcotics.
SAND CRACK	See QUARTER CRACK.
SCAB	See MANGE.
SCABIES	See MANGE.
SCALPING	That condition in which the hairline at the top of the hind foot hits the toe of the forefoot as it breaks over.
SCHOOLING	Training and developing natural characteristics in a pony.
SCLEROSTOMES	See STRONGYLES, LARGE AND SMALL.
SCORING	Preliminary warming up of horses before the start. The horses are turned near the starting point and hustled away as they will be in the race.
SCOTCH COLLAR	Housing over the collar of draft show harness.
SCRAPER	A metal or wooden tool, slightly concave, shaped like a hook at the upper end and used with one hand for scraping sweat and liquid from the body. Also, a thin metal strip with handles affixed at either end, used with both hands for scraping sweat and liquid from the body.
SCRATCHES	See GREASE HEEL.

SCREWWORM	Maggots of the screwworm fly, which require living flesh of animals on which to feed.
SCROTUM	The sac-like pouch that suspends the testicles outside the male animal.
SCRUB	A low-grade animal.
SELF-COLORED	A term applied to the mane and tail when they are the same color as the body coat.
SELL AT HALTER	To sell with no guarantee except the title.
SEMEN	Sperm mixed with fluids from the accessory glands.
SERVICEABLY SOUND	Said of a horse that has nothing wrong that will materially impair its value for the intended use.
SESAMOID FRACTURES	The fracture of one or both of the two pyramidlike bones that form a part of the fetlock or ankle joints (on both front and rear legs) and articulate with the posterior part of the lower end of the cannon bone.
SET-TAIL	A tail in which the cords have been cut or "nicked" and the tail put in a set.
SEX CELLS	The egg and the sperm, which unite to create life. They transmit genetic characteristics from the parents to the offspring.
SHADBELLY	See HERRING-GUTTED.
SHOE-BOIL (or Capped Elbow)	A soft, flabby swelling at the point of the elbow; hence, the common name "capped elbow." It is usually caused by contact with the shoe when the horse is lying down.
SHORT-COUPLED	Describes a horse having a short distance (usually not more than four fingers' width) between the last rib and the point of the hip.
SHOW	Finishing third in a race.
SHOW BRIDLE	Same as Weymouth bridle, but the leather usually is cut finer and the bits often are more severe.
SICKLE-HOCKED	The hind legs set too far forward, giving the impression of a sickle when viewed from the side.

SIDEBONES	Ossified lateral cartilages immediately above and toward the rear quarter of the hoof head. They occur most commonly in the forefeet.
SIDE STEP	See TRAVERSE.
SIGN	The word used when speaking of animal symptoms. Animals show "signs" of abnormality, whereas people can relate their symptoms of ill health. In horses, one must observe these signs.
SINGLE-FOOT	Now called a "rack." See RACK.
SIRE	The male parent.
SISTERS	See BROTHERS.
SKEWBALD	Refers to coat color other than black — such as bay, brown, or chestnut — combined with white.
SKIRT	That part of the saddle against which the knees and calves of the rider are placed.
SLAB-SIDED	Flat-ribbed.
SLEEPING SICKNESS	See ENCEPHALOMYELITIS.
SLOPING SHOULDERS	Shoulders properly angulated and laid back.
SLOW PACE	See STEPPING PACE.
SMOKY EYE	A whitish-clouded eye. See WALLEYE.
SMOOTH	Unshod, "barefoot."
SMOOTH COAT	Short, hard, close-fitting coat of hair.
SMOOTH-MOUTHED	No cups in the teeth. Indicates a horse is 12 years of age or older.
SNAFFLE BIT	A mouthpiece with a joint in the center. The ring may be either circular or D-shaped. The most widely used of all bits.
SNIP	A white mark between the nostrils or on the lip.
SNORTER	An excitable horse.
SOFT	Easily fatigued.
SOLID COLOR	Having no white markings.
SOUND	Said of a horse free from injury, flaw, mutilation, or decay; also one that is guaranteed free from blemishes and unsoundness.

SPAVIN	See BLOOD SPAVIN, BOG SPAVIN, and BONE SPAVIN.
SPAY	To remove a mare's ovaries.
SPECK IN EYE	A spot in the eye, but not covering the pupil. It may or may not impair the vision. See FEATHER IN EYE.
SPEEDY CUTTING	A condition of a horse at speed in which a hind leg above the scalping mark hits against the shoe of a breaking-over forefoot. In trotters, legs on the same side are involved. In pacers, diagonal legs are involved.
SPERM (Sperm Cell)	Male sex cell produced in the testicles.
SPLENIC FEVER	See ANTHRAX.
SPLINTS	Abnormal body growths found on the cannon bone, usually on the inside surface, but occasionally on the outside. They are most common on the front legs.
SPOOKY	Nervous.
SPRINTER	A horse that performs best at distances of a mile or under.
SPURS	The artificial aid worn over a boot, used to achieve a desired result when riding.
STABLE FLY	Biting insects that bite principally on the legs.
STAG	A male horse that was castrated after reaching maturity.
STAKE RACES	A stake, short for sweepstake, is just what the name implies. Each owner puts up an equal amount of money (nominating fees, fees for keeping them eligible, and starting fees) and the winner takes all. Also, the track usually puts up added money. Actually, few stake races are run on a winner-take-all basis; rather, the money is divided between the first four horses.
STALL	Space or compartment in which an animal is placed or confined. It may be a straight stall with the animal tied at the front end (a tie-stall) or a compartment with the animal loose inside (box-stall).

STALLION	A male horse four years old or older; in Thoroughbreds, five years old or over.
STANDING HALTER	Similar to a martingale, it is a strap that runs from the girth to a tight halter on the horse's head. It helps keep the horse from throwing its head up and going into a break.
STAR	Any white mark on the forehead located above a line running from eye to eye.
STAR GAZER	A horse that holds its head high in an awkward position.
STEEPLECHASER	A horse used in cross-country racing with jumps.
STEPPING PACE (or Slow Pace)	A modified pace in which the objectionable side or rolling motion of the true pace is eliminated because the 2 feet on each side do not move exactly together. Instead, it is a 4-beat gait with each of the 4 feet striking the ground separately.
STERILE	A term used to designate a stallion that is infertile.
STIFLE	The counterpart of the knee joint in man. The junction of the horse's tibia and patella in the hind leg.
STIFLED	A horse is said to be stifled when the patella (or kneecap) slips out of place and temporarily locks in a location above and to the inside of its normal location.
STIRRUP IRON	The metal D-shaped device on the saddle through which the leather runs and on which the foot rests.
STOCK HORSE	In the West this term designates a cow horse. In other localities it can also mean a stallion used at stud.
STOCKING	White extends from the coronet to the knee. When the white includes the knee, it is known as a full stocking.
STOMACH WORMS (*Habronema* spp., *Trichostrongylus axei*)	A group of parasitic worms that produces inflammation of the stomach.
STRAIGHT SHOULDER	Said of shoulder lacking sufficient angulation.
STRANGLES	See DISTEMPER.

STRIDE	The distance covered by one foot when in motion. Greyhound, with a trotting record at 1:55¼, had a stride of more than 27 feet.
STRINGHALT	A condition characterized by excessive flexing of the hind legs. It is most easily detected when backing a horse.
STRIPE	A narrow white marking that extends from about the line of the eyes to the nostrils.
STRONGYLES, LARGE AND SMALL (*Strongylus* spp. and others)	There are about 60 species of strongyles. Three are large worms that grow up to 2 inches long. The rest are small and some are barely visible to the eye. Large strongyles are variously called bloodworms (*Strongylus vulgaris*), palisade worms, sclerostomes, and red worms.
STUD	1. A male horse (stallion) kept for breeding. 2. Also, an establishment or farm where animals are kept for breeding.
STUD BOOK	The permanent book of breeding records.
STUMP SUCKING	See CRIBBER.
SUBSTANCE	A combination of good bone, muscularity, and width and depth of body.
SUCKLING	A foal that is not weaned.
SULKY OR BIKE	Light racing rig with bicycle-type wheels used in harness races. The sulkies weigh from 29 to 37 pounds, and usually have hardwood shafts, although aluminum and steel sulkies have been introduced recently.
SUMMER SORES	These are irritated spreading sores which develop from a wound. The sore may be as small as a dime but will enlarge rapidly within a week's time.
SURCINGLE	A belt, band, or girth passing over a saddle or over anything on a horse's back to bind the saddle fast.
SUSPENSORY LIGAMENT SPRAIN	The suspensory ligament is situated over the back of the leg and passes over the fetlock or ankle joint, both in the forelegs and hind legs. Its principal function is to support the fetlock.

This ligament is frequently the object of severe strain; the swelling begins just above the ankle and extends obliquely downward and forward over the sides of the ankle. Should the injury be further up on the leg, the exact location at first may appear obscure, as the ligament is covered by the flexor tendons.

When the suspensory ligament is affected, the swelling will be found right up against the bone. If it is the flexor tendons that are involved, the swelling will be farther back near the surface on the back of the leg.

SWAMP FEVER

See EQUINE INFECTIOUS ANEMIA.

SWAN NECK

A long slim, swanlike neck.

"SWAP HORSES IN MIDSTREAM"

The origin of the saying, "Don't swap horses in midstream," appears to be clouded in obscurity.

Upon being congratulated when renominated for the presidency, Lincoln said, "I do not allow myself to suppose that either the convention or the league have concluded to decide that I am either the greatest or the best man in America, but rather they have concluded it is not best to swap horses while crossing the river, and have further concluded that I am not so poor a horse that they might not make a botch of it in trying to swap." One historian of that period credited the utterance to a Dutch farmer; and H. L. Mencken reports that the phrase was used some 24 years earlier than when Lincoln used it.

SWAYBACKED

Having a decided dip in the back. Also termed "easy-backed" and "saddle-backed."

SWEAT SCRAPER

An instrument for removing excess sweat from a hard-worked horse.

SWEENEY

A depression in the shoulder due to atrophied muscles.

SWEET FEED

Refers to horse feed which is characterized by its sweetness due to the addition of molasses; usually a commercial horse feed mixture.

SWING TEAM

The middle team in a six-horse hitch, or the team in front of the wheelers in an eight-horse hitch.

SWIPE	Racetrack slang for a groom, stable hand, or exercise boy.
SYNOVIAL FLUID	The fluid that lubricates the joint.

T

TACK	Equipment used in riding and driving horses, such as saddles, bridles, harness, etc.
TACK ROOM	Place for storage of tack and accessories used in riding or driving. Also a display room for pictures, prizes, ribbons, trophies, and the like.
TAIL (banged or thinned)	A tail is banged if the hair is cut off in a straight line below the dock; it is thinned if it is shortened; and it is thinned and tapered if the hairs are pulled and broken.
TAIL FEMALE	The female line, or bottom line of a pedigree.
TAIL MALE	The sire line, or top line in a pedigree.
TAIL RUBBING	Persistent rubbing of the tail against the side of the stall or other objects.
TAIL-SET	A crupperlike contrivance, with a shaped section for the tail, which brings the tail high so that it can be doubled and tied down, to give it an "arch" and extremely high carriage; but a tail so set must first be "nicked" to give such results. The set is worn most of the time while the horse is in the stable, and until a short time before the horse is to be shown. Horses with "set" tails are usually "gingered" before entering the ring, in order to assure high tail carriage while being shown.
TALLY HO	The cry of the hunt once the fox is sighted.
TANDEM	Said of two horses, one hitched in front of the other.
TAPADERA	A long, decorative covering over the stirrup used in parade classes.
TAPEWORMS (*Anoplocephala magna, A. perfoliata, Paranoplocephala mamillana*)	Internal parasites of horses, of which there are three species. *Anoplocephala perfoliata* is the most common and most damaging.
TEASER	A horse, usually a stallion or a ridgeling, used to test the response of a mare prior to breeding, or

used to determine if a mare is in heat and ready to breed.

TEMPERAMENT — Refers to the horse's suitability for the job it is to perform.

TEMPERATURE — Normal rectal temperature for the horse is 100.5° F.

TESTICLE — A male gland which produces sperm. There are two testicles.

TETANUS
(or Lockjaw) — Chiefly a wound-infection disease caused by a powerful toxin, more than 100 times as toxic as strychnine, that is liberated by the bacterium *Clostridium tetani,* an anaerobe.

THICK WIND — Difficulty in breathing.

THONG — The lash of the whip.

THOROUGHPIN — A puffy condition in the web of the hock. It can be determined by movement of the puff, when pressed, to the opposite side of the leg. The swelling is more or less rounded or oval in shape and can be observed from both sides.

THREAD WORMS
(*Strongyloides westeri*) — They are known as strongyloides.

THRIFTY CONDITION — Healthy, active, vigorous.

THROAT LATCH — The narrow strap of the bridle, which goes under the horse's throat and is used to secure the bridle to the head.

THRUSH — A disease of the foot, caused by a necrotic fungus characterized by a pungent odor. It is most commonly found in the hind feet and is caused by unsanitary conditions in the animal's stall. Thrush causes a deterioration of tissues in the cleft of the frog or in the junction between the frog and bars. This disease produces lameness and, if not treated, can be serious.

TICKS — External insects, several kinds of which may be found on the horses. The most common ones are the winter tick, *Dermacentor albipictus;* the lone star tick, *Amblyomma americanum;* and the spinose ear tick, *Otobius megnini.*

TIE — To attach or fasten by use of halter and a shank.

TOE WEIGHT	A metal weight (knob) fitted to a spur previously placed on the front hoof to induce a change of balance in motion. Used extensively in the training and racing of harness horses.
TONGUE-LOLLER	A horse whose tongue hangs out.
TOOTH RASP	A file with a long handle, used for floating or removing sharp edges from the teeth.
TOTALIZATOR	The mechanical "brains" of the pari-mutuel system.
TOTE BOARD	The indicator board of the totalizator on which is flashed all pari-mutuel information before or after a race.
TOUT	A low-order con man who peddles tips, betting systems, etc., to the unwary racegoer.
TRACES	The parts of a harness which run from the collar to the singletree.
TRACHEOTOMY	An operation on the throat to cure roaring, or to keep a horse from suffocating in an emergency.
TRAPPY	A short, quick, choppy stride. This condition is predisposed in horses with short, straight pasterns and straight shoulders.
TRAVERSE (or Side Step)	The traverse or side step is simply a lateral movement of the animal to the right or left as desired, without moving forward or backward.
TROIKA	The word "troika" is a Russian word meaning trio or three. A troika hitch is a three-horse combination team hitched to a vehicle; e.g., a carriage, wagon, sleigh, or sled. The carriage is the vehicle of common use and it is known as a caleche. It is a light four-wheeled two-passenger vehicle with an elevated seat for the driver.
TROT	A natural, rapid, two-beat, diagonal gait in which the front foot and the opposite hind foot take off at the same split second and strike the ground simultaneously.
TUCKED-UP	Having the belly under the loin. Refers also to a small-waisted horse. Differs from "herring-gutted" and similar conditions in that a horse may

be "tucked-up" temporarily due to hard work, lack of water, lack of bulk in the diet, etc. Also, called "gaunted-up" or "ganted-up."

TWITCH	A rope run through the end of a stick, used on the horse's upper lip; it is tightened by twisting in order to attract the horse's attention so it will stand still.
TWO-TRACK	The horse moves forward and diagonally at the same time.
"TYING-UP"	The "tying-up" syndrome is characterized by muscle rigidity and lameness affecting the muscles of the croup and loin, accompanied by pain, disinclination to move, a variable temperature, and brownish-colored urine. The cause is unknown, although it does seem to be associated with nervousness.
TYPE	Type may be defined as an ideal or standard of perfection combining all the characteristics that contribute to the animal's usefulness for a specific purpose.

U

UNDERPINNING	The legs and feet of the horse.
UNDERSHOT JAW	The lower jaw is longer than the upper jaw.
UNICORN	An unusual three-horse hitch with two horses hitched as a pair and a third hitched in front of the pair.
UNSOUNDNESSES	Those more serious abnormalities that affect the serviceability of the horse.
UTILITY SADDLE	A saddle that is between the jump seat and the show seat and is designed for general purpose use, except jumping.

V

VESICULAR STOMATITIS	A contagious disease of the mouth caused by a virus.
VETERINARIAN	One who treats diseases or afflictions of animals medically and surgically; a practitioner of veterinary medicine or surgery.

VICE	Any of the multitude of bad habits that a horse may acquire.
VICEROY	A lightweight, cut-under, wire-wheeled show vehicle with curved dash, used for some heavy harness classes, and especially for Hackney Ponies, Shetlands, and Harness Show Ponies.

W

WALK	A natural, slow, flatfooted, four-beat gait; the latter meaning that each foot takes off from and strikes the ground at a separate interval.
WALLEYE (or Smoky Eye)	Also termed glass, blue, china, or crockery eye; refers to lack of color in a horse's eye.
WARM-UP, WARMING UP	The process or routine of graduated exercise until the horse is properly conditioned for a strenuous effort.
WEANLING	A weaned foal.
WEAVING	A rhythmical swaying back and forth while standing in the stall. The prevention and cure are exercise, with ample room and freedom from stress.
WEYMOUTH BRIDLE	A bridle in which the snaffle bit and the curb bit are separate.
WHEELERS	The team on the pole or tongue, hitched directly in front of a rig or wagon in a four-or-more-horse hitch.
WHINNY	The horse's sound that denotes happiness, or anticipation of more pleasure.
WHIP	1. An instrument or device of wood, bone, plastic, leather, fiber glass, metal, or combination thereof with a loop or cracker of leather or cord at the upper end; used for disciplining or goading an animal. Sometimes a required accessory when exhibiting (driving), as in a horse show.
	2. One who handles a whip expertly, one who drives a horse in harness other than racing, or one who "whips in" or manages the hounds of a hunt club.
WHIP (in the Senate)	The term "whip" is derived from the British fox hunting term "whipper-in," the Huntsman's

principal assistant whose job is to keep the hounds from leaving the pack. The principal job of the whip in the U.S. Senate is to round up the party's senators for important votes and to try to make sure that they vote in keeping with the wishes of the party leaders.

WHITE LINE
The union between the sole and the wall of the foot.

WHOA
The command to stop; stand. When repeated softly, means to slow down, but may also mean attention.

WINDGALL
See WINDPUFFS.

WINDING
(or Rope-walking)
A twisting of the striding leg around in front of the supporting leg so as to make contact in the manner of a "rope-walking" artist is known as winding or rope-walking. This condition most often occurs in horses with very wide fronts.

WINDPUFFS
(or Windgall)
An enlargement of the fluid sac (bursa) located immediately above the pastern joints on the fore and rear legs. They are usually the result of too fast or too hard road work, especially on hard surfaces.

WIND SUCKING
See CRIBBER.

WINDY
(or Wind-broken)
Said of an animal that whistles or roars when exerted.

WINGING
Winging is an exaggerated paddling, particularly noticeable in high-going horses.

WRANGLING
Rounding up range horses.

Y

YEARLING
A horse between one and two years of age.

Appendices

Horse Books

Without claiming that either all or the best horse books are listed, the books that follow are recommended as the kind that will provide valuable reference material for the horseman's bookshelf and enhance the home library.

American Horse Breeding, H. H. Reese, Borden Publishing Co., Los Angeles, CA, 1953.

America's Quarter Horses, P. Laune, Doubleday & Company, Inc., Garden City, NY, 1973.

Anatomy and Conformation of the Horse, G. B. Edwards, Dreenan Press Ltd., Croton-on-Hudson, NY, 1973.

Anatomy of the Horse, The, R. F. Way and D. G. Lee, J. B. Lippincott Company, Philadelphia, PA, 1965.

Appaloosa Horse, The, F. Haines, et al., R. C. Bailey Printing Co., Lewiston, ID, 1957.

Appaloosa, The Spotted Horse in Art and History, F. Haines, University of Texas Press, Austin, TX, 1963.

Arab Breeding in Poland, E. Skorkowski, Your Pony, Columbus, WI, 1969.

Art of Horsemanship, The, Xenophon, trans. by M. H. Morgan, J. A. Allen & Co., Ltd., London, England, 1962.

Art & Science of Horseshoeing, The, R. G. Greeley, J. B. Lippincott Company, Philadelphia, PA, 1970.

Asiatic Wild Horse, The, E. Mohr, trans. by D. M. Goodall, J. A. Allen & Co., Ltd., London, England, 1971.

At the Horse Show with Margaret Cabell Self, M. C. Self, Arco Publishing Company, Inc., New York, NY, 1966.

Beginner's Guide to Horses, The, C. R. Melcher, A. S. Barnes & Co., Inc., Cranbury, NJ, 1974.

Biography of the Tennessee Walking Horse, B. A. Green, The Parthenon Press, Nashville, TN, 1960.

Bit by Bit, D. Tuke, J. A. Allen & Co., Ltd., London, England, 1965.

Black Beauty, A. Sewell, Collins, London, England, 1970.

Book of the Horse, The, P. Hamlyn, The Hamlyn Publishing Group, Ltd., New York, NY, 1970.

Book of Horses, The, D. Williams, J. B. Lippincott Company, Philadelphia, PA, 1971.

Breeding and Raising Horses, Agr. Hdbk No. 394, M. E. Ensminger, U.S. Department of Agriculture, Washington, D.C., 1972.

Breeding the Racehorse, F. Tesio, J. A. Allen & Company, London, England, 1964.

Breeding Thoroughbreds, J. F. Wall, Charles Scribner's Sons, New York, NY, 1946.

Buying Your First Horse, P. Bradbury, Cordovan Corporation, Houston, TX, 1973.

Care and Training of the Trotter and Pacer, J. C. Harrison, The United States Trotting Assn., Columbus, OH, 1968.

Cavalry Manual of Horsemanship and Horsemastership, The, ed. by G. Wright, Doubleday & Company, Inc., Garden City, NY, 1962.

Color of Horses, The, B. K. Green, Northland Press, Flagstaff, AZ, 1974.

Complete Book of the Horse, The, ed. by E. H. Edwards and C. Geddes, Ward Lock Limited, London, England, 1973.

Complete Horseshoeing Guide, The, R. F. Wiseman, University of Oklahoma Press, Norman, OK, 1968.

Conditioning to Win, ed. by D. M. Wagoner, Equine Research Publications, Grapevine, TX, 1974.

Dealing with Horses, J. F. Kelly, Arco Publishing Co., Inc., New York, NY, 1969.

Descriptive Bibliography of 1001 Horse Books, A, ed. by W. E. Jones, Caballus Publishers, Fort Collins, CO, 1972.

Diseases of the Horse, U.S. Department of Agriculture, U.S. Government Printing Press Office, Washington, D.C., 1942.

Disorders of the Horse, E. Hanauer, A. S. Barnes and Co., Inc., Cranbury, NJ, 1973.

Elegant Carriage, The, M. Watney, J. A. Allen & Co., London, England, 1961.

Elements of Farrier Science, D. M. Canfield, Enderes Tool Co., Inc., Albert Lea, MN, 1966.

Encyclopedia of the Horse, The, ed. by C. E. G. Hope and G. N. Jackson, The Viking Press, Inc., New York, NY, 1973.

English Pleasure Carriages, W. B. Adams, Adams & Dart, Bath, Somerset, England, 1971.

Equestrian Sport in Five Continents, ed. by E. A. Sarasin, Federation Equestrian International, FEI, Germany, 1963.

Equine Medicine & Surgery, ed. by J. F. Bone, et al., American Veterinary Publications, Inc., Santa Barbara, CA, 1963.

Every Horse Owner's Cyclopedia, J. H. Walsh, Porter & Coates, Philadelphia, PA, 1871.

Fair Exchange, H. S. Finney, Charles Scribner's Sons, New York, NY, 1974.

Famous Horses of America, Porter & Coates, Philadelphia, PA, 1877.

Feeding the Horse, The Blood-Horse, Lexington, KY, 1969.

Feeding Ponies, W. C. Miller, J. A. Allen & Co., Ltd., London, England, 1968.

Feeding to Win, ed. by D. M. Wagoner, Equine Research, Grapevine, TX, 1973.

First Aid Hints for the Horse Owner, W. E. Lyon, Collins, London, England, 1950.

First Horsemen, The, F. Trippet, Editors of Time-Life Books, Time-Life Books, New York, NY, 1974.

From Dawn to Destiny, F. Jennings and Allen F. Brewer, Jr., The Thoroughbred Press, Inc., Lexington, KY, 1962.

Genetic Principles in Horse Breeding, J. F. Lasley, Columbia, MO, 1970.

Genetics of the Horse, W. E. Jones and Ralph Bogart, Caballus Publishers, Fort Collins, CO, 1971.

Great Ones, The, ed. by K. Hollingsworth, The Blood-Horse, Lexington, KY, 1970.

Grooming Horses, R. W. Collins, The Blood-Horse, Lexington, KY, 1959; reprinted under special arrangement, by The Thoroughbred Record Co., Inc., 1971.

Grooming Your Horse, N. Haley, A. S. Barnes and Co., Inc., Cranbury, NJ.

Guide to American Horse Shows, A, D. A. Spector, Arco Publishing Company, Inc., New York, NY, 1973.

Guide for Veterinary Service and Judging of Equestrian Events, American Association of Equine Practitioners, Golden, CO, 1974.

Harper's Encyclopedia for Horsemen, L. Taylor, Harper & Row, New York, NY, 1973.

History of The Arabian Horse Club Registry of America, Inc., The, A. W. Harris, The Arabian Horse Club Registry of America, Inc., Chicago, IL, 1950.

History of Horse Racing, The, R. Longrigg, Stein and Day, New York, NY, 1972.

History of Thoroughbred Racing in America, The, W. H. Robertson, Prentice-Hall, Inc., Englewood Cliffs, NJ, 1964.

Horse, The, J. M. Kays, A. S. Barnes and Company, Inc., Cranbury, NJ, 1969.

Horse, The, I. P. Roberts, The Macmillan Company, London, England, 1913.

Horse, The, P. D. Rossdale, The California Thoroughbred Breeders Association, Arcadia, CA, 1972.

Horse American Made, The, L. Taylor, American Saddle Horse Breeders Association, Louisville, KY, 1961.

Horse Behavior and Training, R. W. Miller, Montana State University Bookstore, Bozeman, MT, 1974.

Horse-Breeding Farm, The, L. C. Willis, A. S. Barnes and Co., Inc., Cranbury, NJ, 1973.

Horse Breeding and Stud Management, H. Wynmalen, J. A. Allen & Co., Ltd., London, England, 1950.

Horse Breeds of the West, F. S. Harris, Cordovan Corporation, Houston, TX, 1973.

Horse Buyer's Guide, The, J. K. Posey, A. S. Barnes and Co., Inc., Cranbury, NJ, 1973.

Horseman's Encyclopedia, The, M. C. Self, A. S. Barnes and Co., Inc., Cranbury, NJ, 1963.

Horseman's Handbook on Practical Breeding, A, J. F. Wall, Thoroughbred Bloodlines, Camden, SC.

Horsemanship, Mrs. A. W. Jasper, Boy Scouts of America, New Brunswick, NJ, 1963.

Horsemanship and Horse Care, Agr. Inf. Bull. No. 353, M. E. Ensminger, U.S. Department of Agriculture, Washington, D.C., 1972.

Horsemanship and Horsemastership, ed. by G. Wright, Doubleday & Company, Inc., Garden City, NY, 1962.

Horseman's Scrapbook in Verse and Prose, A, D. J. Kays, Long's College Book Company, Columbus, OH, 1954.

Horseman's Short Course, Proceedings, Staff, Washington Horse Breeders Association, Seattle, WA, 1968.

Horseman's Tax Guide, J. O. Humphreys, The Blood Horse, Lexington, KY, 1963.

Horse Owner's Vet Book, The, E. C. Straiton, J. B. Lippincott Co., Philadelphia, PA, 1973.

Horse Psychology, M. Williams, A. S. Barnes and Co., Inc., Cranbury, NJ, 1969.

Horses, G. G. Simpsom, Oxford University Press, New York, NY, 1951.

Horses, M. C. Self, A. S. Barnes & Co., Inc., Cranbury, NJ, 1953.

Horses in America, F. Haines, Thomas Y. Crowell Company, New York, NY, 1971.

Horses and Americans, P. Strong, Frederick A. Stockes Company, New York, NY, 1939.

Horse's Astrologer, A, Chadwell and Sellers, Cordovan Corporation, Houston, TX, 1973.

Horse Science Handbook, Vols. 1–3, ed. by M. E. Ensminger, Agriservices Foundation, Clovis, CA, 1963, 1964, 1966.

Horseshoeing, A. Lungwitz, J. W. Adams, Oregon State University Press, Corvallis, OR, 1966.

Horses and Horsemanship, Fourth Edition, M. E. Ensminger, The Interstate Printers & Publishers, Inc., Danville, IL, 1977.

Horses and Horsemanship, L. E. Walraven, A. S. Barnes and Company, Inc., Cranbury, NJ, 1970.

Horses and Horsemanship Through the Ages, L. Gianoli, Crown Publishers, Inc., New York, NY, 1969.

Horses, Horses, Horses, M. E. Ensminger, Clovis, CA.

Horses, Horses, Horses, S. Wilding, Van Nostrand Reinhold Company, New York, NY, 1970.

Horse Shows, A. N. Phillips, The Interstate Printers & Publishers, Inc., Danville, IL, 1956.

Horses' Injuries, C. L. Strong, Arco Publishing Company, Inc., New York, NY, 1973.

Horses & Men, R. Albaugh, The Printer, Davis, CA, 1974.

Horses: Their Breeding Care and Training, H. S. Thomas, A. S. Barnes and Co., Inc., Cranbury, NJ.

Horses, Their Selection, Care and Handling, M. C. Self, A. S. Barnes & Co., Inc., Cranbury, NJ, 1943.

Horses of Today, Their History, Breeds and Qualifications, H. H. Reese, Wood & Jones, Pasadena, CA, 1956.

Horse: Structure and Movement, The, R. H. Smythe and Rev. P. C. Goody, J. A. Allen & Co., London, England, 1972.

Horse Today—and Tomorrow?, The, H. Lange, K. Jeschko, Arco Publishing Company, Inc., New York, NY, 1972.

"Hosses," C. W. Gray, Garden City Publishing Co., Inc., Garden City, NY, 1927.

How to Buy a Race Horse, A. Bower, Cromwell Bookstock Agency, Lexington, KY, 1968.

Introduction to the Wonderful World of Horses, An, Roundup, Inc., McHenry, IL, 1968.

Judging Manual for American Saddlebred Horses, J. Foss, American Saddle Horse Breeders Association, Louisville, KY, 1973.

Keep Your Own Pony, G. Wheatley, A. S. Barnes and Co., Inc., Cranbury, NJ.

Kellogg Arabians, The, H. H. Reese and G. B. Edwards, Borden Publishing Co., Los Angeles, CA, 1958.

Kingdom of the Horse, The, H. H. Isenbart and E. M. Buhrer, Time-Life Books, New York, NY, 1969.

Know About Horses, H. Disston, The Devin-Adair Company, New York, NY, 1961.

Know Your Pony, D. M. Goodall, A. S. Barnes and Co., Inc., Cranbury, NJ.

Lame Horse, The, J. R. Rooney, A. S. Barnes and Co., Inc., Cranbury, NJ, 1974.

Lameness in Horses, Second Edition, O. R. Adams, Lea & Febiger, Philadelphia, PA, 1966.

Law and Your Horse, The, E. H. Greene, A. S. Barnes & Co., Inc., Cranbury, NJ, 1971.

Leg at Each Corner, A, N. Thelwell, E. P. Dutton & Co., Inc., New York, NY, 1963.

Light Horse Breeds, The, J. W. Patten, A. S. Barnes & Co., Inc., Cranbury, NJ, 1960.

Light Horse Management, R. C. Barbalace, Caballus Publishers, Fort Collins, CO, 1974.

Manual of Horsemanship of the British Horse Society and The Pony Club, The, The British Horse Society and the Pony Club, The British Horse Society, Warwickshire, England, 1968.

Mare Owner's Handbook, ed. by T. Rogers, Cordovan Corporation, Houston, TX, 1971.

Mares, Foals and Foaling, F. Andrist, J. A. Allen & Co., London, England, 1959.

Morgan Horse Handbook, The, J. Mellin, Stephen Greene Press, Brattleboro, VT, 1973.

Nutrient Requirements of Horses, No. 6, Third revised ed., 1973, National Academy of Sciences, Washington, D.C.

Old Horseman's 1974 Almanack, The, ed. by S. W. Brotchie, TRT Publications, Inc., Beverly, MA, 1973.

Personality of the Horse, The, ed. by B. Aymar and E. Sagarin, Bonanza Books, New York, NY, 1963.

Points of the Horse, M. H. Hays, Arco Publishing Co., Inc., New York, NY, 1969.

Practical Dressage for Amateur Trainers, J. M. Ladendorf, A. S. Barnes and Co., Inc., Cranbury, NJ.

Practical Horse Breeding and Training, J. Widmer, Charles Scribner's Sons, New York, NY, 1942.

Practical Light Horse Breeding, J. F. Wall, The Monumental Printing Co., Baltimore, MD, 1936.

Principles of Horseshoeing, The, D. Butler and D. Butler, Ithaca, NY, 1974.

Proceedings of the First International Conference on Equine Infectious Diseases, ed. by J. T. Bryans, et al., The Grayson Foundation, Lexington, KY., 1966.

Progress in Equine Practice, ed. by E. J. Catcott, et. al., American Veterinary Publications, Inc., Santa Barbara, CA, 1966.

Racehorse in Training, The, W. Day and A. J. Day, Cassell and Company, Ltd., New York, NY, 1925.

Saddlery, E. H. Edwards, A. S. Barnes & Company, Inc., Cranbury, NJ, 1963.

Saddle Up!, C. E. Ball, J. B. Lippincott Company, Philadelphia, PA, 1970.

Selecting, Fitting, and Showing Horses, J. E. Nordby and H. E. Lattig, The Interstate Printers & Publishers, Inc., Danville, IL, 1963.

Shetland Pony, The, L. F. Bedell, The Iowa State University Press, Ames, Iowa, 1959.

Shetland Pony, The, M. C. Cox, Adam and Charles Black Ltd., London, England, 1965.

Spanish Riding School, The, H. Handler, McGraw-Hill Book Co., Ltd., Maidenhead, England, 1972.

Stable Management & Exercise, Sixth Edition, M. H. Hayes, Stanley Paul & Co., Ltd., London, England, 1968.

Steeplechasing, J. Hislop, J. A. Allen & Co., Ltd., London, England, 1970.

Stud Farm Diary, A, H. S. Finney, J. A. Allen & Co., Ltd., London, England, 1973.

Stud Managers Course, Lectures, Stud Managers Course, University of Kentucky, Lexington, KY, Intermittent years since 1951.

Stud Managers' Handbook, The, ed. by M. E. Ensminger, Agriservices Foundation, Clovis, CA, pub. annually since 1965.

Studies on Reproduction in Horses, Y. Nishikawa, Japan Racing Association, Tokyo, Japan, 1959.

Summerhays' Encyclopedia for Horsemen, Compiled by R. S. Summerhays, Frederick Warne and Co., Inc., New York, NY, 1966.

Tack! Tack! Tack!, M. E. Ensminger, Pegus Company, Inc., Clovis, CA, 1965.

Tales of the King's Horses, L. Rosenvold and D. Rosenvold, Rosenvold Publications, Montrose, Canada, 1958.

Thelwell's Riding Academy, N. Thelwell, E. P. Dutton & Co., Inc., New York, NY, 1967.

Thoroughbred Bloodlines, J. F. Wall, Monumental Printing Company, Baltimore, Maryland, 1935.

Thoroughbred Racing Stock, Lady Wentworth, Charles Scribner's Sons, New York, NY, 1938.

Thoroughbreds I Have Known, R. S. Reeves and J. C. Weyer, A. S. Barnes and Co., Inc., Cranbury, NJ.

Top Form Book of Horse Care, F. Harper, Popular Library, New York, NY, 1966.

Touch of Greatness, A, C. W. Anderson, The Macmillan Company, New York, NY, 1945.

Training the Arabian Horse, H. H. Reese, The Cruse Publishing Company, Inc., Fort Collins, CO, 1961.

Training Horses for Races, G. W. L. Meredith, Constable and Company, Ltd., London, England, 1926.

Training the Quarter Horse Jumper, H. P. Levings, A. S. Barnes and Co., Inc., Cranbury, NJ, 1968.

Training Thoroughbreds, P. M. Burch, The Blood-Horse, Lexington, KY, 1961.

Training Tips for Western Riders, L. N. Sikes, The Texas Horseman, Houston, TX, 1960.

Trotting Horse of America, The, H. Woodruff, University Press; Welch, Bigelow, & Co., Cambridge, MA, 1871.

TV Vet Horse Book, TV Vet, Farming Press Ltd., Ipswich, Suffolk, England, 1971.

Understanding and Training Horses, A. J. Ricci, J. B. Lippincott Company, Philadelphia, PA, 1964.

Using the American Quarter Horse, L. N. Sikes, The Saddlerock Corporation, Houston, TX, 1958.

Veterinary Notes for Horse Owners, M. H. Hays, Arco Publishing Co., Inc., New York, NY, 1972.

Veterinary Notes for the Standardbred Breeder, W. R. McGee, United States Trotting Assn., Columbus, OH.

Western Equitation, Horsemanship and Showmanship, D. Stewart, Vantage Press, Inc., New York, NY, 1973.

Western Horse, The, J. A. Gorman, The Interstate Printers & Publishers, Inc., Danville, IL, 1967.

Wild Horse of the West, The, W. D. Wyman, University of Nebraska Press, Lincoln, NB, 1945.

Wonderful World of Horses, The, ed. by B. Weikel, Roundup Incorporated, McHenry, IL, 1968.

World of Horses, The, J. Campbell, The Hamlyn Publishing Group Limited, New York, NY, 1969.

World of Pinto Horses, The, ed. by R. D. Greene, The Pinto Horse Association of America, Inc., San Diego, CA, 1970.

Young Horseman's Handbook, vols. 1–9, H. Disston, The Jarman Press, Charlottesville, VA, 1961.

Your Horse, A Sporting Life Publication, The Sporting Life, Long Acre, London, England, 1967.

Horse Magazines

The horse magazines publish news items and informative articles of special interest to horsemen. Also, many of them employ field representatives whose chief duty is to assist in the buying and selling of horses.

In compiling the magazine list that follows, no attempt was made to list the general livestock magazines of which there are numerous outstanding ones. Only those magazines which are chiefly devoted to horses are included. Cognizance is taken of the fact that some magazines may not be listed, simply because the author is not acquainted with them.

BREEDS

AMERICAN SADDLE HORSE	*Saddle & Bridle,* 2333 Brentwood Blvd., St. Louis, MO 63144.
APPALOOSA	*Appaloosa News,* Box 8403, Moscow, ID 83843.
	Appy, The, 15039 Rock Creek Rd., Chardon, OH 44024.
ARABIAN	*Arabian Horse, The,* 1777 Wynkoop Street, Suite 1, Denver, CO 80202.
	Arabian Horse News, The, P.O. Box 2692, Denver CO 80201.
	Arabian Horse Times, The, 819 E. Elm Avenue, Waseca, MN 56093.
	Arabian Horse World, 2650 E. Bayshore Road, Palo Alto, CA 94303.

DONKEY AND MULE	*Mr. Longears,* 100 Church Street, Amsterdam, NY 12010.
HACKNEY	*Hackney Journal, The,* P.O. Box 630, Peekskill, NY 10566.
MORGAN HORSE	*Morgan Horse, The,* Box 1, Westmoreland, NY 13490.
PAINT HORSE	*Paint Horse Journal, The,* P.O. Box 13486, Fort Worth, TX 76118.
PALOMINO	*Palomino Horse,* Box 249, Mineral Wells, TX 76067.
PERUVIAN PASO	*Peruvian Horse Review,* P.O. Box 816, Guerneville, CA 95446.
	Peruvian Horse World, P.O. Box 2035, California City, CA 93505.
PINTO	*Pinto Horse, The,* 910 W. Washington Street, San Diego, CA 92103.
PONY OF THE AMERICAS	*Pony of the Americas,* P.O. Box 1447, Mason City, IA 50401.
QUARTER HORSE	*Canadian Quarter Horse Journal,* P.O. Box 65, Ancaster, Ontario, Canada L9G 3L3.
	Intermountain Quarter Horse, The, P.O. Box "O", Sandy, UT 84070.
	Quarter Horse Digest, Gann Valley, SD 57341.
	Quarter Horse Journal, The, P.O. Box 9105, Amarillo, TX 79105.
SHETLAND PONY	*American Shetland Pony Journal,* P.O. Box 435, Fowler, IN 47944.
SPANISH-BARB	*Spanish-Barb Quarterly, The,* P.O. Box 7479, Colorado Springs, CO 80907.
SPANISH MUSTANG	*Newsletter, Spanish Mustang Registry, Inc.* Rt. 2, Box 74, Marshall, TX 75670.
STANDARDBRED	*Harness Horse, The,* P.O. Box 1831, Harrisburg, PA 17105.
	Hoof Beats, 750 Michigan Ave., Columbus, OH 43215.
TENNESSEE WALKING HORSE	*Voice of the Tennessee Walking Horse,* P.O. Box 6009, Chattanooga, TN 37401.

THOROUGHBRED

Walker, The, P.O. Box 286, Lewisburg, TN 37091.

Walking Horse Report, P.O. Box 619, Shelby-ville, TN 37160.

Arizona Thoroughbred, The, 3723 Pueblo Way, Scottsdale, AZ 85251.

Backstretch, The, 19363 James Couzens Hwy., Detroit, MI 48235.

Blood Horse, The, Box 4038, Lexington, KY 40504.

British Columbia Thoroughbred, 4023 E. Hastings Street, North Brunaby, B.C., Canada.

Florida Horse, The, P.O. Box 699, Ocala, FL 32670.

Oregon Thoroughbred Review, 1001 N. Schmeer Rd., Portland, OR 97217.

Thoroughbred of California, The, 201 Colorado Place, Arcadia, CA 91006.

Thoroughbred Record, The, P.O. Box 11788, Lexington, KY 40511.

Washington Horse, The, 13470 Empire Way, South, Seattle, WA 98178.

WELSH PONY

Welsh Pony World, The, 4531 Dexter St., N.W., Washington, D.C. 20007.

GENERAL

American Horseman, 257 Park Avenue South, New York, NY 10010.

Arizona Horseman, The, P.O. Box 1349, Phoenix, AZ 85012.

B.C. Horseman, The, 212–20216 Fraser Hwy., Langley, B.C., Canada V3A 4E7

California Horseman's News, 8808 National Ave., South Gate, CA 90280.

Capital Horseman, 14405 W. 52nd Ave., Arvada, CO 80002.

Chronicle of the Horse, The, Middleburg, VA 22117.

Corinthian, The, c/o Humber College, Box 1900, Rexdale, Ontario, Canada.

Corral, The, P.O. Box 151, Medina, OH 44256

Cuttin' Hoss Chatter, The, P.O. Box 12155, Fort Worth, TX 76116.

Equestrian Trails, P.O. Box 2086, Toluca Station, North Hollywood, CA 91602.

Hoof and Horn, P.O. Box C, Englewood, CO 80110.

Horse and Horseman, 34249 Camino Capistrano, Capistrano Beach, CA 92624.

Horse Lover's Magazine, 651 Brannan St., San Francisco, CA 94107.

Horse, Of Course, RFD, Temple, NH 03084.

Horse & Rider, P.O. Box 555, Temecula, CA 92390.

Horse Show, 527 Madison Ave., New York, NY 10022.

Horse World, P.O. Box 588, Louisville, KY 40501.

Horseman, 5314 Bingle Rd., Houston, TX 77018.

Horsemen's Review, Rt. 1, Box 12, Monroe Center, IL 61062.

Horseman's Gazette, R.R. 1, Badger, MN 56714.

Horsemen's Journal, Suite 317, 6000 Executive Blvd., Rockville, MD 20852.

Horsemen's Yankee Pedlar, 2805 Boston Rd., Wilbraham, MA 01095.

Lariat, The, 12675 S.W. First Street, Beaverton, OR 97005.

Maryland Horse, The, P.O. Box 4, Timonium, MD 21093.

National Horse Journal, The, P.O. Box 927, Toronto 5, Ontario, Canada.

National Horseman, The, Box 4067, Baxter Station, Louisville, KY 40204.

Northeast Horseman, Box 131, Hampden, ME 04444.

Practical Horseman, 19 Wilmont Mews, West Chester, PA 19380.

Southern Horseman, The, P.O. Box 5735, Meridian, MS 39301.

Tack n' Togs, P.O. Box 67, Minneapolis, MN 55440.

Trail Rider, The, P.O. Box 397, Chatsworth, GA, 30705.

Turf and Sport Digest, 704 Norwood Drive, Pasadena, CA 91105.

Washington Horse, The, 13470 Empire Way South, Seattle, WA 98178.

Washington State Horsemen Canter, The, P.O. Box X, Kirkland, WA 98033.

Western Horseman, The, P.O. Box 7980, Colorado Springs, CO 80901.

Index

Protein
   needs, 133
   palatability, 160
   poisoning, 135
   quality of, 134
   supplements, 153
Puffs, 402
Pulled tail, 402
Pulling record, world, 402
Pulse, horse, 250
Pumpkins, 159
Punishment, 88
Purebred, 402
Purebreeding, 102
Purse, 402
Pyridoxine, 146

Q
Quality, 402
Quarter crack, 76, 222, 403
Quarter Horse, 37
Quittor, 74, 403

R
Racehorses, 13, 53
   feeding, 176
Racing, 51
   attendance, viii, 55
   colors, 55
   records, 55
Rack, 80, 403
Random, 403
Rangerbred, 39
Rangy, 403
Rations, 162, 163
   formulation, 168
Rat tail, 403
Rattlers, 403
Reata, 403
Recessive factors, 99, 403
Rectal worms, 277
Red worms, 403
Registrations, 50
Registry, Breed Associations, 55
Reins, holding, 350, 351, 403
Remuda, 403
Reproductive organs, 104

   mare, 108
   stallion, 104
Rewards, 88
Ribbed-up, 403
Rickets, 190
Ridgeling, 404
Riding horses, 12, 346
Right lead, 404
Ringbone, 74, 404
Ringer, 404
Ringworm, 285, 404
Roach backed, 404
Roached mane, 404
Roadsters, 13, 337
Roan color, 82
Roarer, 404
Roaring, 77
Rollers, 404
Rolling, 81, 404
Rolling feed, 168
Roman-nosed, 404
Rope-walking, 81, 404
Roughage, 165
Roundworms, large, 404
Rubdown, 404
Run, 79, 404
Running racehorses, 53
Running walk, 80, 405
Rupture, 405

S
Saddle(s), 320
   blanket, 329
   English, 321
   Western, 322
Saddle seat, 352
Saddling procedure, 322
Sale fitting, 180
Saline, 405
Saliva test, 405
Salt, 136
   deficiency, 190
Sand crack, 76, 405
Scab, 405
Scabies, 405
Scalping, 81, 405
Schooling, 405
Sclerostomes, 405